Indians in Minne

Indians in Minnesota

Fifth Edition

Kathy Davis Graves
and Elizabeth Ebbott

for the League of Women Voters of Minnesota

University of Minnesota Press | Minneapolis | London

The publication of this book was assisted by grants to the League of Women Voters of Minnesota Education Fund by the 3M Foundation, the F. R. Bigelow Foundation, the Mardag Foundation, The McKnight Foundation, the Mille Lacs Band of Ojibwe, The Saint Paul Foundation, and the Shakopee Mdewakanton Sioux Community.

Published by the University of Minnesota Press
111 Third Avenue South, Suite 290
Minneapolis, MN 55401-2520
http://www.upress.umn.edu

Library of Congress Cataloging-in-Publication Data

Graves, Kathy Davis.
  Indians in Minnesota.—5th ed./Kathy Davis Graves and Elizabeth Ebbott for the
League of Women Voters of Minnesota.
    p. cm.
Includes bibliographical references and index.
ISBN-13: 978-0-8166-2732-5 (hc : alk. paper)
ISBN-10: 0-8166-2732-0 (hc : alk. paper)
ISBN-13: 978-0-8166-2733-2 (pb : alk. paper)
ISBN-10: 0-8166-2733-9 (pb : alk. paper)
1. Indians of North America—Minnesota—Social conditions. 2. Indians of North America—Government relations. I. Ebbott, Elizabeth. II. League of Women Voters of Minnesota. III. Title.
  E78.M7G73 2006
  977.6004'97—dc22   2006026403

Printed in the United States of America on acid-free paper

The University of Minnesota is an equal opportunity educator and employer.

15 14 13 12 11 10 09 08 07 06   10 9 8 7 6 5 4 3 2 1

Contents

14   The Criminal Justice System   283

     Conclusion   307
     Glossary   309

Appendix A   Minnesota Indian Reservations: Facts,
             Figures, and Maps   313

Appendix B   Treaties, Significant Federal Legislation,
             and Federal Court Decisions   325

     Notes   341
     Selected Bibliography   369
     Internet Resources   373
     Index   379

List of Tables

Preface

THE LEAGUE OF WOMEN VOTERS OF MINNESOTA published the first edition of *Indians in Minnesota* in 1962, bringing together for the first time comprehensive information about the lives of Minnesota Indians and their relationships with federal, state, and local governments. Revised editions published in 1971, 1974, and 1985 documented major changes within Indian populations. During the previous four decades, the League also has assisted in the establishment of the first state agency run by Indians—the Indian Affairs Council—and provided an impartial presence in several tribal elections.

The 1990s and early twenty-first century have been witness to significant gains and continuing needs of Indians in Minnesota. Creation and expansion of gaming, growing tribal sovereignty, and the 2000 U.S. Census are among the factors necessitating this fifth edition.

The legal relationship between Indians and the U.S. government is complex and often misunderstood. The League of Women Voters of Minnesota hopes that its analysis of issues affecting Indians will give the public a better understanding of Indian needs and a greater willingness to work with Indians toward solutions. The League's goal has been to provide accurate, balanced information that will both document and inform governmental policies.

The League owes deep gratitude to the late Elizabeth Ebbott, who was the author of the 1985 edition and who completed the first draft of this current manuscript in 1998, just a few weeks before her death. Her vision, understanding, and deep commitment to Indians are the foundation of this book.

Numerous other individuals have been involved in the preparation of this book. All eleven tribes reviewed their information and gave great insight to the authors. In addition, five members of Indian communities in Minnesota generously offered to read the entire manuscript for accuracy and fairness. Without them, the League of Women Voters of Minnesota could not have published this book. The League thanks Larry Aitken, Sally Hunter, Tony LookingElk, Laura Waterman Wittstock, and Don Wedll for their honest analyses and helpful comments.

Several League members also spent countless hours reviewing the book. Their assistance was vital in preparing this edition for publication. The League thanks Carol Frisch, Janet Gendler, Judith Rosenblatt, Sally Sawyer, and Marion Watson. In addition, Brigitte Parenteau provided thorough research and a careful eye throughout the revision process.

The strength of the book has been the willingness of Indian leaders and the Indian community to engage in thoughtful discussions about their experiences as Indians in Minnesota. Without this cooperation, this book and the previous editions would not have been possible.

Special thanks are extended to the photographers who granted the League permission to reprint their photographs.

The generous support of the 3M Foundation, the F. R. Bigelow Foundation, the Mardag Foundation, The McKnight Foundation, the Mille Lacs Band of Ojibwe, The Saint Paul Foundation, and the Shakopee Mdewakanton Sioux Community to the League of Women Voters of Minnesota Education Fund has made the fifth edition of *Indians in Minnesota* possible.

Miigwech.

Introduction

WHEN EUROPEANS NAMED THEM, "Indians" did not constitute a group with uniform characteristics. They were separate nations spread over the vast Western Hemisphere, living according to the demands of various climates and food supplies. Political and economic styles, language, dress, and religion differed among each nation. Although many had common characteristics, each nation was distinct.

Early Europeans in contact with Indian nations in the East expressed amazement at the Indians' personal liberty. The American model of democracy, with liberty for the individual and a system of government with divided powers, owes a debt to the Indian example. America's founding leaders, especially Benjamin Franklin, were aware of the governance system of the Iroquois Confederacy, characterized by a federal union of five (later six) nations and a constitution, "The Great Law of Peace." Many features of this system were later incorporated into the government of the United States. As a part of the celebration honoring the two hundredth anniversary of the U.S. Constitution, the U.S. House of Representatives and Senate acknowledged the contribution of the Iroquois Confederacy of Nations in shaping the earlier confederation of the Thirteen Colonies and in contributing to many of the democratic principles in the Constitution.[1]

Indian society had no class stratification, and there was freedom of expression in political and religious matters. The government and military were kept separate, with different leaders chosen for each function. Decision making, in which the entire village participated, was called a "caucus" by the Algonquians; this word later was adopted into the English language.

Early European settlers quickly learned of many Indian-developed foods and products, which have continued in use into the twenty-first century. Many of the ingredients in the foods we eat are from products Indians developed, including corn, potatoes, and sunflowers. Indians also introduced Europeans to squash, tomatoes, pumpkins, chili peppers, beans, tobacco, and peanuts—foods that were to become important not only for white settlers in America but also for the world. Indian herbs, drugs, and flavorings have had great impact—quinine, ipecac, cacao (chocolate), and coca (cocaine).[2] In the lake and forest areas that now include northern Minnesota, Indians harvested and processed wild rice, maple syrup, blueberries, and cranberries. Useful articles such as birch bark canoes, snowshoes, toboggans, moccasins, hammocks, and dogsleds became widely adopted.

Indians' ability to adapt to the rivers, lakes, and winters with portaging techniques and to "live off the land" thanks to wild rice, maple sugar, and pemmican enabled the French and British to develop the fur trade, which for almost two hundred years brought great wealth to Europe and changed the course of Indian history in the Great Lakes area.[3]

In Minnesota, the legacy of the American Indian people is also reflected in place names that are Indian words, names of Indian leaders, or translations of Indian names. *Minnesota* is Dakota for "sky-tinted water"; *Mississippi* is an Algonquian word from the Ojibwe for "great river." Twenty-seven of the state's counties have names of Indian origin, fifteen from the Dakota and twelve from the Ojibwe. Cities are named for important Mdewakanton Dakota tribal leaders, including Wabasha, Red Wing, and Shakopee.[4]

As a people, Indians share a culture and tribal affiliation that make them unique. They do not consider themselves "people of color" or a "minority" but, rather, members of a nation with a sovereign relationship to the U.S. government.

Indians and their communities embody great strengths and are an important asset to the state of Minnesota. They provide a culture and history that can be shared. They contribute the enthusiasm and dynamics of people who know what they want and need and know that they will ultimately achieve it.

An estimated 54,967 Indians were living in Minnesota in 2000. They reside primarily in the major urban areas and on or near eleven reservations (see tables in chapter 6; maps in Appendix A). There is considerable variation in their living conditions. Some Dakota and Ojibwe have achieved middle-class status because of the success of tribal casinos. However, some live in generational poverty, and a very few, benefiting from the highly successful Mystic Lake Casino, have become affluent. Tribal governments have greatly strengthened their administrative role and are developing needed professional staffs.

These developments coupled with successful casino operations have improved employment opportunities. However, depressed economic situations continue to plague many reservations and urban families, and some reservation and urban Indians have not benefited from casinos.

Demographics from the 2000 U.S. Census and other data document the Indians' severe social needs. The casinos have had an impact on the overall picture but do not meet the needs of all Indian communities. Statewide, Indians continue to have social needs in excess of the state's other disadvantaged populations.

- ❏ Indians in Minnesota are a young population, with a median age of 26.3 years, compared to the state average of 35.4 years.
- ❏ There are relatively few Indian elders. Those 60 and over were 6.5 percent of the Indian population; for Minnesota as a whole, 15 percent of the general population was 60 and over.
- ❏ In 2000, Indians were the poorest group in the state. Approximately 28 percent of Indians in Minnesota lived below the poverty level in 2000, a decrease from 44 percent in 1989. Thirty-nine percent of American Indian children in Minnesota were living in poverty in 2000, compared with 6 percent of white children.
- ❏ Indian mothers are young. Twenty-four percent of all Indian births are to women 19 years or younger, compared to 8 percent for the general populations.
- ❏ Educational needs continue to be unmet. Indian students show below-grade-level performance and high absentee and dropout rates throughout Minnesota.
- ❏ Housing is overcrowded and physically unsound. In tribal areas, 40 percent of homes are overcrowded and have serious physical deficiencies. The comparable national average is 5.9 percent for non-Indian housing.
- ❏ Indians are disproportionately involved in the correctional system. Indian adults comprised 1.2 percent of the total state population, yet their arrests and incarceration rates were significantly in excess of their percentage of the population. In 2002, 18.5 percent of the

American Indian population in Minnesota was arrested, comprising 4 percent of all arrests.

Casinos have had a dramatic effect on economic development in Minnesota. Indians have shown they can skillfully administer a multi-million-dollar industry that arose within a short period. They have provided reservations and neighboring communities with jobs and expanded community growth, which years of government programs have been unable to provide (see chapter 9).

Many positive things have occurred for Indians in the twenty years since publication of the previous edition of this book. Most significant have been the increased recognition of tribal sovereignty and the concept of self-governance. Tribal governments are much stronger, and there is a deep resolve to protect and expand Indians' rights to run their own affairs without the threat of federal termination of their status. Increased political understanding has helped Indians to be more effective in protecting their interests, protesting cuts, and demanding a share of general programming. The people's potential creativity and skills are being realized as more are assisted with education and training and allowed to be productive. They provide an economic asset through the programs they administer and the casinos they operate. While many state–tribal jurisdictional issues are still in the courts or are being negotiated between the two governments, both sides have increasingly shown a willingness to agree to an operational settlement for programs while waiting for jurisdictional issues to be resolved.

In spite of many social needs, strong cultural strengths persist for Indian communities, as described by an Indian leader: "The beauty of Indian art, the accomplishments of Indian scholars, the love within Indian families, the dedication of Indian social service workers, the wisdom of Indian elders, the sacrifice of Indian spiritual leaders, and the gratitude of Indian people for being Indian."[5]

In an address to the National Indian Education Association in the mid-1990s, Dr. Jack Weatherford, a cultural anthropologist at Macalester College, said, "At the turn of the twentieth century Indians were almost gone. The elders today know of this, they or their parents lived through it and they have managed to keep their people alive."[6] Today, in the twenty-first century, says John Poupart of the American Indian Policy Center, "Traditional Indian values are being 'rediscovered' and implemented in restorative justice, leadership, alternative dispute resolution, and community development programs."[7]

Chapter 1

Indian People and Their Culture

PRIOR TO THE ARRIVAL OF EUROPEANS in North America, Indians lived holistically, with strong beliefs in the interconnectedness of the physical and spiritual worlds. It often has been difficult for non-Indians to understand the American Indian way of life. Indians lived life at a deliberate, patient pace, synchronized with the rhythms of nature. Indian society was not hierarchical. Rather, decisions were made by consensus, and leaders emerged from group decision-making. Learning focused first on observing and listening to elders. Spiritual ceremonies and oral storytelling were central to Indian life, and restitution was the primary method of resolving conflict.

Indian values ensured survival of the group. Sharing and stressing the group over the individual were necessary to maintain the group's existence. Respect was one of the highest ideals: respect for nature, value of home and employment, respect for elders who embodied the tribe's wisdom, respect for individuals who had skills in healing, and respect for warriors. These values continue as the basis of Indian culture today. Most of the values come from traditional, old teachings, which were embodied in tribal society, clan, and totem systems.

Indian cultures are diverse, and no one person can define values for others. The following discussion of traditions and values is intended only to provide a better understanding of what many Indians cite as important in their culture. Such lists need to be used with caution and should not be assumed to represent all Indians or tribes.

> ❏ Living in balance with nature is desirable, and respect for all things on Earth is vital.
> ❏ Life is cyclical with continuous rebirth. Humankind's role is to respect all living things on the Earth.

1

❏ People and service are valued over goods. Little importance is placed on material affluence, and it is not used to judge community status. Possessions are to be shared, given generously to those in need, and ceremonially used to honor another person.

❏ Indians respect the elderly for their wisdom and look to them for guidance. Age and tradition are highly valued.

❏ Children are taught through example and the use of external consequences, rather than through admonition and punishment. An Indian educator has noted, "Indian people don't teach their children, they story them."[1]

❏ The extended family and the group are greater than the individual. Indians have extensive family responsibilities, and the family interdependence system works much like a form of social insurance.

❏ Although Indians compete fiercely in sports and games with other Indians and wage aggressive political contests, there is a general tendency not to compete to get ahead at the price of another's failure.

❏ Respect for others is manifest in several ways. Instead of aggressiveness and self-attention, there is value in modesty, patience, and waiting one's turn.

❏ Leadership is conferred by the group, and decision-making is often a group process.

❏ Humor is the cornerstone of Indian survival. Indians are told to laugh and enjoy life at least 85 percent of the day.[2]

Indian Culture

Indians have resisted tremendous efforts to destroy their language, ceremonies, values, and beliefs. For many, the scars are deep, and the bitterness is dominant. As Rosemary Christensen of American Indian Associates in Duluth, Minnesota, has said, "Indians are now coming out of 100 years of cultural devastation, the imposed values of another race. They became shorn creatures, stripped of their beings. Now they have to spend the rest of their lives trying to reclaim their values."[3]

However, being a survivor of this past is a source of great pride. Throughout the various Indian communities, there is the determination that culture will survive. In the mid 1990s, Earl Nyholm, then a professor of Ojibwe at Bemidji State University and a consultant to the National Museum of the American Indian, commented that "carriers of tradition" have emerged. "A few clusters of these people survive. They rejected much of the change and kept their old ways. For this they were ostracized, considered outcasts by other Indians of the reservations . . . but now they are honored, for they have preserved something irreplaceable. Now they are the guardians."[4]

At the start of the twenty-first century, John Poupart of the American Indian Policy Center said, "It is important to note that Indians have adapted in varying ways to mainstream social values. Still, most retain the traditional beliefs of their ancestors. They have become masters of a bi-cultural and pluralistic society and have learned to survive in two worlds. It is important to be mindful that Indians who cling to the old ways are likely to be among the most disenfranchised."[5]

In a time-honored address, former Mille Lacs Band leader Marge Anderson spoke words that Indian leaders today still echo: "Art Gahbow, my predecessor at Mille Lacs said, 'We will take it back.' We lost our language, our land and our culture. We will take it back. We lost our way of life, our jurisdiction and our religion. We will take it back. Somewhere along the line, we lost our hope for the future. We will get it back. . . . We must pass on to our children the idea that tomorrow will be a brighter day, and that they have the hearts and the minds to compete with anyone and win. We must, above all, teach our children to walk into the next millennium with heads held high like the warriors that preceded them, and to face each challenge that comes with strength, and with confidence and with hope."[6]

Language

Many Indian leaders believe that the loss of native languages is a threat to the survival of Indian culture and to sovereignty itself. Tribes are taking careful note of their fluent speakers and working to build a larger population that speaks the native languages. Almost all Indian programming in the state's schools and Indian youth programs incorporates some language. The Native American Languages Act administered by the U.S. Department of Education is designed to promote and rescue disappearing Indian languages. It has provided some programming in Minnesota, but very little funding. University-level instruction is offered in Dakota and Ojibwe at several Minnesota colleges, and elders have been included in classroom activities to expand the opportunities to learn.

Conferences on language revitalization and total language immersion schools are gaining strength in Minnesota. The Minnesota legislature passed a resolution in 2004 stating that the Ojibwe and Dakota languages are the original languages of Minnesota.

Powwows

Powwows are an important part of Indian culture and major social events for Indian communities. The word, derived from Algonquian languages, means a ceremonial gathering. Tribes have several powwows every year, with major intertribal powwows. Powwows employ drums, songs, and dances as expressions of sacred prayer, thought, and honor. "Intensity of the dance is meant to restore conditions of harmony within oneself and for the ultimate good of the tribe."[7] Each dance category has its own defined dress with many spiritual and symbolic items and decorations. A powwow signifies more than a celebration. In the words of an Indian leader, "It is a traditional way to commemorate an individual's pride in being Indian, renewing old friendships with other Indian people and an unsaid prayer that the American Indian way of life will continue."[8]

Arts and the Media

Indian expression through visual art is an outgrowth of making traditional ceremonial, ritualistic, and utilitarian objects. Although the objects were prescribed by the culture, technical skill was noted and appreciated. Great skills were also developed in the decorative arts and manufacture of household utensils, clothing, ceremonial dress, jewelry, and other objects.

Minnesota has many good practitioners of the various arts and several who have been nationally acclaimed. They include painters, sculptors, graphic designers, photographers, architects, writers, and poets. Fine crafting and artistic skill are continued in the traditional areas of beadwork, clothing decoration, birch bark items, quilts, and basketry.

A competition for Upper Great Lakes Indian artists, the Ojibwe Art Expo, began in 1974, organized by George Morrison, one of the most noted Indian artists of the twentieth century. The annual show origi- nates at Bemidji State University and then travels to the Twin Cities of Minneapolis and St. Paul.

Native Arts Circle considers itself the only statewide Indian arts organization in America, providing assistance to Indian artists and serving as a clearinghouse for Indian art information. The annual Two Rivers Native Film and Video Festival is organized by the project.

Each Ojibwe reservation has a newspaper. (See the Internet Resources section for a listing of Indian media outlets and other news- papers.) The Minnesota Chippewa Tribe also publishes a paper, *Speaking of Ourselves Ni-Mi-Kwa-Zoo-Min*. *The Circle* is a monthly paper published in Minneapolis. The *Native American Press/Ojibwe News* is published in St. Paul and is not associated with any tribal entity.

Minneapolis is the home of MIGIZI ("bald eagle" in Ojibwe) Communications, a nonprofit organization that produced the first nationally aired Indian news program. MIGIZI continues to produce radio and television documentaries, as well as educate elementary, secondary, and adult students in a communications-related setting. MIGIZI is a member of the Native Media and Technology Network, which is designing new approaches to tribal communications and emerging technological opportunities.

Cultural Issues

Indians vary in their opinions of how best to preserve their Indian culture while living in the white world. One hundred years ago, when some Indians were willing to go along with the white man's ways and others were unwilling, the terms "farmer Indians" and "blanket Indians" were coined. In the 1970s, labels such as "apple" (red on the outside, white within), "Uncle Tomahawk," "conserva- tive," "traditional," and "militant" were used. Today, arguments con- tinue about who qualifies to be an Indian.

In an enduring plea for unity, a Bemidji State University student wrote, "We have all lost land, freedom, and a way of life we will proba- bly never completely regain. . . . However, there is one thing they could not take from us, our spirit. It was and is that spirit that has sustained us through all the years of abuse, continuous neglect, and treatment of invisibility. It should be that same spirit that bonds us together as one. . . . We live in a white dominated society. . . . We must figure out a way to think like the white man while not becoming white. . . . This will take the efforts of all Indians. We have to start looking at our similarities and stop focusing on our differences."[9]

The education system can be a major point of conflict between the two cultures for many Indians. Of his success in being named president of the Urban Coalition and head of Metropolitan Urban Indian Directors, Tony Looking Elk said, "People want to hear it is higher education. That is very often thought of as the only way an American Indian can move forward. . . . It is hard for people to accept that it is my grandparents, parents, brothers and sister, nephews and niece, and many layers of relations that have contributed to my values and beliefs. Whatever is determined to be my level of success has everything to do with what I have been taught by my community, family and culture. Work put food on the table, education created acceptance in the greater world, but my teachings allow me to matter."[10]

The growth of an Indian middle class brings cultural clashes, as the transition to a more affluent lifestyle can conflict with Indian values and upbringing. As a business owner in Minneapolis said, ". . . it's hard for me to call myself (middle class). . . . The way I was raised was that you are no better than the next man, no matter what material things you have."[11]

Minnesota has a law requiring that certain goods made by someone of less than one-fourth Indian blood must be labeled "not Indian made." The 1990 Indian Arts and Crafts Act was intended to be a "truth in labeling" protection for Indian artists from foreign-made goods fraudulently labeled as "Indian made." However, in defining Indian artists solely as enrolled members of a state or federally recognized nation or designated that by their Indian nation, the law has caused problems for some Indian artists, and some Indians consider it demeaning to have to show proof of Indian blood.

Grave Site Protection, Repatriation, and Reburial

Pressure from Minnesota's Indian communities brought passage in 1978 of the Private Cemeteries Act (Minn. Stat. § 307.08, Subd. 7) to stop the desecration of Indian burial sites and to provide for dignified return and reburial of ancestral remains. The statute, as strengthened through the years, includes sites on public or private lands and waters. The State Archaeologist, appointed by the Minnesota Historical Society, is responsible for authenticating burials, and if there is known or suspected association with Indians, the Indian Affairs Council is involved. Identified mound sites are protected and are not to be disturbed. Intentionally disturbing or removing human skeletal remains is a felony.

Federal legislation, the National Historic Preservation Act (§ 406), provides that all federally funded agencies and any program receiving federal funds are required to use archaeologists and confer with Indians before building on or disturbing lands where Indian burials and artifacts might be located. The federal Archaeological Resources Protection Act of 1979 also provides protection for Indian sites.

To meet the needs of these laws, two Indian archaeological firms have been established: Leech Lake Heritage Sites, a tribally owned enterprise, and All Nations Cultural Resource Preservation, Inc., the only 100 percent Indian-owned and-operated archaeological firm in the country.

Since 1978, well over a thousand reburials have been arranged. Among the returns were the bones of Dakota Chief Little Crow from the Minnesota Historical Society and, from the Mayo Clinic in Rochester, the remains of Chief Shakopee and the Dakotas who were hanged at Mankato following the 1862 uprising.

Repatriation of Items Held by Museums and Schools

The Federal Native American Grave Protection and Repatriation Act (PL 101-601), passed in 1990, provides that all federal agencies and federally assisted programs, including museums and schools, must inventory all human remains and funerary, spiritual, and "cultural patrimony" items and then notify the appropriate tribes. As a result, many major museums and other institutions have sent huge volumes of information to Minnesota's tribes. According to Earl Nyholm, adviser to the Smithsonian Museum, "Ownership and intent of items will be hard to determine: medicine men materials could be tribal or of importance only to the individual; burial and other items could be sacred or trade/sale items made for tourists."[12] Each of the state's eleven tribes is making its own repatriation arrangements, some committing major resources. Over the past two decades, several

Indian-connected museums and historical site interpretive centers have been established.

Spiritual Beliefs

In spite of centuries of efforts to impose a new Western culture and spirituality on them, Indians have remained a religious/spiritual people in the Indian way. For example, through prayer they ask the Great Spirit to guide, assist, and provide wisdom. Within some tribes, those who wish to have the floor to address the group are asked to respect the solemnity of the occasion by holding a sacred eagle feather. Sacred drum societies still exist, with the keeper of the drum an honored member of the community.

Among individuals there is a resurgence of seeking out spiritual leaders and participating in vision quests, healing ceremonies, naming ceremonies, and rites of passage. Pipe ceremonies, use of tobacco in prayers, sweat lodges, powwows, drums and dancing, and funeral ceremonies have grown in importance, due in part to the 1978 American Indian Religious Freedom Act. Tobacco is central to praying, talking, and ceremonial activities among most native people. It is a symbol of sincerity and peace, communicated by its offering to invisible forces.

Native American Church

The Native American Church, formalized in 1918, is a structured denomination incorporating traditional and Christian beliefs. The church uses peyote as a sacramental element in its ceremonies as specifically allowed under federal drug laws. There are Native American Church congregations in the Twin Cities, at Red Lake Reservation, and at Prairie Island.

Christian Missionary and Church Activity

Christian churches have been involved with Indians living in Minnesota since 1632.[13] Christian missionaries were among the first white people to come to Minnesota. They played an active role, supported by the federal government, in trying to eliminate the Indians' "pagan" beliefs. Preachers of all denominations shared the view that Christianity was the best means of "civilizing" Indians. Because churches played a large role in the destruction of Indian culture, some Indians still feel hostility and anger at church organizations. Roy Meyers, in his *History of the Santee Sioux*, states that "perhaps the greatest damage was done by those who regarded themselves as their best friends—the missionaries . . . their single-minded determination to Christianize the Indians, born of their unshakable conviction that Christianity—their own particular brand of Christianity—was the true religion, blinded them to everything good in native religions."[14]

Several historical churches and parishes remain on the reservations. The Church of the Holy Rosary at Grand Portage is staffed by the Duluth Roman Catholic Diocese and is considered the oldest Roman Catholic parish in Minnesota. The early Episcopalian parishes of St. Colomba at White Earth and St. Cornelia in the Lower Sioux Community are still active. On Red Lake Reservation, the Benedictine-run St. Mary's Mission remains the Catholic parish, and they operate a day school for the Red Lake community.

Various denominations have congregations and active programs for Indians in urban areas, including All Nations Indian Church (United Church of Christ/Lutheran), Spirit of Waters Indian Ministry (United Methodist/Presbyterian), a Catholic church at the Division of Indian Work in Minneapolis, and Mazakute Memorial Mission (Episcopal) in St. Paul. These churches are increasingly enriching their services and liturgy by incorporating traditional Indian symbols and ceremonies.

Chapter 2

Shifting Governmental Relationships

IN THE CENTURIES SINCE Europeans' first encounter with the peoples of the Americas, the native people have been treated with a varying mixture of conscience and convenience, conflict and domination, but rarely with equality. Formal governmental policies have changed frequently, and there has always been a large gap between those policies and what actually happened to and on behalf of Indians.

To understand how Indians view their relationship with the U.S. government in the twenty-first century, one needs a historical perspective. Once the U.S. government was formed, the view of Indians and their land followed European patterns. An early U.S. Supreme Court decision affirmed the assertion of European nations: Their acquisition of territory on the continent through "discovery" gave them the exclusive right to appropriate lands occupied by Indians. The United States therefore had clear title to the land, subject to the Indian right of occupancy, which the U.S. government could extinguish by purchase or conquest.[1]

Briefly sketched in this chapter are governmental policies from the beginning of white settlement in North America to the present. This historical overview provides a basis for how Indians view their challenges, needs, and opportunities.

Fur Trading: The Earliest Relationship

The fur trade dominated European-Indian relationships for roughly two hundred years, beginning in the early 1600s. To succeed it was necessary for Europeans and Indians to work together. Fur traders needed Indian help in hunting for furs and trading for life needs.

According to researcher Sylvia Van Kirk, the Indian was "neither subject nor slave; . . . the fur trader did not seek to conquer the Indian, to take his land or to change his basic way of life or beliefs."[2] This fur trading partnership undoubtedly protected Indian culture far better than when Europeans began to view native people as a hindrance.

Furs were big business; what happened in the north woods of North America was important to the major markets in London and Leipzig. In the first half of the 1700s, the fur trade provided more than one-quarter of the value of New York's exports to England.[3] But by the 1840s, the fur market had collapsed, and government policies turned away from supporting the fur trade. Land was instead sought for minerals, timber, and farming. The era of initiating treaties to take title to Indian land in the midwestern and western regions of the country began.

Treaties

The European concept of title to land, which could be acquired through purchase, became the basis of Indian-white relationships from the time of earliest European settlement. Treaties became the mechanism for white settlers to acquire land while keeping peace or for traders to get repaid for Indian debts. In contrast, although they occupied defined territory, Indians had no concept of individual ownership and possession of land. As Chief Joseph of the Nez Percé tribe stated, "The country was made without lines of demarcation, and it is no man's business to divide it."

Treaties with Indians were written in English and made promises that were frequently broken. President Andrew Jackson, under the policy of moving all tribes west of the Mississippi River, wrote to the Creek Indians on March 23, 1829, using the phrase that has come to characterize these broken promises. "Your father has provided a country large enough for all of you . . . you can live upon it, you and all your children, as long as the grass grows, or the water runs, in peace and plenty. It will be yours forever."[4]

The reality was quite different. Alexis de Tocqueville, who visited America in 1831, noted,

> The conduct of the Americans of the United States toward the aborigines is characterized . . . by a singular attachment to the

> formalities of law . . . [They do not take] their hunting-grounds
> without a treaty of purchase; and if [the tribes cannot subsist] . . .
> they kindly take them by the hand and transport them to a grave
> far from the land of their fathers . . . Americans of the United
> States have accomplished this . . . with singular felicity, tranquility,
> legally, philanthropically, without shedding blood, and without
> violating a single great principle of morality in the eyes of the
> world. It is impossible to destroy men with more respect for the
> laws of humanity.[5]

The treaty process and the ultimate taking of the land and
resources from Indians is a sordid chapter in European and American
history. Probably no treaty was honestly or fairly handled; frauds,
abuses, and cheating characterized the process. As demands for land
by business interests and immigrants increased, huge areas of
land were transferred by treaty to the United States and opened for
settlement by whites. The federal government paid for the land over a
period of years by providing rations, medical care, education, and assistance in establishing farms and by paying traders' bills. Indians were
to confine themselves to a much-diminished piece of land reserved for
them. This land was called a "reservation." With pressures from whites
wanting more land, from traders wanting bills paid, and from Indians
wanting to ensure continuation of their rations, new treaties were
signed, and Indians were pushed into ever smaller, less viable areas.

Indian sovereignty was acknowledged in law with the Northwest
Ordinance of 1787 (predating the U.S. Constitution), which regu-
lated settlement in the northern Midwest (including a major part of
Minnesota):

> The utmost good faith shall always be observed towards the
> Indians; their lands and property shall never be taken from them
> without their consent, and in their property, rights, and liberty
> they never shall be invaded or disturbed, unless in just and
> lawful wars authorized by Congress; but laws founded in justice
> and humanity shall, from time to time, be made, for preventing
> wrongs being done to them, and for preserving peace and
> friendship with them.[6]

The U.S. Constitution formalized relations with Indian tribes,
granting Congress the "exclusive rights and power of regulating the
trade and managing all affairs with the Indians" (Article IX) and
the power to "regulate commerce with foreign nations, and among

the several states, and with Indian tribes" (Article I). As in relations with foreign nations, treaties were negotiated and considered supreme law of the United States (Article VI). This provision is the basis of Indian tribes' current status in law, recognizing their inherent sovereignty and their powers of self-governance (see chapter 3).

In 1871, the Indian Appropriation Act replaced the treaty-making process. Such agreements, negotiated in the same way as treaties, required approval by both the U.S. House of Representatives and Senate. Legally, the agreements had the same status as treaties, and the change did not affect previous treaties approved by the Senate and signed by the President. But the lands were no longer called "reservations"; instead, they were labeled "communities."

Indian affairs have been almost exclusively a federal responsibility (a few state reservations exist in eastern states). In 1824, Indian affairs were placed in the War Department; they were transferred to the newly organized Department of Interior in 1849. Originally called the Office of Indian Affairs, it later became the Bureau of Indian Affairs (BIA). The head of the BIA was upgraded to Assistant Secretary of the Interior in 1977. Federal law gives to the Secretary of the Interior the task of "management of all Indian affairs" (25 U.S.C. 2).

Reservations

The traditional Indian way of life required very low population density for a sustainable food supply. Leaving the land "unused" was seen as wasteful and even sinful by whites, who wanted the rich, virgin land for timber, mining, and farms. Indians were seen as impediments, to be removed or destroyed.

Confinement on reservations, with their greatly diminished land area, along with white settlement pressures and the destruction of land through logging and mining, greatly limited traditional Indian ways of food gathering. Lack of game and other natural food sources led to a new diet that greatly modified living patterns. The U.S. government deliberately supplied and withheld rations as a way of controlling the Indian population. By the 1890s, it was the practice to deny rations to Indian families who did not send their children away to school.[7]

The BIA sought almost total control over the reservation population. Use of this power, whether by dedicated, honest public servants or by those intent upon less noble purposes, contributed to the destruction of traditional tribal decision-making and individual identity.

Assimilation Policies: Destroying Indian Culture

Missionaries were among the first white people to contact Indians. Believing that Christianity and civilization was the same thing, these missionaries saw their role as converting the "savage" and changing "heathenish" practices and beliefs. Christianity demanded total change, not only in matters of faith, but also in all aspects of life. As a result, missionaries became one of the major threats to the survival of Indian culture and identity.

In 1869, religious groups were given the responsibility for running reservations. The Dakota people, following the Dakota Conflict of 1862, were divided among the Quakers at Santee, Nebraska; the Presbyterians at Sisseton, South Dakota; the Catholics at Devil's Lake, North Dakota; and the Episcopalians at the Lower Sioux Agency in Minnesota. Bishop Henry Whipple, an Episcopalian leader in Minnesota who was considered a friend of Indians, urged in 1885 that all Ojibwe people be made to move to the White Earth Reservation, freeing their other reservations for sale. Indian annuities due from existing reservations had expired or soon would. Unless they moved, the Indian people could not be "led to civilization."[8] Although some did move and formed White Earth Reservation, many did not, so the directive failed. Seven Ojibwe reservations remain in Minnesota today.

Allotments

Allotting land to individual Indian families was seen as the ideal tool for accomplishing the objectives of civilizing Indians, speeding assimilation, and opening the "surplus" reservation land to white settlement. Proceeds from selling the land could fund the cost of administering Indian programs.

The General Allotment Act (Dawes Act) passed in 1887 (25 U.S.C. 331) was intended, according to the Commissioner of Indian Affairs, "to break up reservations, destroy tribal relations, settle Indians upon their own homesteads, incorporate them into the national life, and deal with them not as nations or tribes or bands, but as individual citizens."[9] Although allotments had been made in Minnesota under earlier treaties, the Nelson Act of 1889 (25 Stat. 642) was the major legislation affecting the state (see chapter 3).

Allotments, generally 80 and 160 acres, were assigned to individual families, but title to the land remained with the federal government. The land was held in trust and could not be taxed, sold, or transferred without BIA approval. Certain conditions were imposed before the land could be transferred to fee status, meaning Indians owned title to the land and that land was placed out of trust status. Once this had happened, the land could be taxed, and individuals could dispose of it as they wished. The allotments were handed out randomly, so family members' lands could be miles apart and not near the area they had settled.

The policy of allotment did not work. Indians had a much different value system from European immigrants hungry to farm their own land. Indians did not become farmers. They were subjected to extreme pressures to sell, and non-Indians rapidly acquired land and timber resources. No land was set aside for the benefit of all members on a tribal basis. The allotment process ended with passage of the Indian Reorganization Act (IRA) of 1934. Of the original reservations, only a small percentage of the land still remains in trust (see chapter 3).

Other Pressures to Assimilate

There were other strong pressures on Indians to become "civilized" and assimilate. The federal government established Indian police forces and courts to impose white standards. For instance, in 1884, the Court of Indian Offenses at Red Lake Reservation was established to enforce rules forbidding plural marriages, dances, destruction of property following death, intoxication, liquor traffic, interference of a medicine man with the "civilizing program," and an Indian's leaving the reservation without permission.

Schooling was the major vehicle of forcing conformity and change. Children were sent to boarding schools, completely cut off from their culture, to be taught new ways. Students were punished for speaking "Indian," long hair and braids were cut, and things "Indian" were not allowed. These schools remain a bitter family memory for most Indians.

Citizenship

Indians became citizens when they took title to their allotted land (also known as fee status) or met certain other requirements. For all other Indians, citizenship was forced in 1924 by an act of Congress. Until the late 1920s, very little further attention was paid to Indians. It was commonly assumed that they would vanish. William Folwell, an eminent Minnesota historian, had no doubts in 1930: "The Chippewa Indians are a dying race."[10]

Indian Reorganization Act

In the 1920s, citizens raised concerns about BIA mismanagement, exploitation, and corruption and about the impoverished situation in which Indians were forced to live. An extensive, objective study of reservation conditions published in 1928, *The Problem of Indian Administration,* became known by the name of the survey staff director, Lewis Meriam.[11] The Meriam report had a profound influence on legislation affecting Indians in the 1930s. Besides describing appalling physical conditions, the report cautioned against hasty assimilation.

The Indian Reorganization Act of 1934 marked a major change in federal policy. It became the New Deal program for Indians. Regional hearings soliciting Indian opinions were held before passage of the Act, marking a revival of bilateral relations in the formation of Indian policy.[12] The IRA ended land allotment and the conveyance of allotted land to fee status. The tribal land base was rebuilt by funding $2 million for the purchase of lands to be held in trust for the tribes and returning to the tribes original reservation lands still unsold. In efforts to build an economic base, tribes could charter businesses with the help of a revolving credit fund. Tribes decided by vote whether they wished to come under the Act. All Minnesota tribes accepted (see chapter 4).

The IRA recognized the tribes' right to self-government. However, the standard constitution generally used provided for a very simplified governmental structure: no separation of powers, few checks or balances of officials, and retention by the Secretary of the Interior of significant powers for approving contracts and proposed constitutional changes.

The standard constitution is still causing great stresses on the reservations. The few elected officials control all aspects of government: political, judicial, and administrative, such as running business operations, tribal schools, and housing programs. When government is the only employer on the reservations, a frequent situation, officials have tremendous power over who will have a job. Without checks and balances and with absolute control of the election process, officials are very difficult to challenge in a democratic way. Some Indians believe this system is yet another way of imposing federal domination and manipulation of the tribe's inherent right to run its own affairs. As a result, some reservations have made major adjustments in their governmental structures (see chapter 4).

Termination

By the 1950s, there was a sharp reversal in Indian policy. Termination was seen as the final solution to the "Indian problem," the way to get the government out of the "Indian business." The intent to shift responsibility was most clearly defined in House Concurrent Resolution 108 in 1953. Although it spoke of "freeing" Indians from federal control, the policy's goal was to abolish reservations, subjecting the land to taxation; to end federal programs and the special federal relationship; and to force the assimilation of Indian people. Ultimately, the policy was a failure.

Over fifty tribes were terminated, including the Menominee of Wisconsin (1954). The Menominee had great financial difficulties once they no longer had federal status as an Indian tribe. Land previously held by the tribe had to be sold to meet expenses. An active lobbying effort initiated by Indians was organized, and in December 1973, federal recognition was restored (25 U.S.C. 903).

The goal of termination was also approached from other directions. For many years, tribes had sought redress by filing claims against the U.S. government. Resolution of the claims, it was argued, would eliminate the need for Indians to affiliate with their tribes or reservations. Congress moved to speed the process, establishing the Indian Claims Commission in 1946 (25 U.S.C. 70).

Beginning in 1956, a program originating in the Department of the Interior to relocate reservation Indians to urban areas was also pushed. The BIA assisted in training, moving, and resettling Indians off the reservations, often intentionally far enough away so theoretically they would not return. Start-up services were provided, but support funds were limited, resulting in the transfer and then abandonment of many Indians in urban areas. The federal program moved about one hundred thousand Indians.[13] A large migration of Indians into the Twin Cities of Minnesota began during this era.

Transferring legal jurisdiction to the states was another termination approach, approved by Congress in 1953 as Public Law 280 (Pub. L. 83-280; 25 U.S.C. 1321). Five states that had been most responsive to the needs of their Indian citizens (including Minnesota) were given criminal and some civil jurisdiction on the reservations. The Act was passed without approval of all tribes, but it did protect treaty rights and traditional hunting and fishing rights. The state was not given jurisdiction over taxation or use of trust property. Amendments in 1968 prohibited further transfer of jurisdiction to states unless the tribes agreed to cede state jurisdiction back to the federal government.

The 1960s: Reclaiming Sovereignty

Federal policies triggered the widespread response among Indians that they must organize and aggressively pursue their sovereign rights as nations if they were to preserve their distinct cultural and political communities. In 1961, four hundred Indians from ninety tribes assembled in Chicago and prepared a "Declaration of Indian Purpose." Preserving and strengthening Indian sovereignty was the goal.[14]

Tribal governments, the embodiment of sovereignty, were the major vehicles for improving conditions on reservations. Leaders became more successful in getting assistance programs for the reservations, influencing Congress, resisting federal domination, and using the courts to assert their rights. Indians were returning to the reservations from military service and from war jobs in the urban areas. Increasing numbers had experience administering social, educational, and service programs and were trained as planners who knew how to seek program grants.

Antipoverty legislation, passed in 1964, established a separate Indian Community Action Program (ICAP). For the first time, Indians were identifying their own needs and administering the assistance. Indian communities worked together, and educated Indians returned to help. It was a route to services outside the bureaucratic BIA. Many

Indian community leaders in later decades developed their skills and learned how to be administrators in ICAP.

As Indians came together, they found increasing strength in pursuing united goals. Through the 1960s and 1970s, professional Indian organizations were begun to work on national legislation in education or to pursue issues through the courts. In addition, Indian activists, in the era of the Civil Rights Movement, formed the American Indian Movement (AIM) in Minneapolis in 1968 to dramatize their plight (see chapter 6).

The 1970s: Self-Determination

In 1970, President Nixon, in recommending an end to the policy of termination and the adoption of goals of self-determination and self-sufficiency, said: "Because termination is morally wrong and legally unacceptable, because it produces bad practical results, and because the mere threat of termination tends to discourage greater self-sufficiency among Indian groups, I am asking the Congress to pass a new Concurrent Resolution which would expressly renounce, repudiate, and repeal the termination policy." These policies were designed "to strengthen the Indian's sense of autonomy without threatening his sense of community . . . (to) make it clear that Indians can become independent of federal control without being cut off from federal concern and federal support."[15]

Several important laws followed, one of the most important being the Indian Self-Determination and Education Assistance Act of 1975 (Pub. L. 93-638). The Act allowed tribes on a program-by-program basis to contract to run services previously administered by the BIA and the Indian Health Service (IHS). The Act specified that it did not authorize the termination of any existing trust responsibility. All Minnesota Indian tribes and communities have administered many programs under this authorization.

During the 1970s, several major court decisions further defined Indian rights. Unextinguished treaty rights in hunting and fishing were reestablished throughout the country. Indians were affirmed in their right to have preference in employment in Indian programs. Tribal government jurisdiction was greatly strengthened when the U.S. Supreme Court ruled that the federal government, in most instances, could not interfere when the tribe dealt with its own members in such areas as membership, civil rights, and tribal voting rights.

The 1980s and 1990s: Moving Toward Self-Governance

Federal Policy

In 1983, President Reagan stated that the federal policy was "to reaffirm dealing with Indian tribes on a government-to-government basis and to pursue the policy of self-government for Indian tribes without threatening termination"[16] Presidents George H. W. Bush and Bill Clinton reiterated this official policy.[17] The policy of termination was formally repudiated in 1988 when Congress stated that it:

❏ Reaffirmed the constitutionally recognized government-to-government relationship with the Indian nations, which has historically been the cornerstone of this nation's official Indian policy.

❏ Reaffirmed the trust responsibility of the federal government to the Indian nations.

❏ Acknowledged the need for the utmost good faith in upholding the treaties as the legal and moral duty of a great nation.[18]

A pilot project in self-governance was launched in 1988 (Pub. L. 100-472) and was subsequently made a permanent program. It provided that tribes in direct negotiation could receive direct funding for programs they wanted to run themselves, no longer requiring tribes to deal with subordinate bureaucracies such as the BIA area and agency offices. Reporting was reduced to an annual accounting, with the hope that reducing paperwork would make more money available for programs. The much greater flexibility proved successful, allowing tribes to target their unique needs. The Mille Lacs Tribe was one of the first ten tribes in the 1988 national pilot project. Seven of Minnesota's tribes are now part of this self-governance policy: Boise Forte (1996), Fond du lac (1998), Grand Portage (1997), Leech Lake (1994), Mille Lacs (1991), Red Lake (1997), and Shakopee Mdewakanton Sioux (2004).[19] White Earth operates under the 1975 Self-Determination Act. The other Dakota communities operate with direct services from the BIA.

Indian Gaming Act

An important U.S. Supreme Court case, *California v. Cabazon Band of Mission Indians* (9480 U.S. 202 (1978)), clarified that tribal governments have the sovereign authority to control civil regulatory matters on the reservation; states do not have jurisdiction. Under Minnesota law, this meant that tribes could operate on the reservations, independent of the state. This decision gave legal approval to the tribes to run casinos. Congress responded by passing the federal Indian Gaming Act of 1988, which imposed some limits on tribal sovereignty by providing that there should be negotiated state-tribal agreements. Minnesota's tribes quickly cooperated with each other and entered into state compacts. The tribes had operated "Big Bingo" since the mid-1980s. Building on that experience, tribes built major Las Vegas-type casinos, and a few have been very profitable. The casinos are located on reservation land, mostly in rural areas, and have become the major business in their area, providing work to entire rural communities (see chapter 8).

Legal Directions

Tribal sovereignty continues to be reshaped by the courts. Robert N. Clinton, a professor at Arizona State University, found that from 1959 to 1985 tribal interests won almost 50 percent of cases in the U.S. Supreme Court. But from 1986 to 1990, tribes won only 20 percent of the time, and from 1990 to 1994, only 14 percent. According to Clinton, the decisions disregarded precedent and ignored history and the will of Congress. Of special concern were the cases that ruled against Indians where the treaties had promised tribes federal protection of their sovereign autonomy in exchange for cessions of land.[20]

According to James Genia, an attorney representing several Minnesota tribes and the former Solicitor General for the Mille Lacs Band, an increasing number of judicial appointees to federal benches over the past twenty years favor states' rights, leading to a judicial system that is less receptive to Indian interests. "States' rights are in direct conflict with Indian sovereignty," said Genia. "Tribes want to regulate themselves while states' rights advocates want to regulate tribes."[21]

The Twenty-First Century

Federal Policy

The relationship between the federal programs that serve the tribes and tribal governments continues to change. Self-governance programs have eliminated the need for many services previously provided by federal bureaucracies. Federal funding cuts have raised questions about meeting basic needs. Many of the questions regarding who can best provide services have not been resolved. There are also fears that tribes risk having funding for needed services cut as federal agencies consider them independent enough to take care of their own needs.

Indians are ambivalent about their federal programs, especially the BIA, and there is deep skepticism that the BIA's power will ever diminish. A decade ago, one Indian leader said, "Every era of Indian policy has been ushered in with cheers of hope and salvation, only to find the ideals lost in the myriad red tape and bureaucratic side-stepping. . . . The major continuing factor of Indian policies is the effort of the BIA bureaucracy to resist, insert itself, and do everything to self-perpetuate."[22] That impression continues to be prevalent today among Minnesota's Indians.

Dr. John Red Horse, a professor at the University of Duluth, said, "Indians fear the federal government and the continuing policy threat of assimilation. But on the other hand, the federal government is their guarantee of the trust responsibility and of the programs that follow from that relationship."[23]

State Relations

Indian nations are reluctant to acknowledge any further state jurisdiction over their affairs. They believe it is a threat to their sovereignty. Although Minnesota is considered by Indians to be one of the most cooperative states, the tribes fear any efforts to increase state intrusion over tribal affairs. As they assume jurisdiction over more of their inherent sovereign rights to govern, the tribes face complex issues about how to assert those rights. Despite the fact that federal law and the U.S. Constitution protect Indian rights and sovereignty, many state or local governments still are attempting to exert their own jurisdiction in such areas as law enforcement; courts; levying taxes; regulating zoning, hunting and fishing; and environmental protection rules.

Government and Economics

Casinos have provided needed funds for improvements on the reservations, yet they cannot begin to overcome the economic disparities still existing between most reservation Indian communities and those of the general population. Casinos also provide no financial benefits to the majority of the state's Indians, who live away from the reservations. On reservations where tribal employment is overwhelmingly funded by federal programs, such as the Red Lake Reservation, public support systems play a very large role in the economy.

History has proven the U.S. government's Indian policy is inconsistent. An Indian lobbyist stated, "The one consistent policy that has survived throughout the centuries of contact with Europeans is the greed to take from Indians whenever they have a desirable resource. This is happening again over the successful gambling operations."[24] Indeed, during the 2004 and 2005 Minnesota state legislative sessions, several bills involving Indian gaming were introduced, and Minnesota Governor Tim Pawlenty announced that the state needed to "explore a better deal for Minnesotans than the compacts that were negotiated fifteen years ago."[25] While none of the bills passed, Indian leaders expect that the issue of reopening compacts will arise again soon. According to Indian law expert James Genia, "As long as the casinos are making money and there is a budget deficit, then elected officials are likely to look to gaming for financial solutions."[26]

The memory of how the federal government and Congress have overlooked Indian rights and the fact that these rights continue to be tested in U.S. courts dominate Indians' thinking as they plan for the future. For tribes much more is at stake than just running a government that supplies needed services. Indians have one preeminent imperative, that of cultural and political survival. Very few Indians disagree with this priority, and most view the future with optimism. Tribes are accomplishing great things for their people. On numerous occasions, American Indian scholar Vine Deloria, Jr. has pointed out that self-determination is the Indian genie already out of the bottle and a concept that extends beyond merely political institutions into cultural, religious, and sociological arenas.

Chapter 3

The Tribes and the Land

History

Two major tribes—first the Dakota and later the Ojibwe—occupied the territory known as Minnesota. Both tribes skillfully adapted to the resources and limitations of the cold, water-rich, woodland country. They hunted and fished; gathered wild rice, berries, and maple syrup; built houses of poles and skins or bark in semipermanent villages; and traveled in summer by birch bark canoes and in winter on snowshoes along the countless waterways.

Dakota/Sioux

The Dakota ("friends" or "allies") were called Sioux by the whites, from the French corruption "Nadouessioux" of the Ojibwe word "Nadowa," meaning "snake" or "enemy." Sioux was the name used by the U.S. government in its formal treaty and other legal relations. The people, however, call themselves Dakota, the term used in this book.

The Mdewakanton, Wahpekute, Sisseton, and Wahpeton tribes comprised the Eastern or Woodland Dakota. The Mdewakanton and Wahpekute, called the "Lower Sioux," were located along the Mississippi River, in the St. Paul area, and at the lower end of the Minnesota River. The Sisseton and Wahpeton bands—the "Upper Sioux"—lived further up the Minnesota River and around Lake Traverse on the present-day Minnesota–South Dakota border. Together, these four groups were known as the Isanti or "Santee." Further west were the Yanktons, Yanktonais, and Tetons. Today, those whose ancestors came from the eastern woodlands are known as Dakota; those from the prairie are Nakota or Yankton; and those from the far west are Tetons or Lakota.

The Eastern Dakota were the predominant tribes in Minnesota until the early 1700s, but by 1750, much of northern Minnesota had become Ojibwe homeland. The Dakota were forced to move west, suffering enormous casualties, especially women and children.

Ojibwe/Chippewa

"Chippewa" was the formal name used in treaties, and it remains the legal name for government bodies. It was a corruption, however, of "Ojibwe," the term Indians use (which is used throughout this book). The name for these people in Ojibwe is Anishinabe, meaning "original man" or "spontaneous or genuine people."

There are major populations of Ojibwe in Michigan, Minnesota, North Dakota, Wisconsin, and southern Ontario, Canada. They are in the Algonquian linguistic family, which includes the Ottawa, Potawatomi, Cree, Menominee, Sac, Fox, Miami, Delaware, Shawnee, Cheyenne, Arapaho, and Blackfeet tribes. Before the French arrived, the Algonquian groups extended from Newfoundland to the Rocky Mountains, from Hudson Bay to the Cumberland River in Kentucky.

As middlemen in the fur trade, the Ojibwe moved west along the south shore of Lake Superior. The Northern Ojibwe or Salteaux ("people of the falls" in French) settled in Grand Portage and along the north shore of Lake Superior. The Southwestern Ojibwe moved into the interior through Fond du Lac, settling in central and western Minnesota.

For treaty purposes, the Ojibwe of Minnesota were divided into five large bands: Superior Band (Grand Portage, Bois Forte, and Fond du Lac); Mississippi Band (Sandy, Mille Lacs, White Oak Point, Rabbit, Gull, and Pokegama Lakes in central Minnesota); Pillager Band (Leech Lake, Cass Lake, and Otter Tail Pillagers and the Lake Winnibigoshish Band); Red Lake Band; and Pembina Band (west of Red Lake and into the Dakotas).

The Ho-Chunk

A third group, the Ho-Chunk (or Winnebago), were forcibly moved to reservations in Minnesota from 1847 to 1862, and their descendants are important members of Minnesota's Indian communities. Following the 1862 Dakota Conflict, Congress abrogated their treaty and ordered the Ho-Chunk removed from Minnesota. Currently, two groups have land outside Minnesota: the Ho-Chunk of Wisconsin and the Winnebago Tribe of Nebraska.

Early Contact with Whites and the Formation of Treaties

French traders and explorers were the first whites to arrive in Minnesota, establishing a few trading post forts and claiming the area for France. The British replaced them following the French and Indian War (1763), enjoying the loyalty of both Dakota and Ojibwe during the Revolutionary War. This support continued through the War of 1812.

In 1805, Captain Zebulon Pike signed a treaty with the Dakota (Mdewakanton Band) that ceded a nine-square-mile tract of land for a fort and trading post at the confluence of the Minnesota and Mississippi rivers. Some sixty gallons of liquor and $200 worth of gifts were used to encourage the sale. Although Pike estimated the land was worth $200,000, when the Senate approved the treaty in 1808, they listed it at $2,000. The fort (first called Fort St. Anthony and later Fort Snelling) was built in 1820 and was intended as a base from which to maintain U.S. sovereignty, control the fur trade, and stop intertribal warfare.

In 1825, a treaty was signed with the Ojibwe in an effort to secure peace between them and the Dakota. A line was drawn diagonally across the state, with each group to remain in its own area. Treaties in 1837 ceded large areas of Ojibwe and Dakota land to white settlers and timber seekers. The tribes were not required to move, and they retained rights to hunt and fish and gather. These rights were reaffirmed in a 1999 court decision (*Minnesota et al. v. Mille Lacs Band of Chippewa Indians et al.*) (see chapter 7). In 1847, treaties established new homelands for the Menominee and Winnebago, who were to be removed from their homes in Wisconsin and established as buffers between the Dakota and Ojibwe. The Menominee successfully resisted being moved to Minnesota; the Winnebago came but did not like the land and settled instead in 1855 on land where the Blue Earth River joins the Minnesota River. Many of the Winnebago were subsequently moved by the military to the plains area of South Dakota and Nebraska.

After 1849, when Minnesota became a territory, the pressure on Indians to cede land increased. In 1850, President Zachary Taylor attempted to revoke the Indians' hunting and fishing rights agreed to in the 1837 and 1842 treaties. In 1851, two treaties with the Dakota took all their Minnesota and South Dakota land in exchange for two small reservations—adjacent strips along the Minnesota River, 150 miles long and 10 miles wide on each bank—and the promise of annuities, education, and farm equipment. By 1858, these reservations were reduced by half, to just the southern bank.

In 1854, the Arrowhead region of Minnesota, the triangle of land north and east of Duluth, was ceded. Present-day Grand Portage and Fond du Lac Reservations were set aside, and provision was made for a reservation at Lake Vermilion. After iron ore was discovered in northeastern Minnesota, those lands were taken with the 1866 treaty.

Crowded together and starving, unable to hunt or maintain their way of life, lied to and cheated by the Indian agents and traders, the Dakota vented their anger over their suffering in the war of 1862. In a matter of a few weeks, about 1,400 people—as many Indians as whites—were dead. After the war, 307 Indians were sentenced to death by the U.S. government; President Abraham Lincoln eventually pardoned all but thirty-eight. On December 26, 1862, these thirty-eight Indians were hanged at Mankato in the largest mass execution ever to take place in the United States. In addition, 120 other Indians died in prison, and 350 died in the winter of 1862 at a camp at Fort Snelling.

Congress acted swiftly in 1863, unilaterally abrogating the Dakota treaties, authorizing the sale of the Dakota lands in Minnesota, and providing payment to white victims. The Lower Sioux were forced by U.S. troops to move first to a reserve at Crow Creek, South Dakota, and eventually to the Santee Reservation in Nebraska. The Upper Sioux fled and retreated to Sisseton, South Dakota, and Devil's Lake, North Dakota. In 1861, the Bureau of Indian Affairs enrollment list had over six thousand Dakota living in Minnesota. By the early 1870s, reports showed around thirty-five hundred Dakota in five locations throughout Nebraska, South and North Dakota, and Minnesota.[1] The Dakota people had paid a tremendous price. The money due them from the sale of their Minnesota lands agreed upon in the 1851 treaties was not paid until 1909.

About two hundred Mdewakanton who had not participated in the war of 1862 lived without a homeland in Minnesota for several years. In the late 1880s, Congress authorized the purchase of land for these people, establishing the Shakopee-Mdewakanton Sioux, Prairie Island Indian, and Lower Sioux Indian communities. The Indians who had returned to the Upper Sioux Community area, mostly Sissetons, had land purchased for them in 1938 under the Indian Reorganization Act. After 1871, no reservations could be formed, so their lands are called communities.

The Treaty of 1855 acquired north central Minnesota for the U.S. government, and reservations were established at Leech and Cass Lakes, Lake Winnibigoshish, Mille Lacs, Sandy, Rice, Gull, Rabbit, and Pokegama Lakes. Northwestern Minnesota was obtained through treaties in 1863 (amended in 1864) and agreements in 1889 (Nelson Act) and 1904.

The 1867 treaty established White Earth reservation, where all Ojibwe were expected to move. Under the Nelson Act of 1889, the Rice Commission, created to negotiate with tribes for the relinquishment of their reservation land, used strong and skillful persuasion to convince Minnesota's Ojibwe bands to move to the White Earth Reservation. Most of the Mille Lacs Indians refused to go, as did many on other reservations. The Nelson Act also provided that Indians could take up their individual allotments where they were, preserving the reservations for those who did not move. Lands allotted by the Nelson Act were to be protected for Indians for twenty-five years. However, the Morris Act (1902) and Clapp Amendments (1904 and 1906) removed many of the restrictions on timber sales by Indians and led to a rapid takeover of Indian land and timber resources.

An eighty-five-year-old White Earth Ojibwe woman recalled her mother's experiences:

> My mother told me how she put down her thumbprint on a piece of paper. She couldn't write. She couldn't speak English. My mother lost her land that way. She didn't know she was losing her allotment. . . . She was full blood. She wasn't supposed to be able to sell her land, according to the law. . . . The Indians went through their land money in a hurry. It took maybe a year. They bought horses and buggies and clothes. Then it was all gone and they had to live the way they did before."[2]

The Red Lake Band successfully resisted the pressure to move to White Earth Reservation. May-dway-gwa-no-nind, head chief of the Red Lake Nation at the time of negotiations, stated, "We think it is our duty to protect those that come after us. . . . We want the reservation we now select to last ourselves and our children forever."[3] The Red Lake Nation never accepted allotment and held the land communally. The reservation remains tribally held to this day.

Trust Land

The U.S. government holds two major categories of trust land: land allotted to Indian families and tribal land. Once in trust, land cannot be sold or taken by court action and is exempt from property taxes. Through the generations, allotted lands have been divided among heirs, creating a complicated legal situation. Individuals involved with these lands may apply to the BIA to remove them from trust status so they can be sold; qualified Indians may also apply to have lands they purchase taken into trust. The tribes do not have any control over allotted lands.

Prior to the passage of the Indian Reorganization Act of 1934, very little land was held in trust for tribes. The IRA was very important in enabling tribes to regain reservation land. For example, between 1934 and 1952, the Minnesota Chippewa Tribe (MCT) acquired 91,000 acres that were placed in trust. Through the 1960s and 1970s, most of the trust lands for the six MCT reservations were in the name of the MCT. Additions in the 1990s generally were in the name of the specific reservation; however, most of the lands remain with the MCT.

The tribe's governing body controls tribal land. It may be used for community facilities, economic development projects, leased to members for their homes, or leased to non-Indians for revenue production. For new land to be put into trust, it must be approved by the BIA, a process that can take years if local governments complain about loss of tax base.

The 2003 acreages of tribal, individually allotted, and government-purchased lands and their relationship to the original reservations are shown in Table 3.1. The current land figures are only the acres accepted by the BIA for trust status. All reservations have additional lands that have not yet been processed by the BIA. A further backlog resulted from a decision in 1995 by the U.S. Eighth Circuit Court of Appeals in a South Dakota case, which stopped the processing of Minnesota Indian lands.

Table 3.1. Indian reservations in Minnesota

	2003 acreage compared with original reservation acreage				Original Reservation	
	Indian Trust Lands					
	Tribal	Allotted	Governmental	Total	Acres	%
Minnesota Chippewa Tribe:						
Bois Forte	31,624	12,160	5	43,789	127,000	34%
Fond du Lac	5,634	17,268	—	22,902	97,800	23%
Grand Portage	38,966	7,086	79	46,131	56,512	82%
Leech Lake	16,640	10,916	4	27,560	677,099[1]	4%
Mille Lacs	3,967	140	0	4,107	61,028[2]	7%
White Earth	56,116	2,500	0	58,616	709,467[3]	11%
Red Lake	806,698	0	0	806,698	794,426[4]	
Dakota Communities:						
Lower Sioux	1,785	0	0	1,785		
Prairie Island	1,192	0	0	1,192		
Shakopee-Mdewakanton	661	0	0	661		
Upper Sioux	1,201	0	0	1,201		

[1] The area of Leech Lake Reservation included 212,000 acres in water surface of three big lakes, Leech, Winnibigoshish, and Cass.

[2] The federal government recognizes the original Mille Lacs Reservation, but some local units of government do not.

[3] The White Earth Band considers the four northeastern townships of the reservation (an additional 127,653 acres) to still be reservation although they were sold in 1889.

[4] The Red Lake total includes: lands never ceded, 407,730 acres; water surface of Lower and Upper Red Lakes, 230,000 acres; and ceded lands that were returned (including most of the Northwest Angle), 156,696 acres.

Source: House Research Department, "Indians, Indian Tribes, and State Government," January 2003.

Indians and Reservations Today

On the 2000 U.S. Census, 54,967 American Indians identified themselves in the "race alone" category in Minnesota; in the "race in combination" category, 81,074 people identified themselves as American
Indian and Alaska Native in combination with one or more other
races. Of this latter group, 39,910 identified as Chippewa (Ojibwe),
7,541 as Sioux (Dakota), 2,746 as Cherokee, and thirty-six from other
tribal nations; 9,939 were not specified. Because this was the first census that divided Indians into the "race alone" and "race in combination," it is not possible to compare the state's Indian population to the
1990 census. For many legal purposes, Indians are tribal members or
those eligible for tribal membership. Tribes alone have the authority
to define their own membership.

Minnesota's reservations are discussed in three groups in this book:
the six Ojibwe reservations (Bois Forte, Fond du Lac, Grand Portage,
Leech Lake, Mille Lacs, and White Earth), which have joined together
to form the Minnesota Chippewa Tribe; the independent Ojibwe Red
Lake Chippewa Tribe; and the four Dakota Communities (Lower
Sioux, Prairie Island, Shakopee Mdewakanton, and Upper Sioux).

Reservations are original land reserved for Indians and are areas
where Indian sovereignty is retained. Although there has been extensive transfer of land to non-Indian ownership, this has not removed
the land from the reservation. The U.S. Supreme Court has ruled that,
"the termination of federal responsibility and not the passing of legal
land title within an area . . . determines whether a reservation exists in
the eyes of the law" (*Seymour v. Superintendent*, 368 U.S. 351 (1962)).
Unless Congress specifically acts to extinguish Indian rights, a reservation includes all the land "notwithstanding issuance of any patent"
(18 U.S.C. 1151(1948)).

The following brief descriptions of Minnesota's reservations are
based on a variety of sources, including the Overall Economic Development Plans prepared by the six MCT reservations, numerous articles in tribal newspapers, personal interviews, visits to the reservations,
and many other sources used in preparing this book.

The Minnesota Chippewa Tribe (MCT)

The MCT is the formal governing body of six Ojibwe reservations. The
capital of the MCT is Cass Lake on the Leech Lake Reservation. While

each of the six tribes has its own constitution, the MCT provides the overall governance. Much of the tribes' land is in trust in the name of the MCT, not the individual reservation. Tribal membership is with the MCT, although in practical terms each reservation now deals with its own membership, recommending approval by the MCT.

BOIS FORTE   The Bois Forte Indians lived in the fortress-like forest in the Rainy River watershed of northern Minnesota. The tribe first ceded land in the La Pointe Treaty of 1854. A treaty in 1866 established the Nett Lake Reservation. Reservation land was added by executive order at Lake Vermilion in 1881 and at Deer Creek in 1883.

The reservation is heavily forested with beautiful stands of pine, aspen, cedar, birch, ash, and other species of timber, providing an excellent wildlife habitat. Four independent Indian logging firms do business on or near the reservation. Wetlands cover approximately 50 percent of the land. Nett Lake, covering 7,300 acres, is considered the largest wild rice producing lake in the United States. In 1987, a dam was built to help control the water level.

The Bois Forte Reservation includes three portions: around Nett Lake, 103,000 acres in St. Louis and Koochiching counties, containing the major population and the communities of Nett Lake (forty miles south of Canada), Indian Point, and Sugar Bush; one thousand acres on Lake Vermilion, which have been developed into a casino, hotel-resort complex (Fortune Bay); and twenty-three thousand acres in Deer Creek Township with no population. Orr, the nearest off-reservation city, is twenty-one miles away; Virginia, sixty-five; and International Falls, seventy. The Lake Vermilion portion is sixty-five miles away, located ten miles southwest of Tower and twenty-five miles west of Ely.

The community of Nett Lake contains the tribal headquarters, a medical clinic, and the Nett Lake Education Center, combining elementary school, Head Start, day care, social services, and youth and community centers. The elementary school is a state public school, authorized by special legislation; the Orr high school serves the population. The nearest hospital is in Cook.

The Indian community at Lake Vermilion has a family resource center providing day care and Head Start services, family education programs, and community services, as well as an outpatient health clinic. Fortune Bay Resort Casino, a high stakes casino, opened in

1986, offering blackjack tables, slot machines and other video gaming, bingo, and food service. The 118-room Fortune Bay Resort Hotel and Conference Center opened in 1996.

FOND DU LAC   The 1854 treaty with the Lake Superior and Mississippi bands established the Fond du Lac Reservation. The reservation is located in St. Louis and Carlton counties, abutting Cloquet on the east, with Duluth twenty miles to the northeast. U.S. Highway 2 cuts across the northern part of the reservation and Interstate 35, the southeast corner. The land is rolling hills along the St. Louis River, which forms the eastern and northern boundaries. The eastern part of the reservation is well-settled, sandy farming land; the west is clay soil and wooded. The southern portion is level marshland, with twenty-three lakes totaling over 3,999 acres. Only commercially poor, second-growth timber remains on the reservation.

A new $9 million facility housing tribal government and community sports and social activities opened in 1997 in the Cloquet area. Community centers are also located in Sawyer and Brookston. Human and health services are provided at the Min-No-Aya-Win Health Clinic in Cloquet. The tribe operates a similar Indian health program in Duluth, through the Center for American Indian Resources (CAIR). The tribally run Fond du Lac Group Home for juveniles is located between Duluth and Cloquet. Sawyer is the location of Mash-Ka-Wisen, the nation's first Indian owned and operated residential, primary treatment facility for chemical dependency. The reservation is divided among four Minnesota public schools districts. The tribe has a Head Start program and operates the Ojibwe K–12 school. The unique Fond du Lac Tribal Community College is both a tribal college and a state community college, with a campus in the Twin Cities as well.

The Fond du Lac Tribe operates two casinos. In the only such arrangement in Minnesota, the tribe and the City of Duluth cooperated in building and sharing in the profits of the Fond-du-Luth Casino. It is Minnesota's only casino built on land not originally part of a reservation. The tribe purchased a deserted block in downtown Duluth that now houses 20,000 square feet of gaming and food service. Black Bear Casino and Hotel, the second largest employer in

Carlton County, located at the junction of Highway 210 and Interstate Highway 35, has 82,000 square feet of gaming, food service, entertainment, and a gift shop. The adjacent 158-room Black Bear Hotel opened in 1995.

GRAND PORTAGE   The Grand Portage Reservation, created by the La Pointe Treaty of 1854, occupies the most northeastern portion of Minnesota, encompassing a historic fur trade site, with spectacular woods and rugged Lake Superior shoreline. The name comes from the nine-mile portage necessary to bypass the cascading waters of the Pigeon River, a two hundred-foot drop, to get inland to the highway of lakes and rivers leading to the fur-rich areas of northern Minnesota. The reservation extends eighteen miles along the lake. Highway 61, the route from Duluth to Canada and the circle route around Lake Superior, crosses the reservation. The tribal headquarters is located in the community of Grand Portage. The reservation has no incorporated city; Grand Marais is the closest city, thirty-six miles to the southwest. Duluth is 150 miles away, and Thunder Bay, Canada, is thirty-seven miles farther north.

Grand Portage houses the tribal headquarters, a community store, tribal businesses, and the Gitchi Onigaming Community Center, built with tribal funds in 1994. The center offers recreational activities, a swimming pool, senior and teen centers, computers, a library, and powwow grounds. The center also provides services for the day care center and Head Start program. A new school for kindergarten through third grade students, linked to the center, opened in 1997. Fourth through sixth grade and junior and senior high students attend school in Grand Marais. A health clinic serves the community; the nearest hospital is at Grand Marais.

The Grand Portage area has numerous attractions for tourists. The Grand Portage National Monument features the reconstructed fur trade fort of the late 1700s. Ferries to Isle Royale National Park depart from Grand Portage, and the reservation has over one hundred miles of hiking trails. Grand Portage State Park, opened in 1995 and operated by the tribe, has made the 130-foot Great Falls of the Pigeon River accessible to the public. The Grand Portage Lodge, located on the shores of Lake Superior, opened in 1975; a casino was added in 1990 and expanded in the mid-1990s. It is the largest employer in

Cook County. Additional employment is available in the lumber industry, commercial fishing on Lake Superior, and with the National Park Service. In 2005, with assistance from the Shakopee Mdewakanton Sioux Community, the tribe opened the Grand Portage Trading Post that houses a grocery store, restaurant, post office, Laundromat, gaming area, gas station, and a car repair shop.

LEECH LAKE   The area that includes Leech Lake Reservation in north central Minnesota was the home of Ojibwe bands located around the three major lakes of the region: Cass, Leech, and Winnibigoshish. The Pillager and Lake Winnibigoshish bands ceded the land by 1855, and the treaty of 1864 established the Leech Lake Reservation. The 1864 treaty and executive orders of 1873 and 1874 expanded and consolidated the reservation. The Leech Lake Tribe holds the smallest percentage of its reservation of any of Minnesota's tribes; county, state, and federal governments own well over half the original reservation.

Drained by the headwaters of the Mississippi River, it is a prime sports fishing area, with over 250 lakes. Approximately forty produce wild rice, making Leech Lake one of the largest natural wild rice producers of all the state's reservations. The land is mostly second-growth timber usable for hardwood, wood chips, waferboard, softwood pulp, and sawtimber. Seventy-five percent of the National Chippewa Forest is within the reservation.

Located along U.S. Highway 2, the reservation is fourteen miles east of Bemidji and fifty-three miles west of Grand Rapids. Cass Lake, the largest community within the reservation, is the site of the Leech Lake Tribal headquarters, the offices of the MCT, the BIA Minnesota Agency, and an Indian Health Services hospital and clinic. Other communities within the reservation, many of which have their own community centers and social programs, include Ball Club, Bena, Inger, Onigum, Mission, Pennington, Smokey Point, Sugar Point, Oak Point, and Squaw Lake. The reservation is split among four counties (Cass, Itasca, Beltrami, and Hubbard) and is divided among seven Minnesota school districts (Cass Lake, Bemidji, Blackduck, Deer River, Grand Rapids, Remer, and Walker).

The Leech Lake Tribal Council is the governing body (formerly called the Reservation Business Committee), with offices in Cass Lake.

The tribe provides education and programs for children in two child care facilities, Head Start programs in seven communities, and the kindergarten through 12th grade Bug-O-Nay-Ge-Shig tribal school. The tribe sponsors and provides funding for the Leech Lake Tribal College in Cass Lake, begun in 1990, which offers two-year degrees with credits transferable to Bemidji State University and other higher education institutions.

The tribe operates three gaming enterprises: The Palace Hotel and Casino, the Northern Lights Gaming Emporium, located four miles south of Walker; and the White Oak Casino in Deer River. The casinos have made the tribe the largest employer in Cass County.

Employment is also available in several tribal enterprises in Cass Lake, including a restaurant, service station, convenience store, gift shop, motel, archaeology firm, a major fish hatchery, and the Leech Lake Wild Rice Company. A retail center, built by the tribe, houses Indian-run businesses and provides incubator services for new enterprises. The U.S. Forest Service also is a major employer, as are wood processing plants.

MILLE LACS   The Mille Lacs Reservation area was included in the 1837 treaty with the Mississippi band; the 1855 treaty established the reservation. Some later treaties and acts of Congress recognized the Mille Lacs Reservation, but other interpretations of those same treaties and acts attempted to remove Indians from the land. Allotments were finally provided in the 1920s to those Indians who remained. In recent years, the band has been reclaiming its reservation by purchasing more land. They now own slightly more than 20 percent of the 1855 reservation lands.

The reservation, located one hundred miles north of Minneapolis/St. Paul, is in four counties of east central Minnesota: Mille Lacs, Crow Wing, Aitkin, and Pine. The state's second largest lake, Mille Lacs, dominates the reservation. The land is mainly second-growth forest, swampy tracts, and countless small lakes and streams. For governmental purposes, the reservation is divided into three districts. District I, the largest section, with about 60 percent of the population, is on the southwest shore of Mille Lacs Lake around Vineland. The band government is located here, as are the Grand Casino and Grand

Casino Hotel Mille Lacs, tribal schools, and health clinic. The Minnesota Historical Society, in cooperation with the tribe's elders and artists, has built a $6 million museum. Onamia (twelve miles away) and Brainerd (thirty miles away) are the closest towns. District II is a collection of scattered sites on the east side of Mille Lacs Lake and to the north, including East Lake, the district center, which houses a community center built in 1995. The Lake Lena area is District III, eighty-five miles from Vineland and thirty miles east of Hinckley, near the Wisconsin border and St. Croix State Park. In 1990, 1,500 additional acres of land, including a lake, were added to the reservation in this area. Lake Lena has an award-winning ceremonial center as well as a community center completed in 1995. The Grand Casino Hinckley, with a 281-room hotel, is within this district.

The casinos are the largest employers in both Mille Lacs and Pine counties. The tribe also owns and operates the Woodlands National Bank in Onamia, the first Indian-owned bank in Minnesota; the Lake Mille Lacs Bakery in Onamia; and a service station/convenience store on Highway 169.

Given the scattered nature of the reservation, Mille Lacs children attend several Minnesota public school systems. The Nay Ah Shing tribal schools provide an alternative, with an emphasis on Indian culture and the Ojibwe language.

WHITE EARTH   The White Earth Reservation, established in 1867, was intended to be the home of all Ojibwe in Minnesota. Located in northwestern Minnesota, the reservation is divided among the three counties of Mahnomen, Clearwater, and Becker. Indian communities within the reservation are White Earth, Pine Point/Ponsford, Naytahwaush, Elbow Lake, Beaulieu, and Rice Lake. Other villages include Callaway, Ogema, Waubun, and Mahnomen. The major cities outside the boundaries are Detroit Lakes at the southwest corner, Park Rapids on the southeast, and Bagley to the northeast. From the community of White Earth, Bemidji is eighty miles to the northeast; Moorhead is seventy miles to the west. The land to the east is rolling, second-growth forests, streams, and lakes; on the west are the flat, fertile farming lands of the Red River Valley.

Numerous treaties and unfair negotiations caused rapid division of the reservation, with much of the land passing into non-Indian ownership. In the 1990s, the White Earth Land Settlement Act transferred ten thousand acres of state/county-held lands to the tribe. White Earth has relatively little allotted land remaining in trust. Enrolled members, however, hold significant amounts of privately owned, fee lands equaling about one-half of the reservation's trust property. These are lands that pay property taxes.[4]

White Earth Village is the location of tribal headquarters; the Indian Health Services (IHS) clinic, which had a $10-million, fivefold expansion in 1995; the tribal K–12 school Circle of Life; and a housing project and center for seniors. Because of the widely scattered settlement pattern on the reservation, government services, social programs, Head Start, and day care are provided at four other centers, Naytahwaush, Pine Point, Rice Lake, and Elbow Lake. There is an additional Head Start at Waubun and health stations at Naytahwaush and Ponsford. There is only one hospital located on the reservation, in the city of Mahnomen. Other hospitals are in communities off the reservation. Seven Minnesota public school districts serve White Earth. The Pine Point School is an experimental public school that is now tribally run.

The tribe's Shooting Star Casino and Hotel in Mahnomen is the largest employer in Mahnomen County. The Manitok Mall, also owned by the tribe, offers shops and day care facilities for those coming to the casino. The tribe also owns and operates Ojibwa Building Supplies and Ojibwa Office Supplies in Waubun.

Red Lake

Through treaties and agreements in 1863, 1889, and 1904, the Red Lake Nation gave up land but never ceded the main reservation surrounding Lower Red Lake and Upper Red Lake.

Tribal leadership during the late 1800s and early 1900s skillfully resisted allotment legislation and held the land intact for the tribe as a whole. When land that had been ceded but not sold was returned after 1934, this restored land amounted to 156,696 acres. It included 85 percent of the Northwest Angle of Minnesota, as well as lands scattered between the reservation and the Canadian border. The total land area controlled by the tribe, located in nine different counties, is about the size of Rhode Island.

The tribal government has full sovereignty over the reservation, subject only to federal legislation specifically intended to deal with

Red Lake, which makes it a "closed" reservation. It has never been subject to state law.

The reservation is located in northwestern Minnesota. It completely surrounds Lower Red Lake, the state's largest lake, and includes a major portion of Upper Red Lake, the state's fourth largest lake. Bemidji, the closest city, is thirty-five miles to the south. Thief River Falls is over seventy miles west. The land is slightly rolling and heavily wooded, with 337,000 acres of commercial forest land under management. There are lakes, swamps, peat bogs, and prairies, with some land on the western side suitable for farming. The main population areas are in Beltrami and Clearwater counties. The four reservation communities are Red Lake, Redby, Ponemah, and Little Rock. Red Lake is the location of the tribal headquarters, tribal information center archives and library, tribal court, law enforcement, fire department, social services, natural resources, Boys and Girls Club, gas station, BIA agency office, Red Lake School (K–12), IHS hospital, Jourdain/Perpich Extended Care Facility for the elderly, community center, and Humanity Center, which houses the tribal college, elderly nutrition program, casino, and bingo.

The community of Redby offers a community center, group home and halfway house, as well as employment at a fish hatchery and tree nursery. Redby also is the location of numerous education programs, a child development center, and county and tribal social services. Ponemah offers a day care, K–8 school, fire and ambulance station, health clinic, chemical dependency program, and Boys and Girls Club.

The tribe has Seven Clans Casinos in Red Lake, Thief River Falls, and Warroad.

The Dakota Communities

While some Dakota did not leave following the 1862 war, most had retreated or were taken as prisoners and were placed in reservations in Nebraska (Santee), South Dakota (Flandreau, Sisseton), North Dakota (Devils Lake), and Montana (Fort Peck) or escaped to Canada (Indian reserves in Manitoba and Saskatchewan).[5] By the 1880s, a few Mdewakanton Dakota Indians had returned to their homelands, and by the mid-1880s, the federal government was being urged to do something to provide homes for these people, primarily Mdewakanton Dakota. An 1885 federal law provided some money for the purchase of land for those who had been in the state by October 1, 1883 (a date later extended to May 20, 1886). Additional money was made available in 1886, 1889, and 1890. Most of the current trust land was added under the Indian Reorganization Act in the 1930s (see Table 3.2).

LOWER SIOUX   The Lower Sioux Indian Community, located on the south side of the Minnesota River, is part of the original reservation established in the 1851 Treaty. It is in Redwood County, two miles south of Morton and six miles east of Redwood Falls. Across the river is the Birch Coulee battle site of the 1862 Sioux War. Two Indians, Good Thunder and Charles Lawrence, bought land at the location as early as 1834. Under the land purchase laws of the 1880s and 1890s and again under the IRA, land was acquired for the community.[6]

The land is primarily rich agricultural land. The community, built on the hillside and uplands, centers around the tribal offices, a new community center, Tipi Maka Duta (the Lower Sioux Trading Post), and St. Cornelia Episcopal Church, on the National Register of Historic Sites. There is a public school in Redwood Falls. The tribe manufactures traditional handcrafted Dakota pottery and gets a small amount of revenue from lease of a gravel pit. A major bingo

Table 3.2. Minnesota's Dakota communities, government-held lands (in acres)

	Early 1930s	Purchased under IRA	Total	1963 land in trust
Lower Sioux	470	over 1,200	1,670	1,743
Prairie Island	120	414	534	534
Shakopee Mdewakanton	258	—	258	258
Upper Sioux	—	746	746	746

Source: Adapted from Roy W. Meyer, *History of the Santee Sioux*, rev. ed. (Lincoln: University of Nebraska Press, 1993), 348–349.

facility, Jackpot Junction, opened in 1984 and was expanded into a casino in 1986. The tribe also owns the nearby Lower Sioux Lodge and Convention Center, the Dakota Inn Motel, an RV park, and the 18-hole Dacotah Ridge Golf Club.

PRAIRIE ISLAND   The Prairie Island Indian Community is located on Prairie Island, which is formed as the Vermillion River joins the Mississippi. The land is low-lying, with about half of the community's property in the flood plain. The island is shared with Xcel Energy's nuclear electric generating plant and the U.S. Army Corps of Engineers U.S. Lock and Dam No. 3. The city of Red Wing, without tribal consent, incorporated Prairie Island into the city. This enabled it to collect taxes from the Xcel facility.

Treasure Island Resort and Casino, begun as a bingo operation in 1984, was expanded in 1993. A 250-room hotel and convention center was added in 1996. Casino profits have funded improvements in roads and water and sewer systems. A community center provides kindergarten, licensed day care, and facilities for tribal government. Students attend the Red Wing School District. Programming and congregate dining for the elders are available at the casino. A health clinic funded by the tribe and the IHS brings Mayo Clinic physicians to the reservation several days per week.

SHAKOPEE MDEWAKANTON   Reservation land was first purchased for the Shakopee Mdewakanton in the 1880s. Under the land purchase laws of the 1880s–1890s, land was acquired for community members.[7] The Shakopee Mdewakanton Sioux Community is in Scott County, just twenty-five miles southwest of downtown Minneapolis, their former territory. In 1972, the city of Prior Lake incorporated the reservation into that city. The tribe has taken advantage of its location, gambling laws, and exemption from state liquor and cigarette taxes to develop profitable enterprises. Mystic Lake Casino and Hotel in Prior Lake, one of the most financially successful Indian casino operations in the United States, has its origins in bingo operations, which began in 1982. Today, Shakopee Mdewakanton gaming and nongaming enterprises employ over 5,000 workers. Other tribal offerings include a state-of-the-art child care center,

Playworks LINK Event Center, Dakotah! Sports and Fitness, Dakotah Meadows RV Park and Campground, Dakota Mall shopping center, an $18 million hotel, opened in 1996, with second and third wings and convention facilities subsequently added, and The Meadows at Mystic championship golf course, which opened in 2005. The community also owns and operates a Mystic Lake retail store at the Mall of America. Community students attend Shakopee and Prior Lake school districts. The community also has a health clinic and dental office that serves members, employees, and other Indians living in Scott County.

UPPER SIOUX   The Upper Sioux Community is located in Yellow Medicine County, three miles south of Granite Falls at the mouth of the Yellow Medicine River. Much of the land is in the flood plain and not suitable for building. The area was settled by members of the Sisseton Dakota Band on land purchased in 1938 under the IRA. Community children attend Granite Falls and other area public schools. Firefly Creek Casino was replaced by Prairie's Edge Casino Resort in 2003. In recent years, a community building, powwow grounds, and numerous business enterprises have been built.

Pipestone

Pipestone, Minnesota, is universally revered as a sacred site. The unique catlinite stone of Pipestone made the site an honored place for Indians. They declared it neutral ground and allowed different tribes use of the stone. On his visit in 1836, George Catlin noted, "It is evident that these people set an extraordinary value on the red stone . . . for whenever an Indian presents a pipe made of it, he gives it as something from the Great Spirit."[8]

Through a series of treaties with the U.S. government, this sacred land was relinquished and reacquired. In an 1858 treaty with the Yankton Sioux (11 Stat. 743) that established the tribe's reservation 150 miles north of the quarry, the land was relinquished, and the Yankton were granted the free and unrestricted use of the red pipestone quarry and as much land as necessary for procuring stone for pipes. The quarry was to be kept "open and free to the Indians to visit and procure stone for pipes so long as they shall desire." In 1859, one square mile including the quarry was surveyed as a reservation.[9] In 1928, the Yankton tribe sold the quarry land to the federal government, and a National Monument was created in 1937.[10]

A government boarding school for Indians established in Pipestone drew Indian employees from nearby Flandreau, South Dakota. The school closed in the late 1940s. A Dakota community remains. Indian groups can apply for unused federal land, and there is interest in seeking BIA recognition and the return of this land to the Pipestone Indian community.

Under a permit system, Indian carvers continue to craft items and keep the ancient artistic skill alive. Access is available to any enrolled Indian. Approximately two hundred Indians have permits, but many come only once per year. Less than fifty live in the area and make a living from the quarry.[11] Stone from Pipestone was used in the new Smithsonian Indian museum that opened in Washington, D.C., in 2004.

Pipestone Dakota (formerly Pipestone Indian Shrine Association) represents the carvers group, which organized in 1955. In the mid-1990s, Yankton Dakota tribal members began urging that control of the site be given to their tribe. They view the stone itself as sacred and urge that all quarrying be stopped. There are other Indian voices pointing out the tradition of using the stone for trade and artistic purposes, as well as for sacred pipemaking. They also want to keep the area open to all Indians as a neutral and sacred place.[12]

Land Issues

Original Treaty Claims

The Indian Claims Commission heard claims from 1946 to 1983 to deal with alleged wrongs done to Indians prior to 1946. The issues brought before the Commission dealt primarily with inadequate payment to the tribes at the time of the treaties. Almost all treaties involving Minnesota Indians were reviewed, and awards were granted. Once a claim was settled, no other claim concerning that treaty may be filed.

The settlements, established unilaterally by Congress, provided that no land can be returned and that the settlement be based on the value of the land at the time the treaty was negotiated. Typically 20 percent would go to the tribal government, and the rest would be divided in a per capita payment among descendants. The money paid out in claims was not subject to state or federal taxes, and it could not be used to reduce welfare or payments from other government programs. The process of locating descendants and completing the other paper work dragged the settlements out for years. Payments, when finally received, were often mere tokens, especially when compared to the current value of the land and the cumulative benefits received by the non-Indian parties. Claims not completed by 1983, issues not dealt with by the Commission, and issues arising after 1946 are dealt with in the U.S. Court of Federal Claims, the regular system for suing the federal government.

RED LAKE TRIBE AND MCT INDIAN CLAIMS COMMISSION CASES, 1997   Both the Red Lake Tribe and the MCT had claims (filed by 1951) that had not been resolved by 1983 and were transferred to the U.S. Court of Federal Claims. The claims dealt primarily with mistreatment under the Nelson Act and the subsequent mismanagement of the funds, as well as the handling of forests and trust funds since 1946. The Red Lake Tribe, after forty years with little progress, hired experts to document their case, an expensive process. In 1995, the two tribal groups agreed to cooperate and share information. The MCT agreed to reimburse the Red Lake Tribe for an appropriate portion of their costs, which ultimately came to $2 million for the MCT and $6 million for the Red Lake Tribe.

In 1997, a negotiated settlement was proposed on five of the thirteen pending claims of the Red Lake Tribe and on all of the MCT claims. The $20-million settlement, negotiated with the MCT, was approved in a controversial split decision by the Tribal Executive Committee, speaking for all six reservations. The White Earth Tribal Council rejected it on behalf of its nation.

In June 1997, the Red Lake Tribal Council announced its settlement of $27 million. The distribution, after legal costs and other expenses, was 80 percent to members of the tribe born on or prior to January 27, 1998. It was estimated that the per capita payment would exceed $1,700. Red Lake still has eight claims pending.[13]

DISTRIBUTION OF TIMBER PROCEEDS   At the time of the Nelson Act, the federal government dealt with all Ojibwe tribes as one unit. The Minnesota Chippewa Trust Fund received all the money from the sale of lands and the timber resources. The money was to be held for fifty years at 5 percent interest. Interest was to be distributed on a per capita basis to the Indians, with one-fourth going to schools. At the end of the fifty years, the remaining funds would be distributed in equal shares to all Minnesota Ojibwe. Other funds, from the specific reservations, were added to the joint fund, including the Mille Lacs claim settlement in 1913 for the government's failure to collect money for the sale of lands and pine.

The trust fund became a source of contention, with tribes disagreeing about payment share, who was entitled to payments, and what the timing of distribution would be. The Segregation Bill of 1942 (56 Stat. 1039, Ch. 673) ended the common fund by requiring that each tribe have its own trust fund. It also ended the claims of the two tribes to the revenue gained from the other's ceded lands.

Two other major claim issues are pending against the BIA in its role as trustee of allottee and tribal trust resources. Some 300,000 accounts are included in the case involving allottees and tribes; since 1981, the Red Lake Tribe has been seeking an accounting on its trust funds, primarily from timber and the sawmill operation. The federal government is unable to account for the money.

In 1994, Congress enacted the American Indian Trust Fund Management Reform Act to bring required reforms to Indian trust assets, accounts, and resources managed by the United States. Little progress has been made, however, despite the fact that millions of federal dollars have been appropriated to the Department of the Interior for purposes of trust management reform. In 1996, a class action suit (*Cobell v. Norton*, formerly *Cobell v. Babbitt*) was filed by beneficiaries of Individual Indian Money accounts. The suit continues to be litigated before the U.S. District Court for the District of Columbia, with the courts repeatedly holding federal officials, including two Secretaries of the Interior, in contempt of court for failing to resolve the accounting issues.

Other Trust Land Issues

DIMINISHED RESERVATION SIZE   Since Indian sovereignty extends throughout reservations for some tribal-related issues whether or not the land is in trust, the reservation size is very important to the tribes who feel their boundaries should not be decreased. Reservation boundaries have been an issue with three of Minnesota's Ojibwe tribes—Red Lake, White Earth, and Mille Lacs—who believe their boundaries should be increased or maintained intact.

TRIBAL-STATE LAND PROBLEMS   Generally, the state has no role in tribal trust lands, since the federal status preempts any state involvement. However, circumstances do arise when a state project is on the reservation, and the state requires that it hold title to the property. Public schools, Head Start facilities, and historical society projects have had to deal with this jurisdictional problem. For example, in 1994, state funds were provided for an addition to the Red Lake School, a Minnesota public school. However, the construction was halted when the parties involved realized the land was in the name of the tribe. Eventually, the state negotiated that the tribe would lease the land to the school for fifty years.

RESERVATION LANDS HELD BY FEDERAL AGENCIES   The federal government has been a major beneficiary of Indian reservation lands. The 1908 law that created the Chippewa National Forest on and around Leech Lake Reservation provided that the lands allotted to Indians could be sold or exchanged for allotments outside the forest area. The legislation allowed cutting except for 10 percent, which was to be left standing to reforest the area. This resulted in the rapid harvesting of the virgin pine forests.[14] This process of acquiring the National Forest land, including defective title transfers, has been questioned by Indians.

The White Earth Reservation has over 22,000 acres of national federal wetlands and almost 21,500 acres in the Tamarac National Wildlife Refuge. The Tamarac Refuge, created by an agreement between the BIA and the U.S. Fish and Wildlife Service in the 1930s, stipulated that Indians were to have priority in ricing and trapping in the refuge; they were to be employed in developing it and trained in wildlife management; and ricing privileges were promised on the Rice Lake Migratory Waterfowl Area in Aitken County.[15] Tamarac National Wildlife Refuge is still used by Indians for wild rice and trapping (see chapter 7). The training program for wildlife management never materialized. Some small parcels of trust land remain within the Refuge.

Some land issues have been resolved. On the White Earth Reservation over twenty-eight thousand acres classified as submarginal land were held by the U.S. Department of Agriculture. This was logged land that had been allotted and then went out of Indian ownership. After years of lobbying, legislation was passed in 1975 to return the land to the tribe, and eventually it became trust land. The White Earth Land Settlement Act of 1986, while transferring ten thousand acres of state and county lands to the tribe, also gave non-Indians land inside White Earth borders. Thousands of acres were taken out of trust status and sold to non-Indians living on White Earth trust land.

THE WHITE EARTH LAND RECOVERY PROJECT   The White Earth Land Recovery Project, a private nonprofit group led by Winona LaDuke and White Earth members, is working to recover the original land base of the White Earth reservation. The group is raising money and seeking other donations to acquire White Earth land, stressing the need for Indians to rebuild their land base and to restore traditional practices of sound land stewardship. The group had acquired fifteen hundred acres by 2002.

ADDING TRUST LAND   All Minnesota reservations have made it a priority to reacquire their reservation land. Some tribes, such as Grand Portage—now at 81 percent of its original reservation—have increased their size considerably. Other tribes, such as Leech Lake—which has only 4 to 6 percent of its original land—still have very little of their reservation trust land.

The true importance of trust status is that it signifies and requires the federal government to honor its obligations to tribes and prevents the lands from being sold or taken in the future. Land in trust is no longer subjected to property tax, and the income earned from operations on the property is not subject to state income taxation.

The IRA provided that the Department of the Interior could acquire land for the benefit of Indians within or outside the reservation boundaries. For Indian land purchases to be put into trust, the BIA procedure up until the mid-1990s required that the county be notified when the application was submitted to the BIA and that the land conformed to certain federal policies. Considerable confusion about the trust process was raised by a decision of a three-judge panel of the U.S. Eighth District Court of Appeals in November 1995 (*State of South Dakota v. U.S. Dept of Interior*, 69 F3rd 878, 1995). The court ruled that the 1934 IRA law did not provide the BIA with sufficient guidelines on how to judge what constituted property suitable for trust status and was therefore an unconstitutional delegation of power from Congress to the executive branch of government. A U.S. Supreme Court directive said the BIA should rework the rules, and the issue was sent back to the lower court. The BIA published corrected rules that have allowed for lands to be taken into trust for tribes.

One of President Clinton's final acts in office was issuing a ruling to ease the process by which tribes could get land accepted into trust status, but the rule was rescinded by the Bush administration. At a February 2004 conference, Indian leader Doug Nash noted that the Bush administration was "no longer considering the subject of fee-to-trust lands which basically creates a moratorium on such transactions."[16]

Several major Minnesota purchases are not yet in trust status and are subject to property taxes: White Earth Reservation's casino, Shooting Star in Mahnomen; Leech Lake casino, Northern Lights, near Walker, Minnesota (see chapter 8); Lower Sioux Community's Dakota Inn Motel; Red Lake's Lake of the Woods Motel; and two apartment houses (in Warroad) are not in trust.

New land intended for casinos off the reservation is regulated under the National Indian Gaming Act (1988). The law designates that the Secretary of Interior determine if the land is in the best interests of the tribe, and then the governor of the state is asked for concurrence. The Minnesota tribal–state gaming compacts and unwritten agreements in the early 1990s prevented the expansion of casinos off reservations, but by early 2004, Minnesota legislators and the governor began asking for tribes to renegotiate compacts and for the state to allow expansion of Indian and non-Indian gaming. Some tribes have joined the state in its efforts, while others, through the Minnesota Indian Gaming Association, have refused such entreaties.

The tribes point out that they are sovereign governments and are exempt from property taxes, as are other levels of government. The tribes are repaying the community by providing employment opportunities and expanded business opportunities that do pay a full array of taxes. Several tribes are voluntarily paying for county services.

Indian tax-exempt property is estimated at less than 1 percent of all such property in the state. The most recent Minnesota figures show that nine thousand acres worth approximately $7.5 million were transferred to Indian trust status from 1992 to 1998. Taxes paid on those nine thousand acres prior to transfer totaled $141,000, a small share of the tax bases in the affected counties.[17]

Allotment Issues

Allotment of lands to individual Indians was a very effective tool for whites to acquire Indian land and resources owned by Indians. By numerous manipulations of the law, policies, and illegal dealings, land was rapidly removed from Indian ownership. Generally, the land was to be kept in trust for twenty-five years and then passed to the individual as fee land. These lands were no longer subjected to Indian-specific laws. The land could be sold, mortgaged, taken for debts, and was subject to property taxes.

The Minnesota Supreme Court in *State v. Zay Zah* (259 NW2d 580 (1977)) found that the trust status of Indian land should not have ended unless there was federal legislation authorizing it and there had been Indian consent. Research ultimately found large numbers of land transfers to fee status had been done without meeting those standards. Federal law 28 U.S.C. 2415 was passed to document the extent of land taken or sold without proper compensation prior to 1966. As a result, researchers found a tangled mass of frequent law and policy changes, gross neglect of trustee responsibility, improper law interpretations, and law violations.[18]

White Earth Reservation Problems; White Earth Land Settlement Act (WELSA)

Problems were especially acute on the White Earth reservation, where the special laws resulted in the transfer to fee title for most Indians. When this happened, the BIA ended the trust relationship with these Indians, and after 1915, the BIA no longer probated their estates. These actions were questioned by the *Zay Zah* Minnesota Supreme Court ruling. Some one hundred thousand acres on White Earth had clouded titles (sixty-six thousand acres were in private ownership; twenty-nine thousand acres were held by the state and counties; five thousand acres were federal). The non-Indians on the reservation who now held these lands became very insistent that a legal remedy be found. The result was the White Earth Land Settlement Act (WELSA), passed in 1986 (federal Pub. L. 99-264 and Minnesota Laws 1984, Ch. 539). Clouded titles were declared cleared; the White Earth tribe was paid $6.6 million by the federal government for economic development or land purchase; the state paid an additional $500,000 to help with the computer work; and state and county lands of ten thousand acres were supposed to be transferred to the tribe and put in federal trust. As of 2005, only about nine thousand acres have actually been transferred. Identifying heirs and calculating their payments was the responsibility of the BIA.

It has been difficult to find heirs and do the probate. Claimants are scattered throughout the country, and many are not members of the White Earth Band or any other Indian tribe. Originally in 1986 it was estimated that it would take five years and cost $22 million to satisfy the claims. By the mid-1990s, 1,982 claims had been published, 364 claims had been closed out with one hundred more in process, and $42 million had been paid out. It is estimated it will take at least another twenty years to complete the entire process.[19]

There was strong opposition to WELSA by the Indian community at the time it was passed. Many families still have a deep resentment that their lands had been taken by federal policies and neglect when the BIA was supposedly acting on behalf of the people's best interests. The land could not be restored. The negotiators felt they had no choice but to agree to the settlement, since they were told that Congress would impose the solution whether they agreed or not.

Some heirs challenged the Act in court, realizing that if they lost they would no longer qualify for WELSA reimbursement. They were denied the right to file a class action; it was ruled that neither the U.S. government nor the state had waived immunity so they could not be sued. WELSA itself was upheld by the U.S. Supreme Court, which said that Congress had carefully balanced competing interests (*Littlewolf v. Hodel*, 88 F2d 1058, U.S. D. App. D.C. 270).

Remaining Issues of Lost Land

While WELSA ended the claims on White Earth Reservation, many similar cases remained open throughout the rest of northern Minnesota. All of Minnesota's Ojibwe reservations have unresolved cases. A major group of claims are "Secretarial Transfers." These are sales of trust land the BIA allowed without receiving full consent from all heirs. The BIA did not require consent of all heirs until a policy directive was issued in 1956. Like the court ruling in *Zay Zah*, this interpretation of their trust responsibility has come back to cause problems.[20] The federal government now holds some of the land, such as the Chippewa National Forest. In other cases, the land is in private ownership and may have a clouded title.

By the mid-1990s, the BIA was funding very little research into claims as a result of limited resources and other pressing tribal needs. In deciding whether or not to pursue a claim, the BIA considers only if payment was made. If the property was paid for, even if it was wrongfully taken, they do not pursue it.[21] In pointing out the difficulties of handling these complaints, the Solicitor General for the Department of the Interior in the Minneapolis Area further noted that the portions are so small, documenting the wrong is so difficult, and there is such a small amount due on the claim "it makes it almost impossible to do."[22]

Some tribes are putting their own money into documenting title problems. The Leech Lake Band, which has a large number of problems, has built a database of known Secretarial Transfers. By mid-1997, there were some 960 claims, involving thirty thousand acres of land. In some instances, the claim may mean that the title to property is clouded. A number of the faulty transfers of property went to the Chippewa National Forest.

Heirship Problems

Allotted land has continued in trust through several generations, and ownership is now divided into fractionated interests, sometimes in the thousands. In many cases, the cost of administering these interests far exceeds not only the income derived, but also the value of the property itself. The BIA spends 50 to 75 percent of its realty budget administering these small pieces.[23] To use the land for anything or to convey the property, it is very difficult to secure consent from the numerous other owners. Inheritance follows state law if there is no will.

Congress passed a law in 1984 stating that, in settling estates, ownership of very small parcels would go to the tribe, not to the heir. Future heirs filed legal challenges, and in January 1997, the U.S.

Supreme Court agreed the law was unconstitutional (*Youpee v. Babbit,* 117 S. Ct. 727 (1997)).

Despite this decision, there is general agreement in Indian communities that the ultimate disposal of the land should be to the tribe. However, how to handle this fairly, with understanding and consent of those involved, has not been resolved. Confusion still remains about how to deal with the probates done from 1984 to 1994, when heirs lost their property rights. The Solicitor General of the Department of the Interior in 1997 issued an opinion that those cases should not be automatically reversed but be dealt with only on an ad hoc basis as an individual comes forward to question how the case had been handled. The BIA administration accepted this approach and added that the BIA area directors should withdraw any requests they might have made to reopen cases.

Chapter 4

Tribal Governments, Sovereignty, and Relations with the U.S. Government

The Creation of Tribal Governments

Indian nationhood and tribal governments were European concepts. Prior to the arrival of Europeans, Minnesota Indians (Woodland Dakota) had structured governments, but they were much different from the European system. Tribal governments were based on clusters of families that lived in the same geographical area and formed bands. The Ojibwe had a traditional form of social governance called Clan or Totem divisions.

Political leadership tended to be in the form of consensus, and it changed according to the particular situation. Leadership was considered an awesome responsibility, sometimes a burden. Leaders were to serve the people's needs. Women assumed leadership roles as medical providers, prophets, shamans, spokespersons, hunt managers, and trade negotiators.

With the arrival of the fur traders, Indian decision-making began to change. The traders chose "fur chiefs"—men they could work with or manipulate. These Indians were showered with gifts, uniforms, and other symbols of European ideas of power. Later, U.S. governmental agents seeking treaties followed suit.[1] William Warren, Minnesota's Ojibwe historian, noted in 1852, "The agents and commissioners . . . have appointed chiefs indiscriminately or only in conformity with selfish notices and ends, and there is nothing which has conduced so much to disorganize, confuse, and break up the former simple but well-defined civil polity of these people."[2] Later, to make European-style legal contracts, the United States created a governmental structure for Indians so that the government could choose a limited number of chiefs who were given the authority to speak for an entire tribe or band.

Tribal Sovereignty

Indian people have a unique status because they are members of tribes whose governments are not part of the federal government and are generally not subject to state jurisdiction. Tribal governments form a third, totally unique system in the United States. They retain the inherent sovereignty that is recognized by signing treaties. They are nations within a nation, with limited powers.

Indian treaties remain vitally important because they uphold the concept of sovereignty. Currently, there are nearly four hundred treaties in effect acknowledging that tribal sovereign autonomy and remaining resources will be protected because of the cessions of land exchanged through treaties.

The concept of tribal sovereignty as identified by Felix Cohen, noted authority on Indian legal matters, is considered the standard. There are three fundamental principles:

1. An Indian tribe possesses all the powers of any sovereign state.
2. Conquest rendered the tribe subject to the legislative power of the United States and terminated the external powers of sovereignty (e.g., the power to enter into treaties with foreign nations), but it did not by itself affect the internal sovereignty of the tribe (i.e., its powers of local self-government).
3. These powers are subject to qualification by treaties and by express legislation of Congress, but unless explicitly qualified, full powers of internal sovereignty are vested in the Indian tribes and in their duly constituted organs of government.[3]

Because of sovereignty, tribes define their own conditions of membership, levy taxes, and regulate their own hunting and fishing on reservations. Tribes operate the legal gaming industry. Tribes can use sovereign immunity as a defense against lawsuits, as do other levels of government. The Indian Child Welfare Act, which guarantees the rights of tribes and Indian families to protect their children, is based on sovereignty (see chapter 11).

Most of Minnesota's tribes acquired their present-day constitutions after the passage of the Indian Reorganization Act of 1934. The exception was the Red Lake Tribe, which eventually approved a new government system in 1959 similar to those authorized by IRA constitutions.

The tribal governments approved under the IRA generally have the same provisions in their constitutions and bylaws, based on the Bureau of Indian Affairs' (BIA) federal constitutional and common law notions rather than on tribal customs.[4] The tribes define governmental powers and structures, set membership qualifications, and define election procedures. The government's model for Indians does not have separation of powers; rather, administrative and judicial authorities are placed in the tribal council. For example, the elected council may also be the development commission, gaming board, school board, or housing authority. The Secretary of the Interior retains the power to approve new ordinances, constitutional changes, and appointment of tribal attorneys if required by the tribal constitution. Constitutional changes must be approved by federally called and supervised "Secretarial Elections." The Department of the Interior can reject changes that it believes discriminate against prospective tribal members. This power to overturn constitutional change was upheld in 1996 by the U.S. Eighth Circuit Court of Appeals in a challenge by the Shakopee Mdewakanton Sioux Community.

Tribes' powers to govern are similar to those of a state. They pass and enforce laws; establish courts and appeal processes; have the power to tax and zone, hire staff, and administer programs; enter into contracts; form business corporations; hire counsel; negotiate and lobby with other levels of government; and grant housing and other leases to reservation lands.

Sovereignty Issues

There are many limits on tribal sovereignty imposed by Congress. The Constitution reserves to Congress the power to regulate commerce with Indian tribes, a provision that has been broadly construed to give Congress authority in many areas beyond just regulating commerce. This "plenary power" gives Congress extraordinary control over Indian tribes and has diminished Indian government and its jurisdiction.

TAXES   Because taxation is an inherent governmental power, tribes can tax members and non-Indians on reservations. Courts have ruled that states also have the power to tax non-Indians on reservations. The result is often overlapping and confused taxing authority and an impractical checkerboard of jurisdictions that makes efficient governance almost impossible. For instance, state sales, cigarette, and motor vehicle excise taxes cannot be imposed on Indians within the reservation, but liquor taxes can. In addition, tribal sovereign immunity may make it complicated for states to collect their taxes. On most reservations, these issues have been resolved through negotiated agreements whereby the tribes collect the taxes from everyone on the reservation, remit them to the state, and an agreed-upon amount is returned.

Income earned from tribal businesses by Indians living on the reservation is subject to all federal taxes, but no state taxes. An exception is treaty-guaranteed fishing activities. As employers, tribes are subject to federal withholding, unemployment, and Social Security taxes. State unemployment laws and workers' compensation laws do not apply. However, in operating casinos in Minnesota, the tribes have agreed to comply with state requirements on many employment and other operating regulations.

When Indian property is held in trust by the federal government, it is not subject to property tax. The Leech Lake Tribe raised the issue of taxing reservation land that was owned by the tribe but not held in trust by the federal government. The U.S. Eighth Circuit Court of Appeals said that the Northern Lights Casino was subject to taxes because the land had no restrictions on its sale by the tribe (*Leech Lake v. Cass County*, 108 F. 3d 820, (8th Cir. 1997)). However, a similar decision in the Sixth District court went the opposite way. The issue ended up before the U.S. Supreme Court, which ruled in June 1998 that the land was taxable (*Cass County v. Leech Lake Band*, 97-174).

CRIMINAL PROSECUTION   Congress passed Public Law 280 in 1953, transferring legal jurisdiction to states. Under Public Law 280, Congress delegated to the state criminal jurisdiction over tribal members on most Minnesota reservations. However, the tribe also retains criminal jurisdiction over members. When the dual authority is exercised, an offender can be tried twice for the same or similar offense. Red Lake and Bois Forte are not under Public Law 280's criminal provisions. On those reservations, the federal government deals with major crimes, and the reservation courts deal with the rest. All non-Indians on any reservation are under that state's criminal authority. Some of the Public Law 280 reservations have their own criminal systems with tribal police and courts, which apply to tribal members. Others contract for police services from surrounding cities.

CIVIL DISPUTES   Public Law 280 provides the state with concurrent authority in civil matters that previously had been under exclusive tribal jurisdiction. As a result, Public Law 280 greatly expanded state control over reservation activities.[5]

In civil disputes between Indians on the reservation, the tribes have inherent jurisdiction; jurisdiction over non-Indians is being resolved in the courts. Public Law 280 gave the state some civil jurisdiction over Indians on reservations to provide for private civil litigation. State jurisdiction applies only to general laws; it does not extend to local laws. The state cannot impose its jurisdiction on Indian trust property or personal property. Public Law 280 specifically does not allow the state to tax any Indian or tribal property on the reservation held in trust or subject to restrictions against alienation imposed by the United States (*Bryan v. Itasca County*, 426 U.S. 373 (1976)). Public Law 280 said that the state did not have the power to regulate hunting, fishing, and gathering on reservations or in treaty areas where those rights were never relinquished. Most state pollution laws do not apply to Indian nations.[6]

A major U.S. Supreme Court decision said that a state operating under Public Law 280 does not have civil regulatory authority over tribes or their members on the reservation (*California v. Cabazon Band*, 480 U.S. 202, at 209 (1987)). As a result, Minnesota courts began voiding a wide variety of state actions against Indians on the reservations, resulting in greatly increased tensions because of the non-Indian's view of the special status of Indians.

In the late 1990s, the Minnesota Supreme Court ruled on two cases from the Minnesota Court of Appeals. In the first case, the court ruled the state cannot enforce traffic laws on tribal members on reservations for such charges as driving without a license, speeding, driving with no seat belt, and failure to have a child-restraint seat (*State v. Stone*, 557

N.W.2d 588 (Minn. Ct. App. 1996)). In the second case, the court ruled that the state law on underage drinking and driving is enforceable but the failure to yield to an emergency vehicle is not (*Bray v. Commissioner of Public Safety*, 555 N.W.2d 757 (Minn. Ct. App. 1996)). Tribes have been quick to assure the state that they will address the public safety concerns raised by the decisions by establishing traffic codes, tribal courts, and, in some cases, professional police forces.

PROBLEMS WITH PUBLIC LAW 280   PL 280 has been controversial since it was passed in 1953 and amended in 1968. According to one of the country's leading Public Law 280 experts, Professor Carole Goldberg of the University of California Los Angeles, "Public Law 280 has itself become the source of lawlessness on reservations. . . . First, jurisdictional vacuums or gaps have been created, often precipitating the use of self-help remedies that border on or erupt into violence. Sometimes these gaps exist because no government has authority. Sometimes they arise because the government(s) that may have authority in theory have no institutional support or incentive for the exercise of that authority. . . . Second, where state law enforcement does intervene, gross abuses of authority are not uncommon. In other words, power is uncabined by the law that it is supposed to constrain it."[7]

GAMING   The U.S. Supreme Court decision *California v. Cabazon Band* (480 U.S. 202, at 209 (1987)) set the stage for clarifying the legal status of Indian gaming. Minnesota allowed charitable gambling, including slot machines, presumably with no payoff, and did not outlaw social "Saturday night" gambling, making the state's gaming laws regulatory but not prohibitive. The state did not have jurisdiction over reservation gaming, tribes being free to operate their own facilities. Congress, exercising plenary power, passed the Indian Gaming Regulatory Act in 1988 (25 U.S.C. §§ 2701–2721), which restricted the tribes by imposing some federal and state regulation (see chapter 8).

Sovereign Immunity

Like other levels of government in the United States, tribes must give their consent to be sued. With increased public use of tribal facilities, efforts to sue have increased dramatically in the past few years. Several cases have attempted to use state courts because of the lack of understanding of the special status of Indians. Claims must be dealt with in the tribal court, which has the power to allow or deny being sued. While some attorneys have argued that casinos operate as separate businesses and governmental immunity should not apply, the state courts, including the Minnesota Supreme Court, have upheld the tribes, stating that cases should be taken to tribal courts and that casinos are a part of tribal government and are immune from suits.[8] The courts have stated that unconditional access to state court would impair the tribal court's authority.

According to Vanya Hogan, an attorney with the Faegre and Benson law firm in Minneapolis who is experienced in Indian law, "There is a lot of publicity about tribes asserting sovereign immunity and very little about tribes allowing waivers. It is becoming standard practice to allow waivers. . . . The Minnesota tribal court systems have become experienced in trying these cases and the preponderance of cases has now provided valuable histories."[9]

Current Governments

Minnesota Chippewa Tribe (MCT)

The MCT Constitution governs over forty thousand enrolled members of the Bois Forte, Fond du Lac, Grand Portage, Leech Lake, and White Earth reservations and the Nonremovable Mille Lacs Band. It was approved July 24, 1936, and amended March 3, 1964, and November 6, 1972; Election Ordinance #5 was adopted January 27, 1994. The twelve-member governing body of the MCT is the Tribal Executive Committee (TEC), composed of the chairman and secretary-treasurer of each of the six reservations. In the early 1980s, the MCT provided the major programming on the reservations, but by 2000, the reservations did most of their own programming. As an umbrella organization, the MCT continues to provide economic development, home loans, education, human services, programs for elders, and the operation of a water research laboratory.

The MCT constitution and bylaws govern the elections for the six reservations. The reservation governing body consists of a chairman and a secretary-treasurer elected at large and one to three committee members elected by district. Terms are four years on a staggered basis, with elections every two years.

Tribal government formed an Enrollment Committee that in 1941 established MCT membership. Today, those who qualify were on the 1941 membership roll, children of those members born between 1941 and 1961 who applied for membership by 1962, and children of members born after 1961 with at least one-fourth MCT Indian blood (which can be mixed ancestry from the different MCT reservations) who apply within one year after birth. While the tribe defines membership, the governing body of each reservation determines its own enrollment. Denial of membership can be appealed to the Secretary of the Interior. Adoptees placed outside the Indian community can be enrolled without revealing family names.

INDIVIDUAL RESERVATION VARIATIONS   Under the Indian Reorganization Act of 1934, the governing bodies were called Reservation Councils; in 1963, they became the Reservation Business Committee (RBC); and in 1997, they became the Reservation Tribal Council, with the exception of the Fond du Lac Reservation, which still is governed by the Reservation Business Committee. The Mille Lacs Reservation remains organized under the MCT Constitution, but in 1981, the Band restructured into three separate branches of government with divided powers, becoming the first modern tribal government to develop and implement a separation of powers form of government. On Mille Lacs, the chief executive (elected at large) heads the executive branch and all of the administrative departments; the Band Assembly is the legislative branch; and the speaker of the assembly is the secretary-treasurer of the Band elected at large, with the three remaining assembly members elected by district for four-year terms. The judicial branch consists of a chief justice, appeal court justices, and a district court judge. Mille Lacs has codified its model, and other tribes across the country, including the Navajo Nation, have adopted this model.

Red Lake Tribe

In 1918, Red Lake was the first tribe to organize under a constitution. Unlike other tribes in Minnesota, Red Lake did not accept the Indian

Reorganization Act of 1934. A revised constitution was adopted in 1958 and amended in 1974, 1979, and 1984. The governing Tribal Council is composed of eight district representatives, two from each of four districts, and three officers—chairman, secretary, and treasurer—elected at large. Terms are four years on a staggered basis, with elections every even-numbered year. Seven hereditary chiefs continue to serve lifetime appointments as an advisory council. The tribal constitution defines members as those who were enrolled on November 10, 1958. A Tribal Enrollment Committee was established in 1996 to rule on applicants.

Lower Sioux and Prairie Island Indian Communities

The Lower Sioux and Prairie Island communities have similar constitutions, approved in 1936. They provide for an elected five-member council composed of a president, vice president, secretary, treasurer, and assistant secretary-treasurer. Terms are two years.

Membership in the Lower Sioux Community requires Minnesota Dakota ancestry, as identified by the official census rolls of 1934 and 1935, and residency on the reservation. This includes living within a ten-mile radius, including the nearby towns of Morton, Morgan, Redwood Falls, and Franklin. There is no required blood quantum. However, for children to qualify, their parents had to be members at the time of their birth. Provision is made for nonmembers of Dakota ancestry to become members by a majority vote of the whole community. Residency is also required to participate in community benefits and per capita payments. After an absence of two years, these benefits are lost.

Prairie Island Indian Community has identical provisions, with the exception of a 1991 amendment stating that members who move away for more than two years lose their land assignment but do not lose their right to vote absentee and do retain community benefits and per capita payments.

Shakopee Mdewakanton Sioux Community

The Shakopee Mdewakanton Sioux Community was formed under the Indian Reorganization Act in 1969 on lands in Prior Lake that were originally purchased for the Minnesota Mdewakanton in the late

1880s. The governing body, the General Council, is composed of all enrolled members eighteen years and older residing on Community lands. The members of the General Council elect a three-member Business Council composed of a chairman, vice-chairman, and secretary-treasurer to administer the affairs of the Community. Terms are four years.

Tribal membership consisted of thirty-three charter members at the time the Community was recognized as a tribal government in 1969. The Shakopee Constitution delineated membership eligibility as charter members, children of members with one-fourth Mdewakanton ancestry, persons who are descendants of individuals listed on the May 20, 1886, Minnesota Mdewakanton census with one-fourth Mdewakanton ancestry, and persons enrolled through an adoption law approved by the Secretary of the Interior. In 1993, the Community enacted an adoption law whereby children of Community members were eligible for membership regardless of percentage of Mdewakanton ancestry. Despite numerous challenges, the Shakopee Tribal Court, federal courts, and the Department of the Interior have upheld the adoption law.

Upper Sioux Community

The Upper Sioux Community approved its own tribal constitution in 1996. It has its own tribal enrollment and membership. A board of trustees consisting of five members—chairman, vice-chairman, secretary, treasurer, and member-at-large—runs Community affairs. Members are the original members from 1938, when the Community was formed, and their descendants who are one-fourth Dakota blood. To be eligible for Community benefits, including per capita payments, it is necessary to live within the Community's service radius.

Governance Issues Facing Minnesota Tribes

In her 1994 State of the Mille Lacs Band address, then chief executive Marge Anderson noted, "(w)e have taken things into our own hands. We are governing ourselves. We are rebuilding our nation. . . . We have been ground down by one hundred years of poverty. Now we are building for one hundred years of accomplishment. For the past one hundred years we have been governed by others. For the next one hundred years we will govern ourselves."[10] That statement remains a basic tenet in Indian life in the twenty-first century.

Many of the structures of successful tribal governments are recent additions. An Indian attorney noted, "The last twenty years has been a catch-up of tribes building their own governments, the inherent self-governing powers they have always had. It is a very difficult road to build institutions based on their own needs, not the federally set ones. But there has been light years of changes as tribes are now dealing with their responsibilities in social services, dispute resolution, protection of natural resources, raising taxes, making internal law. There has been a tremendous growth in tribal government and with the economic successes there are now great opportunities for tribal governments to achieve what they always have been able to do."[11]

Two studies done by the Harvard Project on American Indian Economic Development in the late 1990s concluded that until tribes assume primary responsibility for the conditions on their reservations they will continue to reflect agendas of outside agencies, such as the BIA. According to the Project's reports, "This is why tribal sovereignty is so crucial. To exercise self-determination, they must break the dependency on the 'grants-and-programs funnel' attached to the federal apparatus and be armed with capable institutions of self-governance. . . . There may need to be a complete constitutional overhaul and the institution of judicial standards. . . . Problems arise when politicians are in a position to turn authority to personal gain and when claims and appeals can only be made before the tribal council."[12] At the end of the 1990s experts said, "A decade of research by the Harvard Project has been unable to uncover a single case of sustained development that did not involve the recognition and effective exercise of tribal sovereignty: the practical assertion by tribes of their right and capacity to govern themselves."[13]

The IRA acknowledged the right of self-government in the 1930s based on majority rule. Yet many critics believe the system is poorly designed. Robert Powless, a professor at the University of Minnesota Duluth, noted that the U.S. government is saying in effect, "The IRA said you can manage your own affairs as long as you do it our [U.S. government's] way."[14]

Anglo-Saxon concepts of governments do not parallel traditional Indian ways. Traditional government operated by persuasion and total acceptance of the group. Vine Deloria, a professor at the University of

Colorado, has stated, "Majority rule has been destructive. With the only important thing the numbers, an idiot equals an elder. Power goes to the one receiving one vote more from just those who voted that day. This has destroyed traditional governmental processes."[15]

The Department of the Interior (BIA) retains a great deal of control over many major governance changes: the authority to define programs (now greatly modified through self-governance agreements), to control the distribution of money, and to issue operation rules and regulations. In 1994, Congress acknowledged the problem saying, "Federal bureaucracy, with its centralized rules and regulations, has eroded tribal self-governance and dominates tribal affairs." (Tribal Self-Governance Act of 1994, Pub. L. 103-413).

The responsibilities of tribal government have grown tremendously in the last few years. In the past, all programs were governmental, and funding was often inadequate. Tribal government is now big business, some with budgets over $30 million. Reservations may be the largest employer in their communities.[16] Governments must deal with the complex requirements of over one hundred different grants and governmental programs, and they have the responsibility of ensuring the survival of their people and their culture.

There is at times a gap between the political leadership and the traditional Indians who are keepers of the culture. As one Indian leader said, "Tribal members were not that concerned about their government when it had little impact. Now it is all different. It is the tribe's money and the people need to feel that the government is responsible to them."[17]

U.S. courts have acknowledged tribal sovereignty and usually do not interfere in decisions made by elected leaders, who lack checks and balances in the constitutions whites designed for them in 1934. This can result in great abuses. On many reservations, issues of governmental structure and administration remain serious problems. For example, while in office, then White Earth Tribal Chairman Chip Wadena stated, "There is no question I lean toward people who support me for key jobs. Politics are harsh. To the winner goes the spoils."[18] Not surprisingly, when White Earth's leadership changed in 1996, the new chairman found rampant favoritism and financial abuses.[19] Wadena was convicted in federal court of conspiracy, bribery, misapplying tribal funds, and money laundering and spent three years in prison.[20]

Reservation elections are often hotly contested, with challenges of the vote count a frequent occurrence. For the MCT, Election Ordinance #4 requires that the burden of proof of election irregularities "must show substantial and grave irregularities which would affect the outcome of the election." Even when election fraud is documented, if it does not change the outcome, no action is taken. The White Earth tribal court dismissed several election challenges on that reservation in the early 1990s. Following the 1994 election, the U.S. Department of Justice became involved, and indictments were brought in federal court. Flagrant voting abuses were documented, especially with absentee ballots. However, when those responsible for the government are involved themselves in the corruption, correcting fraudulent elections is a difficult task.

Former White Earth Chairman Eugene McArthur pointed out the frustration and dilemma of trying to reform his own government. "Four times I was elected by the people and defeated by the corruption in the election process. . . . Vote fraud was the key." The BIA response was that it was an internal matter, and, according to McArthur, "We have been told to exhaust our remedies at the local level which in effect says, 'present a petition to the Tribal Council to remove themselves.' We have tried that remedy. All too many of our people who had signed previous petitions or protested found themselves out of work, demoted, or denied governmental services by the Tribal Council. . . . The usual remedies of self-help were simply not available."[21]

In early 2004, allegations of election fraud once again resurfaced at White Earth when the tribal council voted 3–2 to allow Chip Wadena to appear on the primary election ballot, opening a heated battle between him and tribal leader Erma Vizenor.[22] Vizenor eventually was elected in 2004, but the election resurrected concerns about abuses in the system.

A situation in the 1980s with the Minnesota Chippewa Tribe led to widespread member interest in changing the MCT Constitution to address powers of reservation governing bodies. During the 1980s, the BIA voided MCT plans for a court system to deal with Indian child welfare cases because the MCT Constitution did not specifically authorize one. The Tribal Executive Committee (TEC) proposed a MCT constitutional amendment to resolve the problem, which gave the TEC "all powers necessary and proper" to carry out other parts of the constitution. Tribal members protested strongly, and when it came before the TEC for approval June 22, 1987, the proposal was withdrawn. The TEC said that instead it would call a constitutional convention. This led to members asking for changes in the MCT Constitution to address perceived excessive powers of the reservation governing bodies, the need to create independent tribal courts, election reform, and the role of the umbrella Minnesota Chippewa Tribe. Members of the six reservations voted 3,182 to 2,093 to authorize that something be done; however, nothing came of the effort.

In 1996, after the entrenched leadership was voted out of office on some MCT reservations, a few policies were rescinded, and primary elections were authorized so that majority elections could be established. A draft of a new constitution was developed in 1999, but no amended MCT version has been passed.

Creative and positive changes are occurring. For example, structured methods of listening to members have been put in place. Petitions for referenda have been honored to give members a chance to vote on governmental decisions. Red Lake organized community town meetings. White Earth Reservation organized community-based input into what kind of government would best suit the needs of the members and how to go about achieving that. On May 13, 1997, the TEC unanimously approved a resolution to review and amend the MCT tribal constitution "to reflect, improve and support self-governance by member reservations." Constitutional reform projects were approved for all six reservations.

On the Mille Lacs Reservation, with the vision of previous leaders and elders and enhanced by their increased economic resources, the tribe has instituted a successful model of Indian government, employing the divided powers of three branches. The Band is successfully involving the whole community, seeking elder guidance and helping the youth learn Ojibwe, understand their culture, and get an education so that they can provide the community's leadership in the future. Mille Lacs Band Chief Executive Melanie Benjamin said in her 2004 State of the Band address, "The tribal government can help us through our problems. But the government cannot solve our problems. . . . (T)his is you and me and everyone here making a commitment to take responsibility for our future."[23]

Current Tribal–Federal Relations

In the 1970s, the U.S. Supreme Court took the lead in asserting Indian sovereignty in many crucial decisions. However, since the mid-1980s, tribes have won fewer and fewer cases, leading Indian law expert Robert N. Clinton, a professor of law at Arizona State University, to conclude, "The Supreme Court recently has disregarded precedent, ignored history and the will of Congress. They have turned on its head the original constitutional understanding of the Indian commerce clause."[24]

Because of Congress' plenary power, Indian tribes have had to become skilled in trying to counter encroachments on tribal sovereignty through formal Congressional relations. The Mille Lacs Band, for instance, has an office in Washington to help with this work. Several tribes have political action committees and support Congressional candidates.

Federal Programs

Legislation through the years has reiterated the commitment to serve Indian needs. The Snyder Act of 1921 (42 Stat. 208; 25 U.S.C. 13) still serves as the authorization for Indian Health Service and Bureau of Indian Affairs programs. As recently as 1988, Congress reaffirmed the trust responsibility and obligation of the U.S. government to Indian tribes "for their preservation, protection, and enhancement, including the provision of health, education, social, and economic assistance programs as necessary, and including the duty to assist Indian nations in their performance of governmental responsibility to provide for the social and economic well-being of their members and to preserve tribal cultural identity and heritage."[25] However, barriers still exist. As pointed out by Indian leader and activist Laura Waterman Wittstock, despite treaties and laws, the payments are not held in a trust account; rather, they are part of Congress' annual appropriation process and thus "subject to all the bombast, posturing, insults and attempts at treaty-busting one cares to imagine."[26]

Bureau of Indian Affairs (BIA)

The Snyder Act of 1921 authorized the Bureau of Indian Affairs to protect and provide for Indian tribes. It sold Indian land and other resources and spent the proceeds to fund governmental services. When these funds were no longer adequate, the funding came from Congress. For Minnesota tribes, the BIA has three levels of administration: Washington, D.C., headquarters; the Area Office in Minneapolis that serves upper Midwest tribes; and the two Agency Offices, one located in Cass Lake for the MCT and another at Red Lake for that tribe. The Dakota communities deal directly with the Area Office.

While tribes require protected trust status and the federal funds channeled through the BIA, very few Indians support how the bureaucracy of the BIA operates. Tribal constitutions give the BIA great decision-making power since ordinances, constitutional changes, and many other tribal activities must have BIA approval. The agency judges whether Indian property is to be taken into trust by the federal government, and it administers the trust property as well as funds generated by trust resources. A wide array of other programs come through the BIA: tribal operations, education programs, tribal courts and Indian police (Red Lake and Bois Forte reservations), natural resources, home improvement assistance for low income, economic development, child welfare, and welfare assistance at Red Lake.

BIA programs generally are restricted to persons who are one-fourth degree Indian or more, are members of federally recognized tribes, and live on or "near" (contiguous land) a reservation. Regular programs available to all citizens are intended to be used first; BIA services are to be provided only if no other assistance is available. With very limited exceptions, BIA programs are not available to Indians in urban areas.

A major first step in moving away from the centralized bureaucracy of the BIA was the Indian Self-Determination Act passed in 1974. Tribes could contract for individual BIA or IHS programs and run them themselves. Minnesota tribes, on an individual basis, contracted for most of their programs, resulting in many improvements.

At tribal urging, the Self-Governance Act of 1987 was implemented as a demonstration project, with Red Lake and Mille Lacs among the first participants. Leech Lake, Bois Forte, Grand Portage, and Fond du Lac soon entered the program; in 1995, the Self-Governance law became permanent. By 1997, of the sixty-eight tribes in the program, six were from Minnesota. Of the Ojibwe tribes in Minnesota, today only White Earth is still using the Self-Determination Program.

Under self-governance, the tribe and the BIA negotiate the programs the tribe wishes to administer. The tribe then receives its share of the funding plus the administrative funds that had previously gone to various levels of the BIA and MCT. The tribe receives a block grant, and paperwork is reduced to one annual report. The tribe has discretion over the funds and can use them for its own priorities. The United States maintains the trust responsibility, and tribes are choosing to leave some programs and funds with the BIA. With so many programs no longer going through the BIA, the agency has taken on a more advisory role. However, the U.S. General Accounting Office (GAO) remains critical of the BIA's functioning. According to the GAO's most recent report in 2001, "the Department continues to struggle with budget formulation problems impeding tribal self-determination policy—a national policy providing for tribal participation in and management of federal Indian programs. . . . According to tribes, these shortfalls in contract support costs limit their ability to contract for and manage their programs."[27]

The function of the MCT government has changed as the tribes adopt self-governance. The MCT handles programs where it is advantageous to do them as a group. It is increasingly utilizing other governmental programs, with BIA funds dropping since 1996. Former Fond du Lac Chairman Robert "Sonny" Peacock commented, "Probably the MCT will become a loose confederacy of the independent bands, where they can come together when it is advantageous to function as one voice."[28]

In its management of proceeds from trust assets, land, timber, and other natural resources, the BIA's role as trustee for the tribes and individuals with allotments continues to be controversial. In the 1990s, Congress discovered that the BIA accounts for these funds had been mismanaged for over one hundred years and that no one was able to state how much was in each individual account. Congress subsequently passed the Indian Trust Fund Management Reform Act of 1994, but the issue remains unresolved and is now in the courts. The BIA also has trusteeship of about thirty thousand Individual Indian Money Accounts. The government acknowledged in 1996 that it had mismanaged these accounts and could not account for them. A class action suit ensued, and the Department of the Interior (DOI) and its secretaries, Bruce Babbitt and Gail Norton, have consistently been held in contempt of court for failing to supply information on the management of these accounts. While plaintiffs and the DOI have been far apart on how much is unaccounted for, at the end of 2003, $13 billion emerged as a figure from which they could negotiate. In April 2004, both sides agreed to mediation in an attempt to end the long-running dispute.[29]

Indian Programs from Other Federal Agencies

The Administration for Native Americans (ANA) in the U.S. Department of Health and Human Services makes community action program (CAP) grants to tribal and off-reservation Indian programs. Indian education has special funding through the U.S. Department of Education. The trust status of the land has made it difficult to get housing programs on reservations, although Housing and Urban Development (HUD) has an Indian program to build housing and establish housing authorities on reservations.

Environmental protection laws first passed in 1970 ignored Indian reservations, but in 1989, the courts ruled that the Environmental Protection Agency (EPA) owed reservation Indians the same commitment to health and environmental integrity. A small amount of funding is now going to the tribes, but it is inadequate to catch up with the water, solid waste, and air pollution problems that have been neglected for decades.[30] To resolve legal problems of dealing with reservation status, the EPA has issued rules stating that tribes have the jurisdiction to qualify as a state for funding and primacy in regulatory authority.[31]

In an attempt to ensure that Indian tribes were involved in decision-making throughout the federal bureaucracy, President Bill Clinton issued an executive order in 1994 that "the head of each executive department and agency shall be responsible for ensuring that the department or agency operates within a government-to-government relationship with federally recognized tribes."[32]

Program Problems

Many Indians acknowledge that dependency on government, while often necessary, can also be destructive. Channels for delivering programs involve a bewildering array of bureaucracies at the federal, state, county, community, and/or tribal levels. For laws that do not specifically include Indians, administrators often overlook the tribes until Indians force inclusion, as with environmental laws. In some cases, legal barriers exist, and it takes years to work out solutions, as in housing assistance and economic development programs. Rigidity in qualifying for state funds has caused school construction problems. State law requires public schools to have title to the land, but tribes will not allow the land to go out of tribal trust status. While state bonding can be extended to "local units of government," Indian tribes are not included in the definition.

Defining who qualifies for Indian programs is another bureaucratic maze. Blood quantum and tribal membership are arbitrary barriers for many Indians. Generally, Indian programs operate only on reservations. However, two courts cases (*Morton v. Ruiz* (1974) and *Rincon v. Harris* (1990)) ruled this too limiting. The Indian Health Service now assists a few urban Indian medical centers, and HUD, after a lengthy court battle, is assisting Indian-focused housing in the Twin Cities. Lack of adequate funding is a major barrier to extending programs to nonreservation members.

Departmentalizing services makes it hard to solve Indian problems in an Indian way. The current delivery systems isolate the person or problem being addressed. Indian leaders would prefer a more holistic approach that involves the whole family and uses the strengths of family and the Indian community. The Healthy Nations Project, a Twin Cities Indian project working with youth, has identified 150 agencies working to reduce chemical dependency among Indians in the Twin Cities seven-county metro area. Yet in spite of the number of programs, Healthy Nations director Melissa Boney says, "There are very few treating the whole family. You cannot heal a child without healing the family."[33]

Most Indian programs are funded with "soft money" for start-up projects that, if proven successful, theoretically would then be absorbed by government and regular funding sources. However, in reality, Indian tribes have never had the resources to absorb such programs even if they are successful. This has made self-government difficult because funding determines priority, making it very difficult to retain professional administrators. In addition, soft money has little protection in times of budget cutting.

Program funding using a per capita basis means that reservations with small populations get so little funding that effective programs are impossible to run. Historically, inaccurate census counts created major distortions in funding. Competition for grants puts a great burden on less organized agencies with small staffs, perhaps the ones in greatest need. There is deep concern that if federal program delivery changes to state block grants then the problems of tribes getting an appropriate share will be greatly increased. Historically, state and local governments have been less responsive to Indians, and block grants have usually meant that less total funding is provided.

The comments of Senator Daniel Inouye, chairman of the U.S. Senate's Select Committee on Indian Affairs, hold true today for most Indians: "It is a mystery to me . . . why Indian people continue to get short shrift . . . These are, after all, the only people in the U.S. for whom this government has a trust responsibility, the people this Nation has, by treaties and statutes, agreed time and again to assist when necessary in return for the cession of millions of acres of land and the promises of peace."[34] One excuse for cuts is that Indians no longer need federal funding because of the success of the gaming industry, but this ignores the fact that Indian program funding is based on the United States repaying tribes for the land the government has received. It is, as Indian leaders point out, like an individual saying: "I no longer have to pay my bill because you already have enough money."

The Director of Human Services on Fond du Lac Reservation commented, "Lawmakers are hearing about Indians rolling in money, so 'Why fund Indian programs?' And they are backing away from it all. This could mean much greater problems. Indian needs are still the greatest of any group, in health, social services and education."[35]

In Minnesota, most of the reservations are using their casino profits to fund a full array of governmental services; building infrastructure; providing programs for education, health, housing, and services to the elderly; and other governmental responsibilities. Tribal members are in effect taxing themselves by forgoing per capita payments in order to provide needed governmental services and to overcome years of neglect. Only the very small Dakota reservations are paying their members (less than a thousand in all of Minnesota) a per capita payment that could be called a living wage. Even one of the most successful reservations, Mille Lacs, documents that gaming cannot begin to fund the needs of its tribe. The Mille Lacs tribe is choosing to rebuild the reservation rather than provide more money to members in per capita payments.

Urban Indians remain the most disadvantaged of Minnesota's minority populations, and leaders fear that the distorted notion of the "wealth of all Indians" from gaming is causing foundations and charities to cut back on their funding of desperately needed urban services (see chapter 5).

Although this book focuses on rights and services uniquely intended for Indians, Indians are U.S. citizens who are fully entitled to all privileges and responsibilities of citizenship. Programs cannot be denied on the basis of race. When programs are designed to help low income, disadvantaged, unemployed, or other citizens with special needs, Indians are included in the distribution formulas. They often add numbers well in excess of their percentage of the population.

A 2003 report by the U.S. Commission on Civil Rights found "evidence of a crisis in the persistence and growth of unmet needs. The conditions in Indian Country could be greatly relieved if the federal government honored its commitment to funding, paid greater attention to building basic infrastructure in Indian Country, and promoted self-determination among tribes. The Commission further finds that the federal government fails to keep accurate and comprehensive records of its expenditures on Native American programs . . . Fragmented funding and lack of coordination not only complicate the application and distribution processes, but also dilute the benefit potential of the funds."[36]

Are Indians being served by governments, as their citizenship status and special needs entitle them? This has been a basic question in the previous four editions of *Indians in Minnesota*, and the answer was clearly "no." In the last two decades, there has been an improvement in Indian set-asides and Indian-focused programs, created with Indian community involvement. However, the answer remains "no." Unless Indian communities aggressively push for inclusion, programs do not reach them in proportion to their numbers in need.

In addition, there is poor utilization of services that is often linked to insensitivity to cultural differences or lack of understanding of Indians, as well as to Indian hesitancy in approaching "white systems." The Director of Indian Programs for the St. Paul Council of Churches put it succinctly, "When Indians don't feel comfortable, they don't go. They critique something by their involvement."[37] The heavy use of programs run by Indians or oriented to their culture indicates that these programs are far more effective. A study done by Joyce Kramer of the University of Minnesota Duluth in the mid-1990s looked at health statistics and health services of tribes that crossed the

U.S.-Canadian border. While Canada provided medical services for the whole population, the United States had the Indian Health Services, focused specifically on Indians. A notable difference in health conditions was found, with Canada ten to fifteen years behind the United States.[38]

As John Poupart, head of the American Indian Policy Center, noted, "Promises made and then broken throughout history have laid a foundation of doubt and skepticism. . . . Effective programs and projects will include Indian community participation from the beginning."[39]

Chapter 5

State and Local Relations

Tribal–State Relations

The U.S. Supreme Court noted in 1887 that tribes are "communities dependent on the United States; dependent largely for their daily food; dependent for their political rights. They owe no allegiance to the States, and receive from them no protection."[1] However, because Indians, as U.S. citizens, have constitutionally mandated rights to both state and county services, states cannot ignore Indian needs.

The role that state governments have played in providing state services to reservations has evolved since the 1920s. Because Indian reservations were located by federal decision within only some state boundaries, those states complained about being expected to provide aid to Indians when other states were free of such responsibility. The 1928 Meriam report noted that several states with fairly large Indian populations still tended to regard services for Indians as purely a federal function. In many of those states, this attitude still dominates.

But the Meriam report found that for a few states, including Minnesota, the state governmental departments concerned with education, health, and public welfare were appropriately concerned. The report stated, "To them the question of whether the responsibility rests on the state or on the national government is very properly being relegated to a minor place and the real question is being faced as to whether these inhabitants of the state are being fitted to be assets rather than liabilities."[2]

Minnesota began extending some programs to Indian residents in the 1920s, when public health nurses were assigned to work with Indians. When the Bureau of Indian Affairs closed its schools in the

1930s, the state took over provision of public education under the federally funded Johnson–O'Malley Act.

In the 1950s, when federal policy encouraged termination of responsibility for Indians, the state assumed criminal responsibility and some civil jurisdiction (under Pub. L. 280) for all reservations except Red Lake. Fearing an end of federal funding of reservation programs and concerned about costs as Indians moved from the reservations, Minnesota began to take a serious look at Indians' status in the state.

Increased Indian advocacy led to greater state awareness and, gradually, the redesign of many state and county programs to reach Indian populations effectively. The process has been mutually beneficial, with Indians having a voice in designing services that serve their unique needs and the state having more effective social programs. A prime example is the state-funded, postsecondary education scholarship program for Indians begun in 1955. This has stimulated the growth of a pool of Indians who are providing leadership and economic advancement for their people.

Some friction remains between the state and its Indian citizens. As the executive director of the 1854 Authority noted in June 1997, "Although our working relationship with the State of Minnesota is not perfect, there are many tribes that have no relationship at all."[3] The 1854 Authority is an intertribal natural resource management agency that manages the off-reservation hunting, fishing, and gathering rights of the Grand Portage and Bois Forte Nations.

Andrea Wilkins of the National Council on State Legislatures aptly described the relationship: "Cooperative state-tribal government relationships are difficult to establish. With slim guidance from the U.S. Constitution and inconsistent foundations in case law, states and tribes are forging their ways in a legal wilderness."[4] While many Indian leaders in Minnesota report improved relations with the state over the past few decades, others point out that the success of gaming has added a layer of strain to those relationships.

Indian Affairs Council (IAC)

In 1963, the Minnesota Indian Affairs Commission (renamed the Indian Affairs Council in 1983) became the first legislated state body to focus on Indians. It is the official liaison between state and tribal governments. The tribal chairpersons from each of the state's eleven reservations are the Council's voting members. Two representatives are also elected for four-year terms by Indians living in Minnesota but enrolled in federally recognized tribes located outside the state.[5] Nonvoting members include three state senators, three house members, and representatives of the governor and of the commissioners of nine state agencies. The IAC appoints the Urban Indian Advisory Council, composed of two representatives each from Minneapolis and St. Paul and one each from Bemidji and Duluth.

By state law, the Indian Affairs Council is mandated to "clarify for the legislature and state agencies the nature of tribal governments and the relationship of tribal governments to the Indian people of Minnesota" (Minn. Stat. § 3.922, subd. 6,1). It has the power to make legislative recommendations, administer programs, establish Indian advisory councils to state agencies, investigate and protect Indian burial sites, and act as an intermediary in Indian–state government questions, problems, or conflicts. The council has been effective in seeking state laws in areas of Indian concern and in administering several programs designed to enhance economic opportunities and protect cultural resources for Minnesota Indians.

State Indian Programs

The state can take credit for several very creative Indian programs, including:

- ❏ A higher education scholarship program and several special K–12 Indian education programs to provide curriculum and staff, thus expanding Indian participation and success in school and improving the public's knowledge of Indians.
- ❏ Supplemental state aid to help reservations with high Indian enrollment provide equal services in spite of a very low property tax base.
- ❏ State support for an Indian-prepared, comprehensive curriculum for K–12.
- ❏ A joint tribal–community college at Fond du Lac.

❏ A chair of Indian Education at the University of Minnesota Duluth, established through the sale of historic salt lands.

❏ An Indian-administered state Indian housing program to assist in home purchases on and off reservations.

❏ A set-aside for Indian economic development loans of 20 percent of the state tax on severed mineral rights.[6]

❏ Chemical dependency and mental health Indian programs using federal and state funds, administered at the state level by Indians.

❏ Labeling laws to protect the identity of Indian hand-harvested natural lake and river wild rice.

❏ Protection of Indian burial sites and a reburial program for disturbed remains.

❏ State funding of an ombudsperson to monitor compliance with child protection laws and support for Indian staff to represent needy Indian Child Welfare Act clients.

❏ A cooperative arrangement with the Grand Portage Tribe to create a state park with the land held by the tribe and leased to the state.

Indians in State Government

Indians are increasingly serving in state government and on state commissions. Indians have headed the Minnesota Departments of Human Rights and Veterans Affairs and served as a judge on Hennepin County Court. Indian advisory groups assist the Minnesota Department of Education, the state's chemical dependency program, the Indian Child Welfare Act advisory board, and the Minnesota Historical Society. Indian elders form an advisory group for the University of Minnesota. Some agencies, such as the Department of Natural Resources, have a designated Indian liaison to advise the Department on Indian views, know the protocol of dealing with the tribes, and lend credibility to state programs in working with the tribes.

Despite these gains, Indians employed by state and local governments tend to occupy lower paid positions, with few in positions of official or administrative leadership.[7]

Government-to-Government Negotiations

Although Minnesota has formally recognized tribal sovereignty, the state does not have a consistent overall Indian policy. Decisions are generally made on an ad hoc basis within various government agencies as programs are funded, rules are written, existing programs are modified, or Indian policies are challenged and tested in the courts. According to the Minnesota Attorney General's Office, the state Legislature "has permitted Indian Band [reservation] issues to pop up almost anywhere in the committee process, with little effort to coordinate the consideration of those issues in a single forum."[8] The IAC is brought in when state-tribal conflicts arise but is generally not consulted as the state makes policy decisions.

In matters of jurisdiction, tribes and states are often pitted against each other. From the tribal point of view, Indians resist state encroachment on their inherent rights to prevent new attempts against sovereignty. Ambiguous laws, complex jurisdictional issues, and vigilance against encroachment often force state/Indian issues into court, especially in the areas of taxation and hunting and fishing rights. The result is polarization rather than encouragement of good government-to-government relations.

Taking issues to court for resolution requires the tribes either to expend a great deal of their limited resources or to postpone exercising their rightful jurisdiction. Indians cite hunting, fishing, and gathering issues as an example, noting that the state has agreed to negotiate a settlement only after tribes have forced the issues into the courts.

Negotiating agreements between the tribes and the state to deal with jurisdictional disputes began in the late 1970s. By the 1990s, the issues being dealt with in this manner expanded to cover a wide range of topics. At a meeting in the late 1990s, state officials and attorneys with the Attorney General's Office noted, "For most of Minnesota history, state policy has run from acting as if tribes did not exist to economic paternalism (social welfare spending) to open hostility. . . . Now, as tribal capacity, both economically and politically, has grown, it is becoming clearer that the better approach is some kind of 'constructive engagement.'"[9] This change in approach requires recognition of tribal sovereignty, establishment of trusting relationships, and building in incentives for compliance outside the courtroom despite disagreements over jurisdiction. For Indians, community leader Laura Waterman Wittstock says, "It is a time of extended sovereignty."[10]

Hunting and Fishing

In the 1970s, after extensive litigation, the state and the Leech Lake Tribe negotiated a hunting, fishing, and harvesting agreement in which the state acknowledged the tribe's right to regulate their own members in the use of the resources. The tribe agreed to give up its rights to commercially take sports fish in the region in return for state payment. In 1988, the state and the affected tribes negotiated a similar agreement for the off-reservation, ceded Arrowhead lands. However, it took Indian court action to force the state to agree to enter into negotiations. Similarly, the Mille Lacs band won a major hunting and fishing rights settlement before the U.S. Supreme Court in 1999, but only after a lengthy court battle with the state (see chapter 7 for further discussion).

Tribal–State Indian Gaming Compacts

The federal National Indian Gaming Act was passed in 1988, and the state responded by authorizing the governor, two senators, and two representatives to enter into compacts by direct negotiations with the tribes (Minn. Stat § 3.9221). Compact agreements that met the parties' priorities and concerns were reached promptly, with both sides making major compromises. Some Indians were very critical of the process because the law took away Indian sovereignty and imposed state and federal regulation over some of the operations. The Red Lake Tribe filed suit but later withdrew it because of the expense of going to court. Other Indians point out that the compacts did force the states to negotiate with tribes as equals.

At the time of the compacts, casinos in Minnesota were seen as financially risky. Few imagined that the new gaming industry would be as successful as it has been. By the mid-1990s, due to the success of the casinos, some policymakers portrayed the compacts as "one of the most favorable deals in the nation" for Indians.[11] Annually, state legislators have sought ways to break the compacts to force renegotiation. For example, during the 2004 and 2005 state legislative sessions, there were several proposals to allow private or state-sponsored gaming and to force Indians to renegotiate compacts or else face a ban on slot machines. All failed, but as Indian attorney James Genia pointed out, "As long as we've got a budget deficit we'll see gaming before the legislature."[12]

Jurisdictional Issues

Public Law 280, which brought state criminal jurisdiction on the reservations, says that the state must give tribal courts "full faith and credit." In a few instances, the state and counties do accept tribal courts; however, generally there is not much reciprocity.

In law enforcement, many changes are occurring. These include cross-deputization as tribes increase their own enforcement, courts recognizing each other's decisions, and courts resolving which is to have first jurisdiction.

In July 1997, state and tribal judges met for the first time to, according to Minnesota Supreme Court Justice Sandra Gardebring, "let our state court judges . . . become acquainted with the other system. We're beginning to get orders from tribal courts and we don't have a full faith and credit mechanism to enforce them." From the Indian perspective, the meetings were an opportunity to educate state judges about tribes' sovereign right to have a judicial system.[13]

For the state, casinos have brought taxation issues to the fore. Although the state has the legal right to collect taxes on reservations from non-Indians, it has had no authorization to get tribes to collect since the state and the tribes cannot sue each other because of their respective sovereignty. The Minnesota Department of Revenue was authorized by law to negotiate with the tribes (Minn. Stat. § 270.60), and in 1996–1997, agreements were reached with most of the tribes on sales, motor vehicle excise, cigarette, alcoholic beverage, and petroleum product taxes (see chapter 8).

Formal agreements between the federal agencies and the tribes had been signed in several areas related to the environment. With tribal sovereignty recognized, this has required the state to adjust its administration under these laws and to negotiate joint implementation of federal environmental programs (see chapter 7).

Tribes have been diligent in trying to help the state and counties understand and cooperate fully with the federal Indian Child Welfare Act (25 U.S.C. 1901 (1978)), which has been expanded by the

Minnesota Indian Family Preservation Act (Minn. Stat. § 257.35 (1985)). Retaining responsibility for making decisions on their children's behalf is one of the most important issues for tribal governments. Although the laws have been in place for over twenty years, many problems with the implementation remain. Over the years, social workers report having a difficult time getting professional recognition from their county counterparts. As Loa Porter from Grand Portage said, "It has been a real struggle to get the county to recognize that there really is a tribal government, with a child protection team in place on the reservation."[14] After agreements on this issue failed to take hold in the 1980s, the tribes and the state renegotiated an agreement in the late 1990s that added a section to the state's social service manual on how to deal with Indian children.

Relations with Local Communities

Indian tribes continue to have their most difficult relations with local governments. Local prejudices and a poor understanding of tribal sovereignty add to the problems. The 1985 edition of *Indians in Minnesota* quoted a Leech Lake official who said, "There has been so much mistrust for so long. It is hard to get across to the county commissioners that they represent Indians, too."[15] Of continuing concern is the lack of understanding and poor communication in some communities.

After annexing the Shakopee Mdewakanton Community in 1972 without Indian consent, the Prior Lake City Council then refused to provide police, fire, and ambulance services. They also refused tribe members the right to vote because there was the possibility they could be elected to a city office and could spend the city's money although they do not pay taxes.[16] The tribe took the issue to federal court, and the U.S. Eighth Circuit Court of Appeals ruled in 1985 that the city's annexation did not affect tribal jurisdiction. Therefore the members had the right to vote, and the city was responsible for the services. The U.S. Supreme Court refused to hear the appeal.

Relations have improved since then. The Community has continually entered into intergovernmental agreements with the city of Prior Lake since 1993 for police and fire services, with the Community paying the cost of these services. While the Community has been unable to get some of the land it owns taken into trust status by the federal government, in part due to city and county opposition, the tribe and

city of Prior Lake made a preliminary agreement to convert 110 acres
to trust status for the tribe to build needed housing. In exchange, the
tribe would build athletic fields on the land for city use. While
the agreement has yet to be fulfilled, Prior Lake Mayor Jack Haugen
stated, "It's a very, very significant intergovernmental cooperative
agreement."[17]

In March 2004, after a two-year legal battle that cost both the Mille
Lacs Band and Mille Lacs County over $1 million, the U.S. Eighth
Circuit Court of Appeals ruled that the county had failed to show that
the Band's reservation boundaries had harmed the county. According
to Joel Patenaude, editor of the *Mille Lacs Messenger*, a previous court
battle in the 1990s over hunting and fishing rights set the stage for the
dispute. "There are people who feel that because the tribe won that
round, revenge ought to be taken. If they can prove in court the
reservation doesn't exist and all sovereign power the band believes
they have can be stripped away, you couldn't beat the band better
than that."[18]

Some reservations have excellent relations with local communities. Fond du Lac Reservation reports cooperative working relations
with its neighbors, the city of Cloquet and Carlton County. These communities, along with the major local industry and the state, put together a "Shared Vision" to build and operate Fond du Lac Tribal and
Community College. Leech Lake Reservation, Minnesota Chippewa
Tribe, and the city of Cass Lake all share the Cass Lake community. The
city's elected officials include reservation residents, and the city provides water to a new residential area of Leech Lake Reservation. In
addition, in 2004, Cass County and the Leech Lake Tribe agreed to
quarterly meetings to resolve differences between the county and tribe.

In May 2003, the city of Minneapolis signed a "Memorandum of
Understanding" with the Metropolitan Urban Indian Directors to create a working partnership between the city and the Indian communities that would focus on building knowledge of American Indians and
understanding of community responsibilities.

Some local officials complain that Indians living on reservations
require services that must be paid for by property taxes, but Indians
do not pay this tax. As the tribes have increased their land holdings
and placed them in trust, negative reactions have increased as well.
This is likely to be a continuing cause of tension. Often overlooked is
the fact that county land was at one time Indian land.

Local programs intended for all people often do not include Indians and do not extend into Indian communities. In an effort to ensure that programs are inclusive, several delivery systems have been legislated to require community/user input. These include the County Social Service Plan, Children and Family Collaboratives, Community Health Boards, and the state's mental health program. However, these provisions are often overlooked, and many areas still lack structured ways for Indians to provide input.[19]

Casinos have had a dramatic impact on local relations. While they have brought much-needed employment and economic benefits to many areas, local reactions remain mixed. However, many communities report improved relations as a result. The mayor of Redwood Falls commented that the casinos have led to "three new hotels, a new Wal-Mart, building contractors have better businesses"[20] From 1991 to September 2003, the Mille Lacs Reservation's two casinos generated more than $49 million in federal and states taxes through employee wages. The net tax capacity of Mille Lacs County has increased by 61 percent since the opening of that community's casino (compared to 16 percent for the state as a whole).[21] In 2004, Granite Falls Mayor David Smiglewski cited numerous contributions from the Upper Sioux Community's casino, including increased tourism in the region, as well as contributions to a state trail along the river and police and treatment centers.[22]

Several tribes have given extensively to local communities. For example, according to the Minnesota Indian Gaming Association, in 2001, the Prairie Island Sioux Community donated more than $2 million to neighboring communities for such projects as an ice arena, a firefighter tanker truck, area schools, and wildlife conservation organizations. During the same year, the Mille Lacs Band donated $1.8 million to northern Minnesota schools and universities, regional tourism events, health clinics, law enforcement agencies, and health and disease prevention organizations.[23]

The Shakopee Mdewakanton Sioux Community made over $50 million in grants to other tribes and nonprofit organizations from 1995 to 2005. The Shakopee Community also has made over $100 million in low-interest loans to other tribal governments in Minnesota and South Dakota to help with economic development projects.

Nongovernmental Sources of Aid

Individuals, foundations, charities, corporations, and other non-governmental bodies have been and are providing start-up and ongoing operations funding for Minnesota Indians on reservations and in urban areas.

Individual Involvement

There are numerous ways individuals are aiding Indians in Minnesota. Mentoring programs link Indian professionals with university students; Indian groups at major corporations provide personal help to Indian-based programs; the Division of Indian Work, a division of the Greater Minneapolis Council of Churches, boasts nearly one hundred individuals involved in a youth tutoring program; and with the help of the Grand Portage Tribe, a volunteer group of Indians is buying and refurbishing homes for homeless persons in Duluth.

The Greater Twin Cities United Way, which collects charitable contributions from individuals and corporations, funds numerous programs specifically for Indians, as well as other social service programs that, although not specifically designated for Indians, have Indian clientele.[24]

Ethel Curry of Rochester, Minnesota, endowed two $1 million funds for Indian scholarships, one at the University of Minnesota Twin Cities and one at the Minnesota Department of Education, to be administered by the state's Indian Scholarship Committee. At Augsburg College, Ada Bakken endowed an Indian scholarship. Shakopee Mdewakanton and Prairie Island Dakota Communities have endowed two more, and comedian Louis Anderson gives proceeds from benefit performances for additional scholarship help. The Shakopee Mdewakanton also made a $900,000 donation to the American Indian College Fund.

Foundations/Private Giving

Foundations and private grantmakers play a crucial role in meeting Indian human resource needs, especially as federal funding declines for existing programs. According to the Minnesota Council of Non-Profits, overall grants to Indians rose from 1.1 percent of total Minnesota grants in 1991 to 4 percent in 2001 (the latest year for which data are available), with grant dollars rising from $6,400,849 to $26,448,413. However, First Nations Development Institute reports, "According to the 2000 Census, Native Americans account for 1.5 percent of the U.S. population. Yet, only one-sixth of one percent of national philanthropic dollars go to Native American communities or organizations."[25]

The latest national figures measuring national foundation giving found that five of Minnesota's foundations were among the top 20 in giving to Indian-related organizations and programs. The 1997 report listed the Bush Foundation with over $6 million as the fourth largest foundation grantor; McKnight Foundation was fifth; Northwest Area Foundation was sixth; Otto Bremer Foundation was fourteenth; and General Mills was seventeenth.[26]

However, private grantmakers often provide funds for new programs, with the hope that the government will then fund successful efforts. But this rarely happens. The result is a steady stream of changing programs with no ongoing support.

The Minnesota Council of Non-Profits has found that grants intended to serve Indians do not necessarily go to Indian organizations. The use of non-Indian agencies to provide services is often a sore point with Indian agencies, which believe they are qualified and can do a better job of reaching the Indian community. Programs serving urban Indians report that foundations are urging them to get funds from casinos, an unrealistic and unlikely funding source.

Chapter 6

Characteristics of the Indian Population of Minnesota

Who Is Indian?

Within Indian communities, both urban and reservation, people are known as Indian because they wish to belong or the communities consider them Indian.

Qualifications for Indian-designated programs vary. For example, the Bureau of Indian Affairs requires an individual living on or near a reservation to have one-fourth Indian ancestry or membership in a federally recognized Indian tribe. The federal Indian Education Act requires only that one grandparent be a tribal member, with no Minnesota residency requirement laws. Minnesota laws, while consistent in defining Indians as having one-fourth or more Indian blood, differ on whether the person needs to be tribally enrolled.

Jimmy Jackson, a spiritual medicine man of the Ojibwe nation, said, "If you have one drop of Indian blood, the spirits will accept you and hear your prayers. Spiritually you can remain an Indian, even if the BIA says you're not."[1]

For the first time, in 2000, individuals filling out the U.S. Census forms for the first time could define themselves as "American Indian or Alaska Native" and as "race alone" or "race in combination." Tribes confer membership, and tribal membership is formal recognition of being Indian.

These multiple definitions can lead to confusion over rights and eligibility for programs as well as denial of services. For example, the Indian Child Welfare Act relies on social workers and court personnel to make the judgment of who is Indian, yet the definition actually is tribally determined. At the same time, a lack of definition can lead to great demands on programs. There are 500,000 Indians not federally recognized, roughly one-fourth of the people who identify as Indian. Indians frequently express concern about individuals who benefit from being considered Indian and receive Indian scholarships or are hired as "Indian" employees but who are not tribally enrolled and are not known to the Indian communities.

Criteria for tribal membership are controversial, especially with tribes whose resources are increasing. In more and more cases, children and grandchildren of members no longer meet the blood quantum requirement for membership. New membership requirements will require changing tribal constitutions. This issue is likely to be an ongoing concern for tribes, the BIA, and U.S. courts.

Profile of Indians in Minnesota: The Numbers

The 2000 U.S. Census counted 54,967 Indians in Minnesota who identified as solely Indian, about 1.1 percent of the state's population, an unchanged percentage from 1990. Nationwide, there are approximately 4.1 million Indians. Until 1950, the enumerator made the decision of who was an Indian. Beginning in 1960, when individuals were free to identify their own race, the Indian population has greatly increased.

With the 2000 census, individuals were allowed to choose American Indian and Alaska Native as well as one or more other races. Though tests conducted before the 2000 census showed that few people selected a multiracial identity, the change still means that 1990 and 2000 race data cannot be directly compared. For example, over 81,000 people identified as either solely Indian or more than one race, including American Indian. Table 6.1 shows the changes in the state's Indian population in the years since 1860.

Historically, Indians have been seriously undercounted by the census. Census takers were often not knowledgeable about Indian communities, and many Indians did not choose to cooperate with the government's request for personal information. Because funding throughout the decade is based on the information in the census, an undercount results in inadequate funding for the actual population. The 1990 U.S. Census was criticized for doing a poor job of identifying homeless urban Indians and undercounting the Mille

Table 6.1 Population changes for Indians in Minnesota, 1860–2000

Year	Number of Indians	% Change from Previous Decade	% of Total State Population
1860	2,369	—	—
1890	10,096	—	0.8
1900	9,182	−10	0.5
1910	9,053	−1	0.3
1920	8,761	−3	0.4
1930	11,077	+26	0.4
1940	12,528	+13	0.4
1950	12,533	0	0.4
1960	15,496	+24	0.5
1970	23,128	+49	0.6
1980	35,016	+51	0.9
1990	49,909	+43	1.1
2000	54,967	+10	1.1

Source: U.S. Census, 1860–2000.

Lacs Reservation. The U.S. Census Bureau used a massive advertising and outreach effort to improve its 2000 American Indian count, especially on isolated and hard-to-reach reservations.

From 1960 to 1990, the Indian population in Minneapolis increased almost 500 percent; in St. Paul and the seven-county metropolitan area as a whole, the increase was over 600 percent. But during the time period 1990–2000, the American Indian population in the Twin Cities metropolitan area declined dramatically; during the same period, the population increased 10 percent statewide. This figure is based on the U.S. Census that counted those who identified solely as Indian (one race). (See Table 6.2.) In cities with a population of 100,000 or more, Minneapolis ranked seventh in the number of Indians, down from a ranking of third in 1990.

The census showed that 32,184 (65 percent) of Minnesota's Indians identified themselves as Chippewa (Ojibwe), with 5,278 identifying as Sioux (Dakota), 643 as Cherokee, and 523 as Winnebago; 9,939 did not identify a tribe.

Table 6.2 Indian population in major cities of Minnesota, 1928–2000
(Percentage of state's total Indian population given in parentheses)

Urban Area	1928	1960	1970	1980	1990	2000
Minneapolis	300 (2%)	2,077 (13%)	5,829 (25%)	8,933 (26%)	12,335 (25%)	8,378 (15%)
St. Paul	300 (2%)	524 (3%)	1,906 (8%)	2,538 (7%)	3,697 (7%)	3,259 (6%)
Suburbs		710 (5%)	2,223 (10%)	4,194 (12%)	7,308 (15%)	8,780 (16%)
7-County Metro		3,311 (21%)	9,958 (43%)	15,665 (45%)	23,340 (47%)	20,417 (37%)
Duluth	150–200 (1%)	402 (3%)	615 (3%)	1,344 (4%)	1,837 (4%)	2,122 (4%)
Total Minneapolis, St. Paul, Duluth	800 (5%)	3,003 (19%)	8,350 (36%)	12,815 (37%)	17,869 (36%)	13,759 (25%)

Sources: Lewis Meriam, *The Problems of Indian Administration* (Baltimore: Johns Hopkins Press, 1928), 197, 727. U.S. Census, 1960–2000.

Since 1920, the U.S. Census has recorded a great deal of fluctuation in reservation populations, with enrolled members of the tribes far exceeding those living on the reservations (see Table 6.3).

Social and Economic Characteristics

The social and economic characteristics of the state's Indians differ from those of the rest of the state's population in significant ways. The following numbers are from the 2000 U.S. Census unless otherwise identified.

Age

Indians in Minnesota are a young population, with a median age of 26.3 years compared to the state average of 35.4 years. Twenty-four percent of all Indian births are to women nineteen years or younger, compared to 8 percent for the general population. Elders (age sixty and older) comprise just 6.5 percent of the Indian population, compared to 15 percent in the general population.

Income

Approximately 28 percent of Indians in Minnesota lived below the poverty level in 2000, a decrease from 44 percent in 1989. Twenty-nine percent of American Indian children in Minnesota were living in poverty in 2000, compared with 6 percent of white children.[2] The median household income for Indians was $28,533, compared to $47,111 for white households.[3] Nearly 20 percent (19.6 percent) of American Indian households in Minnesota received public assistance, compared to 3.4 percent of all Minnesota households, according to the 2000 census.

While income and employment rates on the reservations on the whole rose, mainly due to casinos, officials from the state demographer's office said that this latest round of census data does not tell the whole story of what's happening to Indians in Minnesota. For example, the data do not distinguish between Indians and non-Indians who live on reservations.

Health

There are significant health disparities between the state's Indian population and the general population. Overall mortality rates show

Table 6.3 Reservation population and tribal membership, 1993 and 1991–2000

Reservation	Reservation Population (1993/1991)	Tribal Membership (1996)	Tribal Membership (1999)	Identified by Tribe in U.S. Census (1990)	Identified by Tribe in U.S. Census (2000)
Bois Forte	898	2,690	2,767	397	464
Fond du Lac	1,483	3,638	3,847	901	1,353
Grand Portage	226	1,031	1,097	104	322
Leech Lake	4,289	7,733	8,219	1,784	4,561
Mille Lacs	961	3,080	3,292	670	1,034
White Earth	3,169	20,848	21,083	2,829	3,374
Red Lake		7,950	9,264	4,162	5,071
Lower Sioux		825	930	106	294
Prairie Island		460	582	58	166
Shakopee-Mdewakanton		97	301	54	175
Upper Sioux		169	369	304	147

Sources: Reservation Populations, "Tribal Profile, 1993 and 1991," Minneapolis Area Office, BIA, Aug. 1993.
Tribal Membership–MCT enrollment, Aug. 16, 1993, prepared by Judy Moe, Director of Tribal Operations, MCT.
Red Lake and Dakota Communities, "Tribal Profile," Minneapolis Area Office, BIA, Aug. 1993.
Tribal Membership–MCT enrollment, Nov. 15, 1996, prepared by Judy Moe, Director of Tribal Operations, MCT.
Minn. State Demographic Center, May 2001.

that Indians ages 15–64 years had death rates up to 3.5 times higher than those of whites. The leading factors in death are cardiovascular disease (20 percent), cancers (17 percent), motor vehicle and other accidents (15 percent), and diabetes (6 percent).[4]

Education

The number of Indians twenty-five years or older who had a high school diploma, GED certificate, or further education rose from 55 percent in 1980 to 68 percent in 1990 to 74 percent in 2000. The percentage of Indians in Minnesota with a bachelor's degree rose from 5 percent to 8.8 percent between 1980 and 2000, yet Indians still lag behind all other ethnic groups in the state.

Where Indians Lived in 2000

- ❏ 23 percent lived on a reservation.
- ❏ 21 percent lived in the county in which the reservation they identify with is located.
- ❏ 32 percent lived in Hennepin and Ramsey counties, where the cities of Minneapolis and St. Paul are located, respectively.
- ❏ 25 percent lived elsewhere in the state.[5]

Minneapolis

Fifteen percent of the state's Indian population lived in Minneapolis in 2000. The Phillips and Powderhorn neighborhoods had the largest concentration of Indian people, although the Indian population dropped nearly 50 percent in those neighborhoods from the 1990 U.S. Census.[6] The inner city population is very diverse, with as many as eighty to ninety different tribes represented.[7]

Minneapolis' inner-city Indian population has the greatest need for publicly supplied services. In addition to the census data, other agencies' figures document these needs. The human services chapters that follow also discuss these various problems.

- ❏ In Minneapolis, infant mortality rates are three and one-half times higher in the American Indian community than for whites.[8]

❑ American Indian families have a high number of children eligible for free and reduced lunch: 73 percent compared to 24 percent of whites.[9]

❑ Of the patients served by the Indian Health Board in 2003, 50 percent were Indian; 60 percent were at or below the poverty level; 51 percent were on medical assistance; and 31 percent had no medical insurance.[10]

Twin Cities Suburbs

The Twin Cities suburban Indian population was 9 percent of the state's Indian population in 2000. Indians living in these communities were better educated and had more stable families, less unemployment, and more affluence than the state's average Indian.[11] (See Table 6.4.)

Migration Patterns

According to the 2000 U.S. Census, the American Indian population decreased by 32 percent in Minneapolis and 25 percent in Hennepin County from 1990 to 2000. During the same time period, the Indian

Table 6.4 Comparative social data for Indians in Minneapolis and suburbs, 2000
(Percent of Indians in this category, living in this area)

Indians	Minneapolis	Suburbs
Age, 17 years and younger	38%	24%
Living in poverty	35%	12%
Children under 18 living with:		
Married couple	25%	45%
Female head, no spouse	61%	56%
Nonrelatives	0.6%	0.6%
Those 25 and over without either high school diploma or GED	31%	20%
In the labor force, but unemployed	17%	9%

Source: U.S. Census, 2000.

population statewide grew by 10 percent, with growth occurring largely on Indian reservations and in northern Minnesota.

There is a stereotype that Indian students frequently move back and forth between urban and reservation homes, but studies done on the mobility of Twin Cities Indian students found that while they change schools a good deal, usually they move just a few blocks away.

Importance of Reservations

Despite the fact that only 23 percent of Indians live on reservations in Minnesota, an additional 21 percent live in the same county in which the reservation is located, and the reservation often remains the primary attachment for Indians no matter how long they live in other areas. Local Indian leader William Means said, "Even after living in Minneapolis for a generation or more, when asked, 'Where are you from?' it is the reservation's name that is replied."[12]

For many Indians, reservations represent their spiritual and cultural roots. As an urban dweller commented, "Another meaning of this homing instinct to the reservation is a spiritual cultural tie that exists. It is not recorded or written down. There is a feeling among Indian people that when we lose that chain we've hung on to, there is no more Indian then. No more spiritual connection. To me that is the reservation chain."[13] Life on the reservation means the comfort of an extended family, a community of majority status, strengthened cultural identity, and availability of natural resources, including wood, game, fish, and wild rice. One young person explained, "It's hard to be an Indian in the cities; hard to learn about the culture. You need the living in the woods."[14] In addition, on reservations there are no property taxes, housing assistance may be available, and health care services are provided.

While there has been movement back to the reservations in the last ten years, there can be drawbacks to reservation life. Membership on most reservations far exceeds the capacity of the land. Lack of employment opportunities is an obvious problem, although on some reservations gaming has changed that. With the close-knit community and intrusion of politics, there can be factionalism and nepotism. In the isolation of reservation life, youth especially may feel a lack of excitement and activity.

Urban Life

In 1928, the Meriam report spoke of the Twin Cities urban Indian population as being middle class and fiercely determined to remain Indian:

> One gets the impression in St. Paul and Minneapolis that most of the persons claiming to be Indians have but a slight degree of Indian blood. From 'lists of Indians' furnished by the several reservations, many were reached whose personal appearance indicated French or Scandinavian blood rather than Indian. In a number of cases a claim of only one-sixteenth, one-thirty-second, or one-sixty-fourth Indian blood was made, yet great insistence was put upon the right to be designated 'Indian.' Some of the so-called Indians were found to be persons generally believed to be white, who were living in the type of home that fairly prosperous young professional or business folk generally enjoy.[15]

Throughout the twentieth century, many Indians left reservations to find employment in urban areas. World War II brought many Indians to work in war jobs, and termination policies and depressed conditions on reservations increased the flow in the 1950s and 1960s. At the turn of the twenty-first century, 32 percent of Minnesota's Indians lived in the two major metropolitan counties, Hennepin and Ramsey.

The largest nonreservation concentrations of Indian populations are in the state's major cities. Most of these people, along with the following suburban and other groups identified, have stable lives and do not enter into the troubling statistics that follow in the subsequent chapters of this book. It is a stereotype to characterize urban Indians as an entire group with problems needing the attention of governmental agencies. However, there are Indians, concentrated in the core cities, whose needs have increased during the last two decades.

Those who come to the cities encounter a physical environment, social organization, interpersonal behavior, attitudes, values, and sometimes language that are foreign to what they have known. The traditional source of support—the extended kin group—may be undermined or totally lacking. The sense of community, with family and elders to pass traditional ways on to children, is often disrupted, and people may live in isolation from each other.

However, despite ties to the reservation and the challenges of city life, many urban Indians agree with a young urban Indian who commented, "When I go home [to the reservation] I always feel really welcome but I know that I could never live there. My grandmother and mother's dream is always to move back there. They consider it as home. As I get older I think about it in the same way my parents do. It's hard to give up the convenience of this place. But I don't want to die here."[16]

Urban Indians sometimes worry about being represented in tribal matters, and they point out that being a tribal member means many things: "It means enrollment, and it means political, social, and cultural citizenship."[17]

Indian-Focused Urban Programs

A task force of the American Indian Policy Review Commission argued that because Indian tribes are sovereign, it follows that the individuals who make up the tribe retain that sovereignty regardless of where they live. Therefore, by providing services based on residency, the government is in effect coercing people to return to the reservation to get the services to which they are entitled.[18]

At the same time, as a result of limited funds for reservation programs, many needs go unmet. Serving the urban population, too, is therefore seen as extremely difficult and impractical. Further, any change in current distribution policies would be strongly resisted by reservation leaders, who point out that urban Indians can participate in and are counted for urban-provided services, but urban members are not counted for the distribution of funds to reservations.

Tribes extend a few programs to all members regardless of residency, including the federal higher education scholarship program, Johnson O'Malley elementary education funds to St. Paul and Minneapolis schoolchildren, the Indian Child Welfare Act, and economic development assistance.

Fond du Lac Reservation is operating a clinic in Duluth, funded by the Indian Health Service, as a reservation program. The Mille Lacs Band and the Ho Chunk of Wisconsin fund urban offices with their own funds, and the White Earth and Red Lake Tribes have outreach efforts to assist members with problems, enrollment, and voting. A few federal programs to fund education, health services, and Indian centers specifically include urban Indians, and Minnesota designates urban Indians in some programs. However, most urban Indian programs must rely on patching together a variety of funding sources: regular federal, state, county, and city programs that use Indian agencies; United Way; and foundations and other charities willing to help with unmet needs.

Indian Services in Minneapolis

Since the mid-1970s, the Indian community in Minneapolis has had an advocate in city government to improve understanding and seek better services from the city. The American Indian advocate now is housed in the city's Department of Civil Rights. Hennepin County has several Indian advocates in the Welfare Department and one at Hennepin County Medical Center. In 2002, it joined with the Indian community to launch the American Indian Families Project, a collaboration focused on improving the lives of Indian families. Hennepin County's chemical dependency program has a major focus on Indian patients.

The Minneapolis Indian community can take pride in the leadership that has resulted in many innovative programs:

- ❏ The original service provider to urban Indians, the Division of Indian Work (DIW), offering youth tutoring and activity programs, as well as counseling services.
- ❏ An Indian social service center in North Minneapolis with roots back to the 1930s.
- ❏ The Minneapolis American Indian Center, offering many programs in the heart of the Phillips Indian community.
- ❏ The first federally funded urban Indian health clinic in the nation.
- ❏ The first urban Indian shopping center and a small business "incubator" business center, the American Indian Business Development Corporation, helping to revitalize Franklin Avenue and provide employment.
- ❏ A low-income Indian housing community, which after almost a decade of litigation was again recently confirmed to be Indian-run.
- ❏ A residency and outpatient program to help women with chemical dependency problems and their children.

❏ Several innovative youth educational/cultural programs: Heart of the Earth Survival School (alternative program) and Anishinabe Academy (Minneapolis Public School); American Indian Opportunity Industrial Center (vocational training); and youth programs such as Golden Eagles and MIGIZI.

❏ Safe housing for homeless chemically dependent men.

❏ A residential home for Indians with AIDS.

Numerous Indian programs are focused in the Phillips and Ventura Village neighborhood, where Indians have been leaders in improving housing, providing social services and jobs, and removing liquor stores and bars that contributed to the neighborhood's problems. However, crime and drugs continue to cause fear, and many Indian families seek to move out of the area. This creates concerns that the Indian social programs, built after so much community effort, will be abandoned if too many Indians leave the area. Through its Neighborhood Revitalization Program, the Metropolitan Urban Indian Directors have worked with the city of Minneapolis to designate several million dollars for Indian projects and programs in the area.[19]

MINNEAPOLIS INDIAN CENTERS   Three centers are focal points of Indian activity in Minneapolis. They directly operate a variety of programs and also offer information about accessing other Indian services.

The Minneapolis American Indian Center (MAIC) opened in 1975 and is run by a board elected by Indian residents of Minneapolis or its suburbs. MAIC provides assistance for senior citizens; chemical dependency programs; adult basic education; rehabilitation services; contact with Hennepin County social services; the Healthy Nations Program; Ginew (Golden Eagles) serving Indian youth; and assistance with such issues as funerals, Indian Child Welfare Act, and employment training. MAIC also provides a gathering place for powwows, feasts, and festivals; recreation facilities; a gallery for Indian art exhibits; a craft store; and the offices for *The Circle*, an independent monthly newspaper serving Indians.

The Division of Indian Work began in 1952 to help early post–World War II migrants from reservations adjust to urban life. The

DIW is a division of the Greater Minneapolis Council of Churches, with support also provided by individual denominations, churches, individuals, United Way, government agencies, and foundations for specific programs. Its annual operating budget is approximately $1 million. In 1995, DIW moved into a new $2.5 million facility, designed by Indian architect Dennis Sun Rhodes. Little Six, Inc., which administers Shakopee Mdewakanton Sioux Community businesses, contributed one-half million dollars. The building serves as a community center, used for gatherings, feasts, and Indian-appropriate funerals.

The DIW offers programs dealing with battered women and their children, sexual abuse, and violent partners (for Indian men). A youth leadership development program offers tutoring and activities with the strong involvement of many community volunteers. There is a parent-child learning readiness program and parenting groups for pregnant Indian teens. The DIW also has provided emergency assistance for urban Indians, especially new arrivals, since its beginning.

Upper Midwest American Indian Center is one of the oldest urban Indian organizations, founded in 1961 to help those on north side of Minneapolis. The Indian community elects the organization's board of directors. The Center's recently remodeled building provides an early Head Start program, foster child care licensing and support for Indian families, mental health referral services, a community outreach education program, an alternative high school education, and a gymnasium.

Indian Services in St. Paul

Six percent of Minnesota's Indians live in St. Paul. They constitute a small minority group for the city and are not concentrated in any one neighborhood as in Minneapolis. Because St. Paul distributes funding for community projects on a neighborhood basis, Indians are too small a group to have much influence. The city government of St. Paul has no formal liaison with the Indian community. St. Paul does have several Indian-focused services:

❏ Mother Earth Lodge is a transition home for Indian women and their children adjusting back into the community after chemical dependency treatment.

- ❏ The state's only program and shelter facility for battered Indian women and their children, Women of Nations/Eagles Nest Shelter, is in St. Paul.
- ❏ American Indian Family and Children's Services licenses and supervises Indian foster care.
- ❏ St. Paul Public Schools offers parenting support and other family and youth activity and assistance programs, as well as a magnet school, American Indian/Mounds Park.
- ❏ Ain Dah Yung (Our Home) is a home for runaway and homeless youth.
- ❏ American Indian Family Center provides social services for families and children.
- ❏ In 1994, the St. Paul American Indian Center closed, as did the Red School House, an Indian alternative school, in 1995.

The Department of Indian Work, St. Paul Council of Churches, began serving Indians in St. Paul in 1968. It receives support from churches, individuals, United Way, foundations, and government agencies for specific programming. The Department of Indian Work provides a food shelf program, emergency assistance, and congregate dining. It also educates church groups about Indians and acts as liaison with an Indian burial program to return deceased members to their reservations.

The American Indian Family Center offers youth programming as well as programs supporting women's, prenatal, postnatal, and mental health. The building also houses Ain Dah Yung Family Support Services, the Ain Dah Yung Namadji Project, the Ain Dah Yung Oyate Nawajin Project, in-home and office-based therapy services, the Indian Child Welfare Act Legal Advocacy Project, and Legal Aid services.

Elders Lodge was formed in 1990 in response to Indians' concerns for their community. The project at first focused on family wellness, using elders as teachers. However, the realization that the elders were living in isolation and that their basic needs were not being met led to a project to build housing. In 1994, HUD approved the project, and in 1997, Earthstar Elders Lodge opened. The Lodge has forty-two apartments for elders in a natural setting with space for community activities, congregate dining, and elderly and mental health outreach and counseling.

Services in Other Cities

In Duluth, the Fond du Lac Tribe began providing health and social services for tribally enrolled Indians in 1980 and in 1989 moved into new quarters. The Center for American Indian Resources (CAIR) offers a full-service IHS health clinic, elder outreach program, and a complete array of counseling and social services.

Duluth also has two chemical dependency halfway houses, Indian Legal Assistance services, and a program to help Indian correction system inmates adjust back into the community. Strong Indian programs at the University of Minnesota Duluth and College of St. Scholastica contribute to Indian leadership in the community.

The North American Indian Fellowship Center in International Falls provides Indian programs through the Minnesota Chippewa Tribe, Indian Health Service health clinic services through Boise Forte Reservation, and monthly food commodities distribution. Rainy River Community College offers Indian programming.

St. Cloud recently opened the St. Cloud Area American Indian Center on the St. Cloud State University campus. The Center's purpose is to respond to the educational needs and goals of students and the Indian communities. The Center's outreach activities focus on building awareness and better understanding of American Indian culture.

Bemidji, located near three of the state's major reservations, has a large Indian population, although it has never had an Indian-organized or Indian-run center. Bemidji State University, with a large Indian enrollment and Indian-focused curriculum, is located in the city, as are the state's Indian Affairs Council Office and Indian programs of the Minnesota Department of Education. However, the community provides very little support for agencies serving Indians. For several years, a community race relations committee has attempted to resolve some of the city's race issues.

Indian Research and Advocacy Organizations

Responding to the need to have a ready voice in Washington to deal with Congress and the BIA, Indian tribes have formed several national organizations. The National Congress of American Indians (NCAI), founded in 1944, was the first permanent, national, political, pan-Indian organization. By 2004, its membership consisted of over 250 tribes from every region in the country.[20] The National Indian Gaming Association has a very active role in dealing with the changing tribal-state-federal relationships in controlling gaming.

Minnesota has several professional Indian organizations, including the Minnesota Indian Gaming Association, the Indian Bar Association, and the Indian Chamber of Commerce. The American Indian Research and Policy Institute, founded in 1992 and affiliated with Hamline University, facilitates Indian-directed research and provides a forum for objective discussion and analysis of social and economic issues.

The American Indian Movement (AIM) began in Minneapolis in 1968 as a protest over decades of discrimination in federal Indian policy. AIM leaders spoke out on many issues, including unemployment, housing, racism, and police brutality. The organization used militant tactics, such as occupation of the BIA offices in Washington, D.C., in the early 1970s. While the occupation dramatized the negative role of the BIA in Indian affairs, it also caused extensive damage to records and cultural items. The seventy-one-day occupation of the village of Wounded Knee, South Dakota, in 1973, resulted in violent confrontation with the FBI and the U.S. Army. Some Indians considered AIM's actions violations of their culture, and some reservation leaders were critical of the organization's activities. However, AIM was effective in gaining media attention, which focused on the corruption of some tribal governments, the stifling bureaucracy of the BIA, and the destruction of Indian rights during termination. AIM's emphasis on spirituality and pride in being Indian was a highly effective call to many young Indians who had lost connection with their past.

People associated with AIM started the Red School House and Heart of the Earth Indian survival schools for children in St. Paul and Minneapolis; Little Earth of United Tribe housing development (1975); Legal Rights Center; The American Indian Opportunities Industrialization Center (1979); AIM Patrol; National Coalition on Racism in Sports and the Media (1991), and an annual New Year's sobriety powwow. In 1974, AIM assisted in forming the International Indian Treaty Council (IITC) to focus attention on the needs of Indians throughout the Americas. In 1977, IITC was granted nongovernmental organization (NGO) status at the United Nations and has participated in UN conferences on indigenous peoples. AIM also sponsors the Elaine M. Stately Peacemaker awards annually.

Countering Bias Against Indians

Most Indians acknowledge that they continually face insensitivity, ignorance, and racial prejudice. In spite of laws and court cases, there is some belief in mainstream America that Indians' special relationship with the United States might override the general public's rights. An Indian educator has declared, "What is needed is the understanding that Indians have a political position in this country that no other group has."[21]

Equally ignored are the accomplishments of modern-day Indians. With successes in reclaiming treaty rights and in operating the state's casino industry, Indians face a new barrage of misinformation and stereotyping. Indians observe that when Indians are succeeding, they are seen as threatening competition, and racism and hostility become overt.

Several efforts have been effective in dealing with racial prejudice. For example, when a Twin Cities radio station allowed hostile, racist statements to be made on air, the Indian community reacted quickly by canceling casino advertisements. This brought quick apologies and improved exposure of Indian viewpoints. A spokesperson for one of the tribes involved commented, "Now that we do have some economic muscle, we have an opportunity to stop this kind of thing."[22]

Since 1988, when the Minnesota Board of Education began encouraging schools to drop Indian mascot names and logos, the number of schools using such names and symbols has dropped. But in June 2003, the *Star Tribune*, the largest newspaper in the state, reversed its previous policy of not using Indian nicknames. While editor Anders Gyllenhaal said it was important for newsrooms to reflect reality "as accurately as possible," editorial writers, in opposing the change in policy, said, "All they [Indians] have left is their identity, and they emphatically do not want it expropriated by the white community, especially for commercial use."[23]

Chapter 7

Natural Resources

Plants, animals, grasses and flowers don't need us,
but we need them.

    —Jimmy Jackson, Ojibwe spiritual leader

THROUGHOUT HISTORY, Indians' relationship with the Earth has differed
from that of the dominant culture. Indians were intimately linked to the
natural world around them. They concentrated on their long-term survival by using the diversity of nature, adjusting their lifestyle to focus on
many foods rather than just the few most productive products.

Tribes have always dealt with resources on a communal basis, with
ceremonial taking of fish or animals and ritual ways of collecting plant
materials like sacred pipe stems, medicinal plants, birch bark, and
maple syrup. A wild rice chief or council has traditionally determined
the proper time to harvest. Ojibwe tribes have natural resource departments, employing professional biologists. In the early twenty-first
century, the Red Lake Tribe had eighteen full-time employees dealing
with fisheries, wildlife, waters, wetlands, timber, environmental protection, and conservation enforcement.

Reflecting their sovereign right to protect and regulate natural resources on their reservations, the tribes have greatly expanded their
own laws and administrative capabilities in recent years:

> ❏ Tribes have extensive hunting, fishing, and gathering
> codes, and they license their members. Conservation
> officers and tribal courts enforce regulations. Similar
> programs are active in the 1837 and 1854 Treaty ceded
> areas.

❏ Tribes monitor game harvests; research is conducted on the hunting and fishing codes set by tribal governments.

❏ All the Ojibwe reservations have long-term natural resources management plans, wildlife management programs, programs to protect and clean up the environment, and research projects. Some stock lakes from their own fish hatcheries.

❏ All eleven tribes have an environmental engineer or environmentalist.

❏ Land use zoning and regulatory codes exist on some reservations.

❏ Negotiated agreements now allow for cross-deputization with the state Department of Natural Resources (DNR) and for recognition of enforcement status by the Environmental Protection Agency (EPA).

Hunting and Fishing Rights

In a 1981 decision, Chief U.S. District Court Judge Edward Devitt noted, "It is difficult to conceive of a subject matter in which Indian tribes would have a stronger traditional interest than in hunting, fishing and food gathering" (*White Earth Band v. Alexander*, 518 F. Supp. 536 (D. Minn. 1981)). Hunting, fishing, trapping, and harvesting of wild rice were the sources of survival for early Minnesota Indians; they remain important sources of food.

Since a 1971 U.S. District Court decision in a case brought by Leech Lake Reservation (*Leech Lake Band v. Herbst*, 334 F. Supp. 1001 (D. Minn. 1971)) upheld tribal members' rights to hunt and fish throughout their reservations without state interference, there has been a dramatic expansion of tribes exerting control over hunting and fishing on their reservations.

Tribal–State Agreements

After the Leech Lake court decision, the state and tribe entered into an agreement that was incorporated into state law (Minn. Stat. 97A.151). The tribe agreed to have a conservation code and enforcement procedures acceptable to the state's DNR and to give up its right to commercially hunt and take game fish on the reservation. In return, the state agreed to acknowledge the Indians' hunting and fishing rights. It also agreed to pay the tribe a portion of state-collected license fees to hunt, fish, trap, and take bait, as well as a percentage of the state migratory waterfowl stamp tax (Minn. Stat. 97A.155).

With tensions high about Indians exercising their fishing rights, a group of tribal leaders, county officials, and non-Indian community members came together in the early 1980s to try to defuse the situation, resulting in the Greater Leech Lake Advisory Alliance. Support grew for a tribal fish hatchery to stock the lakes, and the Leech Lake Tribal Fish Hatchery was built in 1984. The state passed legislation authorizing a plan with the White Earth Tribe similar to that for the Leech Lake Tribe, but an agreement was never reached.

The 1837 Treaty Area

The 1837 Treaty included lands in what are now Wisconsin and Minnesota. Some twelve Ojibwe bands signed the agreement specifically reserving the tribes' rights to hunt, fish, and gather in the ceded areas. Major court decisions since the 1970s in Washington state, Michigan, and Wisconsin have upheld tribal treaty hunting and fishing rights.

Tribes retained the right to regulate their own resources, free of state interference. They may net and spear fish and are allowed to sell their share commercially. Under the rulings, Indians are entitled to 50 percent of the harvest. The only justification for state involvement is if public safety is threatened or a species faces extinction. Timber cannot be harvested commercially, but the gathering of maple sap, birch bark, and firewood are subject to tribal regulation. The tribes were not allowed to sue the state for damages from having been denied their rights for more than a century because states have immunity to lawsuits under the Eleventh Amendment to the U.S. Constitution.

Legal battles over major treaty cases have been very long and expensive. Fears of non-Indians that hunting and fishing rights would jeopardize tourist dollars have not materialized, however, and tensions in this first part of the twenty-first century appear to be abating.

1837 TREATY ISSUES IN MINNESOTA   The Minnesota portion of the 1837 Treaty is an area of just over three million acres, including

519 lakes ten acres or more in size. The treaty involves land in the following counties: all of Mille Lacs, Kanabec, and Chisago; nearly all of Benton, Pine, and Isanti; a major portion of Morrison; and small parts of Crow Wing, Aitkin, Sherburne, Anoka, and Washington. Almost all of Mille Lacs Lake, the second largest lake in the state, known for its outstanding walleye, is within the treaty area.

In 1982, the Mille Lacs Band of Ojibwe began negotiations with the state to regain what the tribe believed were its rights. Negotiations failed, with both sides stating that the main reason was strong opposition from those who used the lake for sports fishing. From that point, it took the tribe eight years to prepare its case, at which time Mille Lacs offered and the state agreed to enter into settlement negotiations. While the U.S. Fish and Wildlife Service had recognized the Mille Lacs Nation's right to hunt migratory birds in the ceded area since 1987, resolving questions about fishing required major compromises by both parties. Indians agreed to limit their walleye harvest to twenty-four thousand pounds, less than 5 percent of the average annual catch, and to give up the right to do commercial fishing. The state agreed that tribes could do their own enforcement and not be subject to state control in an area of some six thousand acres of Mille Lacs Lake, about 4.5 percent of the lake, along with six smaller lakes and twenty miles of the Rum and St. Croix Rivers shoreline. The state also agreed to transfer to the tribe seventy-five hundred acres of land, which the tribe agreed would not be used for gaming, and $8.6 million, half of which would be used for protecting the environment and enforcing regulations.

Tribal members ratified the agreement, which then came to a vote in the state legislature in 1993. Despite the support of the governor and the DNR, the agreement was defeated in the Minnesota House by five votes. Steve Thorne, DNR Deputy Commissioner who negotiated the agreement, later commented, "Those people who opposed the deal . . . had convinced themselves that the huge body of Indian law that exists is just plain wrong, but those of us familiar with the law got no real comfort in the arguments we were hearing from sportsmen . . . If we could work something out that protected the resource and gave access to everyone, we felt that was the way to go."[1]

The case then went to U.S. District Court, which ruled in favor of the tribe (*Mille Lacs Band v. Minnesota*, 861 F. Supp. 784 (D. Minn. 1994) on August 24, 1994). A second phase of the trial concluded in

1997, with the ruling that the band's fishing and hunting activities in the twelve-county region were to be regulated by the band rather than by the state.

In April 1997, the Eighth Circuit Court postponed implementing the decision until the appeal was decided; in August 1997, the appeal panel upheld in total the lower court ruling (*Mille Lacs Band v. State of Minnesota*, 48 F.3d 373 (C.A. 8, 1997)). This decision was then appealed to the full Eighth Circuit, which in November 1997, by a 7–2 decision, denied the request to review the decision. A further appeal was made to the U.S. Supreme Court, which ruled in 1999 by a 5–4 vote that the Mille Lacs Band of Chippewa retained the hunting and fishing rights guaranteed to them by the 1837 Treaty. The U.S. District Court ordered the state of Minnesota to pay the legal expenses of the Mille Lacs and six other bands, an amount that totaled $3.95 million.

1837 TREATY ISSUES IN WISCONSIN   The Wisconsin Ojibwe tribes successfully sued Wisconsin in U.S. District Court over the state's denial of treaty rights (*Lac Courte Oreilles Band v. Voight*, 700 F.2d 341 (7th Cir. 1983)). The U.S. Supreme Court refused to hear the state's appeal.

When tribal members exercised their rights under the Wisconsin decision, they were met with strong, sometimes violent, protests at boat landings. Ugly, racial stereotyping typified much of the protest movement.[2] However, a group of white citizens, who organized as Citizens for Treaty Rights, stood peacefully at fishing sites to witness any violent acts against Indians, thus helping to maintain order. Peace was restored when a court outlawed many of the protesters' activities.

Today, there are signs of greater harmony. Indians have proven to be good stewards of the fish resources. They are working closely with state natural resource experts, evaluating the quality of lakes used by the tribes and stocking lakes from their tribal fish hatcheries for the benefit of all. Indian harvesting of the resources is far less than the 50 percent allowed by the court decision.[3] The Lac du Flambeau tribe signed an agreement with the state to reduce its walleye catch in return for state payments. This has allowed the state to raise the bag limit for the area.

1854 Treaty Area

The resolution of Indians' rights under the 1854 Treaty (involving Minnesota's entire Arrowhead region, some five million acres) began in 1985, when a Grand Portage tribal member shot a moose within the treaty area but off the reservation. The three tribes that were party to the original treaty, Bois Forte, Grand Portage, and Fond du Lac, entered the case.

After three years, an out-of-court settlement was negotiated. The tribes agreed to set and enforce all of their harvests, allowing minimal commercial fishing. The state agreed to accept the rights of properly identified tribal members to harvest resources throughout the region and to pay an annual fee to the tribes for their cooperation. The agreement can be canceled by any of the parties upon one year's notice. Both the Bois Forte and Grand Portage tribes accepted the agreement, forming an authority agency to administer their agreement.

Fond du Lac members voted against the agreement on the grounds that their treaty rights were not for sale. The tribe then established its own code and enforcement system for the ceded 1854 Treaty area, foregoing state funds. The state challenged the tribe's right to regulate its members' conduct in the area, but the U.S. District Court ruled that the state could not interfere with the tribe's right to regulate the harvest unless it was necessary for public safety, public health, or to protect endangered species. Subsequently, the tribe and state agreed to let the decision about the harvest be tied to the 1837 Treaty case.

Conservation Codes and Regulation

On all reservations, members come under the conservation codes of their tribe and are not subject to any state regulation. Although tribal codes are quite similar to state law, there are differences. For example, taking fish with gill nets, the traditional harvest method, is allowed. Some tribes have extensive regulations. Photo identification is required of tribal members. Seasons and methods of harvest are defined, with quotas set by areas.

Members of the Mille Lacs, Fond du Lac, and six Wisconsin Ojibwe tribes can hunt and fish in the Minnesota portion of the 1837 Treaty Area under regulations and enforcement established by the tribes. Commercial taking of fish is regulated under terms set by the tribes and has the agreement of the state.

The Peace Officers Standards and Training (POST) Board licenses the conservation officers of Leech Lake, Fond du Lac, and Mille Lacs Reservations, and the 1854 Authority (an intertribal natural resource agency that manages off-reservation hunting, fishing, and gathering for the Grand Portage and Bois Forte Bands). The conservation officers are cross-deputized by the state and empowered to impose state conservation laws upon all non-Band members within the reservation (or the 1854 ceded territory). State conservation officers in the area are cross-deputized and may enforce tribal codes upon tribal members, who are dealt with in tribal court; nontribal members appear in state or tribal court.

All Ojibwe tribes have conservation courts. Red Lake Tribe deals with its conservation code violators in its regular court. For violators in the off-reservation 1854 Treaty area, the 1854 Authority operates a conservation circuit court, moving around the area. Grand Portage members in violation of reservation codes are handled by this court. Fond du Lac has separate courts for reservation and ceded territory violations.

Other Hunting and Fishing Issues

Fishing Methods

Throughout the years, many non-Indians and legal battles have questioned Indians about the use of nets and spears in fishing, Indians point out that they do not fish for sport but for subsistence. Fishing for sustenance is deeply rooted in Indian culture and is verified by the treaties and thus linked to Indian sovereignty.[4] Indians also point out that the same limits apply to taking fish under the tribal codes, whatever method of harvest is used. In reality, the number of Indians who use nets is quite small, and by all accounts, this method has not decreased the availability of fishing in Minnesota lakes.[5]

Other Ceded Lands

As part of the Nelson Act, four townships on the White Earth Reservation were ceded to the government in 1889. Several court cases have debated whether that transfer extinguished reservation status for that land. State and federal courts have consistently ruled against the Indians, the latest being the 1997 Minnesota Court of Appeals ruling that the tribe had ceded the four townships (*State of Minn. v. Butcher*, Minn. Ct. App. C5-96-1076, May 27, 1997).

The Red Lake Tribe also ceded major timber lands to the United States under the Nelson Act, as well as with legislation passed in 1904. The Indian Reorganization Act of 1934 returned to tribal trust status those lands that had not been sold, including most of the state's Northwest Angle. The state and tribe each considered these ceded lands under its jurisdiction, but a 1980 court decision ruled against the Red Lake Tribe (*U.S. v. Minn.*, 466 F. Supp 1382 (D. Minn. 1979), *affirmed on appeal* as *Red Lake Band v. State of Minn.*, 614 F.2d 1161 (8th Cir. 1980)), *cert. denied,* 449 U.S. 905 (1980)).

Indian Rights in the Boundary Waters

According to the 1854 Treaty, tribes have rights to the Boundary Waters that were never relinquished. Indians with proper identification have free access, but they maintain it is the tribe's right rather than the Forestry Service's to define how they use the area. Federal regulation has been challenged and Indians arrested, but the result has been out-of-court settlements rather than a major defining legal decision.

Other Special Arrangements

In 1935, the Tamarac National Wildlife Refuge was established through the Collier Agreement between the BIA and the U.S. Fish and Wildlife Service. A major portion of the reserve is within the White Earth Reservation. The agreement specified that the Indians were to have preference in wild rice harvesting and trapping, which continue to operate with tribal administration. A lottery is required to determine who can harvest the area's good wild rice lakes. Currently, Tamarac is administered as a migratory bird and wildlife sanctuary and used for hunting and logging purposes. Sherburne National Wildlife Refuge, located partly within the 1837 Treaty area, has an agreement with the Mille Lacs Tribe for special hunting rights for tribal members.

Environmental Laws and Regulations

Endangered Species, Migratory Birds

Indian tribes hold the eagle sacred. The Bald Eagle Protection Act
(16 U.S.C. 668a) specifies that Indians have the right to obtain eagle
parts for religious use. The U.S. Fish and Wildlife Service is responsible for collecting the birds found dead on federal lands and distribut-
ing them to qualified Indian applicants.

The U.S. Fish and Wildlife Service controls hunting seasons for
ducks and other migratory birds. Under the Migratory Bird Treaty Act
(16 U.S.C. 703), tribes are able to negotiate control of their own
hunting seasons with more liberal limits. The Mille Lacs and Fond du
Lac tribes, as well as the Ojibwe tribes in Wisconsin, regulate hunting
by tribal members in the territory ceded by the 1837 Treaty. The
federal district court for Minnesota ruled that this federal law does not
apply to tribal members in the 1854 ceded area because, when the law
was passed, Congress did not say it intended to abrogate the treaty
right (*U.S. v. Bresette*, 761 F. Supp 658, (D. Minn. April 9, 1991)).

The Environmental Protection Agency and Tribes

During the 1970s, Indian reservations were left out of the funding
equation for environmental cleanup programs. The Environmental
Protection Agency did not set aside resources for tribes nor did
states channel funds to them. By 1993, there were many serious environmental problems on reservations, including illegal dumping,
inadequate sewage treatment, poor septic systems, and poor drinking
water and air quality. Pollution from lumber companies affected many
lakes and streams. There was a nearly complete lack of administrative
or physical infrastructure to manage or even to influence environmental problems.

The EPA was the first federal agency to respond to the presidential
directive in 1983 that tribes be recognized on a government-to-
government basis. A policy statement in 1984 said the EPA would work
with tribes and incorporate their needs into its policies and budgets.[6]
Amendments in 1986 and 1987 to the major environmental laws (for
example, Safe Drinking Water Act, Clean Water Act, Clean Air Act)
required that tribes be treated as states in order to receive funding.

Tribes have to develop primacy programs for enforcement purposes. However, funding has been inadequate, and as an EPA Indian staff person noted in 1993, "Unfortunately they [the tribes] are getting into the game just at the time the money is running out."[7]

Legal questions were raised as to whether the laws applied to reservations, since that would have required specific Congressional intent to abrogate tribal sovereignty. But combined results of executive directive, legislation, and court decisions made it clear that Indian nations were owed the same commitment to health and environmental integrity as the rest of the nation.

However, it was not until the 1990s that the EPA programs were extended to the tribes. The EPA signed a formal agreement with all eleven Minnesota tribes in 1995, acknowledging tribal sovereignty to deal with their programs. The six Minnesota Chippewa Tribe (MCT) tribes, the EPA, and the state agreed to cooperate on hazardous waste spills on MCT reservations in 1990. For tribes to exert their jurisdiction under EPA programs, they must show they have jurisdiction over the resource and are capable of regulating it. Reservation jurisdiction for this purpose becomes complicated in how or if it extends to non-Indians on the reservation. Supreme Court decisions have not provided a clear way of deciding.[8]

Individual tribes have additional federal agreements. The Prairie Island Tribe, for instance, has agreements with the EPA, U.S. Fish and Wildlife Service, U.S. Geological Survey, Federal Emergency Management Agency, and U.S. Nuclear Regulatory Agency. The Fond du Lac Reservation took over air quality responsibilities from the EPA in August 2003. Regional air permit holders within fifty miles of the reservation now have their applications reviewed by tribal officials. The Band does not have veto power over permits, but their concerns carry the same weight as those of state regulators. The Mille Lacs Tribe's Department of Natural Resources and Environment requested special EPA designation that would protect from contamination the aquifer from which the tribe gets its drinking water.[9] The Mille Lacs Tribe has also developed other programs to protect groundwater.

Regional and Local Environmental Initiatives

Several tribes are involved in regional environmental groups dealing with the St. Louis River, Lake Superior, Leech Lake, and Mississippi

River. Cooperation on a more local level is enabling tribes and neighboring non-Indian communities to deal with needed water and sewage systems. The Leech Lake Tribe and the City of Cass Lake have worked out such an arrangement.

Solid Waste Disposal

The reservations have complied with federal requirements that landfills and open dumps be closed. This has required finding funds from many sources to safely close existing facilities, build waste transfer stations, provide supervision of the facility, and arrange for disposal at an approved landfill. Tribes generally have contracted with haulers to remove solid wastes or have agreed to use the centralized county facility.

The Bois Forte Tribe built a transfer station and properly capped the landfill through funding from several agencies. Grand Portage, however, was unable to find the funds to cap its old landfill dump. The White Earth Tribe funded improvements in its waste and sanitation system with Housing and Urban Development (HUD) funds. Red Lake uses a recycling incinerator facility at Thief River Falls, which reuses some 90 percent of the refuse. In support of this approach to deal with waste, the tribe invested in and now owns 20 percent of the company. The Leech Lake Sanitary Landfill posed major problems for years. An agreement in 1996 between the state and the tribe put the facility into the state's Landfill Cleanup Act program. A few tribes have recycling programs, but generally they lack funds to operate such programs.

Underground Fuel Storage Tanks

Each tribe has been expected to locate underground fuel storage tanks and clean up any leakage. The state has funded the cleanup and regulation of tanks through the Petrofund Program, a dedicated fund (Minn. Stat. 115C.08, Subd. 3). Tribes must enter into and comply with the conditions of this program to be eligible for reimbursement from the state. According to the Minnesota Department of Commerce, many tribes have applied for and received reimbursement for the costs that they have incurred investigating and cleaning up petroleum tank releases.[10] Indians in some cases have dealt with problems caused by non-Indian-owned businesses.

Underground Injection Control Program

The Mille Lacs Band of Ojibwe is developing an underground injection control project to prevent contaminations from seeping into ground-water. The program was approved in 1998 through a memorandum of understanding among the Mille Lacs Band, the U.S. Environmental Protection Agency, and the Minnesota Pollution Control Agency program.

Zoning and Land Use Regulation

The reservationwide zoning and land use code at Grand Portage is one of the most positive examples of cooperation in the very confused area of tribal and non-Indian jurisdiction. The tribe, determined to protect their lands, appointed a committee of tribal and non-Indian community members to prepare a comprehensive ordinance. Areas were defined for human habitation, wildlife management, and timber harvest. Land use permits are required from the tribe for all lands, whether a tribal member or non-Indian owns the land. The ordinance was approved and went into effect in 1996. The county maintains jurisdiction over non-Indians by requiring them to obtain permits.

The Grand Portage Tribe also made a formal agreement in 1996 with the state and the EPA to have joint implementation of federal water quality standards in Grand Portage Bay. In Grand Marais, south-west of the reservation, the city council voted to put undeveloped shoreline into trust so it could not be used commercially in the future. The mayor commented that it was the Grand Portage Tribe's actions that inspired the city.

Grand Portage State Park

In 1989, the three hundred-acre Grand Portage State Park was created by the Minnesota Legislature (Minn. Laws 1989, Ch. 259). In a tribal–state–federal agreement, the land was transferred to the federal government to be held in trust for the Grand Portage Tribe. The tribe leased the land for a nominal fee (not to exceed $100 per year) to the state for a park to be operated in the same way as other state parks. Staff is required under agreement with the Tribal Council to have significant knowledge of Indian culture. In 1997, the tribe also reached agreement to provide maintenance for the facility and to lease a historic nine-mile portage trail for hikers.

Environmental Research

Recent tribal research projects are many, often involving subjects not dealt with by other agencies. Almost all tribes are working with wetlands, lakes, and streams to protect and restore wild rice lakes, encourage migratory waterfowl, and eradicate purple loosestrife.

- ❏ Fond du Lac Tribe studied channel catfish in the St. Louis River and reintroduced sturgeon into the St. Louis River.
- ❏ Grand Portage Tribe has been working for more than ten years to successfully reintroduce the coaster brook trout (rainbow).
- ❏ Prairie Island Community, Shakopee Mdewakanton Sioux Community, and White Earth have restored prairies, and Mille Lacs and Fond du Lac have reintroduced sweet grass.
- ❏ Leech Lake Tribe established a bird sanctuary on Gull and Pelican Island, site for common tern nesting and the federally endangered piping plover.
- ❏ Testing projects for mercury and/or polychlorinated bi-phenyls (PCBs) have been conducted on Lake Vermilion (MCT), Lake Superior (Grand Portage Tribe), and Fond du Lac Reservation.
- ❏ The Mille Lacs Band of Ojibwe, in concern over the lake, has conducted research since the 1980s, analyzing water, mud, and invertebrate samples to build a database so that future changes can be identified. Mille Lacs also has conducted a detailed study of its wetlands.[11]
- ❏ White Earth Reservation, containing major amounts of agricultural land, is studying the use of chemicals, as well as cataloging wetlands.

The Minnesota Chippewa Tribe Research Laboratory is equipped to do a wide range of testing, including analysis of pollutants in water and tissue cultures. The Laboratory does routine water testing of community wells, in schools, and at casinos for the six MCT reservations and contracts with other agencies to provide these services. Leech Lake, Mille Lacs, and Bois Forte also have laboratory facilities.

Bizhibayaash ("Circle of Flight"), a BIA program, is a major funder of reservation resource management and research projects directed to wetland ecosystems. The focus on preserving wetlands and protecting and restoring wild rice lakes fits well with most tribal goals. The BIA also funds the operation of other tribal natural resources programs, as do the Administration for Native Americans, the EPA, and the state Department of Natural Resources.

Several colleges are targeting Indian students to interest and prepare them for careers in natural resources. Programs now exist at Itasca Community College, three vocational schools in the Mille Lacs area, and Fond du Lac Tribal and Community College.

Relations with the U.S. Army Corps of Engineers

The Corps is involved in controlling most of the water in the United States, where many strong, contradictory demands are made. The Corps' extensive involvement with water results in many contacts with tribes. As with other federal agencies, there are presidential and legislative directives to take Indian culture into consideration and to consult tribes on a government-to-government basis. While some recent programs between the Corps and the tribes have been well received, U.S. water policies, as implemented by the Corps, have a history of more than one hundred years of abusing tribal interests.

On projects where the Corps assumes administrative responsibilities, such as dams and wetlands, the Corps usually insists upon ownership of the property. Congress takes the land, with compensation provided, thus overriding tribal sovereignty. This process has led to much mistrust.

Control of water usage has often affected Indian lands, with tribes rarely consulted. Many dams related to the Mississippi River have been built on Indian land without their approval, resulting in the destruction of forests, wild rice habitats, agricultural land, and Indian burial sites. In 1985, the United States settled a claim with the Leech Lake Indians, paying the tribe $3.4 million for damages caused by dams.

During the serious drought in 1988, sharply conflicting views over the use of the Mississippi headwaters being held by the dams led to the development of a water control plan. Protecting tribal interests as a part of the Corps trust responsibility was included as one of the top priorities.

In recent years, the Corps has improved relations with tribes by building waterfowl enhancements, mapping lakes to register changes, and denying building projects that Indians oppose based on environmental concerns.

Nuclear Power Plant on Prairie Island

The Prairie Island Indian Community shares its historic island homeland with a nuclear-powered electric generating plant built in 1973 and operated by Xcel Energy (formerly Northern States Power (NSP)).[12] The city of Red Wing annexed Prairie Island, which enabled it to benefit from the plant's property taxes. Originally, waste from the facility was to be shipped off for reprocessing, but a change in regulations in the 1980s forbade such reprocessing. By 1994, Xcel Energy was running out of storage space at the plant for its spent nuclear waste.

Faced with the possible closure of a plant that produces 20 percent of its power, Xcel Energy approached the Minnesota legislature, seeking permission to store waste in dry casks on Prairie Island. After lengthy and heated public debate, the legislature approved seventeen such casks. The senate majority leader later characterized the passage of this legislation as "the most divisive debate I have experienced in twenty-seven years as a state legislator."[13] An infamous meeting in March 1994 included NSP representatives behind closed doors with the Senate Environmental Committee, while the Prairie Island tribal representative sat outside in the hall. The committee voted that the tribe should move away from its home of nearly 150 years without a single word of testimony or input from tribal leaders.[14] Heavy political pressure also came from the city of Red Wing and Goodhue County, which benefit from millions of dollars of taxes the plant pays and the more than five hundred jobs filled by non-Indians who make a good living from employment at the plant.

The seventeen casks approved by the 1994 legislation were soon filled. During a special legislative session in 2003, a law was passed authorizing additional dry cask storage and allowing Prairie Island's two reactors to continue operating through their license expiration dates in 2013 and 2014. The law also included provisions for renewable energy development and required Xcel Energy to give the Prairie Island Indian Community up to $2.5 million per year. One of the primary uses of that money is to acquire land for the tribe away from the nuclear facility. Future requests for additional nuclear waste storage capacity will be subject to the approval of the Minnesota Public Utilities Commission.

Living next to extremely dangerous nuclear wastes has caused great concern and continual fears for the Prairie Island Community. The possibility of exposure to radiation, a catastrophic accident, groundwater contamination, and the lack of evacuation routes top the list. While some Indians have suggested that the tribe apply to become a nuclear waste depository and be well paid for what they already had to live with, the majority of members rejected that proposal in a community referendum in the mid-1990s. Both Xcel Energy and tribal officials say that the 2003 agreement does not lessen the need for a permanent repository of nuclear waste, which the federal government has been slow to identify and put into place.

Commercial Fishing and Hatcheries

The Red Lakes Fisheries Association, established in 1917, is the only commercial walleye fishery in the United States and the largest tribal fishery on the continent. In the mid-1990s, environmental issues and overfishing led to a crash in the walleye population, and the Red Lakes Fisheries was forced to close in 1997. The closure dealt a serious economic blow to the tribe, which had developed a very profitable fishing and processing enterprise. In addition, the DNR estimated that the economic impact from lost tourism was between $1 million and $2 million annually. For example, Waskish, a Red Lake community that once was recognized as a premier fishing destination, had sixteen resorts/motels in the 1990s; today, only one remains. However, walleye restocking efforts are underway, and the association is on track to reopen the fishery in 2006.[15] The fishery employs five hundred independent fishermen and forty to fifty processors seasonally.

In 1998, the Red Lake Band signed an agreement with the University of Wisconsin System Aquaculture Institute to study the potential for raising yellow perch. The initiative was designed to help revitalize the tribe's fisheries industry, boost the local economy, and offer a fish farming model for other tribes and entrepreneurs to follow. The Red Lake Fisheries is also exploring long-term ways to better utilize their aquaculture products and joint composting with Bemidji State University.

The Minnesota tribes involved in the 1854 Treaty (Bois Forte, Grand Portage, and Fond du Lac) agreed to establish a commercial fishing zone on Lake Superior for tribal members. Grand Portage has been the only one of the three tribes to engage in such commercial fishing. The Leech Lake Tribe, under its agreement with the state, is free to sell nongame fish, but depressed markets for fish have not made this economically feasible.

Several reservations operate fish hatcheries, which in addition to serving tribal subsistence and commercial needs are also contributing significant numbers of fish for lakes and rivers on which anglers are more than 95 percent non-Indian. In 2001, Red Lake hatched over thirty-one million fish, mostly walleye, and the Leech Lake Reservation hatched nearly eight million fish with its state-of-the-art operation. The same year, the White Earth hatchery, active since 1982, hatched 128,000 fish, mostly walleye. Fond du Lac also hatches some walleye for its lakes.[16]

Timber Resources

The value of the white pine forests was a major reason for treaties in northern Minnesota and for policies that led to Indians losing most of their reservation lands.[17] The frenzy to harvest this valuable resource led to innumerable abuses of Indian rights (see the Nelson Act and subsequent legislation in chapter 2). Today, the wounds are still fresh and the issues current, including claims by the Red Lake Tribe and the MCT of improper payment for the lands and timber taken by the treaties and improper accounting for the trust funds.

The treaties that established Minnesota's northern reservations made large timber acreages available to loggers. The government wanted Indians to become farmers to enable the harvest of forested land for white development. Suitable land for allotment was either land without timber or from which timber had been cleared. Indians did not have the right to harvest timber for the sole purpose of selling it (*U.S. v. Cook*, 86 U.S. 591 (1873)).

Forests disappeared quickly (See Table 7.1). By 1912, all but the remote timber areas at Grand Portage had been cut; only small, scattered, and inaccessible timber stands remained on White Earth by 1914; and Fond du Lac Reservation logging was finished by 1917, and Leech Lake Reservation, in 1918.[18] It was not until the Indian Reorganization Act of 1934 that cutting on a sustained yield basis was adopted. In the decades since, management problems, inadequate funding, and the scattered nature of the lands have made administration very difficult.

Policies Today

The Minnesota State Legislature adopted the Minnesota Sustainable Forest Resources Act (SFRA) in 1995 to ensure sustainable use and management of Minnesota's forests. SFRA's twofold program is focused on site-based timber harvesting/forest management guidelines and landscape-level forest resource planning and coordination. SFRA also established the Minnesota Forest Resources Council (MFRC) to develop and implement SFRA initiatives. Additionally, MFRC advises

Table 7.1 Chippewa Tribe forests in Minnesota, 1900–1948

	Before logging, at turn of 20th century	Second growth, 1948
White/Jack Pine	66%	13%
Spruce	12%	10%
Aspen	10%	28%
Mixed Hardwoods	4%	6%
Cedar, Balsam, Other	8%	10%
Brush		33%

Source: Adapted from "Forest Management Problems and Basic Forest Facts," 1950, quoted in Historical Research Associates, Inc., Missoula, Mont., "The Forests of Anishinabe: A History of Minnesota Chippewa Tribal Forestry 1854–1991," 1992.

the governor and federal, state, and local governments on sustainable forest resource policies and practices. Minnesota's governor appoints fifteen members of the MFRC and the chairperson; the Minnesota Indian Affairs Council appoints one representative.[19]

In 1961, the MCT established the policy of setting aside 25 percent of sales for the Forest Cultural Fund to improve timber and cultural resources. The fund is divided among the individual tribes based on their share of the contributing timber harvest. The Grand Portage Tribe has a similar fund.

Tribes do much of their own timber management, setting their own policies and goals, which may focus on protecting wildlife at the expense of timber protection. With the exception of lands held by Red Lake and Grand Portage Reservations, most of the timberland titles are in the name of the Minnesota Chippewa Tribe. Forestry has been an important financial resource for White Earth, Leech Lake, and Bois Forte in particular.

Forest Management Issues

During the last decade, a dramatic change has occurred in the state's timber industry. Prices are good for timber, and a strong market has been found for the rapid-growing aspen and popple, which had previously been considered useless "weed trees." A state study in the early 1990s warned that while these trees could benefit the economy in northern Minnesota, there was the potential for disruption of ecological systems.[20]

Forest resources remain underutilized on some reservations since the amount of logging is far less than the allowable cut set by management plans. Grand Portage's Economic Development Plan noted in 1992 that while the reservation's recommended annual cut was over sixteen thousand cords, the actual average annual cut was just over four thousand cords, almost one-fourth of what it might be.

The Fond du Lac Reservation had a similar situation, with much of its aspen and paper birch past commercial maturity. The trees were becoming infested with insects and disease and, as a result, were posing a wildfire threat. The Fond du Lac Forestry Office undertook a large-scale project to better manage its forests in the early 1990s that has proven successful.[21]

Sawmills

A tribal sawmill is operated on the Grand Portage Reservation, making pallet lumber and wood chips that are sold to paper mills in Canada. The Red Lake Tribal Sawmill, authorized by federal legislation in 1916 (39 Stat. 137) and operated by the BIA, was taken over by the tribe in the 1990s.

Wild Rice

Wild rice ("manomin," the Ojibwe word for "good berry") is an important part of the Indian diet and an integral part of Indian culture. It is a tall, aquatic annual grass (*Zizania aquatica*) that grows in the rich, silted shallows of lakes, rivers, and ponds. Wild rice is referred to as a "spiritual gift from the Great Spirit." It was prophesized during the migration of the Ojibwe/Anishinabe that when you find food growing out of the water, you have found your homeland.[22]

As one Indian researcher said, "It is difficult to overestimate the importance of wild rice to the Ojibwa, or the role rice fields played in the history of the area . . . many battles were fought with the Dakota over control of the rice fields. The Ojibwa depended heavily on wild rice for their winter subsistence."[23] Wild rice lakes determined Indian settlement patterns, and fur traders' survival depended upon Indians providing them with wild rice.

For modern Minnesota, the shallow water wetlands that nourish wild rice are very important in protecting the state's ecology, replenishing the water systems, and providing wildlife habitat, especially for migrating waterfowl. The plant grows in the rich, silted shallows of lakes, rivers, and ponds. About 40 percent of the state's water acres producing natural wild rice are on Indian reservations.[24] The crop is subject to wide fluctuation caused by weather and water level changes.

A variety of wild rice grown in flooded beds, developed by the University of Minnesota, has caused great concern to Indians throughout Minnesota, who see it as an inferior product that has sharply reduced the commercial value of the natural product. One acre of the paddy-grown rice can produce as much as one thousand pounds, while naturally cultivated wild rice yields approximately seventy-five pounds per acre. What is especially troubling to Indians is that, as one Indian wild rice processor noted, "(m)uch of the research on paddy-grown rice was done in Minnesota—a case of the government spending millions of dollars to put a lot of people out of work and out of money."[25]

In 2004, tensions between Indians and University of Minnesota researchers surfaced over the issue of mapping the wild rice genome. University researchers stated that they wanted to understand the wild rice genome for aid in understanding other cereal grains. But Indians argued that it was a major threat to its rice and could lead to battles over a patent. According to White Earth tribal elder Joe Lagarde, "The University of Minnesota School of Agriculture has been involved in research affecting wild rice for the past 50 years. Yet pitifully little was done to assure that the Anishinabe people would have any significant involvement in research with such a direct impact on their lives . . . . Now we are faced with corporations wishing to patent what they consider intellectual property rights as well as the emerging medicinal properties inherent in the manomin [wild rice]."[26]

State law requires that Indian methods be used in harvesting wild rice from all natural lakes and streams in Minnesota (Minn. Stat. 84.111). On reservations, tribes control the harvest, which is restricted to persons of Indian blood or residents of the reservation (Minn. Stat. 84.10). Non-Indians are required to obtain state licenses; on Leech Lake, they are also required to get a tribal license. On lakes outside reservations, everyone must obtain a state license except in the 1837 and 1854 ceded territories, where tribal members are licensed by the tribal government.

Wild rice requires flowing, mineral-rich water that retains a constant level. It does not tolerate chemical pollutants. Several lakes have small dams to maximize conditions for the rice. Many reservations have programs to replant or reintroduce wild rice seed, and several have developed programs to analyze lake inventory and genetic makeup of the rice to protect and preserve it for future generations.

Summary

Nature and its resources have always been of great importance to Indians, both physically and spiritually. Destruction of forests, lakes, and rivers by early Europeans altered Indians' way of life. As the United States industrialized, environmental degradation intruded on the reservations. Reclaiming Indian treaty rights to hunt, fish, and gather has resulted in decades of legal battles.

For the tribes, the underlying issue is sovereignty—the right to make their own decisions on how to administer and protect the small portion of land and resources that remains theirs. Through self-governance contracts and other agreements, tribes are increasingly planning and administering their own natural resources. After decades of being ignored, reservations are receiving the benefit of environmental protection and cleanup programs, with the tribes having increasing authority in the process. Tribal–state cooperation has improved, and while the major problems of insufficient funding and jurisdictional conflicts remain, good will and cooperation have gone a long way toward resolving some very important problems regarding natural resources.

The issues dealt with in this chapter reflect how Indians' understanding of the natural world affects their decision-making. With tribes rapidly increasing their powers and abilities to control their own environments, it is important that non-Indians understand and accept differing views of how to deal with natural resources. As one Indian leader said, "We do not inherit the land from our ancestors, we rent it from our children."[27]

Chapter 8

Economic Development

NO ASPECT OF RESERVATION LIFE has changed as dramatically in the last decade as economic development, a change driven primarily by the casinos. Indian gaming and related economic opportunities have become a major state industry since tribally owned, Las Vegas–style facilities opened beginning in 1990. The financial resources resulting from gaming are helping tribes invest in their reservations, offer expanded employment opportunities to their members and residents in surrounding communities, and provide truly meaningful self-government.

The increased vitality of reservation economies began before the casinos, however, and is traceable to several factors: tribes gradually taking over management of most of their own federal programs; improvement in infrastructure and community services; and the availability of basic resources such as timber, water, and land; and, as Mille Lacs Band Chief Executive Melanie Benjamin commented, "our most important resource—our people."[1]

Economic Development Challenges

Economic development in some areas of Minnesota still faces many barriers. For example, in Northern Minnesota the distance to major markets, an unskilled labor force, steep energy costs, limited investment capital, and a depressed regional economy make economic development a challenge. Lack of good roads, water and sanitation facilities, emergency services, and electric power also contribute to the challenges. The area relies heavily on federal and state funding. In other areas, reservations lack land or have land in parcels too fragmented to permit development.

The reservations and their Indian populations are important economic assets to their local areas. The tribes spend major amounts of money, but because Indians own few retail stores, generally these funds quickly find their way into white-owned businesses.[2] Even though the development of gaming has increased tribal governments' spending, the dollars are still leaving the reservations and therefore are not providing much extra economic benefit for the Indian community. The director of the Minnesota American Indian Chamber of Commerce noted, "In the mainstream community, a dollar will roll over three or four times. But in Indian communities a dollar will roll over one and a half times and then it's gone."[3]

Federal and tribal governments' policies have traditionally focused on social concerns on reservations, not on acquiring the capital for self-sustaining economic development. While gaming has provided cash surpluses for some tribes, research of Minnesota's Indian casinos in rural Minnesota shows that just having a flow of cash may not be enough to achieve sustained development. Rather, real economic growth in a community takes major personal and financial commitments from those willing to risk their capital to invest in businesses.[4] In addition, while casinos have created an enormous number of jobs, the relatively low pay of some of those positions may not support a family or provide a base for further community development through consumer spending.

The Harvard Project on American Indian Economic Development concluded in a 2000 study that the federal government had an important role to play: "Much the way venture capital firms provide managerial talent and organizational advice for their investment of funds, the federal government could accompany its grants and other aid to tribal enterprise with even more readily available and higher quality knowledge, executive education, and information."[5]

In 1995, the Mille Lacs Band purchased the state chartered First State Bank of Onamia (now called Woodlands National Bank), with assets of $20 million, becoming one of the first tribes in the United States to own a bank. The Mille Lacs Band also has formed the Mille Lacs Bank Corporation, a bank holding company, to expand their lending resources. The South Metro Federal Credit Union was established through a capital contribution of $100,000 from the Shakopee Mdewakanton Community.

The status of the land and tribal sovereignty cause unique problems for business investment. Trust land cannot be collateral for a loan, nor can it be sold. Reservations do not have a tax base to pledge for funding. Industrial development bonds, long used by non-Indian governments, are not available for tribes. Although federal law allows the issuance of tax-free bonds, few lenders are interested, except when gaming income can be used as security. In addition, sovereign immunity from lawsuits can be seen as a barrier to investment.

According to Joseph Kalt and Joseph William Singer of the Harvard Project, ". . . tribal self-rule—*sovereignty*—has proven to be the only policy that has shown concrete success in breaking debilitating economic dependence on federal spending programs and replenishing the social and cultural fabric that can support vibrant and healthy communities and families."[6]

However, a major study by the Harvard Project in 1996 and subsequent research stressed businesses that were independently controlled and managed were profitable in thirty-four of thirty-nine cases, while those controlled by tribal councils had only a 59 percent success rate (twenty profitable businesses of thirty-four). Problems with tribal operations included a lack of constitutional checks and balances, a lack of a capable bureaucracy operating under sound administrative procedures, and politicians in a position to turn authority into personal gain.[7]

In Minnesota, the national findings were reinforced by a recent study of the effect of gaming on nearby communities. Among the conclusions, economic development grants and intergovernmental transfers received by communities did not improve their ability to establish self-generating economic development, and government funds did not lead to market opportunities and competitive long-term returns essential for attracting investments in local businesses.[8]

Tribally Generated Funds

Tribal government is a major reservation business and a large employer of Indians. Even though casino profits have enabled some tribes to contribute dollars to needed social programs, tribes are unable to assume all costs. The need for federal and state programs is clear and, as Indian leaders point out, guaranteed through treaties. The White Earth Tribe reported in 1997 that of 350 employees employed in tribal government, 290 of them were funded by federal contracts or grant programs. Even the Mille Lacs Band, with its successful gaming operations, still receives 25 to 30 percent of its annual budget from federal and state programs.[9]

Major Federal Programs

Indian Community Development Block Grants granted from Housing and Urban Development (HUD) provide major funding on reservations, as do development funds from the U.S. Administration for Native Americans, Farmers' Home Administration and Rural Economic Community Development of the U.S. Department of Agriculture, and the Economic Development Administration of the U.S. Department of Commerce. These programs have aided economic planners, sewer and water infrastructure, business developments, community centers, land resource development, and sawmill and other expansions.

Tribal Businesses

GAMING   The major thrust of tribal investments has been to expand resort, tourist, and conference center aspects of casino operations. Legal bodies have been established to insulate Indian gaming business decisions from direct tribal government administration. Most reservations now have major hotels, several incorporating day care centers, youth arcades, swimming pools, restaurants, and facilities for entertainment acts. There are marinas at the Bois Forte, Red Lake-Warroad, and Prairie Island facilities.

CONSTRUCTION   Several construction-related businesses in the state are owned and operated by tribes, including Red Lake, Mille Lacs, Fond du Lac, and Bois Forte. Red Lake Builders, Inc. does residential, commercial, and road construction on and off the reservation.

FOOD AND CRAFTS   Lower Sioux Pottery manufactures handcrafted pottery. The White Earth Land Recovery Project sells wild rice, buffalo sausage, and numerous handcrafted items. Northland Native American Products is an Indian-owned small business that markets gourmet gift packages of wild rice and Indian-produced food products and artwork.

The Leech Lake Reservation is the center of the most dependable wild rice operation, with many productive wild rice lakes. The tribe, through the Leech Lake Wild Rice Company, purchases green, hand-harvested rice at the time of harvesting, in an attempt to stabilize the market by setting a guaranteed minimum price. The Red Lake Tribe continues to operate three hundred acres of commercial paddy rice at a farm it purchased. They sell their wild rice through Red Lake Nation Foods, Inc. on the Web and by telephone. They market the grain through Grey Owl Foods Company, a Canadian, Indian-owned business. A few tribes have built shopping malls to serve the influx of customers from nearby casinos.

TIMBER   Timber is commercially harvested on the Bois Forte, Grand Portage, Leech Lake, White Earth, and Red Lake Reservations. Timber resources provide the MCT about $2 million in total economic return, including payments to Indian employees. The tribes manage the resource and receive payment for their individually harvested timber. For the land held in the name of the MCT, the income is divided 65 percent to the tribe involved, 25 percent to reforestation, and 10 percent for administrative expenses. Red Lake processes timber at its sawmill, and Grand Portage has a sawmill, pallet mill, and chipping plant (see chapter 7).

OTHER TRIBAL BUSINESSES   Most tribes operate service stations and convenience stores on reservations. White Earth Tribe operates the Ojibwe Building Supply Company; Mille Lacs Band owns a bakery and a share of a pizza company. Red Lake has invested $300,000 in a solid waste recycling plant in Thief River Falls. There are commercial gravel quarries on Red Lake Reservation and the Lower Sioux Community.

Urban Indian Business Initiatives

Through great determination, the Indians living in the Franklin Avenue area of Minneapolis have built a unique development project. The American Indian Neighborhood Development Corporation

(AINDC) owns and operates the Ancient Traders Market Place, formerly Franklin Circles Shopping Center (completed in 1982 and updated in 2001), with a grocery store, drug store, bagel manufacturer, and other retail stores. However, nearly all of the businesses in these developments are non-Indian. Nearby is the Franklin Business Center, a business incubator facility offering support services for new, small businesses. AINDC joined with the privately owned Franklin Street Bakery to open a major new commercial operation in 2003. A retail counter at the same site opened in 2004. An area of neglect and blight has been turned into an emerging hub of business activity and hope, with many new jobs created and new development sparked nearby.

Small Businesses

Indians lag far behind all other racial groups in becoming small business operators. For Indians, establishing a small business is a first-generation experience. Indians have the fewest minority firms in Minnesota. The U.S. Census of minority-owned business identified 2,413 businesses owned by Indians in 2000, an increase from 333 in 1987, but this 2000 figure is still only 0.12 percent of the state's businesses.[10]

In 1996, the Metropolitan Economic Development Association began a program with the objective of developing competitive, self-sufficient women and minority-owned general contractors by creating partnerships between them and majority general contractors. Since launching the program, eight partnering relationships have been established, including Adolfson and Peterson Construction and Shingobee Buildings, Inc., a construction company founded and run by Gae Veit. Veit started Shingobee in 1980 with $1,000 and one employee; by 2002, there were twenty-three employees and annual revenues near $10 million. In 1991, she received the Small Business Administration's Women Entrepreneur of the Year award.[11]

Economic Development Assistance Programs

Several programs exist to help guide small business entrepreneurs, including a few that operate especially for the Indian communities. However, in spite of the array of services, the reality is that very few Indians are using the services.

The Native American Business Development Center, located at Cass Lake, is the major program assisting Indians in developing their business plans. The program, funded by the Minority Business Development Agency in the U.S. Department of Commerce, has helped five hundred to six hundred businesses begin operations during the last two decades. In 1997, the Center opened a Resource Center with business machines, computers, and an extensive library at the Cass Lake office. The Center offers support in market research, business plan development, financial management, procurement, franchising, and exporting.

Women's Business Center, in Mahnomen, was a three-year demonstration project, begun in 1993, funded in part by the Office of Women's Business Ownership of the U.S. Small Business Administration (SBA), with matching funds from the White Earth Tribal Council and foundations. Women often have especially severe problems in raising needed capital. Technical help was provided through a variety of training sessions, classes, and group meetings to help women start up new businesses. About 35 percent of the clients were Indian. In Minneapolis, Twin Cities Women Venture provides a similar program, although less than 1 percent of clients are Indian.[12]

The Minnesota Small Business Development Centers are agencies designed to provide technical help to all Minnesotans interested in operating small businesses. The services generally are provided at no cost, with funding from the federal Small Business Administration, Minnesota Department of Energy and Economic Development, local governments, the educational community, and the private sector. The figures for the number of Indians served during 2002–2004 show the program is not reaching significant numbers of Indians, with 1.5 to 2.0 percent of counseling clients identifying as American Indian.[13]

The Metropolitan Economic Development Association (MEDA) and the Minority Business Development Center (MBDC) are two government-funded programs based in Minneapolis that provide business development services to low-income, ethnic minority communities. Approximately 10 percent of MEDA participants are Indians.[14] MBDC racial figures were not available. The Community Planning and Economic Development Agency of Minneapolis makes small business loans; however, it reports serving very few Indians. The Minnesota American Indian Chamber of Commerce works in partnership with numerous community sectors to expand economic opportunities for Indians in Minnesota.

Funding

BIA programs are authorized by the Indian Financing Act (25 U.S.C. 1451) and include loans, interest subsidies, grants, and a federal guarantee for up to 90 percent of commercial loans. This program is the major help to those preparing financial packages through the Native American Business Development Center in Cass Lake and is used by approximately 70 percent of their clients. The BIA guaranteed loan is obtained after the bank approves the financial package.

The Small Business Administration's 7A program is the main loan guarantee program. It is obtained only after a bank has agreed to accept the proposed financing. The required equity is usually around 30 to 50 percent. Statistics show small numbers of Indians—only thirteen during fiscal years 2003 and 2004—made use of the SBA Centers.[15]

The Minnesota Indian Business Loan Program was begun by the state of Minnesota in 1973, when it began taxing severed mineral rights, which are owned separately from the land. The tax currently is forty cents an acre. Twenty percent of the money collected (about $100,000 per year) goes into a fund to be used for Indian business loans. The Indian Affairs Council administers it, with each tribe setting its individual standards. The program requires that applicants be one-quarter Indian and that some money be made available for off-reservation individuals and projects (about 25 percent of the loans).

The program has great appeal because of the low interest and low amount of equity required; however, it has been marred over the years by delays, bureaucracy, and tribal politics. A successful loan application takes over a year to complete.

The McKnight Foundation provided $2.5 million to start the Minnesota Indian Economic Development Fund. Services are available only to reservation Indians and tribes. The program provides technical assistance and some financing necessary to cover the difference between the individual's ability to invest and the cash required for a business loan. Since its inception, the fund has provided more than fifty-five loans to American Indian building contractors, retail food establishments, and clothing makers. By 2003, it had loaned over $3 million to Indian businesses. The program, in association with the Center for Regional and Urban Affairs at the University of Minnesota, offers a professional meeting for reservation planners twice per year.

Government Purchasing Programs

Since the 1930s, federal laws specify Indian preference in purchasing goods and services, as well as in employment practices, in government programs serving Indians (see chapter 9). Federal law, U.S. statute 25 U.S.C. 450e (b) (2) requires that all "federal contracts . . . or grants to Indian organizations or for the benefit of Indians shall require that to the greatest extent feasible . . . preference in the award of subcontracts and subgrants . . . shall be given to Indian organizations and to Indian-owned economic enterprises."

Indian-owned firms are also "Disadvantaged Business Enterprises" (DBE) under federal, state, and local requirements, qualifying for programs designed to overcome past discrimination practices and provide an opportunity to compete in obtaining government contracts. Some Indian businesses have found these programs very helpful; others are very critical that the promise implied is not easily obtained.

Tribal Employment Rights Ordinances

Tribal Employment Rights Ordinances (TERO), approved by tribal councils, enable the tribes to insert their own conditions on projects by defining goals of Indian businesses and employees to be used, Indians to be trained in the trades-skill professions, and so forth. Under a TERO contract, the goal is 50 percent or greater Indian involvement. These conditions become a part of the bidding and negotiating process, which leads to award of the contract. The federal standard provides that a minority firm's bid can be up to 3 percent higher. The administrators of the ordinance can certify Indian firms and workers that qualify and monitor compliance. TEROs have been established on most of the Ojibwe reservations; Mille Lacs and Leech Lake have tribal ordinances similar to TERO dealing with contracts and employment goals under their own self-determination contracts.

Some tribes do not have enough construction to sustain their own TERO office. A statewide TERO office was established to enable construction in the Twin Cities to be identified as "on or near" reservations and subject to the program. TERO has been applied to several important construction projects in the Twin Cities and elsewhere. The Division of Indian Work facility on Lake Street, supported significantly by the Shakopee Mdewakanton tribe, had 58 percent Indian employment. Minnegasco pipeline work and Minnesota Historical Society building construction projects on the Mille Lacs Reservation were under Indian-negotiated contracts. The Minnesota Historical Society work had 70 percent Indian employment. Other projects include the Franklin Avenue home for homeless men, Anishinabe Wakiagun; St. Paul's Earth Star housing for the elderly; the federal prison at Rush City; work for Hennepin County; construction by Artco, Inc. in Thief River Falls; and projects in reservation areas by the Minnesota Department of Transportation (MNDOT).

The Indian preference laws and affirmative action programs described following do not apply to the tribes' business activities, which have greatly expanded because of the gaming industry.

Affirmative Action Programs/Disadvantaged Business Enterprises

Federal, state, and other government levels in Minnesota had used set-aside percentages or other programs to assist minority or other disadvantaged groups in becoming contractors or making sales to governments. These programs were called into question by two U.S. Supreme Court decisions, state and local programs by *The City of Richmond v. Croson,* 488 U.S. 469 (1989), and federal programs by *Adarand Constructors v. Pena* 515 U.S. 200 (1995).

To meet the court's objections, the state analyzed contracting and employment patterns and found that minorities and women were underutilized. This has allowed the setting of specific goals for worker type based on past underrepresentation of the protected groups and their current availability. Today, when a contract goes for bidding, the goals for the specific categories of work are detailed and vary depending upon the job, location, and availability of help. The successful contractor agrees to the goals and complies by using disadvantaged business enterprises as subcontractors. Some Indian businesses have worked out a joint venture relationship with large contractors, becoming full-time subcontractors. The government audits to ensure compliance. Disadvantaged businesses, after being certified, are allowed a 6 percent bidding preference.

Minneapolis has incorporated its previous listing of qualified minority-owned small businesses into a larger "Emerging Small Business

Directory." City contracts require that up to 20 percent of the work go to these listed businesses.

It continues to be government policy to expand opportunities to small businesses operated by previously underrepresented groups. For example, the Minnesota Department of Transportation, following the regulations covering the use of federal dollars, has a goal of 10 percent of the contracts going to disadvantaged business enterprises.

8A is a Small Business Administration program named for Public Law 95-507, § 8 [a], a federal program for small businesses without much equity, owned by racial and ethnic minorities. It is intended to help an emerging business start up and work its way out of the program. If a contract is under $5 million for manufacturing (or $3 million for other types), the contractor or vendor can be designated and the price negotiated. For 8A designated contracts exceeding those amounts, there can be competitive bids, but only from other 8A-approved businesses. There is a nine-year limit to the program. Companies are required to get increasing amounts of outside business, and by the last year, they can have no more than 25 percent of their business from 8A projects. If they do not meet the goals along the way, their participation in 8A will be cut proportionately. The effort is to try to keep the firms stable and to assist so that when they leave, or "graduate," they are viable. It is difficult to qualify for the program, but once on, businesses can gain benefits. In recent years, approximately fifteen Indian firms have been a part of the Minnesota program.[16] White Earth Garment Company was an 8A company in 1995; Red Lake Builders graduated from the program.[17]

Government programs designed to help disadvantaged business enterprises require extensive paperwork. Each governmental level and unit requires a separate filing. Several Indian entrepreneurs have commented that they did not consider the programs worth the effort due to the complex requirements.

The Minnesota Department of Transportation construction projects have a major financial impact in northern Minnesota. The Disadvantaged Business Enterprises program in Cass Lake works in cooperation with the Native American Business Development Center. With the purpose to increase minority and other specified groups' participation in the highway construction industry, the Center provides technical assistance with loans, bonding, and government bid notices.

Business Councils and Organizations

The Minnesota Minority Supplier Development Council (MMSDC) is an effective effort bringing together corporate purchasing people and thirty-five minority businesses. The council is comprised of over 185 corporations and approximately 300 minority companies. The council resulted in close to $1 billion of business for minority firms in 2002. [18] The Indian community has found the program very helpful.

The Minnesota American Indian Chamber of Commerce was organized in 1986 to promote Indian businesses through networking and assistance programs. In addition to encouraging Indian entrepreneurship, the Chamber offers a mentor program linking members with high school and college students to encourage education and familiarity with business enterprises.

The American Indian Corporate Professionals Council is an organization of Indians working in corporate America. They network as an employment referral service, do community service, and are available as a speakers' bureau.

Gaming in Minnesota

Minnesota began the legalization of charitable gambling in 1976, although charitable bingo has been legal since 1945. Subsequent laws allowed gambling to occur in bars. Pull tabs were authorized, and in 1985 and 1989, the state approved video gaming compacts with Indian tribes. Indian Big Bingo began in 1982 and was very successful. In 1990, the first Indian casino opened, and within two to three years, each Minnesota reservation had at least one casino.

Gaming is very big business in Minnesota. Lawful, or charitable, gambling, including pull tabs, paddlewheels, tipboards, bingo, and raffles operating out of 3,216 locations, accepted $1.3 billion in wagers on the various forms of charitable gambling in 2001. With this money, these organizations made $70.1 million in charitable contributions and paid $56.4 million in state taxes.[19]

> ❏ Pari-mutuel horse racing at Canterbury Park recorded wagers of $77 million in 2001, including both live racing and simulcasts.

❏ The card club at Canterbury Park opened on April 19, 2000. In 2001, Canterbury Park's portion of wagers kept by the house exceeded $16 million.

❏ Wagering on the Minnesota State Lottery exceeded $377 million in FY 2002, with total revenues to the state exceeding $81 million. [20]

Wagering at the eighteen Minnesota Indian casinos was publicly estimated at $1.3 billion a year in 2003, the third largest total in the country.[21] Because tribal casinos are not publicly traded companies, they do not have to disclose their finances, so the exact figure is not known. John McCarthy of the Minnesota Indian Gaming Association (MIGA), which represents nine of the eleven tribes, said the figures were overestimated, with totals closer to $700 to $800 million.[22]

The Casino Industry

Casinos have had a dramatic effect on economic development in Minnesota. Indians have shown they can skillfully administer a multi-billion dollar industry that arose within a short period. They have provided reservations and neighboring communities with jobs and expanded community growth, which years of government programs have been unable to provide.

The legal justification for Indian gaming in Minnesota stems from the U.S. Supreme Court's interpretations of Public Law 280. In 1987, the Court defined tribal–state civil jurisdictional relationships in *California v. Cabazon Band of Mission Indians* 480 U.S. 202 (1987). As a result, if the state allowed some form of gaming, tribes within the state could also do so, and using their sovereign powers, they could set their own policies. This assured tribes the right to regulate their own gaming operations. On October 17, 1988, the U.S. Congress passed the Indian Gaming Regulatory Act (Pub. L. 100-497, 25 U.S.C. 2701) to codify the court's decision and provide federal statutory justification for tribal gaming operations. The law, while clarifying tribes' rights to regulate activity on their reservations, also decreased their sovereignty by imposing federal regulation over gaming operations. The law also inserted state authority where it had not been previously with the provision for tribal–state compacts.

The law categorized three kinds of gaming:

> Class I: Traditional Indian social games, where regulation was solely a tribal matter.
>
> Class II: Bingo and "bingo-like" games (including pull tabs, punch boards, etc., when played at the same location as bingo). For Class II, there are federal standards. The tribe regulates, and the state has no jurisdiction.
>
> Class III: All other. This group includes video games, blackjack, lottery, horse race betting, sports betting, and other games. These games are lawful on Indian lands provided that the state "permits such gaming for any purpose by any person, organization or entity" (25 U.S.C. 2710). Federal standards and regulation are required. Gambling can be conducted only on Indian land (land within reservation boundaries or trust land outside the reservation). If land is purchased for a gaming site off the reservation, approval of the U.S. Department of the Interior is required, and there must be acceptance by the state governor before it can be taken into trust status (25 U.S.C. 2719). Minnesota's only off-reservation casino, Fond-du-Luth in downtown Duluth, was taken into trust before the Indian Gaming Regulatory Act was passed.

Minnesota–Tribal Compacts

The compacts covering casino operations and games were signed between the state and Minnesota's tribes from 1989 to 1991 before the U.S. Supreme Court ruled in 1996 that the Eleventh Amendment to the Constitution prevents states from being forced to negotiate with the tribes. Because tribes in Minnesota signed compacts so much earlier, the Indian gaming industry was able to develop in Minnesota well in advance of the rest of the country. By 1993, the Shakopee Mdewakanton Dakota Community had the second largest Indian casino in the United States; the two Grand Casinos of the Mille Lacs Band were fourth and fifth largest.[23] (For brief histories of the development on each reservation see following.)

In negotiating compacts, the tribes were seeking a full array of gaming, including sports bookmaking and off-track betting on horse racing, as well as a wide variety of casino games. The state held that it would negotiate only on video slots because state law generally prohibited other forms of gambling. Although the compacts were later criticized as being too generous to the tribes, at the time they were negotiated both sides found them acceptable primarily because a fixed agreement gave stability to the new industry, and they feared in the future the law could be changed to favor either side. The Minnesota Indian Gaming Association was formed in 1987 to provide a more unified voice to speak for the tribes' mutual interests. This greatly simplified the agreement process.

The tribes agreed to the one game only, reserving the right to have other gaming if the state later authorized the activity. The state has regulatory power over the machines, with the authority to make random checks. The state is paid $150,000 annually by the tribes for enforcement and licensing, with no provision for an increase. The tribes also pay for state and FBI employee checks. Audited financial reports are filed annually with the state for review. These records, similar to private corporation records, are classified "trade secret information" by the Minnesota Attorney General and are not available to the public. No termination date was set in the compacts, but either party may request renegotiation.

Shortly after its video gaming compact was signed in 1989, the Lower Sioux Community sought an additional agreement allowing dealer blackjack. The state refused, holding to the position that any other forms of gambling were prohibited under state law. The tribe sued, and a Federal Court magistrate issued an advisory interpretation that Minnesota was dealing with the tribe in bad faith because social gambling existed and the state was not forcefully prohibiting it. (Private social bets are not illegal, Minn. Stat. 609.75, Subd. 3 (5).) This made state gaming laws civil/regulatory, and the U.S. Supreme Court previously had ruled that states had no power to impose them on reservations under Public Law 280.

Although the U.S. Supreme Court has not ruled on the magistrate's decision, other federal courts have reached similar decisions. The state feared that if the magistrate's decision prevailed, it would be confronted with requests by the tribes to have the full range of gambling, including sports betting.[24] Instead of risking that, a second set of compacts were negotiated, adding dealer blackjack to the casino operations. The blackjack compacts were signed between May 9 and June 11, 1991.

STATE REACTION TO TRIBAL GAMING   An unwritten moratorium on expanding gaming in Minnesota went into effect around 1992. For over a decade, the state refrained from talk of expanding gambling, and tribes informally and voluntarily agreed not to seek off-reservation casino locations. However, in recent years, there have been strong attacks on the Indian gaming industry from many directions. The state at times has sought to impose more control over the operations, to impose more state taxes, and to get more money for crime enforcement. The Federal Indian Gaming law and the tribal jurisdictional powers it protects, however, bar the state from imposing any tax, fee, or assessment on the tribe. The state cannot force the tribes to renegotiate the compacts since there is no termination provision.

Annually legislators have made efforts to unilaterally change the compacts. In 1997, then Governor Arne Carlson wrote the tribes that he would like to discuss "the 'tremendous pressure' for the state to get a piece of the action and funnel the cash into 'public projects' that create economic development." After meeting with the tribes, the governor wrote a follow-up letter that stated because of a "growing sense among many Minnesotans that the tribal casino monopoly should be reviewed . . . I propose that we negotiate an aggregate dollar amount that tribal casinos are willing to remit to the State of Minnesota to preserve the competitive advantage for tribal casinos."[25]

Since that time, pressure to renegotiate gaming compacts has grown. In October 2004, Governor Pawlenty issued a demand for tribes to pay $350 million annually in return for a guarantee of exclusivity on casino gambling. During recent state legislative sessions, several proposals to allow private or state-sponsored gaming and to force Indians to renegotiate compacts were proposed, with Governor Pawlenty's support, including a failed attempt in 2005 by the state, the White Earth, Red Lake, and Leech Lake Bands to operate a metropolitan casino. The Red Lake and Leech Lake bands pulled out of the agreement during the legislative session, and the proposal ultimately failed to gain acceptance. However, most Indians and legislative leaders expect that gaming issues will reappear in future sessions.

While many of Minnesota's Indian tribes viewed the 2005 legislative proposal as an encroachment on their operations, in January 2005, Mille Lacs leader Melanie Benjamin proposed a $50 million tribe-funded foundation to help the poorer tribes, which include White Earth, Red Lake, and Leech Lake. "As a band, we have an obligation to share with people who do not have enough," Benjamin said. "Let's move beyond the schoolyard bullies who want to divide us."[26]

Tribal leaders have frequently commented that they are willing to discuss legitimate expenditure issues with state and local governments. MIGA points out that since gaming began in 1990, tribal gaming has pumped more than $159 million in payments to local governments for services such as police and fire protection.[27] Payments to state and local governments from casinos in 2000 alone was over $15 million.[28]

In addition to resistance from certain tribes, Citizens Against Gambling Expansion, a bipartisan lobbying group, announced in early 2005 that it would launch a grassroots campaign to stop the legislature from approving any gambling expansion. One of the group's leaders, former Minnesota Representative Carl Jacobson, said that state governmental leaders are looking for "easy answers, pain-free answers" to the state's budget problems.[29]

Casino Operations

The seventeen casinos in Minnesota have been planned, built, and are operated independently by the eleven tribes. Video gaming machines provide 70 to 80 percent of the revenue; blackjack is responsible for 10 to 20 percent; bingo, pull tabs, and other activities provide the remainder. While all of the Indian casinos are making money, there are great differences among them, depending upon their access to major population centers (see Table 8.1).

Effects of the Gaming Industry on Indian Life

Tribal Economic Improvements

The Indian Gaming Regulatory Act allows gaming revenues to be used for governmental operations, the general welfare of the tribe and its members, tribal economic development, donations to charitable organizations, or to fund local government operations. From the beginning of the success of Big Bingo, well before the passage of the Act, profits on the reservations had gone to meet previously unfunded needs, such as building infrastructure or repurchasing tribal lands.

Table 8.1 Casino operations, by size, 2002
(Numbers are approximate.)

Very large operations, as many as 3,000 video games

    Mystic Lake and Little Six, Prior Lake, Shakopee Mdewakanton Sioux Community: 4,000 employees, about 10% Indian

Large Operations, 1,000 video games or more

    Treasure Island, Prairie Island Community: 1,400 employees, 2% Indian

    Grand Casino Hinckley, Mille Lacs Tribe: 1,200 employees, over 15% Indian

    Grand Casino Mille Lacs, Mille Lacs Tribe: 1,000 employees, 20% Indian

    Jackpot Junction, Morton, Lower Sioux Community: 900 employees, 10% Indian

    Black Bear Casino, Cloquet, Fond du Lac Tribe: 670 employees, 43% Indian

    Shooting Star, Mahnomen, White Earth Tribe: 1,100 employees, 51% Indian

Medium Operations, 500 to 1,000 video games

    Northern Lights, Walker; The Palace, Cass Lake, Leech Lake Tribe: 900 employees, about 60% Indian

Modest Operations, under 500 video games

    Fortune Bay Casino, Lake Vermilion, Bois Forte Tribe: 580 employees, 35% Indian

    Fond du Luth, Duluth, Fond du Lac Tribe: 360 employees, 10% Indian

    Prairie's Edge Casino Resort, Granite Falls, Upper Sioux Community: 350 employees, 20% Indian

    Grand Portage Lodge & Casino, Grand Portage Tribe: 200 employees, 75% Indian

    River Road, Thief River Falls, Red Lake Tribe: 130 employees, 75% Indian

    Lake of the Woods, Warroad, Red Lake Tribe: 100 employees, 75% Indian

    Red Lake Community, Red Lake Tribe: 40 employees, 100% Indian

---

Sources: Minnesota Indian Gaming Association, various studies, tribal newspapers, tribal reports.

The employment generated by casinos has had a great impact on whole communities, not just the Indian people. Many of the jobs were created in areas that traditionally have had high unemployment. The economic benefits are immediately visible for anyone visiting the rural casinos. The Las Vegas–style facilities and the adjacent hotels with a wide variety of services show the major capital investments that have been made. Stretch limousines and tour buses would have been unbelievable prior to the casinos. Filling stations, fast-food establishments, and additional motels have sprung up around the casinos. The tribal administrator of Shooting Star Casino on the White Earth Reservation commented, "Mahnomen was a dying community. In 1991 Mahnomen was the poorest county in Minnesota. The casino has changed it all dramatically."[30]

In 2003, the Federal Reserve Bank reported that on the Mille Lacs Reservation between 1989 and 1999, per capita income increased 322 percent and median household income rose 213 percent. These increases were recorded despite a large increase in population, drawn in part by new casino jobs.[31]

The success of casinos has brought a construction bonanza to reservations. Profits have funded sewage and water systems, community buildings and tribal offices, recreation facilities, libraries, and clinics. Proceeds have also funded social programs for youth and elders, housing programs, and day care. Several of the smaller tribes extend their casino employees' medical insurance to cover all reservation tribal members. As a result, the Grand Portage tribe has fewer than ten members on Medicaid. Some smaller tribes have a blanket offer of financial assistance for education beyond high school for their members.

Federal law permits distribution of per capita payments to tribal members from gaming revenues, following a plan that must be approved by the federal Bureau of Indian Affairs. All per capita payments are subject to federal income tax and state income tax where applicable.

Serious misconceptions exist about the amount of per capita payments Minnesota's Indians receive from casinos. About half of Minnesota tribes have found it feasible to make per capita payments, but these payments vary greatly in frequency and amount. For example, no Ojibwe tribe had a monthly payment as of 2003, although annual bonuses have been given recently, whereas Dakota payments varied from around $2,000 per month for the Upper Sioux Community to a reported $500,000 or more annually by the Shakopee Mdewakanton Community. The Mille Lacs Band has chosen to invest a significant portion of its gaming proceeds in the reservation's infrastructure, with members receiving approximately $5,000 each in 2003.[32] Most of the Ojibwe tribes have found it much more difficult to make per capita payments because of larger on and off-reservation populations and more extensive infrastructure needs. Within all these communities, many Indians still struggle with poverty because they do not qualify as participating members or because of various lifestyle issues developed through years of living in poverty.

The rapid influx of money has raised many questions. Several studies have been done and countless opinions expressed, but it is clear that casinos have led to tremendous change. A Minnesota Planning Agency study published in 1993 showed that from 1989 to 1991, the overall growth in gross business sales in the ten counties with casinos was almost double the growth rate for the rest of the state.[33] A study comparing data from 1990 to 1995 in rural areas with casinos concluded, "Casinos succeeded in promoting the type of outstate economic development that taxpayer-funded governmental programs have failed to stimulate—and succeeded without the expenditure of any public funds."[34]

An estimated 33,900 new jobs have been created in Minnesota by both direct and indirect effects from casino gambling.[35] Gaming-related construction to date is estimated at over $600 million.[36] In 2000, visitor promotion and marketing expenditures exceeded $29 million. Casinos brought in 3.7 million out-of-state and Canadian visitors who spent over $191 million.[37] Tribal casinos are now second only to the Mall of America in terms of tourist attractions.[38]

In the thirteen counties that have major casinos, there has been a 17.8 percent decline in public assistance 1990 to 2000, while the rest of the state registered a 2.4 percent increase. Similarly, there has been a 58.1 percent decrease statewide in Indians receiving general assistance.[39]

Indian Views of Casinos

Indians are positive about the industry they have brought to Minnesota. There is a sense of pride that they could so quickly and professionally build and operate an industry that in 2004 was the eleventh largest employer in the state.[40] It has enabled many Indians and far more non-Indians to find employment. Tribes have used the profits to do many good things to improve their peoples' circumstances on the reservations and to build for the future. For the first time, tribes can be sovereign in making their own decisions on priorities.

Considering the impact on the reservation, Phillip H. Norrgard, Director of Human Services, Fond du Lac, observed:

> Gambling is causing amazing and wonderful changes. Many families have never had consistent employment, have never known what it means, and what it requires. They are now working, and there is enough opportunity so that anyone can get a job. They are going to work, and it is a matter of pride. They can pay their bills, they can spend money on what they want, they can buy a decent car. People for the first time have checking accounts and they can buy their children nice toys and nice clothes. They are feeling good about themselves. And it is a big help with alcoholism. Some who have been in treatment 15 times are now working, and are working sober. Occupying their time is just one factor, self-image and feeling important are big parts of it.[41]

William Means, Executive Director of the Minnesota American Indian OIC State Council, commented, "Opportunity and hope, these are the biggest things that gaming has brought. It means having a chance. Psychologically it has built Indian pride that Indians can own and operate the casinos. Casino employment has stabilized people's lives, provided a living wage after minimal training and offered the opportunity for Indian people to administer and manage their own multimillion dollar tribal enterprise. There are at least 17,000 employees working in Minnesota Indian casinos and over 80 percent are non-Indian, so once again Indian people of Minnesota are sharing our resources."[42] Laura Waterman Wittstock, retired president of MIGIZI Communications, said, "In a word, gaming has been fabulous. Each tribe has pursued different avenues with its profits and that's okay."[43]

Stresses on Government, Culture, and Individuals

Any change in this dynamic is bound to have multiple effects and cause stresses for individuals and institutions. Many agree that there was not time to prepare the community by acquiring sufficient land and getting infrastructure in place, and there has not been time to prepare all the educated personnel needed.

The success of casinos has added to strains in how reservations are governed. Members are challenging their elected leaders. Some members urge per capita payments. Others support the tribes' priorities in reinvesting in the reservations, building the neglected schools, and providing other services for future generations.

Many members feel they do not receive a full accounting of tribal funds, the amount of casino profits and how they are being used. On the White Earth Reservation, tribal officials were convicted of personally and illegally benefiting from the casino-generated funds. In addition, the casino industry is not attracting increasing numbers of visitors. Many predict that casino profits as they now exist may not last, adding to tensions and uncertainty about the future.

Concerns are expressed that gaming will change Indians' value system. As one Indian commented, "Nothing will destroy Indian culture as much as trying to get rich. Where per capitas are being paid, they are just a more insidious kind of welfare, reinforcing jackpot mentality. There used to be one class on the reservation, all poor. Now there are classes, rich, poor, middle."[44] As Indian leader Jim Northrup, Jr., asked, "Is Indian gambling going to do what assimilation, relocation, acculturation, termination couldn't? Is gambling going to change us from generous people into greedy, money-centered dark imitations of white people?"[45]

However, most of the Indian population in Minnesota will not and cannot receive per capita payments because either their tribes have not earned enough to make any payments or they do not meet tribal membership requirements. The economic benefits of gaming have been slow to reach Indians living in poverty in the urban centers.

Casino Histories by Tribe

Bois Forte Tribe: Fortune Bay Casino on Lake Vermilion, St. Louis County

Big Bingo began in 1984. A $5.6 million facility opened August 9, 1986, and was expanded in 1992 and 1993. In 1996, a $16 million building project included a hotel with 118 rooms, a conference center, and restaurant, as well as water and sewer systems. Casino profits have contributed to a new school, health clinic, and community center at Nett Lake and a community center and day care facility at Lake Vermilion.

Fond du Lac Tribe: Fond-du-Luth, Duluth, St. Louis County, and Black Bear Casino, Cloquet, Carlton County

Fond du Lac owns and operates two casinos, Fond-du-Luth in downtown Duluth and Black Bear Casino near Cloquet. Fond-du-Luth is unique among the casinos of Minnesota, built in cooperation with the City of Duluth and opened in 1986. Profits originally were divided 25.5 percent to the tribe, 24.5 percent to Duluth, and 50 percent for projects mutually agreed upon. After passage of the Indian Gaming Regulatory Act, the tribe brought suit for a distribution of profits more in line with the Act. A settlement agreement in June 1994 gave the tribe full ownership and management control of the casino, machines, and parking ramp and 70 percent of the profits. The city received 18 to 19 percent from the video gaming machines, approximately 30 percent of the profits.

Black Bear Casino opened in 1995, with a 158-room hotel added to the complex later in the year. Casino profits have funded projects of almost $60 million for the Fond du Lac reservations and surrounding community. Among many others, these projects include water and sewer lines, three new community centers, a multimillion dollar health care facility, and school facilities. A Professional Golf Association–approved, eighteen-hole golf course opened in July 2003. The tribe is the second largest employer in Carlton County.

Grand Portage Tribe: Grand Portage Lodge & Casino, Cook County

Gaming at Grand Portage has always been owned and managed by the tribe at facilities that were a part of the Grand Portage Lodge. Video gaming was added to the bingo in 1990, with a separate casino facility attached in 1994 to the former Radisson Hotel and Convention Center, now tribally owned. Tribal operations make them the largest employer in Cook County. The casino draws heavily from tourist trade, estimated at providing 80 to 90 percent of the funds. It is especially popular with Canadians. The casino and hotel recently were renovated with a grant from the Shakopee Mdewakanton Sioux Community.

Gaming profits have funded a community center, and this isolated village (the nearest city forty miles away) for the first time has a place for group activities, indoor sports programs, computer center, and facilities for activities of the elders. In 1996, a new elementary school was built with tribal funds and then leased to the Cook County Public School District to operate for the community.

Leech Lake Tribe: The Palace Hotel and Casino, Cass Lake, and Northern Lights Casino, Walker, Cass County

The tribe's two facilities have always been owned and managed by the tribe. Bingo began on Leech Lake Reservation in 1983. The Palace opened in 1989, with a major expansion in 1992. In 1996, an 800-room motel was added adjacent to the casino.

The Northern Lights Casino was built in 1990, with financial help from the Farmers Home Administration. The tribally owned land is within the reservation but is allotted land in fee status. The Eighth District Court, in a 1997 decision against the tribe, ruled that the casino was subject to property taxes (*Leech Lake Band v. Cass County*, 108 F. 3d 820 (C.A. 8) 1997). However, the issue of taxing Indian-owned, non-trust lands remains to be finally resolved as, in a similar case involving another tribe, the sixth District Court ruled in favor of the tribe. Because of the casino operations, the tribe is the largest employer in Cass County. Casino profits have helped build community centers and improve reservation roads.

Mille Lacs Band of Ojibwe: Grand Casino Mille Lacs, west shore of Mille Lacs Lake, Mille Lacs County, and Grand Casino Hinckley, Pine County

On April 2, 1991, the Grand Casino Mille Lacs began in a converted electronics manufacturing plant on the reservation. An investment from an outside investor, Lyle Berman, made it possible to build a major Las Vegas–style facility. The casino was very successful, and within the first year, investors went public and established Grand Casino, Inc.[46] In 1994, a hotel was added. In 1996, it was expanded to 175 rooms, and a retail shopping center was added.

The public sale of stock helped fund the building of Grand Casino Hinckley on twenty acres of tribal land. The $18 million facility opened May 15, 1992. In 1997, the tribe added a 281-room hotel and convention center.

The two casinos have been very successful. The tribe also raised $20 million in tax-free bonds, one of the first tribes to use its governmental powers this way, to provide for major infrastructure construction. These funds, along with profits from the casinos, allowed the tribe to invest in long-neglected reservation services.

The management agreement between the Mille Lacs Tribe and Grand Casino, Inc. was the last one between Minnesota's Indian tribes and an outside casino company. The terms of the arrangement exceeded those established in the Indian Gaming Regulatory Act, and in 1993, a federal audit concluded that the outside company had benefited more than the tribe.[47] The agreement for the Grand Casino Mille Lacs expired in April 1998, and the tribe decided to operate the Mille Lacs facility. Within a year, the tribe also took over the operation of the Hinckley facility.

White Earth Tribe: Shooting Star Casino & Lodge, Mahnomen, Mahnomen County

The White Earth Band purchased land for the casino in the city of Mahnomen, within the reservation. Before the large casino operation could be built, money had to be invested in the city's infrastructure, a complete overhaul of the telephone system and sewage lagoons and improvements to the state highway and access roads. As collateral for some of the loans on the facility but not the infrastructure, the land was kept in fee status. A management agreement brought Gaming World International in to run the casino. The original agreement had been for 40 percent of the profits for seven years, but since this exceeded federal standards, it was changed to five years, ending March 1997, and 30 percent of the profits. A different proposal was submitted asking for 35 percent of the profits but did not ever receive official approval.

With a change in tribal government in 1996, questions were raised about the financing and running of the casino. The new government removed Gaming World International as managers and had the books audited. Much of the original investment in the casino was from a $12 million federal settlement of the White Earth Land Settlement Act to correct past violations of allottee land rights. Contrary to the management agreement, no repayment of the debt had been made. It also appeared that the management was receiving salaries and other benefits in excess of the agreement, and they had failed to train management employees as required.

Shooting Star Casino opened May 15, 1992. An adjacent 225- room hotel was built in 1994. A convention center and additional hotel rooms were added in 2001, bringing the total rooms to 395. In a separate arrangement, the tribe and the county built a nearby mall of retail shops. As the tribe reduced the outside debt, it began the process of placing the facility into trust. However, the transfer of all Minnesota Indian land into trust was halted until clarification of the law. Property taxes continued to be paid and account for a significant portion of the Mahnomen County budget. The tribe has donated money to various organizations within the White Earth Reservation. Profits also have enabled the tribe to build a recreation building in Naytahwaush and to fund youth and elderly programming.

Red Lake Tribe: Seven Clans Casino Warroad, Warroad, Roseau County; Seven Clans Casino Thief River Falls, Thief River Falls, Pennington County; Seven Clans Casino and Bingo, Red Lake, Beltrami County

The Lake of the Woods Casino, now known as Seven Clans Casino Warroad, opened in 1991, becoming the major tourist industry in Warroad. Since then the tribe has invested $2.5 million in nearby Lake of the Woods Motel with sixty rooms, the Lakeview Restaurant, a bait store, and a motor launch.

Community opposition in Thief River Falls blocked the tribe's original proposal to buy land for the casino. However, a long-neglected parcel of Indian trust land was available, and the River Road Casino, now called Seven Clans Casino Thief River Falls, was built in 1992. The casino now has a 150-room lodge and the world's largest indoor water park attached to a casino. Red Lake also operates Seven Clans Casino and Bingo in Red Lake.

Lower Sioux Community: Jackpot Junction Casino, Morton, Redwood County[48]

The Lower Sioux Community entered the gaming industry in 1984, with Jackpot Junction Casino. In 1991, the Community bought out the management contract with GMT Management Co. and since then has managed the casino, sometimes with the help of outside consultants.

The 1984 facility seated six hundred for bingo and eventually video gaming was offered. It became an early gaming destination for tour bus packages coming from as far away as five hundred miles. Because of limited tourist housing in the area, the tribe purchased the Dakota Inn, a motel in nearby Redwood Falls. When the state compact was negotiated, the Lower Sioux quickly signed it and immediately began the legal process to get the state to enter into negotiations on the blackjack compact, which was signed in 1991.

Jackpot Junction Casino was the first true Las Vegas–style casino in Minnesota, opening in the spring of 1990, with a major expansion in 1991. Jackpot Junction is the largest employer in Redwood County. In 1996, a six-story hotel with 168 rooms and 36,000 square foot convention center was built near the casino. The community also owns and operates the Dacotah Ridge golf course.

Prairie Island Sioux Community: Treasure Island Casino & Bingo, Prairie Island, Goodhue County

The gaming business began on the reservation in 1983 with a $1.2 million agreement with Red Wing Amusement Co. to build and manage Treasure Island. A large facility seating 1,400 was built in 1984. Disagreements with the management company led to a costly legal battle and termination of the contract in 1987. In 1991, the tribe took direct control. Building additions were paid for with profits in 1991 and 1993. In March 1996, members voted to build a 250-room hotel. There also is a 137-slip marina. The casino is the largest employer in Goodhue County.

In 1993, the tribe set a policy to pay out 49 percent of monthly profits. The Prairie Island Community has used $6.5 million of profits for a community center. They also have invested in a safe water system and roads.

Shakopee Mdewakanton Sioux Community: Mystic Lake Casino, Dakota Country Casino, Little Six Casino, Prior Lake, Scott County

Little Six Bingo Palace, named for the Dakota leader, was the first major Indian gaming facility in Minnesota. In 1982, the Shakopee Mdewakanton Community borrowed $1 million from the BIA and established the 1,300 seat Bingo Palace, which was very successful. Within the first year of operation, the loan had been repaid. There were criticisms of the management arrangement with Pan American, and in 1986, the community bought out the contract. Since then, the tribe has managed its own operations. Video slots were added to Little Six Casino in 1984, and blackjack was added in 1991.

The Shakopee Mdewakanton built its first Las Vegas–style casino, the $15 million Mystic Lake Casino, in 1992, at which time the Little Six Bingo Palace was closed with bingo moved to the casino. In August 1993, a large expansion, Dakota Country Casino, opened. It has since become part of Mystic Lake Casino. The Community has continued to operate the more moderate-sized Little Six Casino, known as the Tipi. The Shakopee Mdewakanton Sioux Community, with its gaming enterprise, is the largest employer in Scott County, and the facility is one of the largest Indian casinos in the United States.

Within a year of opening the first bingo facility, the Community had enough profits to begin providing many long-neglected services and making improvements in infrastructure, including water and sewer, roads, housing, and a facility to house government, educational, health, and social services. In 1996, a 216-room hotel opened; a second wing opened in 2000 and a third in 2005. Agreements have been signed to reimburse the city of Prior Lake and Scott County for services provided to the Community.

With the overwhelming success of Mystic Lake Casino, profits soared, as did per capita payments. These payments, made pursuant to a federally approved plan, have allowed individual tribal members to attain a much higher standard of living than they had previously experienced. Financial data regarding the per capita payments have not been made public since the early 1990s.

Upper Sioux Community: Firefly Creek Casino, Granite Falls, Yellow Medicine County

On December 26, 1990, the Firefly Creek Casino opened with 120 employees. The community pays out shares of profits to those registered with the community and living in the reservation area.[49] Profits have enabled the community to improve the water system, roads, sewer system, and community programs and have also provided incentives for youth in junior and senior high school and in higher education. Tribal Chair Helen Blue-Redner said in 2005, "Casino proceeds have greatly enhanced the quality of life for our members and have leveled the playing field, giving our members a semblance of the type of life which has basically not existed here—but elsewhere—for many, many decades."[50]

The Future

In contrast to exotic destination casinos, most of Minnesota's facilities are considered "casinos of convenience," primarily serving local communities. This type of business suffers as casinos closer to large population centers are built.[51] There is widespread agreement that Indian gaming as it now exists will not last. In the early 1990s, William Eadington, professor of economics at the University of Nevada–Reno, estimated that tribes had a "window of opportunity" of about ten years.[52] In acknowledgment of this, the tribes are continually making changes to attract families and conventions and offering nationally known entertainers.

The threats to Indian gaming are many. Federal legislation or the courts may change the legal status. Special interests in the state have concentrated on pressing for more gambling outlets to help bars facing declining revenues. Some believe that threats to expand video gaming will force tribes to let the state and local governments share in the proceeds.

Much is at stake. The casinos have a financial impact well beyond the Indian communities. Local governments and outside investors have an important stake in the future of these enterprises. Millions of dollars have been invested in the industry, casinos have provided thousands of jobs, and non-Indian communities adjacent to the casinos have benefited financially. Both the Indian and non-Indian communities have noted that while punitive policies would clearly be harmful to the tribes, there should be concern that it could harm the economic health of the local areas.[53]

Several years ago, the late Indian spokesman Larry Kitto expressed the fear that remains true for many Indians today: "Tribal gaming is more than just buildings filled with slot machines and blackjack tables—it is empowerment for Indian people. . . . The issue is about power and control. . . . In the history of the relationship between Indian and non-Indian communities, we have been ignored until someone wants something of ours. When we are successful at something, or possess something of value, it has been taken away. It happened 150 years ago in this region and now, if some politicians and other influentials in the non-Indian world get their way, it will happen again."[54]

Indians fear the effect on the culture, the strains put on their governments, and the imperfections of current governmental structures. Some members seek larger per capita distributions. Others appreciate that tribal governments are resisting these pressures and are instead investing in the reservation. However, this latter group points out that many tribes have done a poor job in making long-range policy decisions about the money. The money often is being spent as it is made, and reinvestment is primarily into casino-related projects, which could also suffer if the gaming industry falters.

Concerns are also raised that the gaming industry is not creating enough well-paying positions for an individual to own a home or support a family. More needs to be done to provide a larger range of employment opportunities.

Despite these worries, tribes' financial strengths have grown over the past decade, and they are in a much stronger position than ever before to influence their economic futures. Lasting success in economic development is not easy. Past experiences in manufacturing and other reservation business enterprises have shown that economic development is a slow, difficult process. Gaming has been the exception. Its future in sustaining solid economic growth, however, might be in question either because of political manipulation of the industry or decline due to the cyclical nature of gambling.

Chapter 9

Employment Patterns and Opportunities

UNEMPLOYMENT HAS BEEN a way of life for many Indians in Minnesota due to isolated reservations, discrimination, inconsistent government funding, and lack of education. Reservations have been targeted by a succession of government training programs and government-supported incentives to encourage new industries for more than forty years. Almost without exception, the results have been short-lived and disappointing.

While the unemployment figures of the 1990s and the early part of the twenty-first century show cause for concern, some positive trends have emerged. The gaming industry has dramatically increased employment in the reservation areas of rural Minnesota. Tribal governments are employing more people, and throughout the state, a growing number of Indians with advanced education are filling administrative and professional positions. Of the eleven Minnesota tribes, eight saw a drop in their unemployment rates from 1990 to 2000. The most significant was Prairie Island, which showed a drop from 50 percent in 1990 to 1.6 percent by 2000.[1]

Employment Today

According to the 2000 U.S. Census, the largest groups of Minnesota's Indians were employed in education, health, and social services (22 percent of all Indians) and entertainment, recreation, accommodation, and food services (20.5 percent). In comparison with the general population, Indians were more apt to be employed in health, education, and social services, and they had nearly triple the percentage working in government. An even higher percentage, three times the state figure,

159

Table 9.1 Selected categories of employed Indians, 1999

	Number	Percent Indians Working in Sector	Percent Total State Population Working in Sector
Total	16,831		
Education, Health, Social Services	3,735	22.2	20.9
Public Administration	1,506	. 8.9	3.4
Entertainment and Recreation	3,356	20.5	7.2

Source: U.S. Census: Social and Economic Characteristics, Sample Count, Minnesota, 2000.

worked in entertainment and recreation services, confirming the impact of the gaming industry (see Table 9.1). Most Indians were still employed in low skill groupings such as service, maintenance, and laborers, a pattern remaining unchanged from the previous decade

Unemployment

The 2000 U.S. Census showed Indians in Minnesota dropped in their overall unemployment rate from 20 percent in 1989 to 15 percent in 1999. This rate is still significantly higher than the state average of 4 percent. Stark geographical variations exist. The cities of Minneapolis, St. Paul, and Duluth each had about 22 percent Indian unemployment. Suburban rates were much lower at 8 percent. The very serious problem of northern Minnesota Indian unemployment was reflected in the counties with Indian populations of more than one thousand: Itasca, 18.4 percent; Cass, 17.4 percent; Carlton, 13.9 percent; Beltrami, 20.6 percent; St. Louis, 20.0 percent.[2]

The 2000 U.S. Census showed a drop in the unemployment rates on eight of the eleven Minnesota reservations (see Table 9.2). The average unemployment rate on reservations dropped from 17.3 percent to 10.3 percent. However, while household income rose for most Indians living on reservations, it was still significantly less than the state average; the state average poverty rate was 5.1 percent compared to a range of 6.1 to 38.8 percent on reservations (see Table 9.3).

Table 9.2 Unemployment rates on Indian reservations
in Minnesota, 1990 and 2000

	1990	**2000**
Bois Forte	25.7%	7.9%
Fond du Lac	16.9%	8.8%
Grand Portage	23.6%	10.7%
Leech Lake	18.1%	10.7%
Lower Sioux	8.0%	10.7%
Mille Lacs	2.8%	9.9%
Prairie Island	50.0%	1.6%
Red Lake	24.3%	23.7%
Shakopee	8.7%	7.6%
Upper Sioux	0.0%	13.3%
White Earth	12.6%	8.2%
State Average	5.0%	4.1%

Source: U.S. Census, 1990, 2000.

Table 9.3 Indian household income and poverty rate, 2000

	Average Annual Income	**Poverty Rate**
Prairie Island	$76,186	6.1%
Lower Sioux	$69,792	6.0%
Shakopee	$55,000	18.3%
Fond du Lac	$38,190	11.4%
Mille Lacs	$30,422	13.2%
Grand Portage	$30,326	18.9%
White Earth	$28,487	15.9%
Bois Forte	$28,214	23.7%
Leech Lake	$28,137	18.6%
Upper Sioux	$25,625	21.4%
Red Lake	$22,813	38.8%
State Average	$47,111	5.1%

Sources: U.S. Census, 1990, 2000; U.S. Department of Labor, Bureau of Labor
Statistics.

Tribal Creation of Jobs

Expanding employment has been a primary objective of Minnesota's tribes. Using federal self-governance laws, tribes have taken over the operation of governmental programs and now administer almost all of the Bureau of Indian Affairs programs and many Indian Health Services programs. In addition, tribes are operating their own schools and Indian housing programs, regulating their own tribal hunting and fishing ordinances, and building needed infrastructure. Although tribal casinos have led to tremendous growth in employment since the early 1990s, other tribal jobs remain a very important source of employment, offering increased opportunities for well-educated Indians to return to reservations.

Casino Employment

Tribes entered into the gaming industry with two objectives: to make money for the improvement of the tribal economy and to help members with their own economic futures.

In sheer numbers employed, the casinos have been successful beyond expectations. A study of Indian gaming done in 1992 estimated that just before the great expansion in 1989, 750 people were employed in Indian gaming. By the end of 2000, employment at Minnesota casinos had reached approximately 12,000. These numbers included employment at casino establishments only and not at ancillary establishments such as hotels, dining facilities, and recreational facilities. Over the decade 1990–2000, employment in casinos grew 1,875 percent.[3] Indian gaming currently ranks as the eleventh largest employer in Minnesota, just behind Wells Fargo Corporation. At the local level, tribal casinos are even more important. Twelve of Minnesota's seventeen tribal casinos are the largest employers in their communities; all but one are in the top two for their communities. Twenty-seven percent of casino employees are Indian; 73 percent are non-Indian.

Unemployment figures also tell a compelling story. Prior to the expansion in Indian gaming, rural counties with casinos had much higher unemployment rates than rural counties without casinos. By 2000, the unemployment rate in rural counties with casinos had decreased faster than in rural counties without casinos.[4] Mahnomen County is one of the most dramatic examples. Prior to the Shooting Star Casino's opening, there were 604 private company jobs in the county. By 2000, that figure had increased by 163 percent to 1,590. Wages had increased from $8,106,301 annually to $35,369,055.[5]

Since the beginning of tribal gaming, counties that had casinos showed a 17.8 percent decrease in welfare payments (Aid to Families with Dependent Children/Temporary Assistance for Needy Families (TANF)). Statewide, there was a 58.1 percent decrease in Indians receiving general assistance.[6]

Although casinos have had a dramatic impact, they have not yet overcome years of unemployment on the reservations. The 2000 Census still showed significant employment issues on several reservations, but reservations with small membership report that they now have employment available for all members who want to work in casinos. For the large bands with reservations in more isolated areas, unemployment problems have not been solved. The executive director at Leech Lake said that although their unemployment rate had dropped, "Our labor force is still unskilled, dropping out of schools, and there still aren't enough jobs to go around."[7]

While casinos have had little impact on employment problems of Indians in urban areas, proceeds from Indian gaming have been contributed to address urban concerns. Collectively, Minnesota tribes contribute approximately $1.5 million per year to support off-reservation programs for Indians such as health care services, chemical dependency treatment, job training and placement, and emergency assistance.[8]

The average casino wage ($9.19 per hour in 2004), while above legal minimum, is low.[9] Beginning and average wages including benefits do not equal what a recipient of Temporary Assistance for Needy Families receives, and they are not enough to support a family at a level above poverty. However, casino wages are often higher than those of other jobs available in the community. When White Earth was planning for its facility, the tribe hoped to set the beginning wage at a level that could support a mother with children receiving government aid, but tribal officials discovered the pay level would have been well in excess of prevailing wages in the community.

Barriers to Employment

The success of the gaming industry has clearly shown that, given employment opportunities and dignity in the workplace, Indians can build economically viable futures. In addition, many Indians who have completed professional training and achieved the credentials to find employment anywhere are choosing to return to help their people and assist in tribal businesses.

However, despite gains in the area of employment, discrimination and the negative impact of stereotyping continue to play a role in where Indians are able to work. Various programs designed to overcome past discrimination have done little to help. The most recent report by the U.S. Glass Ceiling Commission, released in 1995, concluded, "By many measures, Indians have gotten less out of affirmative action than any group."[10] Indian leaders say this remains true a decade later.

The state's highest unemployment rates are in the northern counties, where fluctuations in the food processing, wood products, and iron mining industries affect many Indians and non-Indians alike.[11] Tourism has been steadily increasing, but the geographic remoteness continues to be a barrier. Since weather affects business and causes seasonal unemployment, casino operators have found that they must reduce employment as they enter the winter season.

The demographics of the Indian population contribute to employment problems. A high percentage of Indians are young people, which is the largest unemployed group in the country according to the 2000 U.S. Census. The nature of work across the country is changing from unskilled jobs to those requiring special training. Many Indians, especially young people, lack the educational tools or work experience required. According to the 2000 U.S. Census, 87.9 percent of the general Minnesota population age twenty-five and older had an education level of high school graduate or higher, compared to 74.7 percent of Indians. In the general population, 24.7 percent had a bachelor's degree or higher, compared with 8.8 percent of Indians (see chapter 10).

Not only are low skilled manufacturing jobs disappearing, but also many of the new jobs are being created in the suburbs. Yet many individuals who are dependent on day labor or low-paying service jobs can only afford to live in the center city because of lack of transportation options. Metro area casinos provide transportation from the urban centers for their employees, but the commute is long. Lack of transportation can also be a problem on reservations. Both Red Lake and Bois Forte's casinos require a long commute, and neither facility provides transportation for employees.

Indian Preference and Affirmative Action Programs

The Indian Reorganization Act of 1934 and the U.S. Supreme Court (*Morton v. Marcari*, 417 U.S. 535 (1974)) authorized and upheld hiring preferences for Indians. Indians have preference in hiring and promotion by the BIA; IHS, Indian education programs, tribally contracted self-determination and self-governance programs, and in any other Indian-specific federal programs (25 U.S.C. 450e (b) (1)).

Equal opportunity laws and affirmative action efforts to address discrimination in employment have fallen short of expectations in helping Indian people. Information about job openings often comes through word-of-mouth; but with so few Indians employed, this system does not work well. Governmental affirmative action plans, goals, and percentages may be applied in terms of all minorities, but they do not address specific groups.

Tribes as Employers

Tribes have personnel policies that generally conform to prevailing practices in Minnesota. The programs transferred to tribal administration by the Indian Self-Determination and Education Act require equal access to employment for all qualified tribal members. Because of tribal sovereignty and the right to self-government, employment practices may differ among individual tribes. State employment requirements, such as workers' compensation laws, generally do not apply to tribal employees (*Tibbetts v. Leech Lake Reservation Business Committee*, 397 N.W. 883, 886–887 (Minn. 1986)).

Federal employment laws do apply unless Indian tribes were specifically exempted or there would be an adverse impact on sovereign rights. In 1989, the U.S. Internal Revenue Service ruled that tribal employers are subject to federal withholding, unemployment, and Social Security taxes. This has been largely unchallenged by the tribes. The Red Lake Tribe has questioned the Federal Unemployment Tax Act (FUTA) because it allows extensive state jurisdiction, and the issue has not yet been resolved. The law requiring federal construction contracts to follow set wage guidelines, the Davis-Bacon Act (40 U.S.C. 276a), does not apply to tribes. However, Minnesota tribes generally follow the wage provisions. The federal civil rights provisions covering employment practices do not apply to tribes, nor does the law prohibiting age discrimination. Other laws, such as the application of Occupational Safety and Health Administration (OSHA) provisions, are still being challenged in the courts as of 2004.

Most tribal governments have administrative appeals boards to deal with employee appeals to tribal courts. The appeals of tribal employment practices are sometimes difficult due to policy and personality differences. Job security rests with these leaders, and changes in government can mean loss of employment. Some tribes, such as the Shakopee Mdewakanton, have developed their own worker's compensation ordinances and discrimination policies.

Employment Training Programs

The Workforce Investment Act

The federal Workforce Investment Act (WIA) of 1998 replaced the Job Training Partnership Act (JTPA). The purpose of the WIA is to "consolidate, coordinate, and improve employment, training, literacy, and vocational rehabilitation programs in the United States." Federally funded programs conducted under the WIA provide services to youth, adults, and dislocated workers who need assistance to participate fully in the labor force. Youth programs are designed to encourage high school completion, reduce welfare dependency, assist in making successful transitions from school to work, and promote apprenticeships, military enlistment, and postsecondary training. Services provided to adults and dislocated workers are classroom and on-the-job training, vocational and personal counseling, labor market information dissemination, and assessment.

WIA in Minnesota   The WIA requires states to develop a Unified State Plan. Minnesota's stated goals are to empower individuals, provide universal access, increase accountability, streamline services, provide a strong role for local workforce investment boards and the private sector, improve youth programs, and provide state and local flexibility. WIA services in Minnesota are delivered primarily through the fifty-three Workforce Centers, one-stop sites that are intended to provide a seamless and comprehensive system of state, local, county, and private nonprofit workforce development-related services under one roof. Core partners include Adult, Dislocated Worker and Youth

Programs (WIA Title IB), Job Service, Veteran Services (WIA Title III), Rehabilitation Service, and Services for the Blind (WIA Title IV). In addition, other entities and organizations such as Community Action and Welfare-to-Work programs provide their services through the Centers.[12]

In 2000, 9 percent of the WIA Minnesota youth program participants and 4 percent of adult participants were American Indians. However, the WIA does not require federal or state tracking; consequently, since July 2000, there has been no further release of demographic or economic characteristics of persons using the WIA programs.[13]

Funding for JTPA and subsequently the WIA has not been raised in over fourteen years, and in 2006, the federal government proposed and congress passed a 10 percent decrease in funds.[14] Yet according to officials from the Minnesota Department of Employment and Economic Development, "Resources for the WIA youth and adult programs depend upon formulas that rely on unemployment data and are not distributed based on the need for employment and training services."[15]

WIA in Hennepin County   American Indians participate in training and employment programs run by Hennepin County and the city of Minneapolis through the WIA, Minnesota Family Investment Program (MFIP), or additional state-funded programs. American Indians are overrepresented among training and employment program participants, making up 7.2 percent of the participant population in 2000 and 6.0 percent in 2002. This decline does not reflect a decrease in the number of American Indian participants, but rather that the number of participants from other races is increasing at a faster rate. The number of American Indian participants has increased slightly each year.[16]

WIA in Ramsey County   Workforce Solutions provides employment and training programs in Ramsey County under the WIA. Workforce Solutions partners with community-based organizations to provide services such as counseling, outplacement, job placement, and youth development. Data on American Indians served was not available.

WIA IN OTHER AREAS The Minneapolis American Indian Center (MAIC) is a designated Indian and Native American Employment and Training Grantee by the U.S. Department of Labor, Division of Indian and Native American Programs. Since 1974, MAIC has provided employment and training services for the unemployed, underemployed, and economically disadvantaged American Indian population residing within seventy-one county-designated areas (excluding Hennepin County). With funding from the WIA, MAIC added services for youth ages fourteen to seventeen. In 2003, MAIC provided programming to 110 American Indians. There were over three hundred applicants.[17]

Native Employment Works (NEW)

The Personal Responsibility and Work Opportunity Reconciliation Act (PRWORA) of 1996 replaced the Tribal Job Opportunities and Basic Skills Training (JOBS) program with a new tribal work activities program: Native Employment Works (NEW) Program. Funded by the U.S. Department of Health and Human Services, the NEW program provides culturally appropriate employment and training services to all Minnesota Chippewa Tribe (MCT) members in the service area who are Minnesota Family Investment Program participants and are not served by the bands. MFIP, the state's new welfare program (which replaced Aid to Families with Dependent Children), requires job training after a maximum of two years of unemployment. Without MCT's NEW services, those in need would be forced to rely on non-Indian county resources. Services include assessment, counseling, employment planning, job search assistance, referrals, transportation, advocacy, job placement and retention, and technical assistance to reservation employment staff.

Other Employment Assistance Programs

Job training and employment programs serving Minneapolis use federal, state, and city funds channeled through the Minneapolis Employment and Training Program (METP). The intent is to serve low-income, minority communities where unemployment problems have been most acute. In 2002, METP served a total of 19,097 people, of whom 1,131 were Indians, approximately 6 percent of the total. METP also offers year-round youth programs, including the Summer Youth Employment and Training Program (SYETP), in which youth ages fourteen to twenty-one are placed in job settings with mentors while receiving academic support.

Other Employment Programs

In 1979, American Indian Opportunities Industrialization Centers (AIOIC) was founded to train and retrain both the unemployed and under-employed of all ages for productive full-time employment providing a living wage. In addition, AIOIC assists trainees to find meaningful work in culturally sensitive environments. Some of the programs offered are the career immersion high school; a school-to-work program offering small classes, hands-on training, and state-of-the-art computer classrooms; job training and placement services focusing on employment in offices, schools, stores, government agencies, and many other settings where financial, human service, and office support staff are needed; adult basic education; and the School of Business and Office Technology, which helps clients obtain long-term, meaningful employment with opportunities for advancement. Over the years, the AIOIC has developed strong working relationships with employers using its trainees and with companies that provide financial support.

The Anishinabe Council of Job Developers provides an Indian-run job placement program in Minneapolis to help those with limited skills and without a work history. The agency is striving to increase Indian acceptance into higher paying craft jobs and union membership. The city of Minneapolis pays for the program based on actual placements made.

In 1996, Horizons Unlimited (formerly the Emergency Assistance Program) was restructured and includes a self-sufficiency component that provides an intensive case management program for chronically unemployed or underemployed American Indian adults. Successful participants move on to service jobs through Horizons Unlimited Works. Each participant must be an enrolled member of a tribe, complete an intake interview, and attend a twelve-week session of self-sufficiency groups. All programs and services are in the Division of Indian Work building on Lake Street in Minneapolis.

The state's vocational schools operate training programs on the reservations, with Indian educational scholarship funding available. The programs include secretarial courses, child development programs, heavy equipment and machine shop training, building maintenance skills, natural resources management, and business management skills including casino administration (see chapter 10).

The U.S. Department of Housing and Urban Development, through the Minnesota Department of Employment and Economic Development, funds YouthBuild, a program for at-risk youth to teach work skills while refurbishing deteriorating homes. Some of the homes serve as transitional housing for the homeless for up to two years until they can move up to home ownership or subsidized housing. Currently, the program operates in numerous locations in Minnesota, including Bemidji, Chaska, Detroit Lakes, Minneapolis, St. Paul, Monticello, St. Cloud, and Virginia. While not a specific Indian program, some Indians have participated in YouthBuild.

The Hubert H. Humphrey Job Corps Center in St. Paul is a residential program funded by the U.S. Department of Labor providing basic education and job training for disadvantaged, low-income youth, sixteen to twenty-four years old. The program usually takes one and one-half to two years. Vocational education is offered in health services, office services, building and maintenance, printing, and culinary arts. If students meet the qualifications, they can also continue with college studies. A small portion of those served, approximately 2 percent, are Indian.

Summary

There have been encouraging increases in the availability of educated, skilled Indian workers during the past two decades. However, the limited numbers of these trained people and the rapidly expanding tribal needs mean that there is still a considerable gap in meeting the needs of the Indian communities. The casinos, hotels, and other tribal employment opportunities have provided a jump start for entry-level employment; they have created the opportunity for training and decent working conditions; and importantly, they have provided a vision for advancement in rural Minnesota, where few opportunities existed before. But a second reality also exists; those without education and without opportunity are facing an increasingly bleak future.

Chapter 10

Education

THE STATE HAS DONE A POOR JOB educating its Indian students. Minnesota has one of the worst Indian high school graduation rates in the country, most recently reported at 42.8 percent.[1] In Minneapolis, only 27 percent of eligible Indian students (those completing high school in four years) graduated in 2001, according to district officials. With very few exceptions, Indian students show below grade level performance and high absentee rates throughout Minnesota. These figures illustrate a tremendous loss of opportunity and talent that can never be reclaimed.

History of Indian Education

From the beginning of Indian contact with whites, education was seen as the mechanism for "civilizing" and Christianizing the "savages." In 1818, a blunt statement during debate in the House Committee on Indian Affairs: "In the present state of our country, one of two things seems to be necessary; either that those sons of the forest should be moralized or exterminated."[2]

Education of Indians in Minnesota followed the national pattern. Missionaries arriving to convert Indians also offered education. The American fur traders invited the American Board of Commissioners for Foreign Missions (Presbyterian and Congregational Churches) to provide education in the Great Lakes/northern region of Minnesota. Its Sandy Lake School, founded in 1831, was said to be the first school in Minnesota. By 1834, this same mission board was working with the Dakotas in southern Minnesota. From their work, the first Dakota dictionaries were published. Bishop Frederick Baraga of the Leopoldine

Society, Austria, who began working among Indians in northern Minnesota in 1835, wrote the first Ojibwe dictionary. It was published in 1878.

Most of the treaties signed in Minnesota included provisions for education and teaching agricultural skills. Day schools were followed by boarding schools, seen as much more effective because they could remove children from their home atmosphere and totally regiment their lives. Turning over the administration of reservations to church denominations, from 1869–1897, reinforced the message that there must be complete change.

Congress made Indian education compulsory in 1893, denying rations and subsistence to parents who did not send their children to school. Children were taken at an early age, six years or even younger. Absence from home could last the full six years of elementary school. The intent was to replace Indian culture with white values and Christianity. Students were forbidden to speak their language, their hair was cut, and native ways were not allowed. Manual training education was stressed, with students often becoming no more than free labor needed to operate facilities and farms. Boarding schools, representing the worst of the federal coercive assimilation policies, dominated Indian education until coming under attack in the 1920s. The Meriam Report of 1928 documented that boarding schools were suffering from serious neglect and woefully inadequate funding.[3] These schools were replaced by local day schools, the responsibility of state educational systems. St. Mary's Mission Boarding School at Red Lake changed to a day school in 1940, and the White Earth mission school closed in 1945.[4] Today, two much-changed BIA-funded boarding schools in the Dakotas attract sizable numbers of students, especially from Red Lake and White Earth: one at Wahpeton, North Dakota, another at Flandreau, South Dakota, the oldest continuously operating off-reservation boarding school in the nation.

As early as 1899 the federal government was paying to send Indian students to Minnesota's public schools. By 1926, 65 percent of the state's 3,527 Ojibwe students were in Minnesota public schools, 825 (23 percent) were in government day and boarding schools, and 425 (12 percent) were in mission schools at Red Lake and White Earth.[5] The education of Indian students became a full state responsibility in Minnesota in 1936 under a contract between the state and the BIA, as authorized by the federal Johnson O'Malley Act of 1934.

Current Education Systems

Most Indians now attend Minnesota's public school system. In the 2003 school year, American Indian enrollment in grades K–12 was approximately 2 percent of the student population in Minnesota. Sixty-five percent of Indians qualified for free and reduced lunch, compared to 69 percent in 2000; 20 percent were in special education, a 1 percent increase since 2000.[6]

The federal government provides some funding for Indian education to help with special needs. The state has several Indian-specific programs. Other federal and state programs, such as special education, have unusually high percentages of Indians. Since the late 1980s, Public school districts have been offered educational options, several of which are used by significant numbers of Indian students.

❑ Open school enrollment allows a student to switch attendance to a different district. Regular state and special federal Indian funding goes with the child to the new district.

❑ Charter and contract schools, considered part of the school district where they are organized, are under state regulation and receive some state funding.

❑ School districts may operate alternative schools, some specifically geared toward educating Indian students.

Privately organized schools with funding from a variety of sources have contracts with the public school systems and receive some state funding. Heart of the Earth Charter School, The City, Inc., and Nawayee Center School have Indian-focused programs and operate in Minneapolis. Four tribes operate K–12 schools on their reservations, with major funding from the BIA: Ojibwe School at Fond du Lac Reservation, The Circle of Life School at White Earth Reservation, Bug-O-Nay-Ge-Shig at Leech Lake Reservation, and Nay-Ah-Shing at Mille Lacs Reservation.

The legacy of the forced educational experience has left terrible scars on many Indians. Much of the trouble Indians have with current public education stems from the fact that it is still designed to teach white civilization. Parents fear that schools will rob their children of their heritage. Although many of the overtly coercive aspects of education have been eliminated, many Indians believe that American education has not lost its basic assimilative objectives.

Influencing the educational system has become a top priority for many of the state's Indian college graduates over the past thirty years. Education has attracted many Indians who are dedicated to creating an educational system that can truly serve their people and educate the rest of society. Their work has focused on expanding the number of Indian teachers and other Indian presence in schools, preparing curriculum, ensuring that existing teachers know about Indians and the need for different teaching styles, and on pioneering Indian-operated, Indian-focused alternative schools.

Head Start and other early childhood programs have been successful in reaching Indians. Nationally, 3.2 percent of those served are Indian, approximately three times the percentage of Indians in the total U.S. population.[7] American Indian enrollment in grades K–12 for the 2002–2003 school year was 18,184, just slightly over 2 percent of the total enrollment, reflecting little change over the previous five years.[8] High school dropout rates for American Indians far exceed those for whites. By the ages of twenty-five to thirty-four, many Indians return for education, but Indian leaders note that their communities cannot afford this ten- to fifteen-year gap.

Educational Measurements

Methods of evaluating student achievement vary by district, but overall, Indians score lower than non-Indian students in all tests at all grade

Table 10.1 Education, Indians, and general population, 2000, 1990, and 1980

	2000	1990	1980
Indians, less than high school	25.5%	31.8%	45.4%
Indians, high school graduates (or GED certificates)	74.5%	68.2%	54.6%
Total Minnesota population	87.9%	82.0%	73.0%
Indian college graduates, 16 years or more education	8.8%	7.6%	5.0%
Total Minnesota population	27.4%	22.0%	17.0%

Sources: Social Characteristics, Minnesota, 1980, 1990, 2000 U.S. Census sample data; Minnesota State Demographic Center, March 2003.

levels, according to numerous research reports. For example, in 2000, the average reading test score on the eighth grade Minnesota Basic Standards Tests was 71 percent, up from 62 percent in 1996, but still considerably lower than the 84.5 percent for whites. American Indian scores in math for the similar period declined by 4.38 percent to 66 percent, compared to 81 percent for whites.[9]

In Minneapolis in 2002, just 41 percent of American Indian students passed the Minnesota Basic Standards reading test, compared to 85 percent of whites; and 43 percent passed the math test, compared to 79 percent of whites.[10]

Graduation and Attendance

The most recent data show that over 50 percent of American Indian students did not complete high school in four years (see Table 10.1).[11] The latest report from the Minnesota Higher Education Office found that only 43 percent of American Indians who entered high school in 1996 graduated four years later, in 2000.[12] With a high school diploma now a bare minimum for employment at a livable wage, the failure to produce Indian high school graduates is condemning future generations to a continuing life of poverty.

Although graduation percentages are consistently lower than Indians' proportion in the school population, Indians are most successful in graduating from suburban schools and from those in St. Paul and Duluth. In Minneapolis, Indians are more successful in graduating from non-traditional schools.

Dropout rates in Minnesota have changed little since the late 1960s; nearly 32 percent of Indian students then and now drop out, compared to 15 percent of white students.[13] The Indian graduation rate of 43 percent compares with 83 percent for white, 47 percent for Hispanic, 68 percent for Asian, and 39 percent for black students.[14] Dropouts begin early, with about 10 percent occurring in the seventh grade. Nonattendance poses great problems for teaching, and school attendance rates have historically been worse for Indians. However, in Minneapolis, during the 2002–2003 school year, the Indian dropout rate was at an all-time low of 5.8 percent, compared to 5.5 percent for the entire school district, 6.6 percent for African-Americans, and 10.6 percent for Hispanic Americans. Comparatively, in Minneapolis 1994–95, the Indian dropout rate was 24.4 percent; by 2001–2002, it was 8.6 percent.[15]

Disciplinary Actions and Suspensions

Disciplinary actions and suspensions from school result from assault, fighting, carrying weapons, damaging property, disrespect and defiance of school personnel, drug or alcohol use, truancy, or tardiness. In northern school districts, disciplinary actions for Indians far exceeded the percentage of Indian students enrolled. For example, in Mahnomen, a town on the White Earth Reservation, Indians were 57 percent of the enrollment in 2001–2002 but received more than 90 percent of the disciplinary actions reported to the state. In the St. Louis County system, a collection of small-town schools in northeastern Minnesota, American Indian students received 44 percent of the disciplinary actions but were only 9 percent of the student body.[16]

Special Education Programs

Indians are assigned to special education programs well in excess of other racial groups. In 2003, Indians comprised 2.2 percent of the state enrollment but were 20 percent of the state enrollment in special education programs.[17] In Minneapolis, Indian students are 5 percent of the enrollment but comprise 16.5 percent of the special education population; in St. Paul, the figures are 2 percent and 20.5 percent, respectively, in Duluth, 5 percent and 26 percent. Bemidji is the only school district where the Indian population does not have the highest percentage of special education students (16.8 percent of enrollment, 17 percent of special education).[18]

Many Indian children are categorized as having Learning Disabilities (LD) and Emotional/Behavior Disorders (EBD). Some Indians criticize assignment of children to these categories as subjective, dictated by a process that is subject to abuse. A 1993 study looked at the identification of special education students in twenty-five schools within seventy miles of Bemidji, including several schools with very high Indian enrollment. The study faulted the assessment process for not adequately addressing cultural diversity, the primary concern being that the formal and informal instruments used in screening and assessments were culturally insensitive. Indian educators noted that one-third of the schools had no Indian staff, including a predominantly Indian-enrollment school.

Recommendations were made that the materials be revised; that there be more training in culturally appropriate interventions with more cultural awareness; and that Indian staff and parents be involved.[19] One former Minnesota Director of Special Education acknowledged, "For a variety of reasons such as difference in language skills, evaluators who don't know or understand Indians, or outright biases, Indians are probably overdiagnosed."[20] Many Indian leaders fear their children are being labeled and that those labels lead to a sense of failure.

Problems for Indians in the Current System

Conflicting Views of Education

In the late 1980s, one Indian educator bluntly told the Minnesota State Legislature, "The form of public education based as it must be on the values, orientation, and lifestyle of the dominant society uses up Indian children in a way that no war ever has."[21] The Indian School Council, established by the legislature in 1988, thus noted that this culture of "coercive assimilation" can trigger a chain of negative reactions, with the classroom and school becoming a battleground of cultural differences. "Schools fail to recognize the importance of the Indian community. Indians retaliate by treating the school as an alien institution. This results in the dismal record of absenteeism, dropouts, negative self-image, low achievement, and ultimately academic failure."[22]

Based upon recommendations made by the Indian School Council, state policies have been approved that recognize Indians' unique status and establish Indian community committees. As a result, magnet schools have been created in Minneapolis and St. Paul. In 1996, the Blandin Foundation funded planning grants for four northern Minnesota schools to rethink what works in educating Indian students to meet the community's goals. The result was new programs at Nay-Ah-Shing (Mille Lacs Reservation's tribal school); Bemidji Public Schools; Red Lake School District; and a collaboration of Fond du Lac Reservation schools and the Cloquet Public Schools.[23]

In Minneapolis, Four Winds Elementary School was launched in the 1990s with high hopes. But its large size (700 students), location, and combination with a French language immersion program contributed to its failure. Urban Indian leaders then joined with school officials to design Anishinabe Academy, which is headed by a native principal. In its fourth year in 2005, the school was at full capacity with over two hundred students. More than one-half of the staff was

Indian. Tony LookingElk, cochair of the Metropolitan Urban Indian Directors, said that the inclusion of Indians in the design of the school means the program has a promising future.[24]

In 1996, a Saint Paul Foundation report noted that the school system needed to recognize that "less than half the children have ancestral roots in the styles and values identified with the . . . European nations of the world;" that "young people can spend an entire thirteen-year school career without having even one teacher who shares their history or culture;" and that "the daily curriculum contains little of the history or culture of the majority of the children."[25]

Need for Cultural Survival

Although Indians know they need the skills taught by schools, acquiring those skills often means sacrificing Indian identity. As Leech Lake member Dr. Robert Fairbanks said, "Indians have never been against education; they want to learn skills . . . but they don't want their culture taken from them."[26] To address this concern, a committee of urban and reservation educators wrote a curriculum called the American Indian Curriculum Frameworks (see Curriculum and Textbooks later in this chapter).

There is increasing acceptance that Indians must both maintain their culture as well as acquire necessary education credentials to succeed in the dominant society. An Indian physician talked of his cultural conflicts when attending the University of Minnesota Medical school and residency at the Mayo Clinic in Rochester, Minnesota, where he was the sole American Indian in the early 1990s. He noted that aggression and competitiveness are required to succeed in medical training, characteristics not highly valued in Indian culture. However, he said, Indians have always been good warriors, an area in which aggression and competitiveness were viewed as socially acceptable. He came to look on health problems as a challenge to be faced like the warriors of old. "I view cultural survival as our primary goal and responsibility. Education is vital to our adapting to the world around us, but we must use our heritage and its beliefs and traditions as the foundation on which we build our culture of today and the future. We can become Indian physicians and scientists, but we must always remember the Indian comes before the physician and/or scientist."[27]

The Shakopee Mdewakanton Sioux Community's annual powwow, one of the largest powwows in the country. Courtesy of Shakopee Mdewakanton Sioux Community.

TOP: Students and teacher at the Anishinabe Academy, a
Minneapolis Public School. ABOVE: Anishinabe Academy
students. Courtesy of Minneapolis Public School District.

Top: Angela Cavender Wilson, from the Upper Sioux Community, showing the first screen of the Dakota language CD-ROM that she developed. Above: Upper Sioux Community members Harry Running Walker, Chris Mato Nunpa, and Carolynn Cavender Schommer at work on a Dakota–English dictionary. Courtesy of Upper Sioux Community.

LEFT: Members of the Red Lake Band in traditional Indian dress. Standing: left, Matchis Shank (Someone traveling); right, Ta fai wi dang (Sound of someone eating). Seated: Ba shic ta no gueb (High up in the sky), also called Charles Sucker. Courtesy of Smithsonian Institution and Red Lake Archives.

RIGHT: Chief May dway gah no wind of the Red Lake Band, seated in front of a U.S. flag with thirty-eight stars given to him by Abraham Lincoln. Courtesy of Beltrami County Historical Society.

Top: Chores at lakeshore. Above: Mille Lacs Indians gathered near their wigwam. Courtesy of Mille Lacs Band of Ojibwe.

Grand Portage Reservation in northeastern Minnesota. CLOCKWISE FROM TOP: historic fur trade site, rugged Lake Superior shoreline, and spectacular woods. Courtesy of Grand Portage Band of Ojibwe.

ABOVE: Original members of the American Indian Movement (AIM). Standing, from left: Dennis Banks, Syd Bean, Vernon Bellecourt, Bill Means. Seated, from left: Floyd Red Crow Westerman, Clyde Bellecourt. Courtesy of MIGIZI Communications.

RIGHT: Mille Lacs Band members at a Get Out the Vote Rally. BELOW: Mille Lacs leaders at a construction ground-breaking ceremony. Courtesy of Mille Lacs Band of Ojibwe.

LEFT: Construction in the Shakopee Mdewakanton Sioux Community. Courtesy of Shakopee Mdewakanton Sioux Community.

BELOW: Gae Veit, founder and CEO of Shingobee Builders, Inc. In 1991, Veit was honored with the National Female Entrepreneur of the Year Award from the U.S. Department of Commerce. Courtesy of Shingobee Builders, Inc.

ABOVE: Fond du Lac Tribal and Community College, Cloquet, Minnesota. Courtesy of Elizabeth Ebbott.

Control of Education

Indian leadership made a difference at the state level in defining Indian policies and providing funding. Tribal governments now have a much larger role in reservation education programs, operating tribal and Indian-focused schools and administering federal Indian education programs. However, at the local level, state school district boundaries divide the large reservations and make it very difficult to elect Indians to school boards. For example, White Earth Reservation is divided among seven districts, making members a racial minority in each area.

To address the lack of Indian voice in educational programs, several state and federal policies now allow or require Indian input.

❑ Two influential Indian committees are mandated at the state level: The Minnesota Indian Scholarship Committee administers the state's Indian scholarship program, advises on postsecondary educational program grants, and administers the Indian teacher training funds. The Committee has a representative from each of the eleven tribal governments plus one MCT appointee and three Indians at-large who are recommended by the Minnesota Indian Affairs Council (MIAC).

❑ The American Indian Education Committee is an advisory to the Minnesota Board of Education (Minn. Stat. 126.45–126.55), providing the Indian view of major policies and recommending beneficial changes.

❑ Minnesota law (Minn. Stat. 126.51) provides that all public school districts with ten or more Indian students may have Indian Parent Committees to advise on all aspects of a district's education program.

❑ The federal Johnson O'Malley Act allows elected local Indian education committees a major voice in administering the program's funds, independent of the school district.

❑ The Federal Indian Education Act, Title IX, mandates a local Indian education committee for the program.

❑ Minnesota Indian Post-Secondary Preparation Program requires an Indian advisory committee that must be identified on the grant application.

❑ Local schools in which there are ten or more American Indian children enrolled must establish a parent advisory committee (Minn. Stat. 124D.78). This committee must develop its recommendations in consultation with the district's curriculum advisory committee (Minn. Stat. 120B.11).

❑ All postsecondary educational institutions must establish an Indian advisory committee if requested by ten or more Indian students (Minn. Stat. 135A.12).

While Indian leaders believe these committees are often overlooked or not consulted, others believe the committees are one tool available to them as a very small, often politically overlooked group.

Curriculum and Textbooks

Incorporating Indian history and culture in the curricula of all schools has been a major goal for Indians. Critics say many textbooks, focus on the romanticism of the Indians or on the massacres. As a result, most Americans are poorly informed about Indians and have no understanding of treaties and sovereignty. An illustration of the lack of knowledge about Indian sovereignty came from former Minnesota Vikings coach Bud Grant, in the 1990s who said, "The treaties were signed 100 years ago. They don't mean a thing anymore."[28]

Many Indian-prepared materials are available for school use, from teaching specific languages to discussing Indian culture, values, history, and unique governmental relationships. The problem lies in getting schools to use them and persuading teachers to reeducate themselves about Indians. The materials and programs, generally paid for by special Indian funds, are often considered supplementary. Many educators note that Indians frequently are left out of discussions of the history of this country, especially after 1900, and that some U.S. leaders, held up as heroes in textbooks and classroom materials, are officials who were hostile or violent toward Indians.

MULTICULTURAL GENDER FAIR CURRICULUM   In 1988, the state required that all districts prepare MultiCultural Gender Fair Curriculum Plans, specifically requiring information about Indian history, their role and contributions, sovereignty, and treaties. By 1996, all original plans had been completed; the law requires renewal of the plans every six years. While the intent of the inclusive curriculum legislation was worthy, many Indians do not feel that the districts cooperated with the Indian communities as the law envisioned. As a former superintendent of Minneapolis Public Schools said, "To have a group of one background developing a culture-specific curriculum for another is . . . a guarantee that the curriculum will stay on the shelf and never become part of a staff development program or enter into the classroom or enter into any child's life."[29]

AMERICAN INDIAN CURRICULUM FRAMEWORKS   In 1993, the State Board of Education authorized Indian educators to prepare recommended curricula incorporating Indian views throughout all levels of teaching. The American Indian Curriculum Frameworks, approved by each of the eleven Minnesota Indian nations and published in 1996, is a comprehensive curriculum covering eighteen subject areas for primary, middle, and secondary schools. The curriculum was distributed to every district in Minnesota and is now available on the Minnesota Department of Education Web site. It covers topics on Indian culture, language, laws, and treaties and includes sample lessons for students in grades K–12.

Indian School Personnel

Another major goal of Indian educators is to increase the number and professional status of Indians working in the public schools. The 2000 U.S. Census cited 521 American Indians who were primary, secondary, special education, and postsecondary educators in Minnesota. With 104,711 teachers in these areas statewide, Indians comprise just 0.5 percent of educators.[30] The number of Indian teachers had increased slightly by 2003–2004 (see Table 10.2).

    To recognize Indian language teachers who may not have academic teaching credentials, state law provides for American Indian Language and Culture Licensure (Minn. Stat. 124D.75). Individuals with competence in the language, history, and culture of their tribe and approved by their tribal government, as well as another Indian

Table 10.2. Indians employed in K–12 public education
in Minnesota*

Indian Superintendents	3
Indian Principals (assistant and full)	13
Indian Teachers (all forms/full & part-time)	579

*Figures include charter schools but do not include tribal schools.
Source: Minnesota Department of Education, 2003–2004 staff reporting data.

group or academics, can receive a state eminence license. Other
teacher training requirements do not have to be met.

A state law passed in 1988 is designed to help retain beginning
Indian teachers. School districts can keep a probationary teacher who
is Indian even though the individual has less seniority than other similar teachers. The state also has special Indian scholarship programs
to assist Indians in pursuing teaching careers.

Racial Prejudice and Desegregation Laws

Racism severely impacts a student's ability to learn. Dr. Thomas Peacock from the University of Minnesota–Duluth (UMD) says, "The
problems of racism are deep; they are a big factor in schools' problems.
They come from racial attitudes in the dominant society where Indians
are not seen as part of the communities and are not accepted in routine ways. This marginalization is internalized within the Indian community and results in feeling unwelcome, not accepted, looked down
on, as 'different' and therefore inferior. The schools reflect this. Indians and Indian programming have been marginalized. Indian staff and
professionals have not been brought in; attitudes have not changed.
A little bit of change, a program here, a focus there, will not solve it."[31]

Overt racial prejudice in schools continues, often influenced by
the emotional issues of hunting and fishing treaty rights, opposition
to the storage of atomic energy wastes at Prairie Island, and the success with casinos. These tensions have contributed to the creation of
alternative, tribal, and charter schools. For example, in 1993, a racial
clash in the Onamia Public Schools contributed to at least 68 of the
175 Indian students transferring to Nay-Ah-Shing, the tribal school.

The Cass Lake Public School has received the most legal attention, with two major suits alleging educational discrimination filed in

the past fifteen years. Although changes were mandated, many leaders feel the complexity of the issues and history of community attitudes and behavior have proven too large to surmount.

Many Indians oppose mandatory desegregation, instead believing that segregation of Indian children could be beneficial.[32] In addition, Indians have dual status as minority (protected) students and as members of sovereign nations. If a concentration is the result of informed choices of parents and students and is designed to meet their unique academic and cultural needs, the school is not in violation of desegregation rules. [33]

Suggestions for Change

Indian educators and leaders have many suggestions for change:

❑ A focus on improving student achievement, promoting academic success, and encouraging college attendance

❑ A commitment from the top to incorporating and perpetuating Indian cultural traditions, language, history and values into learning

❑ Promotion and respect for the contributions of the native cultural worldview and how it fosters a sense of self, place, community, and global connection

❑ A high percentage of native staff to serve as mentors, role models, and caring people who take time to make students feel worthwhile

❑ More teaching done in Indian learning styles that provide for interaction

❑ Involve families, and make them welcome and a part of the decision process[34]

Educational Programs

Federal Programs

The BIA provides the basic support, transportation, and special education funds for tribal schools. Administration is channeled through the tribal governments. Tribal enrollment or verified blood quantum are required to qualify for these programs.

The Johnson O'Malley Act provides supplemental funds for the unique educational, social, and cultural needs of qualified Indian students who are enrolled in a U.S. tribe. If the student transfers to a different school, the program's funds do not follow. The law provides that if more than ten Indian children are attending a school, there is to be an elected Local Indian Education Committee, which has a say in how funds are to be spent. Although the programs vary, the money (approximately $100 per child) is used for aides, tutors, Indian activities, and equipment.

The Federal Indian Education Act, U.S. Department of Education, Title IX, program provides direct services to Indian students and requires involvement of their parents.[35] It is available to all schools, public or tribal, with ten or more qualified Indian students. Each school sets its own priorities, such as having elders or Indian aides in the classroom or providing educational materials.

Impact Aid, a program of the U.S. Department of Education (Pub. L. 81-874), was expanded in 1958 to include children living on Indian reservations. While impact aid has been declining due to changes in requirements and funding cuts, it is still important to qualifying schools. To be funded, a school district must have policies that give tribal leaders and parents an opportunity to comment on and participate in the educational programs, although the law does not require that the funds be spent exclusively on special programs for Indian children.

Title I, U.S. Department of Education, funds remedial help for low income, educationally disadvantaged children. Funds are used for tutoring and other assistance in reading, math, and language.[36] The program provides major amounts of money to districts serving children living in poverty, which means that Indian students are disproportionately involved. Tribal schools receive the program through the BIA. The dollar amount averages about $1,000 per student. However, due to changes in formulas, Minnesota was losing 10 percent of its Title I funds in 2004–2005.[37]

State Programs

The Office of Indian Education of the Minnesota Department of Education administers the state Indian programs and serves as liaison between the tribal governments/Indian communities and the state's education system. In 2002, the state closed both the Bemidji office of

Indian scholarships and the Duluth office that provided services for grades K–12. According to the Minnesota Indian Affairs Council, "This issue is of great concern to several tribal governments and the MIAC hopes to work together with CFL [now the Department of Education] to address the concerns and loss of services caused by these closures."[38]

In 1982, the State Board of Education adopted a policy to encourage the development of programs and services to meet the unique education needs of Indians and to involve them in developing curricula. The American Indian Education Act (Minn. Stat. 124D. 71-82) funds grant proposals of instruction in Indian language, literature, history, and culture, as well as staff and curriculum development. Each fiscal year, the commissioner of education must make grants to no fewer than six American Indian education programs, three of which must be in urban areas and three on reservations.

The Indian Home School Liaison Program (formerly Indian Social Worker Aide Program) was created to bring Indian community people into the schools as aides to work in special education programs, spending about 60 percent of their time in these programs and the remainder in other Indian programs.

The state provides additional funds for the few small, isolated Indian schools that no longer receive Johnson O'Malley funds: Grand Portage, Mahnomen, Nett Lake, Pine Point, Red Lake, and Waubun. Contracted Assistance for Tribal Schools (Minn. Stat. 124D.83) provides funds to the tribal schools to equalize the level of federal support with the state basic pupil unit general revenue amount. A complex formula provides approximately $3 million annually. The state also funds the Early Childhood Family Education program at the tribal schools.

Indian students classified as needing special education receive funds from federal, state, and local levels. On average, a student with special education needs could add about $2,000 in annual costs, around $1,000 of it supplied from funds outside the district.

In 1997–1998, Aid to Families with Dependent Children (AFDC) revenue was replaced with Compensatory Revenue (Minn. Stat. 126C.10, subd. 3). The formula for allocation was changed from pupils receiving AFDC to those eligible for free and reduced priced lunch.[39] Indians have a disproportionately large number of students in this group. The money must be used to meet the educational needs of pupils with low educational achievement.

When capital bonding needs or debt service costs are greater than the local property tax base can reasonably support, Maximum Effort (Minn. Stat. 123B.63), a state bonding program, can be used. Some reservation school districts, such as Nett Lake, have little or no taxable land and have thus used the program to build educational facilities.

Integration Revenue (Minn. Stat. 124.D.86) funds used for increasing "interracial contacts through classroom experiences, staff initiatives, and other educationally related programs revenue" are provided through state aid and local levies. Funds must be used for programs established under a desegregation plan filed with the Department of Education. The allocation in 2002–2003 was $481 per pupil in Minneapolis, $446 in St. Paul, and $207 in Duluth.[40]

Preschool Programs

The 2000 U.S. Census showed 720 Indian children enrolled in pre-school programs in Minnesota, including Head Start (seven Ojibwe reservations receive the direct Indian-designated Head Start pro-gram). Improved economic conditions in the Shakopee Mdewakan-ton Community have enabled the tribe to provide their own professional, full-service preschool program for three- and four-year-olds, Maga Hota. An Early Head Start program for children under three years of age was initiated at the Upper Midwest Indian Center in Minneapolis in 1997. Minnesota Indian leaders were instrumental in changing the criteria for qualifying for Head Start, with the income limit restriction modified to allow tribes to set their own guidelines. In 1999, an early learning center opened in the Phillips neighborhood of Minneapolis to serve Little Earth residents.

Early Childhood and Family Education

Early Childhood and Family Education (ECFE) is a nationally recog-nized state program for families with children up to age four, designed to strengthen families and their ability to foster the development and growth of their children. Statewide, approximately 2 percent of the participating families are Indian; in the three major cities of Minneapolis, St. Paul, and Duluth, Indian families comprise about 3 percent. The program is supplied to the four tribal schools. The Cir-cle of Life School on White Earth Reservation focuses its program on teenage mothers, encouraging them to finish high school.

During the 2004 Minnesota legislative session, Governor Tim Pawlenty proposed a 50 percent cut in ECFE funding. The House responded by taking $8 million from state Head Start funding to cover the cuts, but the program still lost funds in the overall K–12 education funding decreases.

Early Childhood Disabilities, Interagency Early Intervention

State law requires that any child from birth to age three with disabilities be brought to the attention of community services. The schools are designated as the agency responsible for bringing together the necessary programs and arranging for services to meet the child's needs. Indian children may receive services through county or Indian programming.

Learning Readiness

Learning Readiness is a school-operated medical screening program designed to ensure that students will be ready for school. In 1996, the state authorized a new program to help four- and five-year-olds in schools with the highest numbers of children in poverty develop skills to succeed in first grade. Most of the Ojibwe reservation elementary schools were included.

Public and Charter Schools, K–12

Public schools in Minnesota are financed by a complex arrangement of state and locally raised dollars, with federal funds helping with special programs. All districts with major numbers of Indian children receive federal funding well in excess of the state average. In some cases, as with Nett Lake, Red Lake, and Pine Point, there is little opportunity to raise local taxes; hence, federal funds are very important.

Minneapolis Public Schools

The Minneapolis school district has struggled with educating Indian students over the past decade. Four Winds School opened in 1991, with a waiting list and an almost entirely Indian student population. But school district and Indian leaders say the program lost focus and student achievement fell. In 2003, the school district closed the school and designed a new program with the input of Indian leaders and a pledge to commit adequate resources to the program. Anishinabe ("the people") Academy is now serving approximately 275 students in grades K–8.

Anderson Elementary also enrolls a significant number of Indians, with an 8 percent Indian student population. The school offers The Sacred Circle program for Indians. Three percent of the Anderson staff is Indian. South High offers The All Nations American Indian Small Learning Community. According to former program director Tim Brown (now director of Indian education for Minneapolis Public schools), the creation of smaller learning communities in Minneapolis high schools holds promise for Indian students because "it fits with the American Indian cultural values. Break down these big schools into small, little subsets where there's more of a family connection. It's getting back to what I think a lot of tribal dynamics revolved around."[41] Both South and Roosevelt High Schools offer Ojibwe as one of their world languages.

St. Paul Public Schools

With a smaller proportion of Indians in St. Paul and scattered living patterns, the school district does districtwide identification and tracking of students. Where there are ten or more Indian students, cultural enrichment social workers and other Indian programming are provided. Indian staff are present at every high school, and the school district has a Parent Advisory Indian Education Committee. Mounds Park American Indian Magnet School began in 1991 and became a K–8 school focusing on American Indian culture and language.

Duluth Public Schools

The Indian Education program serves approximately 600 students through home/school liaisons, an elementary teacher/tutor, and a secondary student coordinator. An after-school cultural-specific program is offered to Indian students at Lincoln Park School. The Duluth School District and the Fond du Lac Tribal Government collaborated on opening the K–6 Spotted Eagle School, but funding and organizational difficulties closed the school after just two years. Grant School (K–6) offers Indian language and culture as a focus, originally

offering Ojibwe and Spanish language for one-half-year each. However, due to changing school demographics, the original intent to incorporate Indian students and curriculum into mainstream education
has been weakened.

Suburban Public Schools

Some suburban school districts have growing numbers of Indian students. For example, Indians are 2.8 percent of the student population
in Fridley, 1.5 percent in Brooklyn Center, and 1.4 percent in Anoka.[42]
But often, with low numbers, Indian students are scattered throughout schools, making it difficult to reach them through programming.

Alternative Schools within the Public School System

Generally, alternative programs are for students who do not do well in
the regular public school system. The most recent statistics showed
that Indians made up 3.5 percent of the alternative schools and area
learning centers population but were 2.0 percent of the statewide
K–12 student body. [43]

Indian Charter and Alternative Schools

The value of alternative schools with Indian-focused curriculum and
cultural activities is much debated in Indian communities. For some,
they provide a safe and culturally rich educational environment, and
numerous former attendees have gone on to pursue higher education. But some Indians have questioned whether the alternative
schools are adequately teaching the basic skills necessary to succeed in
advanced education or the competitive job market.

In 1972, Heart of the Earth Center for American Indian Education
(Minneapolis) was begun by the American Indian Movement and pioneered the concept of offering Indian students the opportunity to
strengthen their self-image through learning of their culture, while
learning the basic educational skills to survive in the dominant culture.
The school is located near the University of Minnesota campus and
serves two hundred students K–12. The school is a charter school under
state law, receiving basic pupil unit funding from the Minneapolis school
system and other services such as special education and school busing.

The City, Inc., founded in 1975, is a private, charitable agency with a facility on East Lake Street in Minneapolis, where they have 60 to 70 percent Indian students. The program provides secondary education for inner-city youth, bringing together a variety of social services and Indian cultural programming. Funding comes from Minneapolis School District, Hennepin County, and United Way, primarily. Students graduate with a Minneapolis High School diploma.

Na-wa-yee Center School, an alternative school begun in 1974, is a secondary school (grades 7–12) focused on serving American Indian youth, primarily from the Phillips neighborhood. It has North Central Association accreditation and can award Minneapolis High School diplomas. Funding comes from various governmental social programs, governmental grants, the United Way, and foundations, as well as contract support from the Minneapolis Public Schools. The Upper Midwest American Indian Center houses the Four Directions School, a charter school for grades 8–12 with approximately ninety students.

American Indian Opportunities Industrialization Center (AIOIC). The AIOIC offers a school-to-work Career Immersion High School to support high school graduation, train students in careers, and help negotiate the pathway from student to worker. Enrollment is limited to forty students. Students attend classes plus spend an average of twenty or more hours per week in work settings outside the classroom.

Two Dakota Communities established K–12 state-chartered schools at Prairie Island and in the Lower Sioux (Dakota Open School). Dakota Open School was born of parents' frustration with the quality of education and the perceived hostility in the regular school. The school faced bureaucratic barriers in receiving special Indian education funds.[44] In 1997, the state withdrew sponsorship of the secondary program at the Dakota Open School because academic standards were not strictly enforced, and the school closed in May 1998. The school at Prairie Island closed for lack of funding after one year of operation. Eci' Nompa Woonspe Learning Center, a charter school for grades 7–12, now is serving the Upper and Lower Sioux Communities.

Other Indian Education Programs

Native Academy, run by MIGIZI Communications, received a major $1 million grant over three years from the U.S. Department of Education in August 2004. The program, in business since 1995, is designed to work in Minneapolis Public Schools in classrooms with high American Indian enrollment. Native Academy instructors monitor homework, work with parents, and offer after-school programs, all designed to boost the academic performance of American Indian students. In 2002, Native Academy eighth and ninth grade passing rates on basic skills math tests were twenty percentage points higher than those of other Minneapolis American Indian students. A summer computer program is held to help ease transition for those enrolling in the All Nations American Indian magnet program at South High School.[45] MIGIZI also assists high school students in earning academic credit through after-school and summer programs. Science and math are taught using computers and research projects. Traditional activities are included, such as harvesting maple syrup, blueberries, and wild rice.

Tribal Schools K–12

Tribal schools are authorized by the federal government under the policy "to facilitate Indian control of Indian affairs in all matters relating to education" (25 U.S.C. 2010). Tribal governments administer the schools by contract with the BIA. Tribal councils serve as the elected school boards, with program advisory parent committees. The schools must comply with state standards in curriculum and teacher certification. To meet federal standards, the schools are accredited by Minnesota Non-Public School Accrediting Association and the North Central Association of Colleges and Schools, a higher standard than is required of Minnesota public schools.

Four Minnesota tribes operate large and growing K–12 tribal schools. The federal government has never adequately funded these schools, and it only funds tribally enrolled, one-quarter blood Indian students. Minnesota adds some dollars so that the schools receive the equivalent of the state's basic per pupil unit. Tribal schools receive special need and Indian-focused programs similar to those in the public schools. Special education and transportation funding comes from the BIA.

School construction on the reservations, a federal responsibility, involves a wait of many years on a priority listing. Leech Lake has good facilities built in 1984; White Earth received funds to remodel its school and add an elementary addition in 1995; Mille Lacs sold tax-exempt bonds using casino profits as collateral and invested $6.1 million to build two schools in 1993.

Ojibwe School, Fond du Lac Reservation, serves about three hundred students. The staff is 80 percent Indian, and students are primarily MCT enrollees. In 1995, the elementary facility was remodeled with casino profits.

Bug-O-Nay-Ge-Shig School, Leech Lake Reservation, fifteen miles East of Cass Lake, serves students from the reservation and the surrounding school districts, including Bemidji. To prevent frequent switching back and forth with the nearby Cass Lake Public School, there is an agreement that once children enroll for the quarter they are not allowed to transfer. Approximately 33 percent of the teachers are Indian. In 1996, the middle school was named a "Blue Ribbon School" by the U.S. Department of Education. It is the second largest BIA school in the country, with an annual budget of $6 million. The school has a language immersion program in Ojibwe and began its first kindergarten class in fall 2004.[46]

In 1979, Nay-Ah-Shing, Mille Lacs Reservation, began as a secondary school in response to strong Indian dissatisfaction with the public school. Today, all of the students are Ojibwe. The school has developed numerous Ojibwe materials, video recordings, songs, and books.

Circle of Life, White Earth Reservation, located in the village of White Earth, began in 1978 and added an elementary program in 1983. The school serves 100 to 150 students; approximately 25 percent of the teachers are Indian. A BIA program to rewrite curriculum with measurable goals, stressing academics and imposing stronger standards, was implemented in 1994. The school is currently slated by the BIA to be replaced since the building has been declared unsafe by today's standards.

Boarding and Mission Schools

The BIA operates boarding schools at Flandreau, South Dakota, and Wahpeton, North Dakota. Approximately 100 Minnesota students attend the two schools, most coming from the Red Lake and White Earth Reservations. Both schools offer a four-year program, with general studies and vocational education plus therapeutic and special needs programs. St. Mary's Mission School on the Red Lake Reservation is the only mission school remaining in Minnesota. It has about 120 day students in grades 1–6.

Encouraging Education

Indian Education Associations

In 1969, the National Indian Education Association (NIEA) was founded in Minnesota to ensure that Indians were included in educational policy discussions and to unite Indians in fighting for educational equity. Now headquartered in Washington, D.C., the NIEA is the largest and oldest Indian education organization in the country. The Minnesota Indian Education Association (MIEA), located in Bemidji, supports Indian education in the state and offers an annual conference with workshops, trainings, and a resource fair.

General Education Development (GED) Test

Students can take the General Education Development (GED) test, which provides a standard of achievement that can be used if the person has no high school diploma. The GED program is required by several welfare and jobs programs and is used for acceptance into postsecondary education programs. Many Indians use the GED to get back into the educational system after dropping out of high school.

State-administered funds are used for the Minnesota Indian Adult Education program that serves 350 individuals at four reservations, Bois Forte, Grand Portage, Mille Lacs, and Fond du Lac, and at sites in northeastern Minnesota including International Falls, Cook, and Duluth. Similar funding is used for programs operated by Leech Lake, White Earth, and Red Lake reservations; American Indian Opportunities Industrialization Center (AIOIC) in Minneapolis; a consortium at Granite Falls with tribal participation; Scott-Carver Educational Cooperative working with the Shakopee Mdewakanton Dakota Community; and the Minnesota Corrections Department, which handles the prison programs. The St. Paul Public Schools have an Indian-run Native American Special Adult Program. Funding from the federal program also comes directly into the state for the programs at the Minneapolis American Indian Center, Upper Midwest Indian Center, and MIGIZI Communications, Inc. Minnesota's Indian Adult Basic Education program serves more Indian adults than any other state program in the country.

Programs to Encourage Postsecondary Education

Several programs have been designed to reach Indian students while they are still in school to establish relationships, present the possibilities of future education, and help overcome the barriers to seeking a university or other postgraduate career.

The Post-Secondary Preparation Program (Minn. Stat. 124.481) is a state-funded grant program to assist secondary students in graduating and seeking advanced education. The Minnesota Indian Scholarship Committee awards the grants.

Trio Programs serve numerous Indian students from low-income families and those whose parents did not graduate from college; Talent Search serves students in grades 6–12 with counseling and support for applying to college and obtaining scholarships and financial aid. In 2001–2002, the program reached 997 Indian students in Minnesota, approximately 11 percent of the total served. Student Support Services helps students stay in college through tutoring, counseling, and remedial instruction. In 2001–2002, the program served 370 Indians in Minnesota, 7 percent of the total served. Upward Bound programs help prepare students for higher education through instruction in literature, composition, math, and science on college campuses after school, on Saturdays, and during the summer. In 2001–2002, 147 Indians participated out of a total of 1,213 (12 percent).[47]

The University of Minnesota–Duluth has offered Indian students a successful sequence of programs for many years. The programs encourage Indian students to enter medicine and associated scientific fields. The program now boasts numerous Indian graduates from medical school. The Twin Cities Chapter of the American Indian Science and Engineering Society provides a summer math camp for high school students. The Multicultural Center for Academic Excellence offers classes for freshmen minority students to develop college level writing and math skills. The Minority Encouragement Program (MEP) is a collaboration with St. Paul Public Schools to increase the enrollment of academically prepared students of color and to promote their retention through to graduation.[48] An Elders Council advises the president of the University of Minnesota and works with Indian students attending college.

Other Academic Encouragement

The American Indian Natural Resources Careers Program is a unique program put together by the Services to Indian People Program at Itasca Community College. The five-week summer program encourages high school youth to prepare for college by linking the enrichment curriculum and Ojibwe culture to forestry work. The program is supported by the BIA Forestry, U.S. Forest Service, Itasca Community College, University of Minnesota College of Natural Resources, Minnesota Department of Natural Resources, U.S. Fish and Wildlife Service, and the White Earth and Leech Lake tribal governments.

The Anishinabe Computing Sciences and Engineering Project, with National Science Foundation funding, is run by the Fond du Lac Tribal and Community College and the reservation's Ojibwe school. It offers summer camp experiences for youth beginning in fifth grade, to develop interest in careers in technology and engineering.

The federally funded Schools to Work program for students in the Cloquet Public School and the Ojibwe Tribal School focuses on developing interest in technology and health careers in the early grades. AmeriCorps, with federal funding, places young people in service jobs with deferred wages to be used for education. The Red Lake Tribe operated Partners in Service to America with about twenty-nine youth in 2004–2005.[49] The youth are seventeen years and older, and if they have not graduated from high school, they must work on obtaining a GED during the program. Twenty percent of their time is spent on education, 80 percent doing community service. After completing a year's work, participants receive a voucher for further education.

The Ronald E. McNair Post-Baccalaureate Achievement programs, part of the federally funded Trio Programs, are designed to encourage low-income students and minority undergraduates to consider careers in college teaching as well as prepare for doctoral study. Participants are offered research opportunities and provided with mentors. In 2001–2002, thirteen Indians participated, approximately 15 percent of the total participants.[50]

Higher Education

The number of Indians enrolled in postsecondary educational institutions increased from 2,555 in 1988 to 2,927 in 2002. During the time period 1993–2002, African-American higher education enrollment increased by 79 percent; Hispanic by 30 percent; and Asian by 35 percent; but American Indian enrollment grew by just 7 percent.[51] However, the Minnesota Minority Education Partnership reported that of those American Indians who graduated, participation in higher education immediately following high school rose from 31 percent in 2000 to 40 percent in 2002.

Much of the postsecondary student increase has been attributed to efforts by tribes to encourage youth to pursue a college education. For example, the Mille Lacs Band is using casino revenues to provide college subsidies for tribal members.[52] The leader of the Band's effort, Eric North, invites speakers to talk about college options and organizes visits to colleges and universities. "We talk to students about going to college," said North. "Career choice is really what we're looking at. 'What do you want to do when you grow up?' and, 'What do you need to do in order to get the position you want?' "[53]

Indian students have significantly different patterns of postsecondary enrollment than the general population. The choices reflect the need to deal with poorer high school preparation and the lack of a high school diploma, the desire to remain closer to Indian communities and in smaller institutions, the need to economize on expenses, and the preference for programs that provide strong support for Indian students. They are more apt to choose two-year technical and community colleges. For example, in 2002, 44 percent of American Indian enrollees chose a four-year institution; 56 percent chose a two-year program.[54]

Over the eleven-year period 1992–2002, the choice of institution changed. After Indian enrollment nearly tripled during the early 1990s, community and technical colleges saw a 12 percent drop by 2002, from 1,577 students to 1,386. Private career college enrollment dropped from 197 to 91 Indian students; private college and university enrollment rose 47 percent, from 296 to 437. State universities' enrollment increased from 398 to 417 students. University of Minnesota Indian enrollment rose 38 percent, from 399 to 551 students. Graduate/professional school enrollment nearly doubled, from 26 to 45 students.[55]

Not as well documented is the importance of Indian-run institutions. For example, the Leech Lake Tribal College serves approximately 270 students, most of whom are American Indian, and Fond du Lac Tribal and Community College tripled its student body during the years from 1987 to 2003.[56]

American Indian students in Minnesota graduate from four-year institutions at a lower rate than African-American, Asian, Hispanic, and white students, according to the Minnesota Higher Education Service Office's most recent report, in 2000, 29 percent of American Indian students graduated, compared to 38 percent of African-Americans, 49 percent of Asians, 45 percent of Hispanics, and 52 percent of whites. [57]

For degrees requiring four years or more, the proportion of students completing programs who are Indian is very low, ranging from 0.8 percent in private colleges and universities to 1.1 percent at the University of Minnesota–Twin Cities.[58] In the shorter, more technical categories, including associate of arts degrees, Indians earned 1.1 percent of the degrees awarded, but just 0.6 percent of bachelor's degrees.[59] There has been dramatic growth in the one-year degree program in business management and administrative services, designed to train casino employees.

Barriers to a Postsecondary Education

There are several formidable barriers for Indians to completing a postsecondary education, primarily need for financial assistance, poor academic preparation, lack of support in mainstream institutions, and family responsibilities.

NEED FOR FINANCIAL ASSISTANCE   Most Indian students cannot afford advanced education without outside help. They frequently have family responsibilities, yet they increasingly must work to get through college. Often studies must be interrupted by work to earn money to continue. A study of Indian students at the University of Minnesota showed that the more hours worked, the lower the grade point average.[60] A 1999 study by the American Indian Urban Higher Education Initiative found that students cited the need for more help in resolving financial aid problems as the major factor in their ability to remain in school and complete their degrees.[61]

As tuition increases and demand for college loans grows, there are concerns about how the costs can be met. Annually, the Indian Scholarship Program grants over $1.8 million to nearly nine hundred students. This figure has not increased since 1994. The maximum amount a student can receive is $3,300. The program is unable to fund all who apply.[62] A continuing problem is that increasing numbers of Indian students do not qualify for special assistance because they are unable to verify membership in a specific tribe or one-fourth ancestry.

In November 2004, a private donation to the University of Minnesota made possible $100,000 in scholarships for American Indian students attending the University's General College. Approximately 12 percent of the University's American Indian students are enrolled in the General College.[63]

POOR ACADEMIC PREPARATION   High schools are often faulted for their poor preparation of Indian students. Educators cite poorly acquired basic skills and study habits, counselors who discourage Indian students from attempting the challenges of postsecondary education, and smaller rural schools with limited funding that may lack science laboratories and technical equipment to provide a competitive education.

In its 1999 report, the American Indian Urban Higher Education Initiative (AIUHEI) recommended a stronger student recruitment program using staff from postsecondary institutions, as well as increased coordination and communication about Upward Bound, Talent Search, and other college preparatory programs. In recent years, summer and other programs have been created to help with remedial tutoring, exposure to the college environment and potential career opportunities, and job-shadowing opportunities. For example, in August 2004, Carleton College hosted the five-day College Horizons, a crash course on how to apply to elite colleges.

FAMILY RESPONSIBILITIES   Indians have a much higher ratio of students with families and dependents than does the general population, adding an additional layer of concerns about housing, health care, child care, public assistance programs, and special needs for social services. Family ties are very important to Indians, and family needs may interfere with school, placing enough of a burden to cause withdrawal from college. In addition, many Indian students are the first in their families to attempt a postsecondary education, and they are often unfamiliar with what it takes to complete such a course of study.

LACK OF INDIAN FACULTY AND STAFF   A few institutions have made major efforts to provide an Indian presence, as reflected in the following tables (see Tables 10.3 and 10.4).

Table 10.3 Indian faculty and staff at postsecondary institutions in Minnesota, 2003

Institution	Faculty*		Staff**	
	Number	Percent	Number	Percent
University of Minn–Twin Cities	21	0.8	161	0.7
University of Minn–Duluth	8	2.0	24	2.0
Bemidji State University	5	2.8	18	3.1
Augsburg College	2	1.3	10	1.6
Macalester College	3	1.9	5	0.9
University of St. Thomas	2	n/a	0	0
Fond du Lac Tribal College	9	34.0	36	28.0
Leech Lake Tribal College	8	53.0	30	60.0
White Earth Tribal College	2	33.0	17	65.0

*Full and part-time, tenured and nontenured teachers
**Full and part-time employees
Source: National Center for Education, 2003.

Table 10.4 Tenured Indian faculty at postsecondary institutions in Minnesota, 2002

Institution	Number Tenured*
University of Minnesota–Twin Cities	10
University of Minnesota–Duluth	2
University of Minnesota–Morris	3
Augsburg College	2
University of St. Thomas	1
(Fond du Lac, Leech Lake, and White Earth Tribal Colleges do not offer tenure track.)	

*Tenured assistant, associate, and full professors
Source: U.S. Department of Equal Employment Opportunity, 2002.

NEED TO INCORPORATE INDIAN CURRICULUM   Institutions vary in their willingness to accept the academic value of Indian classes. St. Scholastica requires a freshman survey class that includes an Indian professor as one of the team teachers. At the University of Minnesota–Twin Cities campus and Southwest State University, Indian classes qualify for required diversity of cultures and human relations credits. Several institutions allow the use of Indian curriculum to meet specific academic discipline requirements. At other institutions, these classes can only be used as electives, which severely limits their use. Indian language classes are often not accepted for language credits outside of Indian Studies.

INDIAN CONFLICT WITH ACADEMIC TRADITIONS   Indian studies programs represent a different cultural and intellectual approach, one that is not always readily accepted by universities. As noted Indian educator and leader W. Roger Buffalohead said, "While teaching styles in mainstream colleges and universities have become more diversified in recent years, no Minnesota institution, with perhaps the exception of the Indian-controlled colleges, is noted for pioneering teaching strategies that resonate with Indian people."[64] Progress has been made at the University of Minnesota–Twin Cities where the American Indian Studies Department now has a department chair and tenure track, as well as four full professors and numerous adjunct professors after many years of struggle to prevent the department from being absorbed by other departments.[65]

Academia has also been at odds with Indian interests. For example, University of Minnesota research created paddy wild rice, which had a dramatic negative effect on the market for Indian-harvested lake rice.[66] In addition, academia can place extraordinary demands on Indian faculty. They are often expected to serve as the Indian spokesperson on administrative and academic governing committees, and with such few numbers, the time demands are significant.

Ingredients of Success

A strong, ongoing commitment by top administrators is vital to the success of attracting and retaining Indian students. That commitment entails Indian faculty, Indian support programs, and acceptance of an

Indian curriculum. Programs in several private colleges to attract Indian students were successful but have disappeared because of lack of commitment and funding.

INDIAN SUPPORT SERVICES   The recent American Indian Urban Higher Education Initiative study found that "students, administrators, student support staff, and faculty all agreed that there is a significant correlation between Indian student retention and graduation rates and the presence of Indian support and cultural programs on their campuses."[67] Many of the state's institutions of higher learning and community colleges with significant numbers of Indian students have Indian-staffed programs that generally include counseling, referral to needed services, tutoring, and assistance in adjusting to college. Most institutions have Indian student clubs and cultural activities, providing important social outlets for Indian students. Indians reject the notion that one umbrella "minority" support program can provide adequate services for Indian students because of the need to understand complex tribal and Indian-specific needs.

INDIAN SCHOLARSHIP PROGRAMS   Funding for low-income students is available through federal Pell Grants, federal Supplemental Education Opportunity Grants administered by the college, Minnesota State Grant in Aid, and federal student loans. Special categories of assistance may be available from veteran benefits, Social Security assistance, and various private and institutional grants. In addition, Indian students may apply for the Minnesota Indian Scholarship Program (MISP) and the federally funded (through the BIA) and tribally administered Indian scholarship program.

The Minnesota Indian Scholarship Program is for students who are at least one-fourth Indian ancestry and who have a high school diploma or a GED. They can be from tribes throughout the United States and Canada but must have been a state resident at least for the prior year. The program has assisted more than five thousand Minnesota Indian students since its inception in 1955. The scholarships can be available for up to five years of study. In addition, the Ethel Curry American Indian Scholarship Fund, established in 1995, is administered by MISP as a separate program. The MISP has been an important source of funds for many Indian educators and leaders over the past fifty years.

The BIA Scholarship Program is a federally funded program for tribally enrolled Indians. Red Lake, Fond du Lac, Mille Lacs, Leech Lake, and White Earth handle their own programs; the MCT administers for Grand Portage and Bois Forte. There is close cooperation with the state program, but unlike the state program, the scholarships can follow the member regardless of residency. The funds are split 60 percent for higher education and 40 percent for vocational education. The Dakota Communities also administer BIA higher education grants.

The BIA also provides "critical professions scholarships," which include a stipend in addition to the scholarship. They are granted to students in professions that are of special importance to the tribes, such as accounting and education. In return for the assistance, the graduate works two years for the tribe.

Teacher Training Incentive Programs, such as the Minnesota Indian Teacher Training Program at the University of Minnesota–Duluth, Bemidji State, Moorhead State, and Augsburg College, provide scholarships and stipends to those students who want to enter the teaching profession. Teachers of Color is a similar state program for all minority students.

Minority Fellowship Grants is a state program for people with college degrees who link with a public school, receiving practical experience and one year of courses to complete the needed classes to become a teacher. St. Thomas University offers this program.

The American Indian Graduate Center in Albuquerque, New Mexico, provides assistance for graduate students in the priority careers of health, education, business, science, law, and natural resources. About three-fourths of the students in the UMD–UMTC health professions program finance their education through the Indian Health Service, which then requires a three-year payback of service to the IHS.

Private scholarships are very important, and several play a crucial role in assisting Indian students to meet higher private college tuition costs. Augsburg College offers several scholarships designated specifically for American Indians; St. Scholastica and the Prairie Island Dakota also offer scholarships. The Shakopee Mdewakanton Sioux Community helped found the Augsburg scholarship program, donated $900,000 to the American Indian College Fund for a scholarship endowment, and helps fund Catching the Dream scholarships.

Entertainer Louis Anderson has established an Indian scholarship fund to honor his brother, Kent Smith. Since 1997, the Saint Paul Foundation has awarded scholarships through its Spectrum Trust Two Feathers Scholarship Fund program. The United Church of Christ's special American Indian ministry program provides scholarships for seminary students at United Theological Seminary of the Twin Cities. The Bush Leadership Fellowship Program has made possible the advanced education of many of the state's Indian leaders. Education costs are covered for up to eighteen months, and recipients are challenged to broaden their experience before returning to serve Indian communities.[68]

Because of casino profits, the Dakota Communities and Mille Lacs are able to encourage advanced education by helping any member who needs additional assistance. Leech Lake Reservation has an annual summer golf tournament as a scholarship fund-raiser. MIGIZI offers scholarships for studies in natural resources, journalism, and culture and language studies.

Higher Education Institutions

Most tribes have arrangements with postsecondary institutions to conduct classes on the reservations. Technical and community colleges provide several degree programs in such areas as building services, heavy equipment, secretarial and clerk/typist, natural resource technology, wildlife, and casino management. Colleges and universities provide classes on the reservations for credit. The University of Minnesota and Mankato State University have offered extension classes at the Shakopee Mdewakanton Community Center; Moorhead State University has staff on the White Earth Reservation, where it offers liberal arts classes; and Bemidji State University teaches business classes on Red Lake Reservation.

Tribal Colleges

Minnesota has four tribal colleges, Fond du Lac Tribal and Community College, Leech Lake Tribal College, White Earth Tribal and Community College, and Red Lake Nation College. In just over a decade, Minnesota Tribal Colleges have become a major factor in

Indian education. As explained by Larry Aitken, a professor at Itasca Community College and former president of the Leech Lake Tribal College, "For Indians, a university must be authenticated to Indian lifestyle, culture and spirituality. We need an education that stresses feeling whole, with spiritual values; where cultural and academic values are integrated, and teaching native language leads the way."[69]

Fond du Lac Tribal and Community College, chartered in 1987 by the Fond du Lac Reservation Business Committee and established in 1988 as a tribal college, is one of thirty tribal colleges nationwide. As a unique part of the Minnesota Community College System, it is supported through state funding and enrolls both Indian and non-Indian students. Since it opened, enrollment has more than tripled, with approximately 850 students enrolled in 2003. The campus was built on land donated by the Potlatch Company, with city, county, and utility company support in providing the needed services and state funding for the $7 million facility. The college offers Ojibwe language classes and an Anishinabe associate arts degree.

Leech Lake Tribal College was chartered by the Leech Lake Band of Chippewa in 1990 and is governed by the sovereignty and constitution of the tribe. The college's board consists of enrolled members of the Leech Lake Nation. The college awards two-year degrees with a mission to transmit the Anishinabe language and culture. In 1994 it was designated a land grant institution. The college enrolls approximately 270 students, the majority of whom are Indian. Leech Lake offers four-year degree programs in early childhood education and studies of indigenous people, jointly offered through an arrangement with Sinte Gleska Tribal College on the Rosebud Reservation in South Dakota.

White Earth Tribal and Community College was founded in October 1997, with the mission of providing training for jobs on the reservation. The college serves approximately ninety students in education, technology, Indian Studies, and other programs. The college is in the process of seeking accreditation and was recommended for initial candidacy in May 2004. The college works closely with Moorhead State University and Bemidji State University. Articulation agreements were signed so students can transfer their credits to those four-year institutions after completing studies at White Earth.

Red Lake Nation College opened in January 2004. According to President Renee Gurneau, the college expects to be accredited in four to five years. The college has working partnerships with Fond du Lac, Bemidji State University, and Turtle Mountain. Classes are offered in computer technology, Anishinabe studies, writing, algebra, drumming, and moccasin-making.[70]

Native American Educational Services, Inc. (NAES), a four-year private American Indian college that began a program in the Twin Cities in 1987, lost accreditation effective June 2005. It had offered a bachelor's degree in community studies, as well as Dakota/Lakota and Ojibwe languages instruction.

Minnesota State Colleges and Universities System (MnSCU)

Indian studies classes and programs are offered in several of the colleges and universities in the Minnesota State Colleges and Universities System. American Indian/Native American Studies focusing on the history, society, politics, culture, and economics of the original inhabitants of the Western Hemisphere, including American Indians, Aleuts, and Eskimos, are offered at Bemidji State University (BA in Indian studies); Central Lakes College, Brainerd Campus (certificates in American Indian, Ojibwe studies); Fond du Lac Tribal and Community College, Cloquet Campus (certificate in Anishinabe); Itasca Community College, Grand Rapids Campus (certificate in American Indian studies); Minnesota State University Moorhead (multicultural studies: American Indian studies minor); Rainy River Community College, International Falls Campus (certificate in indigenous studies); Southwest State University (minor in American Indian and Dakota studies).

Bemidji State University, located near the state's three largest reservations, has the second largest number of Indian students at a postsecondary institution. In 2001, Indians made up slightly more than 5 percent of the student population. The University established an Indian studies program in 1969, which was made a freestanding academic program in 1972, and now is one of two such programs in the state. A strong Ojibwe language program, begun in 1971, is part of the Modern Language Department. The 3M Corporation endowed the first chair of accounting in the nation designated to foster minority interest in corporate America.

Minneapolis Community and Technical College (MCTC) currently has the state's third largest number of Indian students at a postsecondary institution. The college's American Indian support program is well known in the Indian community and is a strong factor in the college's Indian program. Many of Augsburg College's Indian students come from MCTC.[71]

University of Minnesota System

In recognition of the University of Minnesota Morris campus's history as an Indian Boarding School in the 1800s and the fact that the campus was built on Indian land, the Minnesota Legislature mandated that American Indians attending Morris are not required to pay tuition. To be eligible for the tuition waiver, students must show membership in a state or federally recognized American Indian tribe or provide other documentation or certification of American Indian ancestry/heritage. Applicants are not required to be residents of Minnesota.

University of Minnesota–Duluth began a tribal/community advisory council in 1977, and its success led to a state law later mandating the right of Indians to request similar councils at all facilities serving ten or more Indian students. Programs in health, social welfare, and education work closely with the Fond du Lac Tribe and use the reservation's programs for student placement. A major in American Indian Studies is offered in the College of Liberal Arts, and approximately 50 percent of the students in these classes are Indian. UMD also offers a graduate program in social work with Indian emphasis, as well as training through the Center of American Indian and Minority Health. UMD has an endowed chair of Indian education that focuses on helping teachers serve different learning styles of various cultural groups.[72]

According to Dr. Thomas Peacock, a professor at UMD, the university started a unique partnership program with Fond du Lac Tribal and Community College to keep Indian students enrolled in higher education. "It's a very white campus and therefore it's hard to build a supportive community for Indians," Peacock said. The new program graduated twenty-four Indian students in its first master's degree in education cohort and twenty-seven in its most recent, second round. Peacock reported that UMD extended the program to include doctoral students, with over twenty doctorates in education awarded by 2004. In 1998, UMD also added the Duluth Bridge Program to increase the number of American Indian/Alaska Native scientists.

The University of Minnesota–Twin Cities Department of American Indian Studies, founded in 1969, is the oldest such program in the country with departmental status. The program is committed to studies that reflect American Indian perspectives and to embracing "ways of knowing that stand in contrast to the linear analytic Euro-American studies typically found in colleges and universities."[73] Indian community leaders, artists, and elders supplement the department faculty. Classes are offered through the College of Liberal Arts and through Continuing Education and Extension, both on the Twin Cities campus and at the Community Center established by the Shakopee Mdewakanton Sioux. Major and minor degrees are offered. Course offerings focus on Dakota and Ojibwe languages, American Indian literature, art, philosophies, and socioeconomic issues. UMTC offers an American Indian Learning Resource Center to provide support services for Indian students.

Private Colleges

Augsburg College offers a major in American Indian studies. Ojibwe language is one of the most popular language courses offered. Each year, approximately fifty-five Indians are enrolled both full-time and part-time. The college participates in the Minnesota Indian Teacher Training Partnership in conjunction with Minneapolis and St. Paul public schools. In an agreement with the Fond du Lac Tribal and Community College, the tribal college offers courses on the Augsburg campus for students working for their two-year tribal college degree. The American Indian Student Support Program helps students develop an education plan and provides counseling and financial assistance advice. The retention and graduation rates are about 85 percent, the highest for postsecondary institutions in Minnesota.

With a strong Indian faculty, St. Scholastica College in Duluth offers a minor in Indian studies, which is usually linked with an education or social work major. The school's teacher training program integrates Indian language and culture classes. Indian students also are enrolled in the nursing and physical therapy programs.

Concordia College in Moorhead offers classes in Indian education and social work and has two Indian professors. The Indian programs and student bodies at Moorhead State University, North Dakota State in Fargo, and Concordia College work together on social activities.

Summary

Minnesota Indians know they have tremendous challenges ahead of them to educate their children. They envision an education that will teach the skills to enable their children to receive equal treatment in society, and they seek an education that will allow their children to retain their Indian values and culture. Improving overall education and graduation rates are vital for helping to solve the many other problems facing Indians. A strong Indian presence, institutional commitment, financial support, and staying power can produce positive results. But the programs that offer these successful ingredients are too few. The ultimate cost is many missed opportunities to increase the professional staff of tribal government; to provide an Indian aspect to programs in health, welfare, education, and social welfare; and to train members ready to make valuable contributions to their communities.

Chapter 11

Social Services

American Indians over time, through many struggles,
worked to preserve the integrity of Native culture. We must
fully appreciate the conditions under which our ancestors
were forced to live. Using the cultural traditions that they
fought to preserve we must continue to build the future for
our children. Social indicators that outline the needs of
the American Indian community cannot be the sole driver
of policy; we must continue to utilize cultural values as
assets for designing effective social programs, especially if
we are to strengthen American Indian families.
                    —John Poupart, American Indian Policy Center

EVER SINCE TREATIES forced Indians onto reservations, native people
have had to depend in large measure on support from the government. Geographic restrictions and the destruction of timber and
other natural resources denied Indians access to income and traditional food supplies. Increasingly, Indians had to pay for their own
government programs funded through the sale of Indian lands. When
the money ran out and starvation became imminent, government
food rations began.

The supplying of rations continued until criticized by the Meriam
report in 1928, which concluded, "It worked untold harm to the Indians
because it was pauperizing and lacked any appreciable educational
value."[1] During the many years of federal domination on the reservations, Indians were not allowed to make their own decisions; the
government acted for them. These experiences robbed many Indians
of the expectation that they would manage their own lives and

established the pattern of dependency. By the time of the nationwide welfare programs of the 1930s, Indians had been declared U.S. citizens, eligible for all state and national services.

Current Economic Status

Lack of employment opportunities, limited education, poor health, substandard housing, discrimination, alcoholism, and teenage pregnancies are some of today's realities in Indian communities. These multiple problems, combined with scars from past treatment and visions for a better future, contribute to the need for assistance.

Though Indians in Minnesota face considerable difficulties, Marge Anderson, former Chief Executive of the Mille Lacs Ojibwe, underscored the beliefs of many Indians today when she said, "We have weathered the storms of injustice. We have lived through plagues of diseases unknown to our ancestors. We have seen our darkest hour. We have much to be proud of. We have a heritage in America that is second to none. We are in a state of crisis. That is true. But we have faced much worse and survived."[2]

The expanded powers of tribal government to control political and economic decisions are making a difference in the lives of many individual Indians. Casinos have for the first time provided employment for many Indians living on or near reservations. With work has come increased self-esteem and stronger families. Gaming has built economic strength because Indians have demonstrated successful ownership and operation of businesses. Returning to the reservations to live and work has become a viable alternative to urban poverty.

But these changes reveal the deeper social problems. Tribes struggle to provide housing and other services for many new residents. Blending different lifestyles can create social problems, and gambling addiction dominates some lives. Importantly, for most Indians in Minnesota, there is little or no direct financial impact from the casinos. Even for tribes experiencing the most successful economic development and self-governance, human needs remain substantial.

As mentioned in previous chapters, there is a great deal of confusion in the public mind about the use of casino profits. Publicity about the successful casino operation at the Shakopee Mdewakanton Dakota Community in Prior Lake, with its large per capita distribution of profits, has created the notion that all Indians are wealthy, yet census data and other social status research find there has been no measurable impact from casinos for many Indians in Minnesota, especially those living in urban areas. The problems and needs in the new century are just as great, if not more so, than they were in 1990 before Indian gaming began in earnest in Minnesota.

Chapter 10 notes that the education level of Indians is much lower than that of other population groups, leading to higher unemployment rates and lower wages. Discrimination, poor health, and chemical dependency issues continue to contribute to the poverty that made Indians the poorest racial group in the state according to the 2000 U.S. Census. While the percentage of the state's Indians living in poverty dropped from 44 percent in 1989 to 24.5 percent in 2000, the 2000 figure compares to 7.5 percent for whites, 21.2 percent for Hispanics, and 22.1 percent for African-Americans. In addition, Indian families made up 10 percent of Minnesota's homeless families, far in excess of their percentage of the total population.[3]

Federal and State Funding

Federal welfare reform was enacted beginning in 1996. Temporary Assistance for Needy Families (TANF) replaced Aid to Families with Dependent Children (AFDC). The new legislation stresses employment and limits the time allowed on public assistance. Under TANF, Indian tribes are eligible to apply to the U.S. Department of Health and Human Services to create and administer welfare programs.[4] When accepted, tribes have the flexibility to establish their own participation rates and time limits, which may vary from federal requirements. All of the tribes are participating in TANF programs to some extent. However, as of 2003, only the Mille Lacs Band has had a formal plan approved, which allows the flexibility previously mentioned.

The Mille Lacs Band operates an Independent Life Skills Center that serves as a one-stop service center for TANF recipients. In 2003, the Mille Lacs Band also began the process of expanding TANF programs and services to the urban area. The Band started with a demonstration project to serve all Minnesota Chippewa tribal enrollees living in Hennepin and Ramsey counties. According to the tribe's Chief Executive Melanie Benjamin, "This is a good opportunity to have a more culturally specific, compassionate and effective way of serving Indian people."[5] The BIA approved of the Band's administration in 2005.

TANF funds also are available to tribes beyond the creation of a tribe's own program through such assistance as the TANF Home Visiting Program, Cash and Food Assistance, Child Care Assistance, Employment Services, Housing Services, and Refinancing. In 2002, the state issued new guidelines for Indians, providing time limit exemptions for adults living on an Indian reservation of over one thousand people with at least 50 percent joblessness.[6]

With the creation of the TANF block grant system, the existing JOBS programs were terminated, except for Indian tribes. The Tribal JOBS Program was replaced with the Native Employment Works (NEW) Program, which funds tribal work activities programs. As of 2001, the Minnesota Chippewa and Red Lake Band were participating. Their federal funding level was just under $1 million.

Minnesota passed welfare reform legislation—Minnesota Family Investment Program (MFIP)—in 1997 to comply with TANF. The new legislation requires county governments to cooperate with tribal governments in implementing MFIP. The Commissioner of Human Services is also authorized to enter into agreements with tribal governments to provide employment and training services. From December 1998 to December 2002, the number of American Indian adults eligible for MFIP dropped 9 percent, but Indians still made up 8.5 percent of the MFIP caseload.[7]

Tribes have deep concerns about all these changes, especially mandating employment on reservations where no employment opportunities exist. Tribes also fear that block grants to states will mean that their needs will be ignored. Most programs do not require that Indians' unique status be taken into consideration.

State records show that Indians have difficulty leaving welfare after two or three years, which is the goal of MFIP/TANF. Of all those receiving MFIP assistance in January 1998, 55 percent of American Indians were still receiving assistance more than two years later (in May 2000), compared to 35 percent of white participants, 53 percent of African-American participants, and 61 percent of Asian participants.

In analyzing these data, Wilder Foundation researchers found that most American Indians enrolled in MFIP had gotten or tried to get a job and that they valued work and the freedom it gave them from MFIP rules and paperwork. But many participants said the time frame of MFIP was not long enough to get the necessary education for jobs; that jobs available to them were often temporary, unstable, or low paying; that new casino employees often had to work the night shift; that they encountered discrimination in interviewing for employment; and that suitable child care was often not available.[8]

The Minnesota Indian Family Preservation Act (MIFPA) of 1985 (Minn. Stat. 257.35) supplements the federal Indian Child Welfare Act (ICWA) and provides major funding that has enabled the state's tribes to establish social welfare departments. In 2003, the amount of funding was $2.1 million for family preservation, reunification services, and special focus grants to all eleven Minnesota Indian tribes and four urban American Indian agencies, including the Indian Child Welfare Law Center.[9] The stated intent of the Act is to protect the long-term interests of Indian families and children by maintaining the integrity of Indian families, extended families, and tribal communities. The Act provides for an American Indian Child Welfare Advisory Council, composed of representatives of the eleven tribes (authorized by tribal resolution), as well as one representative from Duluth, three from Minneapolis, and two from St. Paul.

Community Social Programs and Collaboratives

The state has transferred to local communities the responsibility for setting spending priorities for several programs such as Community Social Services, Community Mental Health Adult and Children's Advisory Councils, Community Health Services Board, and Community Corrections Advisory Board. While the intent is that all people are to be heard and the programs should deliver services to those in need, there are few provisions to insure inclusion of minority groups.

To simplify systems, promote collaboration among governmental agencies at the community level, and respond to communities' unique needs, the state began funding Family Services and Community-Based Collaboratives in 1994, administered through the Minnesota Department of Human Services (Minn. Stat. 124D.23). Examples of Indian-oriented programs that have been included in the collaborative efforts include:

> ❏ The Cass County/Leech Lake Reservation Children's Initiative worked with the county's four school districts to give more convenient access to social programs through local Family Resource Centers. The collaborative has

been successful in its goal of reducing out-of-home placements by providing more support for families.

❏ The Mille Lacs Tribe developed Indian community-county collaboration with each of its three widely scattered districts of the reservation by improving links between services from Mille Lacs, Pine, and Aitken counties.

❏ The St. Paul/Ramsey County Children's Initiative was a collaborative project with an Indian board, working to provide appropriate and needed services to Indian families in St. Paul through Family Centers. In 2003, the Initiative dissolved, and its Family Center services for Indians were transferred to the American Indian Family Center.

While tribes realize that collaboratives make good sense, they are very aware that the state cannot be allowed to assume powers that would diminish tribal sovereignty. Many of the Indian-run social service programs have taken years of effort to establish, and convincing federal, state, and local governments that Indians must direct services if they are to reach Indian people has taken time.

Even with governments that have the best and most understanding relationships with tribes, there can be problems with lack of sensitivity in dealing with Indians. A tribal social service director who has worked extensively with other agencies commented, "Collaboratives bring together the agency people, police, schools, social services, etc., but the problem is that tribes are not in the bureaucratic loop. The agencies do want the tribes to be there, but for the Indian representative, it is not a comfortable place. The agency people are vocal, and if there is a big group, the Indian gets lost. If one or two Indians use the program, the agency assumes there is no problem. However, there may be many other Indians who have rejected the service because they did not feel comfortable or welcome. It then becomes the Indian's fault for not participating and they become the ones to blame."[10]

Tribal Social Service Programs

All the reservations have their own social service programs, primarily providing children's services. (See ICWA programs, at the end of this chapter.) Each tribe sets its own employment standards, ranging from those with Master's of Social Work degrees to paraprofessionals. Most tribes administer domestic abuse, mental health, and chemical dependency programs.

In addition to the Indian Family Preservation Act funding, the BIA provides funding for children's services and to help with the Indian Child Welfare Act. The tribes also use some of their own funds to provide emergency assistance, as well as programming for elders and children.

The Minnesota Chippewa Tribe (MCT) social service program is the contact point for identifying Indian children in need of services and referring them to the proper tribe. Urban workers help tribal members in child protection cases. Other programs include those for Indian elders, employment, education, child care, chemical dependency, and youth projects. The six individual tribes that make up the MCT vary in which programs the MCT administers for them and which ones they contract for and run independently.

The Fond du Lac Tribe is unique in that it serves not only Indians on the reservation and in Carlton County but also in southern St. Louis County and in Duluth. Fond du Lac operates a full range of medical and social services, offering several approaches to strengthening families and working with children. The tribe offers support groups for chemical dependency, anger control, grief and loss, gambling addiction, foster parenting, dealing with fetal alcohol syndrome, and diabetes.

The Red Lake Tribe and Beltrami and Clearwater counties provide children's services on the reservation. The state, recognizing the excessive financial burden this might impose on these two counties, provides supplemental funds, and the BIA helps fund child protection workers. The tribe has several people working on child protection, family preservation, and foster care.

Other Assistance Programs

Food

More Indians use Food Support than any other income assistance programs. In February 2003, 18,500 Indians were in the program, 6.3 percent of the total participants in the state. Based on the estimated Indian

population in Minnesota in 2000, almost one-third of Indians in the
state were using Food Support.[11]

The federal Commodity Distribution Program (7 U.S.C. 612c),
administered by the U.S. Department of Agriculture, specifically authorized the program for Indians and directed that the variety and
quantity of commodities supplied to Indians be improved to provide
a more nutritious diet. (The health aspects of the program are discussed in Chapter 12.) To many Indians, the commodity program offers more benefits than using Food Support. The program has strong,
political support. While the qualifying income level is at 100 percent
of poverty, in contrast with 130 percent for food support, other more
lenient standards allow families with higher income levels to qualify.
Once the family has qualified, the full monthly food package is available, while with Food Support the benefits diminish as income level
rises. The extensive list of food is accessible on the reservation; in contrast, grocery stores willing to accept food stamps are often a long
drive from the reservation. In addition, administering the commodity
program adds employment opportunities for tribes. Only the Dakota
communities no longer offer the commodities program, since member per capita payments have raised incomes above the poverty level.
In fall 2001, approximately 2,500 Indians participated in this program
on the Ojibwe reservations.[12]

The food shelf program offered at Little Earth in Minneapolis is
designed to help people within a designated community. Use is limited
to once a month, the food generally lasting a family one week or less.
In Minneapolis, the Division of Indian Work (DIW) provides a food
shelf that in 2002 fed 23,450 American Indian people, 12,455 of whom
were children. According to DIW Executive Director Noya Woodrich,
the food shelf usage grew by 105 percent from 2001 to 2002.[13] In
St. Paul, the Department of Indian Work provides food shelf and
clothing assistance. In collaboration with the Episcopal Church and
Mazakute Memorial Mission, they also serve nearly 1,000 households
annually with food and clothing.

Energy

The Energy Assistance Program, administered by the tribes or Community Action Agencies, helps approximately 25 percent of the state's
Indian population cover the costs of heating. The seven Ojibwe,

Prairie Island, and Upper and Lower Sioux reservations each have the program.[14] Funding uncertainties beginning in 1995 and continuing today have resulted in a sharp decline of applicants for the program.

The Weatherization Program operates in a similar fashion to fund insulation and repairs that reduce fuel costs. However, of the federal funds coming to Minnesota, only 2 percent have been used for reservation programs. In 2003, the Department of Energy funded eighty-six American Indian households, both on and off the reservation.[15]

Homelessness and Emergency Needs

As of late 2000, American Indian adults made up 10.5 percent of the Minnesota homeless population, and American Indian youth made up 20 percent of the homeless youth population. Both figures are far in excess of their percentage of the total population.[16]

A worker with Indian people in the inner city of Minneapolis commented, "These are families on the brink. They are just barely coping and then something comes up and they get pushed over. They have become a permanent underclass. They either do not qualify for general assistance or have exceeded the program's limit. They may try the shelters, but these run out of space. They may be put in a hotel, but this is limited to a very short stay. The families are expected to quickly solve their problems, which is often unrealistic."[17]

Domestic Violence and Sexual Abuse

People working in the field of abuse and neglect report that Indians, in dealing with their past victimization and uncertain futures, sometimes direct their anger at those closest to them, resulting in abuse of family members. Indian leaders agree that a large percentage of Indian families have had some history of family violence including child abuse or neglect, sexual abuse, and/or battering. As Indian researcher and educational expert Dr. Tom Peacock of the University of Minnesota–Duluth commented, "The wounds inflicted on Indian families in the past continue to be passed on to the young ones."[18]

Major legislation (Indian Child Protection and Family Violence Prevention (Pub. L. 101-630)), passed in 1990, was intended to deal with reservation child abuse and provide for reporting of abuse, checking backgrounds of people working with children, and helping with treatment. The Act led to the Domestic and Child Abuse Initiative in 1996, to more directly address abuse and neglect against American Indian women and children. The focus is on improving health care providers' capability to identify and respond to violence in culturally appropriate ways.

Battered Women

Female Indian victims are often without adequate protection, emotional support, information, and legal resources. Some have chemical dependency problems. Obtaining help may mean getting another Indian into trouble with white authorities. Indian women are also fearful of finding racism, insensitivity, and misunderstanding in the public-supported, non-Indian focused shelters. Many also fear having their children taken away.

For reservation women in a rural setting, shelters and services often are not available, and the individual who has no resources must leave the community. In urban centers, there are more programs available, but there are crucial gaps in services, programming, and housing options.

Child Abuse

Neglect and abuse of Indian children are very serious problems. In 2001, there were 683 confirmed maltreatment cases of American Indian youth in the state. While this reflects a drop from the 2000 statistic of 827 cases, it still represents 7 percent of all cases in Minnesota, a significant overrepresentation of American Indians. American Indians represented 33.1 per 1,000 cases compared to white youth, who make up 4.7 per 1,000 cases. Only African-American children have a higher rate.[19]

Programs

According to most social workers, family abuse is a very sensitive issue within the Indian communities, but there is growing realization that the problem exists. The tribes are dealing with these issues with more training of Indian social workers and Indian school personnel, through strengthening tribal codes and ordinances, and with increases in services to help children who have been abused.

Numerous programs both on and off reservations have emerged to deal with abuse and neglect. For example, Mending the Sacred Hoop, an Indian program in Duluth not associated with any tribe, provides training nationwide to tribal government personnel on how to curb domestic violence against women. It also offers a local criminal justice intervention program.

Over the past decade, the MCT, Bois Forte, Fond du Lac, and Leech Lake Reservations have received grants to educate reservation, school, and county social service staff about identifying child sexual abuse and supporting victims. On Wings of an Eagle is an independently operated crisis shelter on the White Earth Reservation. The Evergreen House similarly serves the Bemidji area. Ain Dah Yung (Our Home Shelter) in St. Paul provides the only Indian-operated shelter for Indian youth in the metropolitan area.

On the Fond du Lac Reservation, the Min No Wii Jii Win House provides services to victims in a relaxed, homelike atmosphere. In 1997, Red Lake Reservation's Women's Advocacy Program began with a sixteen-bed shelter. White Earth Healing Families Sexual Assault Program is an Indian-run, multilevel program, helping to provide the basic needs of food and shelter while providing support in dealing with oppression, economic problems, and victimization.

Eagle's Nest, a culturally supportive women's shelter in St. Paul, opened in 1991 as one of the first Indian-run shelters in Minnesota. The facility serves hundreds of women and children with thirty full-time and twenty-five part-time employees.

The Division of Indian Work in Minneapolis provides Indian-focused domestic abuse programming, with counseling, legal advocacy, support groups for the victims of domestic violence, including children and the violent partner, and assistance with filing for court protection orders. The Resident Association of Little Earth housing complex offers a broad variety of education, support, and assistance programs, including family counseling, conflict resolution, and early intervention.

Indian Elders

The 2000 U.S. Census documented that 3,600 Indians in Minnesota, approximately 6.5 percent of the Indian population, were sixty years or older. Indian elders are most apt to live on reservations. Their small numbers and scattered locations make programming a major problem in the metropolitan area.[20]

Indian elders face many difficulties. The 2000 U.S. Census reported that nearly 18 percent of their households had incomes below poverty. They have difficulties with daily living tasks, such as preparing meals, shopping, doing housework, and obtaining transportation.

Historically, the role of Indian elders has been advisory as keepers of the Indian traditions and history. Respect and honoring of elders and their role in family life is often not understood nor incorporated into programs run by service agencies.

In 1984, the Minnesota Indian Council of Elders was begun to help coordinate and give greater voice to Indian elders. In 1991, state legislation authorized the Indian Elder Services Task Force to make recommendations on how to improve Indians' access to services. Barriers the Task Force identified included:

❏ Many Indian elders live in isolation and are unaware of available services.

❏ The use of programs is seen as complicated and often intimidating; there is a lack of trust.

❏ Many Indians do not feel comfortable receiving services from white providers. They often feel like outsiders at congregate dining programs, and no efforts are made to provide their traditional foods.

❏ There is need for more transportation and areas to congregate.

❏ In areas such as the Phillips neighborhood in Minneapolis, the elderly are hesitant, even fearful, of going out to existing programs.

There are too few acceptable housing choices for elders in urban areas. Indian elders have many problems with existing senior housing facilities. According to Betty Greencrow, an Indian social worker in St. Paul, "Elders will not go to public elder high-rise housing. They are considered unworthy and unsafe. They want to be close to the earth. And the rules are unacceptable. They can't have family and young people with them, which is opposite to their culture where extended families are welcomed and Indian elders frequently raise their grand-children. So the elders have remained with the families to take care of them. The families are busy and the elders live in isolation, dealing with their problems alone."[21]

The Minnesota Indian Council of Elders consists of representatives from the eleven reservations and the three urban areas. In response to their advocacy, the 1995 state legislature established a position of Indian Elder Specialist at the Minnesota Board of Aging to represent and work with the Indian communities. The Council has an Indian Elder Desk that offers support in a variety of areas, including access to and enrollment in health programs.

The federal Older Americans Act, under the U.S. Department of Health and Human Services and supplemented by state money, funds several programs for the elderly. Tribes may receive funding directly from Washington (Title VI), as do the Fond du Lac, Mille Lacs, and Red Lake Nations and specific programs on Leech Lake and White Earth Reservations. The Minnesota Board on Aging (Minn. Stat. 256.975) allocates federal and state funding to regional Area Agencies on Aging, which in Minnesota channels the programs to the Bois Forte, Grand Portage, Leech Lake, and White Earth Reservations. Elders in the Dakota Communities, Twin Cities, and Duluth are served by the state's area agencies in their regions.

The federal law provides for services, including transportation, for homebound and elders with disabilities. It also funds nutrition programs (Title III C) that provide congregate dining and home-delivered meals. The U.S. Department of Agriculture provides either commodities or cash, and the state supplements the home-delivered meals funding. The congregate dining program is usually a noon meal, five days per week, with social activities often included. The program may also include transportation, outreach, information and referral, advocacy, and other supportive services.

The federal act also provides assistance for those fifty-five years and older who want to reenter the employment market through the Senior Community Services Employment program. Part-time employment of twenty hours per week is provided through sixteen positions on the six MCT reservations.

All the Ojibwe reservations have congregate dining, provide social services, and support elders' activities. Fond du Lac and White Earth Reservations have housing complexes for the elderly, and Red Lake has the state's only Indian-run, Indian-focused nursing home, with forty-seven beds. Many communities have elders' centers. Grand

Portage, Bois Forte, and Mille Lacs have built facilities for dining and social activities into their new community centers. At Red Lake, the elders have their own building by the lake. In the Leech Lake Reservation community of Onigam, the elders raised money to remodel a building for the Gi-Tee-Zee Center, which serves elders.

The congregate dining program in Cass Lake is operated by the MCT for the whole community, including equal attendance from elders of the Indian and white communities. White Earth Reservation provides community dining and transportation in five communities, as well as home delivery of meals and commodities. Red Lake has two congregate dining sites, home-delivered meals, programming for the elderly, outings, home health services, and transportation. In the Dakota Communities, such as Prairie Island, tribes have elder dining programs at casinos.

The Minneapolis American Indian Center has the major Indian congregate dining program in the Twin Cities, operated by the Volunteers of America. Indian Family Services (IFS) in Minneapolis provides outreach, homemakers' services, transportation, social activities, and a health clinic. IFS also offers programming for Indian elders with disabilities. The Leech Lake Tribe funds a program of social activities for elders in the Twin Cities, operating out of its tribal urban office.

Beginning in 1986, the St. Paul Indian community sought to honor their elders and help them in their isolation by building an Indian-focused elders housing project. After many years of planning, the $2.9 million project was accepted for funding by HUD and was opened in 1997. Elder Lodge has forty-two one-bedroom apartments in a circle of life design; within the circle is a community activity area with trees and natural landscaping. Residents are sixty-two years or older, and have an income that is 125 percent of poverty or lower. Congregate dining, transportation, home chore, and social programs are located at the project.

Burial Assistance

A transportation service to return bodies to reservation homes up to four hundred miles away is provided in the Twin Cities communities. The program, *Miigeweyon* (I am going home), operates with volunteer drivers and is provided at no charge. It is administered through the Office of Indian Ministry of the Catholic Archdiocese located in

Minneapolis. *Miigeweyon* also provides space for wakes and memorials, assistance with caskets, food for wakes and funerals, and help with funeral notices. In addition, the Leech Lake Tribe provides burial insurance for all members regardless of residency, funded by casino profits. The Indian Burial Assistance program also provides low-cost casket and headstones, as well as transportation funds.

Children and Families

Many Indian children are at risk, facing the effects of poverty, child abuse, neglect, low birth weight, and premature births. Many are born to young mothers who lack parenting skills, and many face out-of-home placement. According to the 2000 U.S. Census, over 65 percent of Minnesota Indian children lived 185 percent below the poverty line in 2000. Indian youth show much greater use of alcohol, drugs, and tobacco (see chapter 12).

Funding to help Indian families and children comes from many sources: federal, state, county, city, school district, tribal, foundations, and charities. Many agencies volunteered that there is too much fragmentation and a need to simplify and coordinate programs. Tribes also face difficulties in delivering human services efficiently. Given the complex and confusing web of programs, it has been difficult to track whether and to what extent the needs of Indians are being met.

Promoting resiliency has become the focus of many programs. Specifically, effective programs have focused on strengthening the parent-child relationship; building self-esteem with rewards and positive feedback; increasing knowledge and appreciation of Indian culture; providing positive role models; and, if necessary, offering culturally sensitive intervention.

Increasingly, Indians agree that they must look to the old ways for answers as they address the problems of the future. They urge using such techniques as involving the extended family, sharing child-rearing responsibilities, valuing children as gifts to the entire community, and respecting the wisdom of elders.

Programs to Strengthen Indian Families

Help with parenting skills for expectant mothers and families with young children is available to most Indian communities through

regular social services, health programs, and Head Start, which
requires parental participation. The reservations receive Early Childhood Family Education through school districts or tribal schools.
Through schools, the state offers the Early Childhood Special Education program to help identify children with disabilities at an early age
and arrange for necessary assistance.

Twin Cities Healthy Start, a federally funded program administered by the Minneapolis Department of Health and Family Support,
works with Indian mothers in Minneapolis and St. Paul to reduce
infant mortality in the American Indian community, which has the
highest infant mortality of all racial groups (see chapter 12). The program provides home visits, connections with social service agencies,
and help in obtaining health care and insurance.

Because of the need to provide positive Indian child-rearing
images, the state Adult Indian Education program in Duluth prepared
the publication *Positive Indian Parenting* in 1992 and developed a program for parents that focuses on traditional Indian values and
strengths. Workshops to train individuals have helped to take the program back to many communities. The Nawayee School in Minneapolis
offers a class based on the findings from this book.

Several programs in urban areas focus on strengthening Indian
families. In 2002, the Hennepin County Board established the American
Indian Families Project (AIFP) at the request of the Indian community and the Metropolitan Urban Indian Directors. The program's
mission, according to Project Director Justin Huenemann, "is based
on the premise that solutions rest within the strengths and assets of the
American Indian community itself." Through research and collaboration with more than fifty organizations, the AIFP strives to improve the
quality of life for Indian families in Hennepin County.

The DIW has a Teen Indian Parents Program, which works with
pregnant teenaged girls throughout their pregnancy to develop
health and parenting skills. Program results show that 90 to100 percent of the babies are born healthy and remain in good health
through the first year of life. Ninety-five percent of the girls do not get
pregnant again in their teenage years. The DIW also offers a group to
help Indian fathers improve relationships with their children.

Running Wolf Fitness Center has partnered with the Indian
Health Board, AIFP and the Mille Lacs Band of Ojibwe to strengthen
the health of Indian families.

In St. Paul, the American Indian Family Center offers pre- and postnatal support programs, as well as mental health services. The Department of Indian Work of the St. Paul Area Council of Churches operates a family aide program to help in child neglect situations referred by Ramsey County Human Services. In Minneapolis, the Minnesota Indian Women's Resource Center offers several programs, including day care for children of women in treatment and alternative response systems for those at risk for further involvement with child protection.

Youth Activities

The reservations have youth programs to provide sports, cultural and spiritual experiences, education, and other activities to encourage healthy lives. The details and funding sources vary by reservations, with the tribes and casinos often providing major support. Several tribes have built community centers that are staffed and provide organized programs for all ages.

Fond du Lac Reservation offers a continuum of programs for children, ranging from weekly meetings with constructive activities to discussions on drug and alcohol use to help in building decision-making skills. The Tribe operates a camp in northern Minnesota and has helped the community of Brookston establish a youth center.

Grand Portage organized a summer mentorship program in the late 1990s, linking youth with employees on a one-to-one basis to gain experience through work at the health clinic, education office, community center, in forestry, and in the office at Grand Portage Lodge.

Shakopee Mdewakanton offers tribally sponsored youth programs, including after-school programs, tutoring, field trips, and summer youth work, culture, and art programs.

In Minneapolis, several Indian youth programs operate outside of the schools. Ginew/Golden Eagle is an after-school youth development program serving more than four hundred youth, ages five to eighteen, annually out of the Minneapolis American Indian Center. The program focuses on building academic success, attachment to Indian ways, and healthy lifestyles. There is also a component of the program to work with youth who have completed treatment programs for chemical abuse.

MIGIZI began with radio broadcasting in 1977 and has since added educational programs to its services. In addition to operating Native

Academy, MIGIZI offers internships and programs stressing healthy living for students after school and in the summer (see chapter 10).

The DIW has a tutoring program for Indian children in elementary school, working one-on-one with a child for a whole semester in an after-school program. The volunteers come from the universities and adolescent groups. Reports in recent years show that over 60 percent have improved their grades and school attendance. Besides academic help, the DIW provides after-school cultural activities and summer camping.[22]

Elaine M. Stately Peacemakers Center is housed in a Minneapolis park building. It provides a recreational center and a safe haven for inner-city Indian youth. The program, a partnership of MIGIZI Communications, the AIM Patrol, and the Legal Rights Center, provides a quiet place to do homework and participate in, sports, games, and cultural activities.

The Little Earth housing complex, with nearly four hundred resident children, offers sports and recreational programs, a drum and dance group, and other youth activities. They have a drop-in center and a staffed education center with computers and media materials. A cultural coordinator works with the youth. Outside groups, such as Youth Care, also offer programs through Little Earth.

Programs for Indian youth in St. Paul have been offered by Earth Star through an intergenerational program to learn from elders, with sports activities, a garden project, and scouting through the American Indian Scouting Association. The St. Paul School District offers a summer camp for youth to provide an Indian cultural experience with elders, and the Amherst Wilder Foundation offers an elder-youth, weeklong camping experience for Indian youth ages ten to eighteen.

First Call for Help was created to assist people in accessing the complex array of social programs in the Twin Cities. Healthy Nations in Minneapolis operates the American Indian Resource Help Line, serving a similar purpose for Indians.

Indian Child Welfare Act (ICWA)

For many years, large numbers of Indian children were taken from their parents and placed in boarding schools, often not returning home for years. This separation was made for the "benefit" of the child and to "civilize" the race; parents were often viewed as unsuitable to raise their own children. In recent decades, Indian children were placed in white foster care or adoptive homes for their "own good" or until a "better" environment could be provided.

Before the passage of the Indian Child Welfare Act in 1978, white systems and white personnel often applied cultural values and social norms inappropriately to Indian life to remove children from their parents. Poverty, poor housing, lack of modern plumbing, and overcrowding were used as proof of parental neglect. Child-rearing practices of another culture were misinterpreted as neglect or letting the child "run wild." Whereas abuse of alcohol by a parent was one of the most frequently advanced grounds for removing children, this standard was rarely applied to non-Indians. Parental rights were often terminated without due process and true understanding. The children involved were denied their rights to tribal membership and an Indian heritage.

Minority children who came into the child protection system were placed in white homes.[23] The adoption rate of Indian children was eight times that of non-Indian children. Approximately 90 percent of Indian placements were in non-Indian homes.[24] The program to actively promote cross-racial adoptions ended in the late 1970s, when Indians and other minorities raised strong objections.

In 1978, Congress passed the Indian Child Welfare Act (Pub. L. 95-608, 25 U.S.C. 1901–1963) to end the abuses by giving tribes the opportunity to control what happened to Indian children. The act states, "no . . . resource is more vital to the continued existence and integrity of Indian tribes than their children." A national evaluation of ICWA after ten years showed that "in less than a decade after ICWA's passage, Indian tribes achieved substantial control over foster care and adoptive placement of Indian children."[25] Nearly all adoption of Indian children had stopped, and placement in foster homes had greatly decreased. Minnesota's adoptions declined from 8.13 Indian children per 1,000 Indian population in 1975, the second highest rate in the country, to 0.67 per 1,000 by 1988, a 92 percent decline. During the same decade, Minnesota's foster care rate declined 66 percent from 58.16 Indian children per 1,000 to 19.67 per 1,000.[26]

ICWA and Minnesota Indian Family Preservation Act[27]

Indian children in Minnesota came under ICWA in 1978. In 1987, the state took the federal law, strengthened it, and made it a state law: the Minnesota Indian Family Preservation Act (MIFPA)

(Minn. Stat. 257.35). Minnesota remains the only state to have done this. Where the state law imposes higher standards, those requirements must be followed.

Federal law deals with all Indian children up to age eighteen who are members of federally recognized tribes or are eligible for membership and who are biological children of members when they are subject to removal from their homes (in cases of abuse and neglect, placement in foster care, termination of parental rights, and adoption). It does not apply to divorce or juvenile delinquency proceedings. State law only requires eligibility for membership, the tribe having sole authority to define membership.

On reservations, generally tribal social workers handle child welfare cases, doing intake, acting as case managers, licensing foster care homes, supervising placement, and, in case of adoptions, doing home studies. Where the tribe has a fully operating tribal court, such as on Red Lake, Bois Forte, and Mille Lacs Reservations, that court may take responsibility for the children. Tribes that have contracted the power to administer their own child protection programs as a part of self-governance, such as White Earth and Leech Lake, provide the same services, with state courts handling legal procedures. The Dakota Community courts deal with children's issues.

In cases originating in the counties, tribal officials must be notified and have the right to participate from the time of the first hearing through the final decision. The tribes have concurrent jurisdiction, and they can intervene at any point in the state proceedings. The law provides that in most instances cases can be transferred to tribal courts. In 2003, amendments made to the state statutes enabled tribal courts to make adoptive placements for children in their jurisdiction, without termination of parental rights of the child's birth parents. This maintains the child's cultural heritage and permits the child to be raised in a permanent family.[28] There is increasing pressure from counties for the tribes to take jurisdiction. While the tribes want to exercise this authority, they do not have the financial resources to fund a full child protection and child placement system. In cases arising in the Twin Cities, tribes accept very few transfers.

The intake worker is responsible for identifying a child as Indian. If there is the possibility that the child might be removed from the home at any stage in the process, the tribe is to be notified. While the federal law does not specifically deal with voluntary placements or adoptions, state law requires notification of the tribe before making any removal decision. If the tribe is not known, the BIA is responsible for locating and notifying the tribe and the parent. The BIA Agency Office, the administrative level closest to the tribe, handles ICWA referrals. The MCT processes the cases of its members and then transfers them to the individual tribe.

The law requires that active efforts must be made to help the family avoid removal of the child. To place the child in foster care requires clear and convincing evidence. To terminate Indian parents' rights, there must be proof beyond a reasonable doubt that the action is necessary. These requirements are all legally more stringent than for the general population. The testimony of a qualified expert witness, approved by the tribe, is required before removing a child. Foster care and adoption placements must follow a sequence of preferences: The first choice is in the child's immediate family; second is the child's extended family; third is a member of the child's tribe; fourth is with a member of any other tribe; and the final choice is with a non-Indian family. Social service agencies are responsible for locating extended family members in both voluntary and involuntary cases. Approval of placement decisions rests with the tribe, and in cases of voluntary placements, the tribe can overrule the wishes of parents.

Minnesota Heritage Act

In 1994, federal legislation (Pub. L. 103-392) made it illegal to consider race in placement decisions, which would have nullified the state law. The state asked to be exempted, and federal legislation allowed states to consider race as long as it did not delay placement.

Minnesota law (Minn. Stat. 259.29, 260C.193, 260C.212, subd. 2;) stipulates that religious and cultural needs be considered in making placements that are in the child's best interest. Children eligible for the ICWA law are excluded from this Act; however, these laws are important to Indian children who do not meet the federal "Indian" standard of being enrolled or eligible for enrollment.

Tribal–State Agreements

In 1998, the state and the tribes entered into an agreement that outlined a process for implementing the ICWA. The main objective was to draft a step-by-step procedural manual to ensure that county social services and court personnel follow the laws. In addition to clearly defining responsibilities, it is intended to ensure that Indians are included as a part of the decision-making process; under available funding resources, the state will purchase services from the tribe; the state must extend full faith and credit to tribal courts; tribes are required to provide information on a timely basis; the cultural experts who are required to testify before a child can be removed are to come from a list acceptable to the tribe; and a yearly evaluation is to be done jointly between the tribes and the state on how the Act is working. The agreement also required the formation of a Compliance Review Team, whose overall function is to monitor county compliance with ICWA and make recommendations regarding best social work practices for working with tribes.[29]

ICWA Legal Challenges

The Minnesota Supreme Court upheld the importance of placing Indian children in tribally approved circumstances with *In the Matter of the Custody of S.E.G.* (521 N.W.2d 357 (Minn. 1994), appeal to the U.S. Supreme Court denied). In reversing the lower courts, the court said that a child's need for stability and permanence are not more important than other factors.

Some state court decisions are imposing on the ICWA their own standard of what constitutes an "existing Indian family." The protections of the law are being denied in cases where the courts ruled that because Indians were not living in an Indian home or in a state-defined Indian way they were not to be considered Indian. The U.S. Supreme Court has not yet reviewed these cases.

In the past few years, several amendments to the ICWA have been proposed in both the U.S. House of Representatives and Senate, some with the support of tribes and others greatly opposed by Indians. To date, none of the amendments has passed, including one serious challenge that would have denied rights to parents who had not maintained "significant social, cultural or political affiliation with the tribe," while leaving open to state courts to define what constitutes "significant." The most recent amendment, which many Indians still hope will be adopted, was proposed by the National Congress of American Indians (NCAI) to protect Indian children and families and formalize a substantial role for Indian tribes in cases involving child custody proceedings, while ensuring fairness and swift action in custody and adoption cases involving Indian children. The National Indian Child Welfare Association and the American Psychological Association support this bill.[30]

If prior enrollment were to be imposed as a requirement for ICWA coverage, it would have grave consequences for the effectiveness of the law. For example, in Hennepin County courts, of over 1,500 Indian children involved in child protection cases over a recent two and one-half year period, only 16 percent had actually been enrolled, while an additional 80 percent were eligible for enrollment and came under the Act.

Procedural Requirements

Child protection laws require many procedural steps; ICWA adds several additional requirements if there is the possibility that the child might be removed from the home. When the child enters the system, a case plan is to be prepared within thirty days detailing the steps to be taken. Indians are critical of this process because the plans are often made without Indian input, since county social service departments frequently do not have Indian employees. The plan becomes the basis for a quarterly review of the case, and noncompliance can mean removal of the child.

A state law passed in 1993 requires a permanent solution within twelve months (six months for children less than eight years of age) when a child is removed from the home. This can be extended six months if the court explains why the extension is in the child's best interest. The twelve-month limit is not realistic for parents in many Indian cases. If the problem is chemical dependency, it is usually a matter of years before the needed changes can be made. Permanent solutions for the child include being returned to the parents, having a relative assume guardianship, being adopted, or being put in long-term permanent placement if the child is twelve years or older. As tribes are usually unwilling to terminate parental rights in most cases, it is not clear how state policies deal with the Indian children under age twelve who continue to require child protective services in excess of the eighteen months.

Tribal Involvement

In addition to making decisions about how and if the tribe should be involved, tribes can identify members, gather background information about the situation, locate extended family, supervise out-of-home placements, and work with the parent and child in prevention and reunification efforts. The MCT has one child adoption and two child protection workers dealing with Twin Cities and southern Minnesota cases; the Mille Lacs Tribe has its own staff responsible for Twin Cities and Duluth cases; the Red Lake Tribe has a staff of two in the Twin Cities and an off-reservation person to work in the northern counties. Tribes also receive notices about their members throughout the country, but lack of financial resources often hinders their ability to assist in these out-of-state cases.

Parties Involved

In ICWA cases several parties may be involved in the court sessions, including a social worker and attorney from the county, parents, the child if he or she is twelve years or older, tribal advocates, a guardian *ad litem* appointed to represent the child's best interests, and often a public defender serving as attorney for the parent. Many Indians involved professionally with the court process feel that the public defenders generally do not understand the laws, which limits their effectiveness in representing Indian clients. Many have turned to the Indian Child Welfare Law Center, founded in 1993 by the American Indian Attorney Association of Minnesota to improve legal representation in ICWA cases. With funding provided by state legislation, the Public Defender Program, and foundations, the Center enables low-income people involved in child protection proceedings to have Indian legal representation.

The guardian *ad litem* is required by law to be appointed in all cases of removing a child from the home and terminating parental rights (Minn. Stat. 260.155 subd. 4). The counties vary in how the program operates. In some instances, they are paid. Some have legal training, but most have limited understanding of Indian culture. Very few of the guardians *ad litem* are Indians themselves. While the law mandates a guardian *ad litem* in all cases, in reality this does not happen.

There is a basic conflict between the purpose of the guardian *ad litem* and ICWA legislation. The guardians are to represent children at their present time in life, while one of the purposes of ICWA is to allow children the opportunity to be brought up within Indian culture. At the young age many children come into court, they are not able to judge the importance of this culture and as a result may be denied the opportunity to have an Indian future. A legal services attorney testified to a task force investigating racial bias in the Minnesota judiciary system in the early 1990s, "Guardians *ad litem* have demonstrated, in most of the ICWA cases I have worked with, hostility toward Indian families which results in recommendations contrary to the spirit and letter of the law."[31] While Indian leaders cite some improvements over the last decade, there is still a gap in cultural understanding on the part of many non-Indians in the legal system.

State legislation created the position of Indian Ombudsman (Minn. Stat. 257.0755–.0769) to help people deal with problems they may have had in child protection and placement services. The program works with the Minnesota Indian Affairs Council and has an Indian community board to advise the program.

Placement Options

Increasingly, out-of-home placements are with a relative. Relatives can qualify to receive payment as a foster care home if they go through the process of becoming a licensed care home. Licensure requires meeting the county standards and takes three to four months of training. Outside of the bureaucratic difficulties, Indians have two other problems with current policies regulating placements with relatives: One is the financial burden it places on families; the other is that regulations designed to force speedy permanent solutions for the child make it difficult to work out family care.

The law's intent is to have out-of-home placement end within twelve months. The county pressures the family to assume legal guardianship, which provides the permanent solution. It also ends any support payments if the family had become a licensed foster care home. If the child is twelve or older, a permanent solution may be placement in a long-term foster care home. Policies, however, prevent relatives from serving as that home; it must be with a nonrelative. This usually means that the child ends up going into a non-Indian long-term foster care home, while an interested relative who is financially unable to take guardianship responsibilities is denied the child.

Most of the tribes are licensing foster homes under their own codes. Generally, they are similar to state requirements with the priority of protecting the children's interests. They may be more flexible in standards such as required square feet and number of bedrooms; they may be more stringent with other requirements, such as with the Bois Forte Tribe's requirement of two years of prior sobriety compared to the state's one year. The Leech Lake Tribe can license off-reservation homes. An independent Fond du Lac Foster Care Licensing and Placement Agency licenses homes in Duluth and is used by MCT to license homes elsewhere in the state. Two urban Indian agencies have been licensed by the state to recruit people, assist them in obtaining licensing, and monitor the operations of foster care homes. Counties and other foster home agencies also license Indian homes.

Counties set their priority on the most vulnerable children, namely infants to five-year-olds, with less attention being paid to children over fourteen years old. Annually, substantial numbers of children leave the child protection system at age eighteen without any services arranged for them.

New Approaches

In an effort to improve compliance with ICWA, Hennepin County designated a team of social workers to work just with Indian cases, enabling them to become more familiar with the laws. The tribal-authorized advocates are consulted on placement options. The initiative aims to provide a nonadversarial program that avoids removal of children. With a prior agreement to accept court intervention, the child can remain in the home and not be sent to a foster care home while the family receives needed services.

The Fond du Lac Foster Care Licensing and Placement Agency was established by the Fond du Lac Tribe as a nonprofit organization that contracts with the tribe's human services agency to provide programmatic and administrative services. With the establishment of the off-reservation placement agency, many Indian families stepped forward to be considered for licensure. In the last decade, the agency has helped assure that fewer Indian children in Minnesota grow up in non-Indian homes. The Agency has licensed fifty-eight off-reservation Indian homes since its inception; it has placed more than seventy children each year since 1995; and as of 2003, nearly 60 percent of the Indian children in out-of-home placements in St. Louis County were in Indian homes. The Band says its success is due to highly qualified employees and creating good working relationships with county social workers. The program won a 1999 Harvard Project Award.

Problems with ICWA

Since its passage in 1978, ICWA has been upheld by both the U.S. and Minnesota Supreme Courts. According to the Minnesota Department of Human Services, Child Safety and Permanency Division, "Although county social workers are experiencing greater exposure to ICWA and the Minnesota Indian Family Preservation Act requirements through training provided at the county and state level, many counties are still in the process of internalizing policies that enforce ICWA compliance."[32]

Indians point out that there are still few sanctions for failure to comply with ICWA. Very few Indians are employed as intake workers, causing concern in the Indian community that many Indian children are not being identified. Indians urge that counties with major Indian populations seek Indian staff who know the communities.

Many children do not qualify for ICWA. For example, in Hennepin County in 2000, 2001, and 2002, approximately 50 percent of American Indian children in out-of-home placement were eligible for the ICWA.[33] Indian children who do not have documentation are not protected by the Act. The Act also does not apply to Indians who are members of Canadian tribes. Minnesota Indians from the Canadian border region are very concerned about this because their extended families may be on either side of the border.

The ICWA requires communication and cooperation between professional representatives from Indian tribes and county professionals. Established systems have had to change, and the law has often been resisted or ignored. Some hold the false belief that other Minnesota laws supersede the ICWA and the Minnesota's Indian Child Preservation Act. Indian professionals report difficulties in gaining acceptance. As one director of tribal human services commented, "The county believed it had jurisdiction on the reservation and that the federal ICWA law did not apply. It has been a real struggle to get the county to recognize that we are a tribal government with a child protection team in place."[34]

The Minnesota Supreme Court Task Force on Racial Bias in the Judicial System in the mid-1990s reported testimony of noncompliance. "[T]here is clearly a great deal of hostility among some judges and court personnel as it related to Native American foster care placement. . . . There was greater noncompliance in cases involving Native Americans than other people of color." A legal services attorney testified, "[T]he misapplication or nonapplication of the ICWA (in

the state court system) is appalling. . . . [C]ounty workers are still culturally ignorant at best and racist at worst. . . . The courts are unpre-
dictable: some know and apply the laws, some don't. The courts are
sometimes less than respectful toward tribal representatives."[35] Unfortunately, these concerns are still present for Indians in the twenty-
first century.

The ICWA represents a different approach to dealing with human
needs. A professional review of the effectiveness of the legislation
stated, "ICWA stands as an anomaly in child welfare policy because it
is an apparently effective community-based policy surrounded by a
dominant culture that most values individualism and individual
autonomy."[36] This may cause philosophical problems for the social
worker, and it results in a loss of authority.

According to Esther Wattenberg from the University of Minnesota, "As tribal governments in Minnesota have increasingly
exercised their jurisdiction, there has been some uncertainty about
county responsibility for payment and services for children under the
jurisdiction of a tribal court. Issues on assessment of need, placement
decisions, availability of services, and placement costs are constantly
under review between counties and Tribal Family and Children's
Services.[37]

Several counties have good cooperation with tribes. The director
of Fond du Lac Tribe's social services stated that from the beginning
Carlton County has been willing to consider Indian needs and to
incorporate them into their county responsibility. For child protection, the tribe and the county comanage the cases. Mahnomen and
Cass Counties are also mentioned frequently as cooperative. Although
violations of the ICWA continue in Hennepin County, Indian moni-
tors note that procedures incorporating a commitment to the law have
improved dramatically.

As they face cuts in welfare budgets, counties are reviewing the
high costs of child protection services and out-of-home placements.
However, there is skepticism over the family preservation solution.
A professional working with Indian adolescents commented, "Is it
a good tool that they know is really helpful, or is it because budgets must be cut and it is a way to cut costs, but perhaps also harm
the child?"[38]

Many Indians still deeply distrust systems that were created with
little Indian input. Case plans and bureaucratic "red tape" may set

unreasonable expectations. Voluntary placements turn into involuntary ones; ongoing foster care is used to justify terminating parental rights. Once an Indian family is caught in the social service system, it is difficult to get free.

While Indians have concerns about the current child protection system, they know that out-of-home placement is necessary in some cases to protect the child. The director of the Indian Child Welfare Law Center stated, "We see a number of cases of children who are in imminent danger who aren't being removed from their homes."[39]

Many Indians believe that tribal courts should deal exclusively with cases involving Indian children. Yet tribal courts, lacking funding, are reluctant to assume the responsibilities. Stable funding for a child protection program is crucial for success. Indians need to be involved in designing and administering the programs so that they are better accepted by Indian communities.

Changes have been made. Placements with relatives and use of licensed Indian foster care homes have led to great improvements. Some tribes have strengthened codes to protect against abuse and to insure enforcement. Most reservations are working on expanded court capabilities, and some prevention and family preservation programs extend to the reservations.

Because counties and the courts have sometimes failed to follow ICWA, tribes have at times found it necessary to spend significant funds on identifying Indian children and seeing that the laws are followed. This marks a waste of very limited resources, but many Indians believe that without the expenditures there would be even poorer compliance.

Adoptions and Out-of-Home Placements

According to the 2000 U.S. Census, American Indian children were six times more likely to be adopted than white children relative to their proportion of the population. The incidence of adoption was 1.8 per 1,000 for American Indian children, compared to 0.29 per 1,000 for white children. Just over 10 percent (725 children) of all children in the Minnesota foster care system were American Indian. Of the children deemed "waiting children" (children who have a goal of adoption and/or whose parents' rights have been terminated), 8.4 percent (154 children) were American Indian.[40]

A major concern is for Indian children whose parents' rights have been terminated and who are under state guardianship and considered "free for adoption." These children include those with special needs who are waiting for a permanent situation.

In 2003, a legislative change was made that expanded the definition of an adoption agency to include federally recognized Indian tribes in Minnesota. This change enables children adopted through a tribal social service agency to be eligible for Adoption Assistance. All children in need of adoptive placements are on the State Adoption Exchange Web site. Adoption Assistance provides reimbursement for adoption studies of a specific child by agencies in other states. The Department of Human Services is able to contract with tribal social service agencies to assist in the adoption of American Indian children under state guardianship.

As of 2000, there were 1,903 Minnesota Indian children in out-of-home placements, a rate of 92.3 per one thousand and the highest rate for all population groups. These children represented 10 percent of the caseload.[41] Dr. John Red Horse, noted professor of social work and Dean of the College of Liberal Arts, University of Minnesota–Duluth, commented, "The number of Indian children involved just keeps growing. Minnesota is unbelievable . . . California with the second largest Indian population in the United States has rates far lower than in Minnesota."[42]

Summary

Indians in Minnesota remain a group with proportionately great needs. In category after category, government programs designed to help are not resolving the problems or adequately improving the lives of Indians. The1985 edition of *Indians in Minnesota* noted, "Until agencies realize that Indians must be involved meaningfully in the decision-making process and that there must be Indian outreach, sensitivity to Indian culture, willingness to modify bureaucratic procedures if necessary, and additional Indian staffing, the cost of Indian services will continue to rise but their effectiveness will not."[43] Unfortunately this conclusion remains true.

Marge Anderson, former chief executive of the Mille Lacs Band, speaking at the National Indian Family Preservation Conference in 1995, noted that, "We must be creative in preserving families. We must encourage young people to get married and stay married. . . . We must teach better child care to our young mothers. We must ensure that abuse is prevented and treated. Above all, we must be creative in instilling into our tribal members and their children a sense of self-esteem. Let them know they are survivors. Let them know they have the blood of warriors in their veins. Let them know that their generation must pick up the torch that is Indian culture and tradition and carry it into the 21st Century."[44]

Chapter 12

Health

Although Indians' health has improved greatly over the past two decades, significant disparities remain in causes of death and sickness between Minnesota's Indian population and the general population. Most tribes are now running their own health programs, with a major portion of the funding coming from the Indian Health Service (IHS), making culturally appropriate services available to tribal members. But government funding cuts have affected the quality and availability of health care for Indians, resulting in a failure to keep up with the health needs of the population.

Introduction of Diseases

Diseases introduced to the Indians by white Europeans devastated Indian communities. Diseases quickly spread from tribe to tribe, wiping out whole communities and leading to major changes in tribal territories far in advance of the actual presence of Europeans. Most notorious was the smallpox epidemic of 1781–1782, which spread from the upper Missouri River to northern Minnesota and the Red River Valley, killing one-half to three-fifths of the population.[1]

Alcoholism, unknown until white contact, added to health problems. As Indian health declined, the reservations' close proximity to white settlements raised concerns that disease would spread to them. The Meriam report of 1928 urged expanded federal programming: "Both the Indians and their white neighbors are concerned in having [Indians] live according to at least a minimum standard of health and decency. Less than that means not only that they may become a menace to the whites but also that they themselves will go through a long drawn out and painful process of vanishing. They must be aided for the preservation of themselves."[2]

Providing Health Care

Treaties often promised health care, and as with other services, the federal government initially did provide it with money due the Indians from the sale of their lands. The 1921 Snyder Act (25 U.S.C. 13) provided open-ended and permanent authorization for programs "for the benefit, care, and assistance of Indians," with funding appropriated by Congress. Indian health programs are not entitlements; their funding level is at the discretion of Congress.

Responsibility for Indian health services, first provided by the BIA, was transferred in 1954 to the Indian Health Service, U.S. Public Health Service, under what is now the Department of Health and Human Services (Pub. L. 83-568). The 1976 Indian Health Care Improvement Act (Pub. L. 94-437) expanded and clarified the law to authorize funding urban Indian programs (25 U.S.C. 1651). In 1988, funding was provided for alcohol and substance abuse treatment, allowing the IHS and tribes to receive third-party reimbursement for their services (Pub. L. 100-713). Comprehensive mental health programs were added in 1990.

Self-determination and self-governing laws gave the tribes the option of contracting to operate specific health programs, with the IHS continuing to administer and staff the remaining services. The federal government provides funding for both. The state has played a lesser role in providing health services to Indians than it has in areas such as education and welfare. As early as 1911, however, Minnesota was working with the state's Indians in controlling tuberculosis and trachoma (an eye disease causing permanent injury). In 1923, the state became the first in the nation to have a public health nursing program to work with Indians.

In the mid-1990s, major changes in funding for health and welfare programs forced changes in the responsibility for meeting Indian health needs. The IHS, tribal, and urban Indian programs now receive substantial payments from third-party billings such as Medicaid, Medicare, and private and worker's compensation insurance. However, medical costs have escalated, patient numbers have increased, and funding has not kept pace with need.

In 1976, Congress declared that it is the nation's policy, in fulfillment "of its special responsibilities and legal obligations to the American Indian people, to meet the national goal of providing the highest possible health status to Indians and to provide existing health services with all resources necessary to effect that policy" (Pub. L. 94-437, 25 U.S.C. 1602). Medical statistics indicate that a wide gap still exists between the health of Indians and that of the general population, and Congress has not provided the funding necessary to achieve the goal it set in 1976.

Vital Health Statistics

There have been tremendous improvements in Indian health, although significant disparities remain in causes of death and sickness between the state's Indian population and the general population. Diabetes, cardiovascular disease, suicides, and HIV/AIDS rates continue to be much higher for Indians in Minnesota than for the rest of the state's population.

Mortality

Overall mortality rates show that Indians ages fifteen to sixty-four years had death rates up to 3.5 times higher than those of whites. The leading factors in death are cardiovascular disease (20 percent), cancers (17 percent), motor vehicle and other accidents (15 percent), and diabetes (6 percent).[3]

Morbidity

Respiratory illnesses such as colds, bronchitis, asthma, influenza, pneumonia, and emphysema were the reasons for 13 percent of visits to IHS clinics and 11 percent of visits to the Minneapolis Indian Health Board (IHB) clinic. However, almost as many visits were for diabetes mellitus, a serious disease that significantly impacts Indians. Seeking medical help for hypertension ranked third in reasons for clinic visits. Cardiovascular disease remains a serious issue for Minnesota Indians, with American Indian death rates 33 percent higher than state general population figures and 44 percent higher than rates among the total U.S. American Indian population.[4]

Infant Mortality

In their first year of life, Minnesota's Indian babies die at a rate more than three times higher than that of whites. Deaths due to sudden infant death syndrome (SIDS) are three to five times the rate for whites. In 1998, the National Center for Health Statistics reported that this infant mortality rate was the highest among all states with large Indian populations. As a result, public health programs have put increasing emphasis on reducing infant mortality in Indian communities, especially in the metropolitan area, through such programs as Healthy Start and Back to Sleep.[5]

High-Risk Pregnancies and Births

Children of teenage mothers are at higher risk for poor prenatal and neonatal care, low birth weight, infant mortality, and living in poverty. The teen pregnancy rate for American Indian girls ages fifteen to seventeen in Minnesota fell during the 1990s, from 99.6 per 1,000 girls in 1992 to 75.9 in 2000. This rate is lower than rates for African-American and Hispanic girls, but much higher than the 15.0 per 1,000 for white girls. In 2000, American Indians in Minnesota ages eighteen to nineteen had the highest unintended pregnancy rate (177.6 per 1,000).[6]

Since 1990, the percent of low birth weight Indian babies (5.5 pounds or less) has risen from 6.1 to 7.3 percent while remaining the same or falling for all other minority groups. Prenatal care, considered a vital component of a healthy pregnancy, is a leading indicator for low birth weight, and far fewer Indian women receive such care. While eight out of ten white women receive first trimester prenatal care, the figure for American Indian women is only five out of ten.[7]

Table 12.1 Infant mortality in Minnesota (deaths per 1,000 births)

	1992	1995	2000
African-American	21.9	18.1	15.1
American Indian	17.4	16.5	14.4
White	6.6	6.5	5.1

Source: Minnesota Department of Health, Center for Health Statistics, 2000 Report to the Minnesota Legislature.

A majority of Indian children in the state are born to unmarried couples. In 1978–1980, 53 percent of the state's Indian children were born to unmarried women. By 1993–1995 this number had grown to 72 percent, and for mothers under 20, it was 95 percent. At the time of the 2000 U.S. Census, 37.3 percent of American Indian children lived in a household headed by a single mother, compared to 15 percent of other Minnesota children. Across the state, American Indian fathers made up the largest percentage of households headed by single parents, compared with other races. More than 10 percent of American Indian families are headed by single fathers, compared to 6.9 percent of Hispanic, 5.4 percent of African-American, and 4.6 percent of white households.[8]

Immunization Rates

Immunization against preventable diseases has a major role in reducing serious illnesses and death. However, in studies of kindergartners done by the Minnesota Department of Health (MDH), fewer than 50 percent of American Indian children were current with immunizations. Less than 50 percent of American Indian elders were vaccinated against pneumococcal disease.[9]

Disabilities

Over 12 percent of Indians in Minnesota noted some form of disability on the 2000 U.S. Census, slightly higher than the 11.6 percent figure for the total population. For disabilities that prevented working, the figure was 9.3 percent of Indians ages sixteen to sixty-four years, compared to 7.3 percent for the total population.[10]

While Indians have comparable or lower rates of genetic and congenital disabilities for which causes are unknown or difficult to prevent, Indians are at greater risk from preventable problems such as maternal diabetes, accidents, cigarette smoking, and prenatal exposure to alcohol.[11]

Causes of Death

Indians have the same two leading causes of death as Minnesota's general population: major cardiovascular disease and cancers. The other major causes of death reflect Indians' more severe problems, with

Table 12.2 Causes of death for Indians and whites
in Minnesota, 1997–2001

Cause	Indians Rates per 100,000 Population	Whites Rates per 100,000 Population
Heart Disease	246.2	183.9
Cancers	228.7	184.6
Diabetes	94.4	23.0
Cirrhosis	38.4	6.4
Influenza/pneumonia	26.9	21.0
Unintentional Injury	81.7	33.9
Suicide	19.1	9.1
Homicide	13.8	1.6

Source: "Populations of Color in Minnesota: Health Status Report Fall 2003,"
Center for Health Statistics, Minnesota Department of Health, 10.

motor vehicle accidents, diabetes, suicide, chronic liver disease, and homicide significantly higher for Indians than the rest of the population.

Health Issues of Youth

Suicide and Injury

American Indian males ages eighteen to ninteen have suicide rates six times higher than in any other age or population group.[12] Alarmingly, 16 percent of Indian sixth-graders in Minnesota reported that they attempted suicide in the past year, compared to 5 percent of other youth.[13] American Indians in Minnesota have rates of traumatic brain injury more than four times higher than that of the rest of the population.

Alcohol, Drugs, and Tobacco Use

Indian youth show much higher use of alcohol, drugs, and tobacco. Approximately one-half of ninth and twelfth grade Indian students reported having five or more alcoholic drinks on one occasion within the past month, and 16 percent of sixth grade Indians had at least one alcoholic drink during the same time period, compared to 9 percent of other youth. One-fifth of sixth grade Indians had smoked a cigarette within the past month, almost three times as many as other sixth-graders. By twelfth grade, 60 percent of Indians smoked, compared to 40 percent of other twelfth-graders. Fifty percent of ninth and twelfth grade Indian students had used marijuana in the preceding year, compared to 25 to 30 percent of other youth.[14]

Pregnancy Prevention for Teenage Girls

In a 2000 survey of ninth and twelfth graders in Minnesota, American Indian ninth-graders used contraceptives at a rate consistent with the overall population's use (45 percent), but twelfth grade American Indians used contraceptives at a rate (56 percent) lower than that of the overall population.[15]

The teenage birthrate has declined among American Indian girls ages fifteen to seventeen in Minnesota. While Indian teens are still twice as likely as whites to have children during their teen years, the Indian birthrate declined from 131 per 1,000 in 1993 to 102.5 per 1,000 in 2000.[16]

The IHS, IHB, and other community clinics offer family planning services. Special family planning projects have been funded for the Fond du Lac and Leech Lake Reservations. The Division of Indian Work in Minneapolis has a Teen Indian Parent Program that works with pregnant teen girls to build parenting skills and to keep them in school.

Special Health Issues

Diabetes

Type 2 diabetes, which typically occurs after age thirty, has grown to epidemic proportions within Indian communities. The disease can lead to infections requiring amputation, blindness, severe kidney damage, heart disease, and strokes. The prevalence of diabetes in Indians is almost three times higher than for whites.[17]

Diabetes develops among Indians at a younger age and progresses faster than in the general population. In 1985, the National Institutes of Health estimated that one-third of American Indians will develop type 2 diabetes by the age of thirty-five, attributing this directly to diet and obesity.[18] Indian leaders point out that today's poverty-driven diet of fast food contributes to this condition.

The Indian Health Care Improvement Act of 1978, § 204, set up a centralized program in IHS to provide surveillance and strategic help with diabetes (25 U.S.C. 1621c). A patient registry has become a useful tool for reservations to track and coordinate care for individuals with diabetes. Nutritionists and dietitians are available on all reservations and in urban Indian programs, and good foot care—vital for reducing the need for amputations related to diabetes—has been available on reservations since the late 1980s.

The Minnesota American Indian Diabetic Nephropathy Project is a combined effort of the Leech Lake and Red Lake Reservations, IHS, Hennepin County Medical Center (HCMC), and the University of Minnesota. The program uses aggressive interventions, including medications to control blood pressure, reduce cholesterol, and prevent kidney disease, as well as smoking cessation efforts. The American Diabetes Association, Minnesota Affiliate, funds a part-time Indian employee for the Minneapolis American Indian Center. The Red Lake Tribe's Million Miles Against Diabetes seeks to change lifestyles to fight diabetes.

Smoking

Indians smoke in much greater numbers than the general population, with the rate approximately three times the rate for all Minnesota adults. The Centers for Disease Control noted in 1999 and 2000 that 60.8 percent of Minnesota American Indians smoked, compared to 23.5 percent of Hispanics, 19.2 percent of whites, 15.9 percent of African-Americans, and 13.3 percent of Asians.

Because smoking is closely linked to cardiovascular disease, the leading cause of death for Indians, smoking cessation programs on reservations are increasing, funded by the state and the Centers for Disease Control. The Golden Eagles program at the Minneapolis American Indian Center has a Legal Eagles youth group that has done a compliance project checking on sales of tobacco to underage people.

Chemical Dependency

Fur traders introduced alcohol to Indians in Minnesota, using it to create loyalty and to build kinship-like ties. The use of alcohol and the disease of chemical dependency contributed to abuses in Indian–white relations and demeaning stereotypes. One of the most destructive aspects of this stereotyping is that alcohol is seen as Indians' biggest problem, allowing society to overlook the mistreatment of Indians throughout U.S. history.

Today, the abuse of alcohol contributes to a variety of persistent threats to Indians: death and injury, alcohol-related birth defects, unintended pregnancies and sexually transmitted diseases, crime, family violence, child abuse, fetal alcohol spectrum disorder (FASD), and the burden of continued chemical dependency problems. All have tremendous economic impacts on health care, social welfare, and criminal justice.

While enduring decades of abuse, displacement, racism, and broken promises, "Many of our people found comfort in alcohol," Indian leaders Priscilla Day and Thomas Peacock pointed out.[19] Today, among those whose parents, grandparents, and other family members had drinking problems, there is a high level of chemical abuse. Children may be fifth or sixth generation problem drinkers, and professionals working in Minnesota Indian communities assert that 95 percent of Indians are personally affected by chemical dependency.

Data from Minnesota's Drug and Alcohol Abuse Normative Evaluation System show that Indians use all forms of chemical dependency treatment at a greatly disproportionate rate to their numbers in the general population. American Indians constituted 9 percent of treatment admissions but were only 1 percent of the state population age eighteen and older and 2 percent age seventeen and younger.[20] Among Indian women, cirrhosis was the leading cause of death for ages twenty-five to forty-four and the third leading cause for ages forty-five to sixty-four.[21]

Despite these statistics, there are many positive signs of progress in ending chemical abuse within Indian communities:

❏ Tribal leaders speak openly and often about the negative effects of alcohol, and many tribes have committed themselves to paying 100 percent of treatment costs if other program funding is not available.

❏ Powwows forbid alcohol, and several casinos, including Mystic Lake Casino, Little Six Casino, and Grand Casino Mille Lacs, are alcohol-free.

❏ Economic improvement on the reservations has brought self-confidence and dignity, leading more Indians away from alcohol.

TREATMENT PROGRAMS   A continuum of chemical dependency services is available to Indians: prevention and education programs; intervention (referral) and advocacy; detoxification; primary treatment (either inpatient or outpatient); aftercare, which includes halfway houses that provide support in returning to the community; and support groups, such as Alcoholics Anonymous or Alanon (for family members).

The federal government funds prevention programs in public and tribal schools through the Drug Free Schools and Communities Act of 1986. Federal funds also go to the IHS, BIA, and Indian Housing and Urban Development (HUD) for chemical dependency programs serving Indians. The IHS provides some services on all the state's reservations, although funding is very limited. In addition, the federal governments funds adolescent group homes with treatment components for Fond du Lac, Leech Lake, and Red Lake Reservations, the Indian-administered primary treatment facility Mash-Ka-Wisen, and a program for Indian women in Cass Lake. Urban programs are funded through the IHB (Minneapolis), Juel Fairbanks programs (St. Paul), and the Fond du Lac Tribe's program in Duluth.

At the state level, the Department of Human Services targets American Indians through the Consolidated Chemical Dependency Treatment Fund (CCDTF), which pays for treatment for low income people through a combination of state, federal, and county funds. Rather than having treatment decisions driven by cost considerations, the CCDTF arranges for treatment best suited to the needs of the individual. This has been important to Indian people because it made it easier to use Indian-staffed treatment programs. In 2002, 1,288 Indians used the program on Minnesota reservations. For fiscal year 2002, the Minnesota legislature appropriated slightly more than $41 million for CCDTF and an additional $1 million for American Indian prevention, treatment, and support.[22]

The change to prepaid managed health care made treatment decisions for many Indians the responsibility of the HMOs, which have usually funded primary treatment and not halfway houses or extended care.

OTHER INDIAN-FOCUSED PROGRAMS   A recent study by the Minnesota Department of Health found that 71 percent of Indians were likely to abstain when in culturally specific programs, compared to 54 percent enrolled in traditional, general population programs. The research also showed that adolescents with a strong cultural identification were less vulnerable to risk factors for drug and alcohol use. In response in 2002, MDH allocated 6 percent of its chemical health budget for culturally specific prevention programs. MDH has provided approximately twenty prevention grants, with tribal and urban Indian communities using approaches built on tribal values and traditions. Services provided include access to medicine men and women, healing ceremonies and practices such as vision quests, sweat lodges, talking circles, making crafts and powwow regalia, drumming, and singing.[23]

Numerous programs to treat chemical dependency in Indians are offered both on and off reservations. All tribes have prevention and intervention programs, do assessments, and offer aftercare services. Tribes provide outpatient programs on all reservations except the Upper Sioux and Shakopee Mdewakanton Dakota Communities.

The Four Winds Lodge at Brainerd, a state-operated treatment program, offers Indian chemical dependency counselors and a culturally based program. Hennepin County has an Indian Chemical Dependency program providing a full range of counseling and case management services. This includes providing halfway houses for Indians.

Minneapolis programs include a youth chemical dependency program at the Minneapolis American Indian Center, American Indian Services, and Kateri Residence, a program for Indian women operated by the Church of St. Stephen. Fairview University Riverside Medical Center has a Native American Program with Indian staffing. In St. Paul, The Juel Fairbanks Aftercare Residence, Inc. provides a comprehensive rehabilitation program, and Ain Dah Yung, a youth shelter program in St. Paul, provides chemical dependency services.

In northern Minnesota, Duluth's programs include the Fond du Lac tribal services offered through their CAIR Center, Wren House for girls, Thunderbird House for boys, and Equaysayway, an outpatient treatment program for Indian women.

Mash-Ka-Wisen on the Fond du Lac Reservation was the nation's first Indian-owned, Indian-operated primary inpatient chemical dependency treatment program. The board is composed of tribal chairmen from Minnesota's reservations. Treatment emphasizes Indian culture along with conventional chemical dependency treatment.

After documenting that Indian women in Minnesota had unmet chemical dependency treatment needs, the Minnesota Indian Women's Resource Center received state support in 1984. Its facility in the Phillips neighborhood, which includes housing for fourteen families, opened in 1992. The Center has pioneered primary outpatient treatment for American Indian women, serving approximately 150 women per year. Circles Beginning is a supplemental program targeted to the specific needs of addicted pregnant women. The Center also provides training for professionals to increase their ability to help Indian women.

DUAL DISABILITIES   Of special difficulty is treatment of Indian patients diagnosed with "dual disabilities," primarily those with chemical dependency and mental illness. Professionals from each discipline agree they have difficulty treating these types of patients. The state's Chemical Dependency Division in the Minnesota Department of Human Services is working toward changes in the treatment systems to allow greater flexibility and choices so that the focus is on the patient's individual needs rather than the patient fitting into the established treatment system. The American Indian Mental Health Advisory Council, which helps formulate policies and procedures relating to Indian mental health services and programs, has helped advance these changes.[24]

DRUG USE BY THE YOUNG   Throughout the last two decades, all Indian communities experienced a rapid increase in youth violence, gangs, and the use of drugs. What had previously been considered primarily an urban problem is a growing concern to reservations. The White Earth Chemical Dependency Coordinator commented, "The problems are getting worse out there: eight to ten-year-olds are experienced pot smokers and crack users."[25]

Studies have documented the need for, but a distinct lack of, treatment programs for youth. According to a study in Minnesota in the late 1990s, only one-fourth of youth ages fourteen to seventeen who need substance abuse treatment received it.[26] According to Ken Winters, a researcher from the University of Minnesota, "The gap between treatment need and treatment availability appears to be significantly increasing for adolescents, particularly for those who present with mild or moderate substance use behaviors. Fortunately, brief and relatively inexpensive interventions have been shown recently to be effective as stand-alone therapies for adult substance abusers and early investigations with young adults are promising."[27]

CHRONIC ALCOHOLICS   Statistics from Hennepin County show that some of its most stubborn cases are chronic homeless inebriates who may be admitted as many as fourty to fifty times per year to detoxification programs and emergency rooms. A disproportionate number, approximately 90 percent, are people of color, predominantly American Indian.[28]

In addressing the fact that the system of medical detoxification and intervention was not working for chronic Indian inebriates, the American Indian Chemical Task Force developed Anishinabe Wakiagun ("The People's Home") to provide dignified housing, clean clothes, and meals for an estimated 450 chronic Indian alcoholics in Minneapolis. The facility is a permanent residence, not a treatment program, with the goal of reducing chemical use through a more stable life. As reported in 2002, prior to moving into Anishinabe Wakiagun, residents had an average of eighteen detox episodes per year, which accounted for forty-two days. After entering Anishinabe Wakiagun, this number dropped to two and one-half admissions, or six and one-third days, on average.[29]

In 1992, the Hennepin County detoxification facility had its license revoked due to charges in the Indian community that clients were subjected to physical abuse and treated in a humiliating manner. State legislation was passed in 1993 to allow the county to conduct a pilot project of a nonmedical, secure program. It required "a culturally targeted detoxification program" and that video monitoring be allowed to ensure the safety of clients and staff (Minn. Stat. 254A.085–.086). In 1995, Hennepin County reopened its facility, operated by the Salvation Army until 2002. Over the six years of operations, numerous disputes arose over funding and labor, with the Salvation Army ultimately declining extension of its contract. Beginning in 2004, the County reorganized its chemical health division and formed an alliance with the County's mental health divisions to provide culturally appropriate assessments and referrals, detoxification services, in- and out-patient treatment, and extended care for people with substance abuse issues.

Mental Health Needs

Indian patients frequently have multiple and interrelated problems such as substance abuse with other mental disorders or other medical conditions and social problems. A confusing fragmentation of programs adds to the difficulty of finding help. More than a decade ago James Thompson, MD, a member of the Association of American Indian Physicians, said, "Separate programs deal with general health, mental health, alcoholism and social services, often with separate budgets, administrations, staffs, services and ideologies. . . . Anyone who has treated Indian people can attest that these co-morbidities are present. . . . For no other population is the need to coordinate services more obvious."[30] Unfortunately, this fragmented situation remains true today as well.

When they are unable to meet their needs with reservation services, tribes can link their mental health services to the county regional centers. Major facilities serving northern Indian reservations are Range Mental Health Center, Virginia (Bois Forte Reservation); Duluth Human Development Center (Fond du Lac Reservation); and Northland Mental Health Clinic (Mille Lacs Reservation). Leech Lake and White Earth Reservations have IHS-funded professional staff. The Red Lake Tribe generally cares for its patients with a staff of psychologists.

MENTAL HEALTH FUNDING FOR INDIANS   Mental health programs serving Indians in Minnesota are partially funded by the Minnesota Comprehensive Adult and Children's Mental Health Act, 1987, 1989 (42 U.S.C. 300X; Minn. Stat. 245.461-245.846, 245.487-245.4887) On advice from Indians, programs for adults and children were combined to provide a continuum of services.

Minnesota statute (Minn. Stat. 245.699) requires an Indian advisory council to assist in formulating policies and procedures relating to Indian mental health services and programs. The council consists of one member appointed from each of the Minnesota reservations; one representative from the Duluth urban Indian community; two from the Minneapolis urban Indian community; and one from the St. Paul urban Indian community.

The local advisory councils mandated in the Act are required to take into account cultural or racial groups in planning, but by most accounts, there is widespread noncompliance, with counties varying greatly in how they acknowledge Indian needs in their plans.

Mental health block grants to Minnesota are provided through the federal Substance Abuse and Mental Health Services Administration. In allocating funds in 2006, the U.S. House of Representatives specifically called for grants to go to organizations with a history of providing culturally competent services to communities of color, including American Indians.

The Minnesota Indian Mental Health program funds mental health workers on the reservations and in urban areas. The program operates on the seven Ojibwe reservations, Upper Sioux and Shakopee Mdewakanton Dakota Communities, and at the Upper Midwest American Indian Center and Indian Health Board in Minneapolis. A St. Paul program ended with the closing of the St. Paul Indian Health Clinic.

HIV/AIDS

The Minnesota Department of Health reported that the cumulative rate of AIDS for American Indians is 154.1 per 100,000, a rate 2.4 times higher than the rate for whites. Cumulative rates of non-AIDS/HIV infection are 119.2 per 100,000, 3.1 times higher than the rate for whites. The state reports indicate major differences between Indian and white patterns of infection, with Indian women much more likely to be infected and drugs playing a major role.

The Indian Health Service requires a designated AIDS coordinator for each reservation, usually an additional duty for an existing staff member.

The Indigenous Peoples Task Force (IPTF, formerly the Minnesota American Indian AIDS Task Force) is providing educational materials and outreach throughout the state to prevent the further spread of HIV to Indians. IPTF also operates Maynidoowahdak Odena (A Place Where the Ceremonies Happen), a fourteen-unit permanent housing program for families living with HIV. The project received the "Design of the Year Award for Affordable Housing" from the Minnesota Housing Finance Agency. The Ogitchidag Gikinooamaagad Players are also a program of the IPTF. The troupe uses storytelling, music, and dance to teach youth about AIDS/HIV.

Fetal Alcohol Spectrum Disorder and Fetal Alcohol Effect

Both Fetal Alcohol Spectrum Disorder (FASD) and Fetal Alcohol Effect (FAE) are associated with the use of alcohol during pregnancy.

Alcohol usage causes problems with the infant's physical growth and the development of the central nervous system, resulting in significant learning and behavior problems for the remainder of the child's life. FASD and FAE are preventable by avoiding alcohol during pregnancy.

While actual FASD and FAE rates have been difficult to track due to varying definitions and data sources, research has shown a high incidence of both conditions in Indian populations. The Centers for Disease Control has found the highest rates of FASD in the American Indian and Africa-American populations.[31]

After publication of Michael Dorris's book *The Broken Cord*, an account of an Indian family's struggle to help a child with FASD, Indians began to focus on prevention through health and chemical dependency programs and outreach through newspaper articles.

Because FAE in particular is not well-defined in the medical community, problems may be ignored, or children may be labeled with attention deficit or behavioral disorders. As one professional working with the program on the Fond du Lac Reservation commented, "With a wrong diagnosis or a lack of one, it becomes as damaging as treating an illness with the wrong medicine. While FAE has no cure, with the proper information it can be treated."[32] The Minnesota Organization on Fetal Alcohol Syndrome is part of a consortium that is studying incidence of substance use during pregnancy, incidence of FASD diagnosis, and intervention plans that target high-risk women, including American Indians.

Thunder Spirit Lodge in St. Paul provides training, tutoring, medical advice, support for families, and testing by the University of Minnesota to identify FASD/FAE. About 80 percent of the program participants are Indian. On the Fond du Lac Reservation, a FASD/FAE Guardian Support Group meets twice per month.

Traditional Indian Medicine

A strong spiritual component and extensive knowledge of herbs and natural remedies are the foundations of traditional Indian medicine. The non-Indian medical profession has been slow to recognize the validity of much of this knowledge. The Indian healer deals with all of life—the natural, spiritual, and physical—to cure illness and return wholeness and harmony. One does not go to school to become a medicine man; rather, those who become healers have been chosen through dreams, visions, or other personal experiences to receive healing powers as a gift from the Great Spirit. Elders, greatly respected and honored for their powers, transmit their knowledge to younger tribal members.

Traditional healing practices are receiving increasing attention. At the Fond du Lac Clinic, traditional Indian medicine is included in services, and the staff can make referrals. Mille Lacs Clinic has a full-time traditional practitioner. At Indian Health Service operations, traditional healers are not funded, but assistance is provided in connecting Indians to such practitioners. The same holds true for the Indian Health Board in Minneapolis. Indian students in the University of Minnesota Medical School program can do field work and internships with Indian physicians, helping students learn about traditional healing practices.

Environmental Concerns

Lead Poisoning

Lead eaten or inhaled can cause severe damage, especially if ingested by young children and pregnant and nursing mothers. Low-level exposures, which have a cumulative effect, have been correlated with lowered IQ, as well as hearing, growth, and behavior problems. While major sources of lead—in paint, water pipes, lead solder, and gasoline—have dropped sharply since the late 1970s, the contaminants remain in many older structures and in soil along streets. The only recent studies, conducted in the early 1990s, of children affected by lead poisoning found Indian children in the Twin Cities were greatly overrepresented.[33] The IHB makes testing for lead a part of its routine examinations for children. Dealing with the problem is very expensive, and efforts to correct the environmental problems have proven to be beyond the financial resources of the Indian community. While lead poisoning is often considered just an urban problem, many reservations have housing likely to contain unsafe levels of lead.

Mercury

While mercury emissions declined substantially between 1990 and 2000, the level of mercury in the fish population remains high enough for the Minnesota Pollution Control Agency to maintain its warning to limit fish consumption.[34] Numerous tribal lakes have been identified as having mercury pollution. Indian populations are considered especially at risk because of their large fish consumption. Tribal members annually consume fish well in excess of recommendations.

Radiation Dangers and the Prairie Island Nuclear Powered
Generating Plant

An important part of the discussion of the future of the Prairie Island nuclear power plant has been Indians' concern about its effects on their health and safety (see chapter 7). As one leader said, "We live next to a nuclear neighbor twenty-four hours a day, seven days a week. Our homes, our school, our community center, our church and our tribal business are all located less than three blocks from a nuclear power plant and a nuclear waste storage site."[35]

Many residents believe that miscarriages, infant deaths, and sudden brain tumors in their community are possibly radiation-linked. However, the Minnesota Department of Health (MDH) reanalyzed breast cancer data and concluded, "This analysis provides a clear and unambiguous conclusion: breast cancer mortality trends over the period 1950–1992 in the ten counties near nuclear power plants show no discernible difference from statewide trends. There were also no differences found in the rate of newly-diagnosed breast cancers during the period 1988–1992. . . . Furthermore, no differences in mortality trends or recent incident rates could be found for several other cancers sensitive to exposures to ionizing radiation."[36]

A state health official also noted, "As for evaluating risk to the Indian population at Prairie Island, it can't be done. The population is just too small to make any statement, even with extensive medical data collection."[37] The Agency for Toxic Substance and Disease Register, U.S. Public Health Service, is funding tribal monitoring of radiation.

Tribal and Indian Health Services

Indian Health Service

Since the IHS assumed responsibility for Indian health programs in 1955, delivery of services has greatly improved, resulting in better Indian health. Because of the obligation to serve all health needs and the reality that in isolated, rural reservations no alternatives are available, a full range of services is provided. With tribes now contracting to run their own programs, most services are the tribe's responsibility, with a major share of funding provided by the IHS, so that each reservation has a unique health program. Services include primary medical care, pharmacies, dental care, optometry, audiology, podiatry, radiology, laboratory services, prevention programs, community health and education programs, nutrition, immunizations, chemical dependency services, mental health, environmental health, construction and maintenance of IHS facilities, and funding to certain urban programs serving Indian communities. The tribes are responsible for public outreach, clinics, programming for people with specific diseases, and health promotion activities.

Eligibility for IHS health care funded services varies with the type of program. Facilities on the reservations—hospitals, clinics and their associated programs—are available to all U.S. tribal members and their children or grandchildren, whether or not they live on the reservation (25 U.S.C. 1603). For non-Indian women pregnant with an Indian child, reservation programs also provide prenatal services through postpartum care.[38] Urban programs have the same tribal membership requirement and require residency in the urban center.

Because all qualifying Indians may use reservation clinics, workloads are especially heavy at the Mille Lacs and Fond du Lac Reservations because of their proximity to the Twin Cities. Indian elders living in the Twin Cities are free to use reservation pharmacies to obtain expensive medicines at no charge.

When medical services are not provided on the reservation, care is provided through contracts that have been made with non-Indian service providers. Only tribal members who reside on or near the reservations are eligible. Funds for this program have been severely limited. Tribes administer the programs from a lump sum payment, with each tribe establishing its own priorities for services. On most reservations rationing is necessary. For example, on Red Lake Reservation the contract fund year starts October 1, and by April 1, only emergency care services are usually authorized. To fill the gap, some tribes pay for selective services from their own funds.

The IHS categorizes its services into three areas: traditional IHS hospitals and clinics, tribally operated hospitals and clinics, and the urban Indian health programs. Nationwide, about 46 percent of IHS resources are allocated to IHS facilities, 53 percent to tribally operated facilities, and only 1 percent to urban Indian programs, a percentage that has remained the same since 1979.[39]

IHS AND TRIBAL FUNDING   Funds provided through the IHS often are not sufficient. While Congress has declared the "national goal of providing the highest possible health status" to Indians (25 U.S.C. 1602), funding has never matched the rhetoric, nor has Congress ever specifically detailed guaranteed services for Indians as it has done with Medicaid. According to the U.S. Commission on Civil Rights, "The federal government spends less per capita on Indian health care than on any other group for which it has this responsibility, including Medicaid recipients, prisoners, veterans, and military personnel. Annually, IHS spends 60 percent less on its beneficiaries than the average per person health care expenditure nationwide. . . . The anorexic budget of IHS can only lead one to deduce that less value is placed on Indian health than that of other populations."[40]

In Minnesota, shortages in IHS budgets have forced tribes to supplement funds as they attempt to administer health programs according to their members' priorities. Health services have been a priority for the use of casino proceeds.

THIRD-PARTY FUNDING   Beginning in 1983, the IHS implemented policies to collect reimbursements from third-party sources of funding such as Medicaid, Medicare, and employment, automobile, private, and workers' compensation insurance. Nationally, third-party payments in 2002 comprised 13 percent of IHS budgets. The Veterans Administration (VA) cannot be billed, but patients qualifying for VA services may be referred there.

Tribes generally have regular health insurance programs covering casino and other tribal employees. The insurance reimburses tribal clinics for services. The Dakota Communities are using insurance to cover all their resident members. The reaction has been very positive since members now have some choice in health care and are no longer restricted to the limitations of the IHS contracted provider. However, 16.2 percent of Indians in Minnesota remain uninsured, compared to 4.6 percent of white Minnesotans.[41]

OTHER FUNDING SOURCES   Federal and state monies for special programs are provided by such agencies as Centers for Disease

Control, U.S. Public Health Service; Alcohol, Drug Abuse, Mental Health Administration, U.S. Public Health Service; U.S. Department of Agriculture; Minnesota Departments of Human Services and Health (which channel several state and federal programs to reservations), University of Minnesota, American Diabetes Association, and private foundations.

Tribal Health Programs

Facilities

Most tribal medical facilities are modern, and most are new or newly remodeled. The $6.7 million Ne-ia-shing, the health center on the Mille Lacs Reservation, and the $3.5 million expansion of Fond du Lac's Min-no-aya-win clinic and expansion of the clinic at Nett Lake were all done in the 1990s, funded by tribal casino profits. After waiting more than ten years on an IHS priority list, the White Earth Tribe received $8 million in federal funds in 1995 for a new clinic.

The IHS administers the state's two Indian hospitals at Red Lake and Leech Lake Reservations. In addition, IHS is responsible for a clinic at Ponemah on the Red Lake Reservation and the health center on White Earth Reservation. Tribes administer all other programs.

Medical Professionals

The major source of physicians to staff IHS facilities are those who received their education through National Health Service federal scholarships and are then required to pay back the cost through service of two to four years. There have long been complaints about this system because the doctors are young and inexperienced and their pay is low compared to doctors in other practices, a strong disincentive for physicians to remain in the IHS system. In addition, finding doctors for all rural practices, not just for Indian reservations, remains a challenge, making good medical care in such areas difficult to provide. Aggressive efforts are being made to encourage Indian students to become physicians and medical professionals (see chapter 10).

Community health representatives and technicians are trained reservation residents who have proven valuable in dealing with Indian patients. They provide a link between the professional medical staff and the community in helping with advocacy, referrals, clinics, screenings, youth programs, transportation, health education events and in making treatment more culturally sensitive and understandable.

Sanitation Programs

The IHS is responsible for constructing water and sanitation systems, providing safe drinking water, and meeting environmental health needs (Pub. L. 86-121, Pub. L. 94-437). The recent Safe Drinking Water Act requires costly upgrades to meet new standards.

On several reservations one of the first uses of discretionary funds from casino profits was upgrading or providing new water and sewage systems to correct poor water pressure, contamination, foul odors, and unsanitary disposal systems. Mille Lacs, Fond du Lac, Grand Portage Tribes and Red Lake have made these improvements a priority. In the 1990s, tribes were included in closing existing land dumps and establishing transfer stations to haul trash to federally funded, centralized county landfills.

The IHS funds environmental health workers for the state of Minnesota whose responsibilities include food sanitation, insect and rodent control, safety of water and waste systems, building inspections, helping to develop codes and ordinances, and working to prevent injuries. At the casinos, they ensure that tribal, state, and federal health and safety standards are maintained.

Veterans Administration Medical Assistance

The Veterans Administration operates medical hospitals, chemical dependency treatment, counseling, and other services for veterans. While the VA plays a very small role in providing medical help to Indians, some efforts have been made to incorporate Indian veterans. The VA medical facility at St. Cloud offers a sweat lodge. In an effort to make services more available to Indian veterans of the Vietnam War, a counseling program was established in St. Paul with an Indian coordinator.

Urban Programs Serving Indians

Indian Health Board of Minneapolis (IHBM)

The Indian Health Board of Minneapolis (IHBM) was incorporated in 1971 to serve the many hidden and unmet health needs of the Indian community in Minneapolis. Located in the Phillips neighborhood, the program provides a medical clinic with family practice physicians, pediatrician and internist, dental services, immunizations, family planning, counseling, referrals, and Women, Infants and Children (WIC) services. Meeting with a traditional medicine man can be arranged. IHBM primarily serves a low-income population, with more than 60 percent at or below 100 percent of poverty level. Thirty-one percent of IHBM clients do not qualify for any state or federal insurance program.[42] In addition to the payment received for welfare recipients, insurance, and other third-party payments and fees, IHBM receives about one-fourth of its funding from the IHS.

IHBM records approximately 20,000 office visits annually. Fifty percent of IHBM clients are American Indians. Grants from such sources as the Indian Health Services, Bureau of Primary Health Care, United Way, and Minnesota Department of Human Services cover 70 percent of costs, with 30 percent coming from patient fees.

Other Urban Programs

The Community University Health Care Center is also a community health service provider in the Phillips neighborhood. Approximately 15 percent of patients are Indian. The full medical clinic offers programs in mental health, for substance abuse, and for pregnant women. The Center receives special state Indian funding and has numerous Indians on staff.

The Native American Community Clinic on Franklin Avenue in Minneapolis provides family health care. It was designated a federally qualified health center in 2004.

Hennepin County funds an Indian advocate at Hennepin County Medical Center. Slightly less than 1 percent of the staff is Indian. The hospital has an Indian rights policy, allowing consideration of spiritual values. HCMC will help obtain a spiritual healer or traditional medicine man, and arrangements can be made to hold healing ceremonies.

The Fond du Lac Tribe's Center for American Indian Resources (CAIR) program provides health care for Duluth Indians. CAIR offers the same full line of services as on the reservation. The Leech Lake Tribe extended medical services to a clinic in Bemidji in 1996, and the Bois Forte Tribe provides a monthly health clinic at International Falls.

Other Programs

Commodities and Good Diet

Proper diet is a problem for many Indians because of low income. On the reservations, the commodity food program is very popular; although when commodities are the sole food supply, the diet can be high in fat, starch, sugar, salt, cholesterol, and calories. Given the selection of foods, a participant with a good understanding of nutrition can have a properly balanced diet. However, the commodity program has no provision for meeting the needs of those requiring special diets, including people with diabetes.[43]

Women, Infants and Children

The Special Supplemental Food Program for Women, Infants and Children (WIC), funded by the U.S. Department of Agriculture, provides vouchers that can be exchanged for highly nutritious food for low-income pregnant women, nursing mothers, and children to the age of five who are considered to have special nutritional needs such as anemia. For those using commodities, the Commodities Supplemental Food Program makes extra foods available, including milk, cheese, juice, eggs, dried legumes, and iron-fortified infant formula. The program also provides nursing and nutritional education with referral to needed medical and social services. The Minnesota program reaches about 4,475 Indians monthly, 4 percent of the state total; in the month of September 2003, it served 994 pregnant and postpartum women, 1,036 infants under one year of age, and 2,446 children ages one to five. About 70 to 80 percent of all Indian births receive WIC services.

Community Health Services

Public health programs at the local level are administered by community health organizations to provide home health care, pregnancy and early childhood care, vaccinations, family planning, environmental health programs, and emergency medical care. Most funds are raised locally, about 75 percent through third-party payments, fees, and local taxes.

Biannual community plans prepared with "full community participation" set program priorities. The program to fund services for off-
reservation Indians requires that the plan document the involvement
of the Indian community (Minn. Stat. 145A.14 Subd. 2).

Reports show that large numbers of Indians are using some of the
services offered by community health organizations. The programs
serving families, pregnant women, and children helped 11,000
Indians, 7 percent of those using the programs. The 627 Indian
children under one year of age were 46 percent of the yearly births of
Indian children.[44]

While counties generally provide very little health programming
for reservation Indians, some counties do offer services, usually by
public health nurses and home health aides. Examples include
diabetes control projects on the Fond du Lac and White Earth Reservations and breast and cervical cancer screenings on several Ojibwe
reservations.

Project Grow

Project Grow began in 1990 on the Fond du Lac Reservation to
provide nutritious vegetables, exercise, and the experience of working
together to grow and share in produce from a community garden. The
program had spread to all Ojibwe reservations (except Grand
Portage) by the end of the 1990s, with nearly 1,500 families participating. The program receives support from tribes, foundations, and
the University of Minnesota Agricultural Extension Office. In
Minneapolis, the Peacemakers youth program operates an organic
garden project for inner city youth.

Barriers to Serving Indian Patients

Impact of Health Care Reform in Meeting Indian Health Needs

In Minnesota, Medicaid and General Assistance Medical Care pay for
many of the health services for qualifying Indians. In addition,
Minnesota Care serves those who do not qualify for either of the afore-
mentioned programs, but who have limited incomes and no health
insurance. In 1997, the state began requiring that the Medicaid
program be offered only through prepaid, managed-care Health

Maintenance Organizations (HMOs). The program pays a negotiated rate to the HMO based on the number of patients selecting that program and the cost of care. The HMO is responsible for deciding the type of care and providing for all medical needs according to the contracts.

Minnesota tribes, asserting sovereignty, protested the planned expansion of prepaid managed care to eligible Indians living on reservations, since they estimated the changes would reduce their funding. Ensuring adequate funding while respecting tribal sovereignty and Indian jurisdiction remains a challenge in the statewide HMO reimbursement system.

Several Indian programs qualify for the designation of Federally Qualified Health Centers, including the Indian Health Board in Minneapolis and Fond du Lac, Mille Lacs, and Leech Lake tribally run clinics. A special federal year-end payment is made to cover costs unmet by reimbursement programs. It is important to Indian patients that HMOs managing the Medicaid health program allow them access to their chosen Federally Qualified Health Center.

Other Barriers

The clash of cultures often makes use of the medical system difficult for Indians. As noted by Dr. Gerald Hill from the University of Minnesota, "Medicine is a white system, based on assumptions that are not Indian. Indians live in a different culture. The expectation is that you can take health care and transfer it to another cultural context."[45]

Indians often have multiple health and social needs. As Hill explained, "The Indian patient, for example, with diabetes, no reliable transportation, inadequate resources to buy appropriate food for a diabetic diet and perhaps also afflicted with substance abuse difficulties or depression, presents the picture of a multi-need patient who must be served by an integrated system."[46]

Transportation also is a serious problem for Indians seeking health care. Many studies cite the difficulty in finding transportation as a barrier to getting health care. The Minnesota Department of Health's American Indian Goals lists help with transportation a necessity in nearly every category.

Summary

Minnesota Indians have greater health needs than the general population. They die younger, with higher rates of infant death and deaths from violence and alcohol use. The large numbers of Indians living in poverty and the social factors that relate to that economic condition, especially in urban settings, contribute to health problems. Indians' health care is highly dependent upon services provided by governments, and its quality and availability has declined as programs have failed to keep up with needs or have been limited or cut.

There are some bright spots. As they increasingly run their own health programs, tribes are identifying their own priorities and delivering health care in more culturally meaningful ways. Innovative programs to help people with diabetes, programs to improve nutrition and exercise, and effective treatment programs for chemical abuse are showing results.

Despite these gains, great disparities in health still exist between many Indians and the general population in Minnesota. Much remains to be achieved to meet the federal goal of providing the "highest possible health status to Indians and to provide existing Indian health services with all resources necessary to effect that policy."

Chapter 13

Housing

TO MEET THE GOAL of adequate, safe, and healthy housing for all citizens requires many complex public policies and programs to fit a wide array of human needs. For the state's Indian population, in spite of several innovative programs, the needs far outstrip the resources being allocated.

Characteristics of Indian Housing

Housing statistics from the 2000 U.S. Census show substantial differences in living arrangements between Indians and the state's total population. The rate of Indian home ownership is about two-thirds that of the state average; in Minneapolis, it is even lower, about one-half (see Table 13.1). However, the percentage of Indian, owner-occupied housing units increased 6 percent statewide since the 1990 U.S. Census; in Minneapolis, St. Paul, and the suburbs, the increase was 5 percent.

Table 13.1 Owner-occupied housing, 2000

	Indians	**Total Population**
State of Minnesota	49%	74%
Minneapolis	23%	51%
St. Paul	31%	54%
Duluth	23%	64%
Cloquet	52%	73%
Bemidji	39%	54%

Source: U.S. Census, 2000.

The average home ownership rate on reservations is 76 percent, slightly higher than the overall ownership for the whole state. The census figures show the dramatic impact on home ownership when a tribe has the resources to help its members achieve a middle-class standard of living. For example, in Scott County, where the Shakopee Mdewakanton Dakota Community operates the Mystic Lake Casino, 95 percent of Indians were homeowners, exceeding the state's average.

Much of the state's reservation housing is old and in need of extensive repairs. Many homes built under government programs twenty to twenty-five years ago are of low quality. In tribal areas, 40 percent of homes are overcrowded and have serious physical deficiencies. The comparable national average for the general population is 6 percent.[1] Indian leaders in Minnesota estimated in 2004 that it would take $120 million to renovate and build new housing on reservations to adequately house the population.[2]

Measuring Reservation Housing Needs

Housing needs have increased rapidly since 1990. All reservations report increases in members moving back due to the possibility of

Table 13.2 Real median values of owner-occupied homes on reservations, 1990 and 2000

Reservation	1990	2000
Bois Forte	$16,900	$41,400
Fond du Lac	$70,200	$84,500
Grand Portage	$59,500	$68,000
Leech Lake	$52,400	$47,800
Lower Sioux	$26,000	$66,400
Mille Lacs	$50,800	$86,400
Minnesota Chippewa	$57,600	$63,500
Prairie Island	$31,600	$68,800
Red Lake	$51,200	$54,900
Shakopee	$89,800	$210,700
Upper Sioux	$20,300	$61,700
White Earth	$47,400	$51,500

Source: U.S. Census, 1990, 2000; Northwest Area Foundation, Web site data, 2005.

employment. Affordable housing on the reservation is another big draw.[3] The per capita payments from casino profits for some Dakota Community members are not available until they meet reservation residency requirements, making this an incentive to return.

Overcrowded housing remains a continuing reality on the reservations. In a nationwide survey by the National American Indian Housing Council in 2004, more than half (59 percent) of respondents reported that housing is overcrowded on their reservation. An overwhelming majority (83 percent) said housing is substandard on their reservation. Nearly all (94 percent) said that substandard or overcrowded housing has had an impact on tribal members' health or the well being of their children.[4]

Financing Housing

While Indians spend less money on housing than the rest of the state's population, it costs them a larger portion of their income. In 2000, nearly 9 percent (8.6 percent) of the state's Indians used over 50 percent of their incomes for housing, compared with 4.7 percent for the general population.[5] Many Indians do not have the income to obtain housing by conventional means or even from governmental programs. In 2002, a family of four with two full-time wage earners needed to earn a combined annual salary of $47,436 (or a wage of $11.41 per hour for each worker) to afford the basic cost of living in Minnesota.[6] A household needed to earn $50,542 to afford the median-priced home ($154,900 in 2001–2002).[7] A significant portion of the state's Indian population (71 percent) earns less than $25,000 (see Table 13.3).

Table 13.3 Income comparisons, Indian and white households in Minnesota, 2000

	Indians	Whites
Median Income	$28,533	$47,111
Income less than $35,000	58% (9,614)	36%
Income less than $25,000	44% (7,387)	24%
Income less than $15,000	27% (4,430)	12%

Source: U.S. Census, 2000.

While the casinos have provided employment and have been a tremendous help for many reservation residents, casinos cannot solve all of the housing problems. Most casino employees are not highly paid, and even at a wage of $8 per hour, a family with one wage earner does not have sufficient income to qualify for a home mortgage loan. Many reservation residents will continue to need public housing programs.

Indians face discrimination in the housing market due to a variety of factors: race, family size, single parent status, and neighborhood choice.

❏ From data required by the Home Mortgage Disclosure Act, in 2003, 24 percent of American Indian applicants were denied conventional home purchase loans, compared to 12 percent of white, 11 percent of Asian, 18 percent of Hispanic, and 24 percent of African-American applicants.[8]

❏ In a 1993 study done by Humphrey Institute graduate students of the availability of home loans for people of different races but with identical credentials, the study found "persistent discrimination in mortgage lending against people of color across the upper Midwest . . . The amount of discrimination apparently due to racism was 65% among American Indians and 33% among African-Americans."[9]

On reservation lands, conventional channels for funding housing are not an alternative. As a federal trust responsibility, the land cannot be mortgaged voluntarily or involuntarily. In case of default, the land cannot be taken in foreclosure. For tribal lands, individual families can only lease use of it. If a private financial institution is to invest, the federal government has to act as the guarantor, and the tribe must be involved. While laws have existed for several years to allow such arrangements, they have been used infrequently.

Housing and Urban Development (HUD) and the Minnesota Housing Finance Agency programs that assist with rental and home ownership are major suppliers of existing reservation housing. The overwhelming reliance on these programs is illustrated by a survey of housing on the Red Lake Reservation, published in 1995. Federal or state-funded rental units served 41 percent of the reservation's population; 20 percent were in the "rent-to-own" home-ownership program of HUD. Of the remaining homes, 11 percent were privately owned with private mortgages and 28 percent had no mortgage debt.[10]

Federal Housing Programs

Federal assistance for housing began in 1937, but it was not until the early 1960s that efforts were made to expand programs to Indian reservations, with the Bureau of Indian Affairs (BIA) determining tribes had the legal authority to develop and operate public housing. In 1968, assistance to low-income families on Indian reservations was authorized, and funds were set aside (42 U.S.C. 1437). The resulting programs, however, often have requirements that make them difficult for Indians to use.

Housing Authorities

A separate HUD Office of Indian Housing was established in 1975, with programs for Minnesota's tribes and all tribes east of the Mississippi River administered from Chicago. Each Minnesota tribe has a housing authority to administer its programs. The Indian Housing Authorities (IHA) are tribal government subdivisions with independent boards. Under contract with HUD, IHAS own and manage the projects. They build and operate rental units. Rent is based on adjusted income, set to a maximum of 30 percent. The housing authorities are responsible for utilities and maintenance.

Home Ownership

The Mutual Help Homeownership Program funds new housing, which is leased to the purchaser for up to twenty-five years. The program usually involves the buyer providing payment in some form of mutual help, such as providing the land, participating in the building, performing maintenance, or paying for utilities. The program has not had any additional funding beyond the initial grant in 1995.

In Minnesota, The HOME Investment Partnership Program, a HUD-block grant, is targeted for rehabilitating housing and helping first-time home buyers through grants and low interest loans. While it is not designated as an Indian program, it has been used by the White Earth and Bois Forte tribes for home construction and rehabilitation and for Indian housing in Duluth.

Housing and Urban Development

Many Indian housing authorities have difficulty collecting rents and homeowner payments and ensuring homes are maintained. Extreme poverty and nonexistent or unreliable employment opportunities exacerbate the situation. Tribal leaders and courts may be reluctant to enforce collection and eviction policies because often there are no other housing options on the reservation for evicted people.

Housing authorities that do not fulfill their responsibilities may face sanctions from HUD. In 1997, HUD removed the White Earth Housing Authority Board and management and took over the operation. HUD charged that the White Earth board had failed to provide oversight and to get competitive bidding; homes had been unfairly distributed to friends and relatives; and housing had been allowed to become defective and hazardous. HUD agreed to fund all but twelve of the original seventy units.[11]

In 1996, heeding requests to allow tribes more say in shaping housing programs, Congress passed the Native American Housing and Self-Determination Act (NAHASDA). As a result, almost all of the Indian housing programs administered through HUD were placed in a formula-allocated block grant given directly to tribes, allowing them a great deal more flexibility in setting priorities and incorporating other funding into housing programs.

The Native American Housing Enhancement Act (NAHE) of 2003 amended NAHASDA to ensure that participants do not pay more for housing than the fair market rate and to prevent reduction of grants. The bill clarifies Congress's requirement that HUD gives housing authorities the ability to retain program money for successive grant years, ultimately providing tribes and tribal entities more flexibility in planning. NAHE also amends the Civil Rights Act (CRA) so Indian tribes qualify for U.S. Department of Agriculture (USDA) funding without violating the CRA, and it amends the Cranston-Gonzalez National Affordable Housing Act so that Indian tribes, tribally designated housing entities, or other agencies that primarily serve Indians can qualify for Youthbuild grants (see chapter 10).

Funding continues to be an issue, despite the amendments to NAHASDA. According to the Native Housing Council, "Although tribes through NAHASDA have self-determination in their housing developments, the level of funding available at the tribal and federal levels is impeding necessary progress." In 2003, the U.S. Civil Rights Commission released a study on unmet needs in Indian country. In the category of housing, the study found:

> [T]he basic standard of living of Native Americans remains well below that of the rest of the nation . . . For FY2005, the president has proposed $647 million for Native American Housing Block Grant (formerly the Indian Housing Block Grant) funding. Yet in FY2001, the actual amount received was $648.6 million. Factoring in inflation and consecutive years of stagnant funding, Indian housing appropriations are losing ground and, because of this, tribes continue to struggle to meet housing demands. . . . FY2005 funding would have to increase to $715 million simply to adjust for the impact of inflation, and that does not take into account population growth.[12]

Other Federal Programs

The Housing Improvement Program (HIP) of the Bureau of Indian Affairs began in 1964. It provides minimal funding directly to tribal governments for repair and rehabilitation of existing homes and is used only as the last resort if assistance is not available from other sources.

The federal system designed to provide housing for Indians on reservations delegated to the Indian Health Service (IHS) the responsibility for safe water supplies and sanitation. While the IHS funding for these programs has increased, it has not kept up with demand. The priority is for communitywide facilities; very little attention is paid to individual housing. Improved water and sewage disposal systems have been a high priority on all reservations. Existing systems are old, inadequate, and may be polluted. In the 1990s, new homes and major building projects put a tremendous strain on existing facilities. IHS and the Farmers Home Administration have helped on some reservations. Some of the tribes, unable to get federal help for water and sewage systems, have funded major systems on their own. However, adding such costs to individual housing programs reduces the number of homes that can be built with the limited funds available.

Indian Housing Programs in Minnesota

Since 1971, the Minnesota Housing Finance Agency (MHFA) has helped low- and moderate-income people purchase, construct, or improve decent housing through private lenders, local governmental units, and nonprofit organizations that administer the programs throughout the state.

In 1976, the Minnesota Indian Housing Programs (Minn. Stat. 462A.07 Subd. 14, the urban program Minn. Stat. 246A.07 Subd. 15) were the first nonfederal, publicly funded Indian housing programs in the U.S. and are considered a national model. Nearly thirty years of stable funding and consistent administration have done a great deal to increase home ownership in Indian communities. Loans are limited to tribal members and are primarily focused on mortgages for home ownership or home repair, for low- and moderate-income tribal members on and off reservations. Policies for the programs are developed in consultation with the Urban Advisory Council of the Minnesota Indian Affairs Council.

The American Indian Community Development Corporation builds and operates culturally specific housing and supportive services for American Indians in the Twin Cities metropolitan area, including a self-sufficiency program, tenant training, and rental housing programs.

Housing on Trust Lands

In an attempt to resolve the problem of providing security for the lender when the land is in federal trust and cannot be sold or foreclosed, several programs have been structured to combine agreements among the tribes, government agencies, and private lenders. There has been limited acceptance of this approach by both lenders and tribal officials due to tribal codes and lack of enforcement of the agreements.

Some Minnesota tribes have been certified for federal programs (Indian Housing Loan Guarantee Program, § 184 and § 248) guaranteeing loans to Indians on trust land; however, they have had little use.[13]

In the late 1990s, two demonstration programs allowed pooling of funds for home ownership loans on trust lands. The Minnesota Chippewa Tribal (MCT) Housing Corporation entered into an agreement with Federal Home Loan Bank of Des Moines, joining the bank as a nonmember borrower able to make low interest loans. These funds are pooled on a one-to-one basis with state housing funds. Those using the program need not be low-income. The home must qualify for a Federal Housing Administration (FHA) guaranteed loan, which is used as collateral. The MCT Housing Corporation becomes the party obligated to repay the loan if foreclosure becomes necessary. Neither the tribe nor trust land is involved.

The Minnesota Dakota Indian Housing Authority developed a program with the state to fund mortgages on the reservation. The tribes match state funds one-third to two-thirds, and income limits do not apply. With the high per capita payments from casino profits to Shakopee Mdewakanton Dakota Community members, the tribe has switched to providing members with its own home purchase guarantee program.

Department of Veterans Affairs (VA) Loan Guaranty Program

The VA guarantee for housing loans for qualifying veterans uses a Memorandum of Understanding with several Minnesota tribes. However, the loan limit of $80,000, requirement of a good credit history, and steady income often present a challenge for Indians. Indians have used the program very little.[14]

Rural Economic and Community Development Agency,
U.S. Department of Agriculture

Formerly known as the Farmers Home Administration Rural Housing Program (42 U.S.C. 1471), the Rural Economic and Community Development Agency serves low-income, rural populations. With generous lending terms, it works with projects on trust land under a Memorandum of Understanding agreement with the tribes. In Minnesota, it has directly funded several major building projects, including a congregate housing project for the elderly on the White Earth Reservation and water and sewage systems for the Mille Lacs and Bois Forte tribes.

Housing Programs Initiated by Tribes

Several tribes are using some casino profits to regain reservation land and build units in order to accommodate demands for housing.

Woodland National Bank, owned by the Mille Lacs Band, now has a housing mortgage program with investment capital provided by casino profits. The Shakopee Mdewakanton Dakota Community deducts tribally issued loans from per capita payments and has used casino profits to build several housing subdivisions solely for members. The Grand Portage Tribal Council has contributed funds to purchase duplexes and land in Duluth for rental housing and an elders lodge.

Urban Housing for Indians

Indian leaders cite the lack of affordable housing in the Twin Cities as a critical issue facing the Indian community. According to the Indian Health Board of Minneapolis, Indians in urban areas, especially those with large families, have great difficulty finding affordable housing that is free of health and safety hazards. Moreover, Indian people experience discrimination when seeking housing based on race, children, and welfare status. Many of the multiunit dwellings in which Indians live contain housing code violations: poor waste disposal, inadequate plumbing, rodents, insects, faulty and exposed wiring, shared toilets, and poor heating.[15] Such conditions are strongly linked to other social ills, including poor health conditions, chemical dependency, criminal activity, and violence.

A Wilder Research study completed in December 2003 found that only 23 percent of American Indians in Duluth owned their own homes and that one-third of the homeless in the city were American Indian. City officials said that lack of job opportunities and the fact that 57 percent of Indians in Duluth under age eighteen were living below the poverty level contributed to the housing problem.[16]

There are many city, state, federal, community groups, nonprofit agencies, and religious groups involved with the various facets of urban housing. However, few are focused on Indian needs.

Minneapolis and St. Paul

The city of Minneapolis, through its Housing Services, offers an Indian outreach worker who spends a great deal of time working out difficulties between landlords and tenants. The American Indian Community Development Corporation is a nonprofit organization providing housing advocacy in Minneapolis.

Little Earth of United Tribes, in the Phillips Neighborhood, was the first HUD-financed urban housing project for low-income Indians in the nation; it has continued to be the only Indian-controlled one. The complex has faced problems with poor construction, rapid deterioration of facilities, and insufficient funds to keep up repairs or repay the mortgage. The U.S. Eighth Circuit Court of Appeals upheld foreclosure in 1989, but Indian activism and political pressure put the decision on hold. In 1993, the U.S. Secretary of HUD agreed to return the project to Indian management. The city of Minneapolis and the state's Urban Indian Housing program committed $3.1 million to rehabilitate the buildings. HUD agreed to provide $31 million in Section 8 rent subsidies until 2009.[17] Despite all the difficulties, the project remains an important symbol to Indians.

Elder Lodge is a lodge for elders in St. Paul developed by the St. Paul Indian community for low- income elders. The forty-two one-bedroom apartment complex has been designed by an Indian architect to incorporate nature, community participation, and other Indian values.

Duluth

The Greater Duluth Grand Portage Enrollees Program, comprised of tribal families, buys, repairs, and rents duplexes to Indians in Duluth. As a completely volunteer-run organization, it has been cited nationally as an exemplary program of community and cultural cooperation.

Other Nonprofit Urban Organizations

Project for Pride in Living receives state Indian housing funding to help low-income Indian families in scattered site individual homes. The program begins with the option to convert to ownership. Habitat for Humanity uses volunteers and donated materials to buy and fix up vacant houses. Indian people have worked and obtained homes through the Minneapolis program and on the Mille Lacs Reservation. Phoenix Group refurbishes houses in the Phillips neighborhood.

Programs for Populations with Special Housing Needs

Anishinabe Wakiagun, a facility to provide safe housing for homeless, chemically dependent Indians, opened on Franklin Avenue in

Minneapolis in 1996 (see chapter 12). Maynidoowahdak Odena, a fourteen-unit home for Indian HIV/AIDS patients and their families, was built in Minneapolis in the late 1990s with funds from HUD, the state, the Phillips Neighborhood Revitalization Program, and the Minneapolis Community Development Agency.

In March 2005, a twenty-six apartment complex for elders living on reduced incomes was constructed as an addition to the Jourdain/Perpich Extended Care Facility in Red Lake with a $1.9 million grant from HUD and more than $500,000 in rental subsidies. Residents must be sixty-two years or older and live on low income but able to pay 30 percent of income in rent. Electricity, water, heat, and laundry facilities are provided at no extra cost.[18]

Housing Issues

There are many barriers and hurdles as Indians seek satisfactory housing, including insufficient incomes, underfunded housing programs, and cultural differences.

Lack of Funds and Housing

In 2003, the National American Indian Housing Council estimated that 200,000 housing units were needed immediately in Indian communities to provide adequate housing.[19] The lack of HUD Section 8 rental subsidy housing, plus rigid program requirements, continue to plague low-income Indians. Many Indians remain on the waiting list for years. This is especially troubling for people dealing with domestic abuse or chemical dependency recovery, whose housing needs are often immediate.

Home Ownership

Owning a home in an urban area is a relatively new concept in Indian communities. In interviews with urban Indians, the American Indian Research and Policy Institute found that ownership was not the important thing; rather, feeling a sense of community and belonging to a place were most significant. Communal, supportive solutions to housing were deemed important. Indians also noted that HUD houses were rarely viewed as truly belonging to the family.[20]

Although fewer than half the state's Indians live in homes they own, surveys show that home ownership is the preference of most Indians. For example, a survey done in 1993 of Leech Lake tribal employees found that 77 percent preferred living in a single family home; 78 percent wished to own their home.[21]

Legal Challenges

Court cases have challenged the St. Paul Housing Board and Little Earth of United Tribes housing project on the grounds of racial discrimination. In *St. Paul Housing Board v. Reynolds* (564 F. Supp. 1408 (D. Minn. 1983)), HUD challenged the Indian administration of the state program to renovate and rent homes. HUD argued that the Indian-only program discriminated against non-Indians. The court ruled, and the U.S. Eighth Circuit Court of Appeals upheld, that the program was not a violation of racial discrimination laws but was politically justified as compensation to federally recognized Indian tribes for taking their land.[22]

Beginning in 1982, HUD issued a series of challenges to Little Earth, saying its preferential policy for Indian tenants was discriminatory. The U.S. District Court in Minnesota upheld the policy because of Indians' special relationship with the federal government. However, HUD continued to maintain that Little Earth was violating the laws until the Secretary of HUD personally intervened in 1993, stating that the Little Earth housing project could have a "policy giving American Indians preference for admission to the project."[23] While the future of Little Earth seems more secure, Indians remain fearful that another administration may reverse the decision.

Summary

Casinos have had a major impact on housing on reservations. The need for housing has increased dramatically, and members are increasingly able to consider home ownership as income increases due to expanded employment opportunities. Utilizing casino profits, tribes have much greater flexibility to seek outside funds and to use their own funds as investment in reservation housing.

HUD, the major federal supplier of housing funds, in its change to a program of tribal block grants, has given tribes much greater flexibility in terms of housing. But funding remains inadequate to deal with the quantity of housing needed and the repairs necessary for aging and ill-constructed homes.

Many Indians do not have the income to obtain housing by conventional means or even from governmental programs. Lenders have shown reluctance and, at times, discrimination in issuing mortgages to the state's Indian population.

The state has been helpful in its continued stable funding of creative and flexible programs for Indian housing. The programs have proven to be the most effective way to channel to Indian communities their share of the state housing funds.

Urban housing problems for Indians are formidable. Very low-income families with a wide variety of the most pressing needs have no decent housing or rent support options available, and the Section 8 program intended to help these people is woefully underfunded. Affordable housing, to rent or own, is a growing problem for those with more moderate income levels.

Chapter 14

The Criminal Justice System

BEFORE THE IMMIGRATION of Europeans to America, Indian tribes had well-established codes of conduct and ways of dealing with crime. If a person violated another's rights, penalties were culturally sanctioned. Crimes against another individual called for restitution to the injured party. When the price was paid, the matter was settled. Public shame and humiliation were major punishments exacted by the group. Tribal elders counseled until the behavior changed.

Other penalties included spiritual disenfranchisement, prohibition from participation in ceremonies, isolation, and temporary banishment. Banishment was the ultimate punishment because it represented the loss of one's people and status, as well as almost certain death in the hostile environment of northern winters. It was used for the most serious crimes in the most extreme situations.

Individuals were taught by example to become personally responsible for their conduct. An individual's conscience included not only personal values, but also those of the entire culture. During the frontier years, whites were amazed when an Indian voluntarily rode miles unescorted to appear in court to be sentenced.

With the reservations came pressures to extinguish traditional Indian society. Formal legal systems with police enforcement were set up under civil and criminal codes devised by the Secretary of the Interior. These legal systems imposed an alien culture and form of government on Indian society.

Courts of Indian Offenses, with Indian judges, were established in 1883; Indian police imposed the laws and federal agency regulations. This legal system further destroyed Indian traditions.[1] In 1881, when Crow Dog killed Spotted Tail, a Brule Sioux chief on the Sioux

Reservation in Dakota Territory, the courts realized they lacked jurisdiction to prosecute. As a result, in 1885, Congress passed legislation giving federal courts responsibility for handling major crimes on the reservations (18 U.S.C. 1153).

Allotment and the subsequent sale of major portions of the reservations brought jurisdictional problems. Tribes do not have criminal jurisdiction over non-Indians within the reservation, and the state handles these legal issues. Because most tribal police officers are cross-deputized, they can arrest non-Indian violators under state law. County enforcement officers can also send tribal members into tribal courts.

In 1953, criminal jurisdiction on all Minnesota reservations (except Red Lake) was transferred to the state under Public Law 280, partly to deal with the problem of lack of law enforcement. Public Law 280 weakened tribal sovereignty and did not necessarily lead to improved law enforcement. Counties complained that the federal government did not provide the necessary funding to hire additional personnel. The Indian communities often considered the county sheriff and legal systems prejudiced. In 1973, the Minnesota legislature approved the request by the Bois Forte Tribe to return to federal–tribal jurisdiction in criminal matters. Both Bois Forte and Red Lake Reservations have their own criminal codes, tribal courts, and BIA-funded police forces. In 1990, the Mille Lacs Band requested the right to return to the federal–tribal system, but this was not approved by the state.

Indians and Crime

Crime is a major concern for all Indian communities. Based on the 2000 U.S. Census, Indian adults were 1.2 percent of the total state population, yet they made up 4.5 percent of the criminal cases in Minnesota in 2002.[2] In 2002, 18.5 percent of the adult American Indian population in Minnesota was arrested, comprising 4 percent of all arrests.[3]

From 1994 to 1998, 55 percent of American Indian youth ages fifteen to twenty-four who died were victims of homicide. While the percentage of murder victims who were Indian dropped from 11 percent in 1992 to 6 percent in 2002, that figure is still far in excess of their percentage of population in Minnesota.[4]

Many factors not related to race correlate with a high crime rate. A disproportionate share of the Indian population falls in categories with higher crime rates, including youth (crime correlates with age), those living in poverty, the unemployed, alcohol and drug abusers, and the poorly educated.

Indian communities, from isolated reservations to central cities, have expressed deep concern about increasing crime among their young people. The problems are taxing the state and tribal courts as well as human and financial resources.

Gangs continue to be an enticement for young urban Indians. An Indian professional working with Indian inner-city youth explained:

> These people live a third world existence with no economic re-sources. There is no employment that pays decent wages . . . They know that even with both working at McDonalds (minimum wage) they cannot make enough to meet the lifestyle that Amer-icans expect . . . They don't want to accept their poverty. Gangs and the violent way of life is a decision to "do what I have to do to survive . . . and I will survive." They come together in gangs for collective survival.[5]

State Criminal Procedures

City, county, and state law enforcement, as well as courts and correc-tional systems, deal with most of the criminal acts involving Indians. Exceptions are the Red Lake and Bois Forte Reservations, the regula-tion of hunting and fishing laws on reservations and in certain treaty areas, and the expanding jurisdictional responsibilities being taken by the tribes.

Today's criminal prosecution system is complex, involving five or more separate systems: the police; those making decisions about pros-ecution; those defending the accused; the courts with their judges and probation officers; correctional institutions, jails, and detention facil-ities; and possibly social services agencies, schools, and a wide variety of public and private alternative programs.

Arrest data are reported in two groups for adults. Part I Violent Crimes against persons include murder, rape, robbery, and aggravated assault, and property crimes include burglary, larceny, motor theft, and arson. They can result in felony charges and imprisonment in state prisons. Part II Crimes include driving under the influence, simple assault, fraud, disorderly conduct, narcotics, and sex crimes. Most are misdemeanors, with jail terms under one year, which are the responsibility of local government. Status offenses are crimes that apply only to juveniles, such as truancy, curfew violation, and running away.

Issues with the Criminal Justice System

The state's criminal justice system is primarily non-Indian, and most Indians expect racial bias. The Indian's response may be to withdraw. Common comments from attorneys representing Indians in court are that they are not active in their own defense, that cultural factors affect communication, and that witnesses frequently do not appear. Lack of trust in law enforcement is an obstacle to those trying to prevent criminal activity.

Indians claim that law enforcement neglects their communities, not giving them equal protection from those breaking the laws. In the northern reservation areas, distance adds to the problem. For instance, Grand Portage Reservation is served by the Cook County Sheriff's Department, forty miles away from the reservation.

County sheriffs note that Indian people are reluctant to pass on information or to testify for fear of retaliation or, perhaps, because kin or friends are involved. Although more than one-half of Fond du Lac Reservation members responded on a survey that they had personal experience with a crime in the previous two years, 78 percent said they did not report the crime to a law enforcement agency.[6] A 1999 nationwide study showed that only 45 percent of American Indian victims of violent crime reported the crime to police. Nearly half of those not reporting the crime said they considered the matter "private or too minor to bother police."[7]

According to Joe Day, Executive Director of the Minnesota Indian Affairs Council, "The philosophy from the American Indian perspective is why go up and file a complaint? It's not going to go anywhere anyway. It's going to get shoved under the rug and nothing will improve if we do complain. And, as a matter of fact, there might be some retribution."[8]

The complex legal status of Indians adds to the problem. An Indian is confronted by multiple jurisdictions, different laws, and even different definitions of "Indian." On reservation lands, in addition to tribal laws, some state laws apply, while others do not, and still others are in the courts being challenged. Whether one is a tribal member of that specific reservation may make a difference. Being an unenrolled child of a reservation member or being a member of a different tribe may subject the person to state laws that do not apply to enrolled members of that reservation. Many jurisdictional issues are unresolved, and tribal actions or court decisions can cause sudden changes in the laws and their enforcement. Knowing what is the law and whose law it is places an especially heavy burden on reservation Indians.

Bias in the Justice System

Many Indians report negative experiences with the criminal justice systems, including racial prejudice. As the director of Anishinabe Legal Services said, "We glibly assume people are being treated in an unbiased way. But Indians experience racism in a thousand different ways every day."[9]

It is difficult to prove bias because of the complexity of the systems and the many subjective decisions that are never publicly recorded. Who stays in jail, who receives bail and how much it will be, the quality and dedication of legal counsel, the nature of the charges brought, how plea bargains are negotiated, and who goes to alternative, diversionary programs are all factors. In addition, where police enforcement efforts are concentrated, there often are higher arrest rates in general, which may be unrelated to racial bias. If those making decisions do not understand cultural factors, Indians can be disproportionately affected.

African-Americans and Indians are arrested in far greater numbers on more serious charges than are whites. This is true not only as a percentage of the arrest category, but also as the proportion of their racial group.

The percentage of American Indians convicted of felonies in Minnesota makes up a larger percentage than their representation in the population. In 2002, 5.5 percent of the convicted felony offenders were American Indian, compared to 1.8 percent Asian, 5.4 percent Hispanic, 26.7 percent African-American, and 60.1 percent white. Their incarceration rates were also higher than those of the white (20.7%) and Asian (24%) populations, similar to those of African-Americans (27.7%), but lower than those of Hispanics (31.3%). American Indians

Table 14.1. Percentage of arrests in Minnesota, by category, 2000

| | Juvenile Arrests | | |
	Indian	White	African-American
% of population			
Part I Violent Crimes	4.9%	67%	21%
Part II Crimes	4.0%	80%	12%
Status Offenses	4.7%	61%	24%
Total Juvenile Arrests	4.3%	74%	16%

| | Adult Arrests | | |
	Indian	White	African-American
Part I Violent Crimes	5.1%	6.6%	26%
Part II Crimes	4.0%	78.0%	16%
Total Adult Arrests	4.1%	77.0%	17%

Note: Total will not equal 100% since other races have been omitted.
Source: State of Minnesota, Bureau of Criminal Apprehension, Arrest and Apprehension Data 2000, prepared by Criminal Justice Center.

also received the least number of "dispositional departures," a judge's willingness to depart from the sentencing guidelines.[10]

Racial Profiling

Officials with the American Civil Liberties Union (ACLU) of Minnesota report that the arrest numbers of American Indians in relation to their percentage of the population show law enforcement agencies in Cass and other northern counties are unfairly targeting Indians. According to Chuck Samuelson of the Minnesota ACLU, "The statistics just reek of wrongness. It's one of the biggest disparities in the whole country."[11]

As a result of its investigations, the ACLU launched the Greater Minnesota Racial Justice Project in 2004. With a satellite office in Bemidji, the ACLU is targeting counties surrounding Minnesota's three largest Indian reservations: Red Lake, Leech Lake, and White Earth. The project is focusing on monitoring the courts in northern counties and helping educate Indians about their civil rights.[12]

A racial profiling study released in 2003 sparked widespread protests by American Indians who believe they are unfairly targeted by law enforcement. The study examined data on traffic stops collected over one year in Beltrami County (where Bemidji is located and the county with the second largest American Indian population in Minnesota). Indians stopped in Beltrami County were approximately two and one-half times as likely to be arrested as white drivers (17.1 percent compared to 6.1 percent). The study also showed that Bemidji police searched Indian drivers at three times the rate of white drivers.[13]

In contrast to the racial profiling in Beltrami County, data from traffic stops in 2000 in Minneapolis showed that Indians were stopped in equal measure to their population: 2.0 percent of stops and 2.2 percent of the population.[14]

Minnesota Supreme Court Task Force on Racial Bias

A state study was conducted in 1991 to determine why youth of color were overrepresented at every point in the Minnesota Juvenile Justice System. The Minnesota Supreme Court subsequently established a task force to evaluate racial bias throughout the judicial system. A thorough analysis was done of the "funnel effect, starting with arrest and charging and ending with sentencing, through which a disproportionate number of people of color get caught up in the system and a disproportionate number are eventually sentenced." The final report stated that "more than 75% of the attorneys, judges and probation officers responded that bias against people of color exists in the court system. Nearly 90% said the bias is subtle and hard to detect. [But] [d]espite the fact that racial discrimination in the courts is often subtle, its ultimate effects are anything but."[15]

Two years later, after questions were raised about the speed of and commitment to implementing the task force's recommendations, the Minnesota Supreme Court and the state lower courts began joint discussions with tribal courts to understand better their workings and how to interrelate the systems. In 2001, the Minnesota Judicial Branch began collecting self-reported race information at the first appearance in criminal, juvenile, and traffic cases. Minnesota courts are the first in the country to have an ongoing, statewide self-reported race data collection project. According to Chief Justice Kathleen A. Blatz, "The Minnesota state court system understands that we cannot begin to determine if and where bias or disparate treatment exists nor can we address problems of bias without hard data . . . The Judiciary is committed to making the race data collection project a permanent step in the court process so we can watch trends over time, examine the impact of new legislation and other factors related to people of color in the justice system, and move us from anecdotes to empirical evidence and from empirical evidence to action."[16]

Reports and Fears of Police Mistreatment

In 1968, at a time of elevated police brutality in the Minneapolis Indian community, the American Indian Movement (AIM) responded by organizing its own protective street patrols. When a serial killer was causing great fear in the Indian community in the late 1980s, the AIM patrol concept was reactivated. Since that time, men and women of all races have volunteered to patrol in cars at night in the high Indian population, high crime areas of Minneapolis.

The Minneapolis Civilian Police Review Authority was established in 1990 to deal with complaints about police conduct, especially in communities of color. Few Indians have filed complaints with the Authority, which has been unpopular with police and criticized by community leaders for its lack of effectiveness. A working group from city government began crafting changes to improve the troubled Authority in 2006.

A 1993 incident focused widespread attention on treatment of Indians. Two Indian men, who were drunk and incapacitated, were taken to Hennepin County Medical Center in the trunk of a squad car instead of by ambulance. The county attorney found no basis for a criminal complaint, but the Minnesota Department of Human Rights ruled there had been discrimination based on race and the disability of alcoholism. In a civil suit in June 1995, the courts held the police and city of Minneapolis liable for major civil damages.

A 1997 survey of youth involved in the Minneapolis American Indian Center's Ginew/Golden Eagle youth program found that 62 percent of eleven- and twelve-year-olds do not feel they can count on police for help; the percentage increased to 75 percent among thirteen- to seventeen-year-olds.[17] The Minnesota Supreme Court Task Force on Racial Bias reported that 47 percent of Hennepin and Ramsey County judges agreed "minority defendants are more likely to be physically mistreated during custody"; 41 percent of public defense attorneys agreed.[18]

Juries

Juries are selected from lists of voter registrations, driver registrations, and Minnesota identification cards. Many Indians may not be in either group. As a result, Indians are greatly underrepresented in juries, even in areas that have significant Indian populations. Court policy in Beltrami County of granting a four-year exemption from jury duty for having served on the Red Lake Tribal Court further reduces potential Indian jurors there.

In 1990, Minnesota mandated that jury composition reflect the proportion of majority and minority groups in the general population. The Minnesota law was rejected in 1999 on racial quota grounds. In 2001, the Minnesota Supreme Court amended the rules to allow Hennepin and Ramsey County District Courts, on a pilot basis, to adopt new jury selection procedures guaranteeing minority representation on the grand jury equal to the percentage of the minority adult population of each judicial district.[19]

Employment in the Criminal Justice System

There are many barriers to increased Indian employment throughout the justice system. While Indian culture honors the warrior and many Indians have given outstanding service to the U.S. military, Indians tend to shy away from jobs that make them "the enforcer." They may be reluctant to enforce laws and policies that Indians have had little say in or those they believe show racial prejudice. Required educational standards may also be a barrier, as is a previous criminal arrest record.

The 2000 Federal Equal Employment Opportunity Report noted that Indians made up 1.4 percent of Minnesota's protection services personnel. Minneapolis reported that 3 percent of their police force was Indian in 1996, the same percentage as the Indian population in the 2000 U.S. Census.[20] However, this is three to four times lower than the percentage of the city's arrests of Indians. Indian employees comprised 2 percent of the Minnesota Department of Corrections in the late 1990s.[21]

There have been improvements. Indians have served as head of police and sheriff departments in the city of Bagley, Clearwater County, and Beltrami County. Fond du Lac Tribal and Community College offers an academic degree in law enforcement, qualifying graduates for special police training and employment as police officers.

Over the past twenty years, the number of American Indians receiving law degrees has increased, but as of 2002, American Indians still were only 0.2 percent of the legal profession in the United States.[22] In 2003, only eighteen out of 297 Minnesota state court judges were people of color (thirteen African-American, two Asian, two Hispanic, and one American Indian).[23]

While the number of Indian lawyers in the state is still small, their willingness to become involved in the judicial system has begun to make a difference and has the potential for major changes. A major milestone was the appointment of the state's first Indian district court judge in Hennepin County in 1995.

State Correctional Systems

State correctional facilities house adults who are sentenced to one year or more in prison. Sentences of less than one year of incarceration or longer ones that have been stayed by a judge are served in county jails. Youth offenders are placed in residential facilities, group homes, alternative, and nonresidential programs operated by public and private organizations or in out-of-state institutions. As of 2000, there were 414 American Indian adults and twenty-three juveniles in Minnesota correctional facilities, comprising 17 percent of the facilities' populations.[24] American Indians make up 33 percent of the juvenile resident population at the Red Wing Correctional Facility.

The Northwest Minnesota Juvenile Training Center in Bemidji has 40 to 50 percent Indian youths at its primary facility and five satellite units. The staff is about 35 percent Indian. They also operate a home for four to five youth on the Leech Lake Reservation, staffed by Indians. The Arrowhead Juvenile Center provides both correctional and detention facilities. In the Twin Cities, the Hennepin County Home School has 12 percent Indian youth.

State-Funded, Indian-Specific Corrections Programs

On release from state prison, some Indians are assigned to the ninety-day Walks Tall program, which provides assistance and informal support from a fellow Indian to help in the transition. The program operates in the Twin Cities, Duluth, and Bemidji and deals with fifty to sixty parolees at a time. State Corrections assists a few Indians at the Juel Fairbanks program in St. Paul, a structured residential program for adults.

Indian Cultural and Religious Freedom in Prison

Minnesota law requires the commissioner of corrections to set aside time and space for religious worship, and clergy are allowed to visit inmates (Minn. Stat. 241.05 and 243.48). There also is authorization for the state to contract for American Indian counseling programs and services at state correctional facilities, including providing Indian spiritual leaders and developing cultural pride (Minn. Stat. 241.80). By the late 1990s, most of the state and federal and some local institutions had access to Indian spiritual leaders and ceremonies. The availability of Indian groups in prison has helped many Indian prisoners learn for the first time their culture and its spiritual strengths.

However, there have been numerous charges over the past decade that Indians have been harassed or ridiculed for their spiritual ways and use of pipes, sweet grass, and sage, leading to further racial tensions. In addition, the state budgets for only one Indian spiritual leader to serve all state institutions, while more generous funding is provided for ministers of other faiths.

The Minnesota Department of Corrections has adopted religious policies that give the wardens a great deal of discretion to regulate spiritual practices based on safety and security considerations. While the regulations may be "reasonably related" to administering prisons, they put severe limits on Indian religious practices. Other major religions are not similarly affected. Many issues regarding freedom of Indian religious practice in prisons still are being debated in state and federal courts.

Legal Services

Indians who cannot afford an attorney are entitled to a publicly funded defense attorney, but Indians are critical of the program because the usually non-Indian attorneys are not knowledgeable about Indian issues. Dealing with Indians in the courts, especially in jurisdictional cases, is a very specialized area of law; most people are not familiar with it. In addition, the sheer number of cases and the limited funding for attorneys combine to put a great burden on the defense services.

State-Assisted Programs

The state responded to Indians' need for independent legal assistance by funding five special public defense programs for underserved populations: Legal Rights Center in Minneapolis, Neighborhood Justice Center in St. Paul, Indian Legal Services in Duluth, Leech Lake Criminal and Juvenile Defense Corporation, and White Earth Criminal and Juvenile Defense Corporation.

The Legal Rights Center in Minneapolis was begun in 1969 with AIM backing to provide legal services in criminal cases to low-income people. Directed by a community-based board, the program is well-known in the Minneapolis Indian community.

Indian Legal Services in Duluth provides legal assistance for Grand Portage, Bois Forte, Fond du Lac, and Mille Lacs Reservations as well as for Indians in Duluth. In addition to criminal cases, the office handles civil cases involving divorce, domestic abuse, and landlord–tenant problems.

Federally Funded Legal Services

Legal Services programs are available statewide to provide assistance for low-income people in civil matters such as domestic relations, cases involving children, landlord–tenant disputes, consumer problems, problems of the elderly, and issues concerning taxes, Social Security, welfare, and public benefit programs. These programs are prohibited from using funds to provide counsel in criminal cases, except for charges of criminal misdemeanors in tribal courts (42 U.S.C. 2992 f(b)(2)).

Anishinabe Legal Services in Cass Lake is the federally designated Indian program in Minnesota. It provides legal services primarily targeted to Indians, serving the Leech Lake, White Earth, and Red Lake Reservation areas. It also serves as the Legal Services office for the area. Other general public legal service programs serving major numbers of Indian clients include: Northwest Minnesota Legal Services for the Moorhead and Bemidji areas; Northeastern Minnesota Legal Services in Duluth, providing assistance in eleven counties west to Grand Rapids; Legal Aid Society of Minneapolis, covering a twenty-county area with three offices; Southern Minnesota Regional Legal Services in St. Paul serving thirty-three counties, as well as the Indian community in St. Paul.

Juvenile Justice System

The juvenile justice system is intended to help youth overcome criminal pasts through rehabilitation rather than punishment. The process allows flexibility to tailor programs to meet individual needs. As the growing juvenile criminal statistics show, many facets of the system are not working well.

The percentage of American Indians in juvenile correctional facilities grew from 12 percent in 1995 to 18 percent in 1999. In contrast, the white juvenile population decreased by 27 percent over the same period. American Indian juveniles made up 27 percent of the juvenile population in Beltrami County, 3 percent in Hennepin County, and 1 percent in St. Louis County. However, American Indian juveniles were 49 percent of juveniles arrested in Beltrami County, 7 percent in Hennepin County, and 13 percent in St. Louis County.

According to a long-time worker with inner-city Indian youth, "The law system doesn't work for the kids. Indian children are powerless. They get stopped for all kinds of things. They get things pinned on them. They don't know their legal rights. They can't speak for themselves; they need to be represented."[25]

Youth charged with felonies or gross misdemeanors are entitled to the same legal representation as adults. There is no provision for an attorney in misdemeanor cases, and approximately 50 percent of children do not have lawyers. Minnesota Supreme Court Justice Sandra Gardebring commented that this is one reason for the high number of Indian children in the court system. "If they are charged with

misdemeanors, they should at least see a lawyer. But there is no funding
. . . Once in the court process, it is all secret and there is very little
appeal possible. This makes bias particularly grievous in the juvenile
system."[26] Since the time of Gardebring's comment in 1994, juvenile courts have opened their doors in some, but not all, judicial
districts in Minnesota.

In spite of the system's goal to rehabilitate, an audit done by the
legislative auditor in 1995 showed that this clearly was not being
achieved. Over 90 percent of males released from Red Wing and
Sauk Center had adult arrests by their twenty-third birthdays, and 85
to 89 percent were arrested for felonies.[27]

The audit in 1995 also found that it appeared that placement
decisions were being made based on financial considerations, not necessarily on what is best for the child. Sauk Center and Red Wing are
intended to house youth who have had the most extensive and serious
criminal records. They are also the only state institutions totally state-
funded for counties that did not accept the Community Corrections
Act (CCA). On the other hand, the CCA counties are required to pay
about 75 percent of the costs for their youth. The study found that the
non-CCA counties were sending a much larger share of their juveniles
to state institutions, and these youths' records indicated they had
committed fewer serious offenses, although the institutions are
intended to take the most serious offenders.[28] While racial figures
were not a part of the study, Indian youth comprise approximately 12
to 15 percent of the two facilities' populations.

Indians also criticize juvenile release programs. Responding to
the problems of dealing with released youth, the Minnesota Department of Corrections established an advisory group that included five
Indians to advise on improving services closer to the communities to
which Indian youth are returning.

Limited Juvenile Justice Programming for Indians

There are very few juvenile diversion programs with an Indian focus,
and there is a major gap in programming for young people fifteen
years and older. A study by the American Indian Research and Policy
Institute of state juvenile justice programming concluded that there
are no state standards defining what is culturally specific programming and that there is a distinct lack of Indian programming in
Minnesota's juvenile justice system.[29]

The 2003 Juvenile Justice Advisory Committee in Minnesota reported there were no programs funded that specifically targeted American Indian youth.[30] At the federal level, the Native American Juvenile Justice program's budget was slashed by 80 percent from 1998 to 2003.

Ain Dah Yung "Our Home Shelter Center" in St. Paul provides a residential correctional program for a few youth in minor criminal cases. The City, Inc. operates two nonresidential Indian-focused programs in Minneapolis. AIM operates the Indian-oriented Elaine M. Stately Peacemaker Youth Center in Minneapolis. It provides an after-school drop-in center and programming for Indian youth on a gang-neutral basis. Its goal is crime and violence prevention for the Indian community's most at-risk youth.

Tribal Courts

In exercising their sovereignty, all reservations have court systems to resolve internal tribal disputes, resolve election challenges, and enforce tribal laws and regulations. Appeals are possible to judges appointed by tribal governments for this purpose.

For those designated by Congress as coming under Public Law 280 (Fond du Lac, Grand Portage, Leech Lake, Mille Lacs, White Earth, and the four Dakota Communities), the state has responsibility for criminal prohibitive laws, although the tribes retain concurrent jurisdiction. Most state civil regulatory laws cannot be enforced by the state against tribal members on the reservation. On Bois Forte Reservation, criminal jurisdiction was returned to tribal and federal jurisdiction in 1973. The Red Lake Tribe was never a part of Public Law 280, and all jurisdiction on the reservation is either tribal or federal.

Each tribal court has considerable variation in jurisdiction. Conservation courts and tribal wardens operate on Bois Forte, Fond du Lac, Leech Lake, Mille Lacs, White Earth, and Red Lake Reservations. A separate conservation court and wardens operate for the Arrowhead 1854 Treaty Area, serving the Bois Forte and Grand Portage tribal members. The court acts as Grand Portage's conservation court. Fond du Lac has separate wardens and a court for the same 1854 Treaty region.

While severely limited by lack of funds, Red Lake, Bois Forte, and Mille Lacs Reservations provide some court services for families and children. The four Dakota courts provide broad civil jurisdiction. Major changes have begun occurring over the past few years: Bois Forte Tribe has started to delve into civil jurisdiction matters; Grand Portage Tribe has begun its own court to deal with civil matters; Mille Lacs Band handles not only natural resources and family and children services, but also probate, debt collection, and employee grievances; and the White Earth Tribe began its court in December 1997 and is building a professional police force.

Casinos have their own security staff, although criminal violations are usually dealt with in the state courts for the Public Law 280 reservations. Tribal courts deal with civil matters from the casinos, such as alleged human rights violations and other civil suits.

In March 2003, the Minnesota Supreme Court rejected a rule proposed by the Tribal Court/State Court Forum, which would have mandated state courts' rubber stamping of most tribal court actions, both criminal and civil, giving them the same force as state court actions. The Supreme Court said while it was not ready to adopt the proposal of the Court Forum, it directed the advisory committee to develop a framework for the recognition and enforcement of tribal orders and judgments where there is an existing legislative basis for doing so.

The Indian Child Welfare Act (ICWA) and the Violence Against Women Act (VAWA) do provide for limited acceptance of tribal court orders and judgments, generally based on potential emergency situations.[31]

The Indian Civil Rights Act

The Indian Civil Rights Act (ICRA) (Pub. L. 90-284; 25 U.S.C. 1301–1341 (1968)) was passed to extend most of the U.S. Constitution's Bill of Rights to individual Indians on reservations and to limit the powers of tribal governments over their members, an intrusion on tribal sovereignty criticized by many Indian tribes. Arthur A. Fletcher, Chairman of the U.S. Commission on Civil Rights, after extensive hearings on the implementation of the act, testified, "The act reflects the bias that the non-Indian adversarial judicial system was somehow superior to the tribal government's judicial system."[32]

A review of tribal courts in the 1980s by the U.S. Commission on Civil Rights concluded that "prior to any further intrusion by Federal Government into tribal justice systems . . . tribal forums be first given the opportunity to institute proper mechanisms that would operate with adequate resources, training, funding and support from the Federal Government."[33] Federal legislation (Indian Tribal Justice Act) followed, which authorized major funding to upgrade tribal courts.

The ensuing court actions as well as voluntary changes have:

❏ Affirmed that federal courts can only be used for appeal on issues of habeas corpus, testing the legality of imprisonment (25 U.S.C. 1301–1303).

❏ Affirmed that a trial by jury of no fewer than six persons must be available if requested for any defendant accused of an offense punishable by imprisonment as required in the ICRA (*Good v. Graves,* Civ. No. 6-85-508 (D. Minn. 1985); *Cook v. Moran,* No. 6-85-1513 (D. Minn. 1986)).

❏ Retained the policy that defendants have a right to counsel at their own expense under ICRA. However, because of their limited finances, Indian courts are not required to pay legal fees. Legal Services attorneys are available for low-income people in tribal court civil cases.

❏ Allowed non-Indian lawyers to practice in tribal court. Red Lake Tribal Court allowed this in 1991. However, what qualifications an individual must have to represent someone in tribal court is established by tribal law.

❏ Upgraded the courts with assistance from the National Indian Justice Center. With help from the Bush Foundation, all reservations have acquired law libraries.

Difficulties of Applying the U.S. Court System on the Reservations

The nature of reservation life makes it difficult for police or courts to provide services that are viewed as fair and impartial. Factionalism, extended family kinship systems, or resentment of outside interference may lead to charges of harassment or excessive leniency. Tribal sovereignty legally rests with the elected councils that can control the court system through passing laws, appointing and removing judges, funding the court, and authorizing who can appear in court. In some instances, these governments have used their powers to ensure reelection through manipulating laws and operating fraudulent elections, which in turn were not challenged by appeals court judges who were appointed by the same government officials. These abuses were documented in the 1996 trials of some of the leadership on the White Earth and Leech Lake Reservations.

JURY TRIALS   The Indian Civil Rights Act requires that an accused person in a criminal case be given the right to a trial by a jury of not fewer than six persons if the offense is punishable by imprisonment. This has put an increasing financial burden on the courts and is making it difficult to bring all cases to trial. A tribal judge testified that nearly everyone asks for a jury trial, knowing that the chances of being brought to trial are slim.[34]

The chief judge of the Bois Forte Tribe also commented that Indians find it difficult to act as a judge and interfere in others' lives, especially restricting their freedom. "No one on the reservation, sitting face to face with another person wants to vote to put them in jail. It is just not in Indian culture to do that."[35] It is also difficult to find impartial jurors who are not family, related to the police, witnesses, or otherwise potentially prejudiced.

To deal with these issues, some reservations are convening a "standing jury," similar to a grand jury. Respected members of the community are specifically chosen to act as the jury. While some have suggested that difficult cases be transferred to another tribe for an impartial hearing, this can interfere with tribal sovereignty.

AN INDEPENDENT JUDICIARY   Providing a judiciary independent of the tribal governing body has been difficult. For a brief time, the Mille Lacs Band tried electing judges but reverted to using appointed courts in the mid-1990s. Some tribes, including the Dakota Communities, Shakopee Mdewakanton, and Prairie Island, have combined to establish an appeals court.

FUNDING   Inadequate funding is at the heart of many problems with the tribal justice systems. In its 1991 report, the U.S. Commission on Civil Rights stated that tribal courts should be funded in an amount equal to an equivalent state court, salaries need to be increased, and public defenders should be funded.[36]

In response, Congress passed the Indian Tribal Justice Act (Pub. L. 103-176, 25 U.S.C. 3601 (1993)) and authorized $58 million per year to professionalize Indian courts. However, the funds were never made available, and by the time the act expired in 1999, only $5 million had actually been appropriated. The National American Indian Court Judges Association noted that if the originally promised $58 million was not going to be appropriated, then tribal courts should at least be funded at $15 million per year, more than twice the 2003 appropriation, to ensure their continued operation.

The effects of inadequate funding of tribal courts are far-reaching. With underfunded tribal courts, the burden for criminal justice will continue to fall on the federal court system, where sentences are typically harsher, perpetuating a system of dual justice for Indians. In addition, developing systems that effectively resolve civil disputes is an essential component of tribal self-governance and therefore self-sufficiency.[37]

Enforcement Issues

Under federal laws, any non-Indian who commits a criminal offense on a reservation is under state jurisdiction. However, Indians have long believed that the federal government is reluctant to get involved and slow to act. Acknowledging that "crime on Indian reservations has been neglected," the U.S. Attorney for Minnesota increased prosecutions throughout the 1980s and 1990s.

Basic law enforcement is one of the most urgent needs on reservations. The U.S. Commission on Civil Rights estimated in 2003 that tribes have between 55 to 75 percent of the resources available to non-Indian communities. "Large cities such as New York, Washington, D.C., and Detroit provide between four and seven officers per thousand residents, whereas few departments in Indian Country have more than two per thousand."[38]

While casinos have their own security employees, county sheriffs and other local officials have law enforcement responsibilities at the casinos. However, a survey done by the Gaming Enforcement Division, Minnesota Department of Public Safety, found that casinos were a low priority, with officers reporting they had more serious crimes with which to deal. From the tribal point of view, tribal police lack the authority to deal with disruptive behavior by non-Indians.

Minnesota Statute 626.84 recognizes tribal government law enforcement and allows cross-deputization. This has provided for more effective law enforcement on the reservations and helped tribal law enforcement officers work more closely with county officers.

Reciprocity and Jurisdiction

The Indian Child Welfare Act requires that state courts accept tribal court decisions. Red Lake court decisions are generally accepted throughout the state, and the Mille Lacs court has reciprocity with some counties. However, there is not uniform acceptance, and jurisdictional problems remain. There are no other federal or state laws mandating reciprocity.

Major Changes

Strengthening Laws and Enforcement

Major changes have been made in recent years to strengthen laws affecting Indians. Juveniles can be fined, and their trust account can be taken and used for restitution. Parents may be liable for injury or property damages caused by their child. To deal with the intimidation of jurors who fear possible retaliation from the defendant's family, a guilty verdict no longer requires a unanimous vote of the jury. Judges have been given the power to overturn jury verdicts. Sex offenders can be tried in tribal court and sentenced to imprisonment for up to one year for each offense, with the additional sentences added on after the first year. These types of crimes had previously had poor federal prosecution, with action often delayed one year or more.

The U.S. Attorney can still prosecute under federal laws. Because Indian tribes are separate political communities, the U.S. Supreme Court ruled (*U.S. v. Wheeler*, 435 U.S. 313 (1978)) that an Indian defendant found guilty by a tribal court can be prosecuted again by the United States.

Alternative Sentencing/Restitutions

At the time it established their Court of Central Jurisdiction, the Mille Lacs Band included the flexibility to use the more Indian approach of a Cultural Court, where the parties involved can talk informally through the problems and arrive at an acceptable solution. This concept was expanded in 1996 with a Restorative Justice Project designed to make the offender accountable to the entire community and to provide restitution to the victim. It is available on a volunteer basis for those who have pled guilty to certain misdemeanors.

Sentencing Circles bring the offender, the victim, elders, community members, and social services specialists together on a volunteer basis to arrive at an appropriate punishment. Since Mille Lacs is a Public Law 280 reservation under state criminal jurisdiction, the county court retains responsibility for the case, making the decision to refer to the Project and to accept the Sentencing Circle's recommendation. Healing Circles will also be implemented to provide immediate support to the victim, bringing community members into the process.

Red Lake has piloted a restitution program for youth, Creating Restitution and Following Traditions (C.R.A.F.T.). On assignment by the tribal court, the youth attends sessions to receive instruction in traditional skills with the obligation that a gift be made for the victim. The goal is to expand cultural skills and appreciation for them and to bring the offender and victim together to create peace and harmony.

Banishment

At least seven of Minnesota's eleven Indian bands have either passed or used banishment-type laws within the past decade. In 2003, the Grand Portage Band of Ojibwe approved a law that revived the practice of banishment as a penalty for violent or gang activity. According to Band Chairman Norman Deschampe, "When people cross that line and the community says we've had enough, it's a process we can use to deal with it."[39]

Expanding Jurisdictions

Tribes are expanding their police and court systems in several ways:

> ❏ As more tribes use cross-deputizing with the State Department of Natural Resources, game warden responsibilities have increased, and new courts have been established to deal with members' use of off-reservation treaty-provided rights.

❏ Courts capable of dealing with family matters and Indian child welfare issues have long been a goal of the tribes, and counties are increasingly turning to tribes for these cases.

❏ Frustration over perceived inequities in county-provided protection in criminal matters is leading to state-negotiated arrangements, returning more of the jurisdiction to the tribes.

❏ To protect sovereignty, the necessity of business codes and courts capable of dealing with financial issues, especially as they relate to casino operations, have led to improvements of these services.

Gaps

CIVIL REGULATORY LAW   As they increasingly acknowledge that the state lacks authority over civil regulatory matters on reservations, state court decisions are leaving a legal vacuum. Dealing with these issues remains a challenge. A series of court decisions during the mid-1990s ruled that state civil regulatory laws could not be enforced against tribal members by counties on reservations. A great deal of confusion has resulted, and in some counties, sheriffs continue to make arrests. In other areas, enforcement has stopped, but tribes are not yet equipped to deal with the issues. If there is final agreement by the courts that the state has no jurisdiction in civil regulatory areas, it will mean changes in law enforcement and court responsibilities on most of the state's reservations.

To deal with these and other issues, state law was changed to allow tribal police officers to be cross-deputized. These tribal officers meet state requirements, including post-board certification; therefore, they can arrest individuals under state law where state law applies.

WHITE EARTH RESERVATION   Public Law 280 created special problems on White Earth Reservation. The law sent all civil jurisdiction to the tribe, but criminal jurisdiction remained with the three counties encompassing the reservation. With these three entities responsible for portions of the reservation and because each had limited funds, issues of responsibility are clouded. As one White

Earth council member testified, "The problem is getting worse and no increase in law enforcement money is in sight."[40]

White Earth currently has law enforcement agreements with both Mahmonen and Becker Counties, which allow county and tribal officers to have concurrent criminal and civil jurisdiction. White Earth has a police department, established in 1995, which has grown and supplements area counties.

White Earth also has a court system that operates on a shoestring budget provided primarily from casino profits and the BIA. Where it once handled only hunting and fishing cases, its jurisdiction has expanded dramatically in recent years. The court now handles traffic violations, child protection, juvenile justice, and a variety of civil cases and is planning to take on domestic violence codes.[41]

Summary

Reservation communities continue to seek better law enforcement and justice alternatives more in line with Indian culture. The present criminal justice system has many inadequacies for Indians that may be causing more problems than it is solving. The number and treatment of Indians throughout the criminal justice system raise questions of racial bias.

Tribes are taking increasing responsibility for their own law enforcement and punishments, but in doing so, tribes face tremendous legal, jurisdictional, and financial challenges. Tribal courts are underfunded, and the nature of reservation life can make it difficult for police or courts to provide services that are viewed as fair and impartial.

The underrepresentation of Indians employed in the criminal justice system is of continuing concern, although the numbers of Indian lawyers, judges, sheriffs, and police officers is increasing. Also of concern is the lack of Indian programming and personnel in Minnesota's juvenile justice system.

The strong correlation between criminal behavior and other social problems means that improvements in Indian education, employment, housing, and chemical dependency prevention and treatment are essential to reducing crime in Indian communities.

Conclusion

IN ITS JULY 2003 evaluation of the federal government's programs to assist Indians, the U.S. Commission on Civil Rights concluded, "Measured by honor of funding commitments, none of the agencies reviewed has met its obligations to Native American tribes. . . . The government's failure has resulted in services that are of lower quality than those provided to other Americans and inequitable access to much-needed programs." Importantly, the Commission said that new agreements and studies were not what were needed; rather, "swift and decisive action oriented to fulfilling existing federal responsibility must be taken."[1]

Indians' relationship to the federal government is unique and complex. They are a sovereign people, but they rely on the government's protection and assistance. Long ago, the federal government promised, through treaties and laws, to support and protect Indians in exchange for their lands and in compensation for forcing them onto reservations. The very existence of the tribe depends on the federal government continuing to honor these past treaties and legal commitments. Yet Indians are continually threatened by unilateral government actions.

Maintaining their sovereignty, their culture, their language, their tribes, and their reservations are the top priorities for Indians in Minnesota. There are many encouraging signs as tribes extend their sovereignty and build brighter economic futures while preserving their traditional ways. But many distressing signs remain, since Indians in Minnesota continue to rank at or near the bottom of many social, health, and economic indicators.

Government actions have in many ways shaped today's problems for Indians; therefore, the government has an obligation to help provide solutions. For many of the very pressing and debilitating human problems in the Indian community, government assistance is the only way to obtain sufficient help. This help, if it is to be truly beneficial, must involve Indians in the planning, directing, and staffing of programs—programs that are shaped to Indian culture and unique Indian needs.

Indians are gaining increasing control through self-governance programs, which allow tribes to contract directly to receive all of a program's funds and to set their own spending priorities. Funding levels are a continuing problem since programs are cut while growing needs are not addressed.

Because government relations are so fundamental to Indian existence, it is important that all Americans have a more accurate understanding of Indians' unique status and needs. Annually, state and federal legislative proposals severely encroach on the sovereign rights of tribes and threaten the already inadequate funding tribes receive. With a better-informed public, these issues would not have to be revisited year after year. The greatest long-term contributions to the needs of Indians will be acceptance of their sovereignty and commitment to consistent, long-term, and adequately funded programs.

Indians' challenge to themselves was eloquently and insightfully summarized by Marge Anderson, former Chief Executive of the Mille Lacs Band of Ojibwe:

> We are the survivors. . . . We have weathered the storms of injustice. . . . We have seen our darkest hour. . . . All of the answers to all of our problems come from us. We no longer look to Washington for answers. We look to tribal self-governance. We look to our own economic development. We look within our traditions for the answers. . . . We must, above all, teach our children to walk into the next millennium with heads held high like the warriors that preceded them, and to face each challenge that comes with strength, and with confidence and with hope.[2]

Glossary

Bureau of Indian Affairs (BIA)

In 1824, Indian affairs were placed in the War Department; they were transferred to the newly organized Department of the Interior in 1849. Originally called the Office of Indian Affairs, it later became the Bureau of Indian Affairs.

ceded lands

In the treaties, American Indian tribes ceded vast segments of their homelands in exchange for honoring their right to retain small segments of this land for tribal members in common. The treaties included provisions that guaranteed the tribes government services in the areas of education, health, and technical assistance. Some of the treaties guaranteed tribal members the right to hunt, fish, and gather resources in a customary manner on ceded lands.

closed reservation

On a closed reservation, tribal government has full sovereignty over its land, its members, and other American Indians within its boundaries, subject only to federal legislation. The reservation is not subject to state law. Red Lake is the only closed Minnesota reservation.

Dakota

The Dakota ("friends" or "allies") were called Sioux by the whites, from the French corruption "Nadouessioux" of the Ojibwe word "Nadowa," meaning "snake" or "enemy." Sioux was the name used by the U.S. government in its formal treaty and other legal relations. The people call themselves Dakota, the term used in this book.

fee lands

Privately owned lands within the boundaries of the reservation. Despite treaties that "reserved" such lands for Indians, the U.S. government sold selected parcels to non-Indians. Fee lands are subject to property taxes.

Indian Affairs Council (IAC)

The first legislated state body to focus on Indians and the official liaison between state and tribal governments.

Indian Child Welfare Act (ICWA)

In 1978, Congress passed the Indian Child Welfare Act (ICWA) (Pub. L. 95-608, 25 U.S.C. 1901–1963) to end the abuses by giving tribes the opportunity to control what happened to Indian children.

Indian Reorganization Act (IRA)

Passed in 1934, this law marked a major change in federal policy and became the New Deal program for Indians. The IRA ended land allotment and the conveyance of allotted land to fee patented status. The tribal land base was rebuilt by funding two million dollars for the purchase of lands to be held in trust for the tribes and returning to the tribes original reservation lands still unsold. The IRA recognized the tribes' right to self-government. See chapter 2.

Minnesota Chippewa Tribe (MCT)

The formal governing body of six Ojibwe reservations: Bois Forte, Fond du Lac, Grand Portage, Leech Lake, Mille Lacs, and White Earth.

Minnesota Indian Gaming Association (MIGA)

Formed in 1987 to provide a single voice to speak for the tribes' mutual interests and to help member tribes exchange information, address shared concerns, and educate the public, media, and elected officials on tribal gaming and other issues of importance to tribal governments. MIGA represents nine of the eleven Minnesota tribes.

Ojibwe

"Chippewa" was the formal name used in treaties and remains the legal name for government bodies, but it was a corruption of "Ojibwe" (the term used by Indians and throughout this book), meaning "puckered toe," which describes the moccasins they wore. The name for these people in Ojibwe is Anishinabe, meaning "original man" or "spontaneous or genuine people."

Public Law 280

Congress passed Public Law 280 in 1953, transferring legal jurisdiction to states. Congress delegated to the state criminal jurisdiction over tribal members on most Minnesota reservations. The tribe also retains criminal jurisdiction over members. When dual authority is exercised, an offender can be tried twice for the same or similar offense. Red Lake and Bois Forte are not under Public Law 280's criminal provisions. On those reservations, the federal government deals with major crimes, and the reservation courts deal with the rest. All non-Indians on any reservation are under that state's criminal authority. All of the Public Law 280 reservations have their own criminal systems with tribal police and courts that apply to tribal members.

reservations

> Reservations are original land reserved for Indians where Indian sovereignty is retained.

self-governance

> Tribes in direct negotiation can receive direct funding for programs they want to run themselves; tribes are no longer required to deal with subordinate bureaucracies, such as BIA area and agency offices. Reporting is reduced to an annual accounting, with the hope that reducing paperwork would make more money available for programs. This much greater flexibility has proved successful, allowing tribes to target their unique needs.

sovereignty

> Indian people have a unique status because they are members of tribes whose governments are not part of the federal government and are not subject to state jurisdiction. Tribal governments form a third governing system in the United States. They retain the inherent sovereignty that is recognized by signing treaties. They are nations within a nation, with limited powers.

trust land and allotted land

> The U.S. government holds two major categories of trust land: land allotted to Indian individuals and tribal land held in trust. Once in trust, land cannot be sold or taken by court action and is exempt from property taxes. Income earned from operations on the property is not subject to state income taxation. Through generations, allotted lands have been divided among heirs, creating a complicated legal situation. Individuals involved with these lands may apply to the BIA to remove them from trust status so the land can be sold; qualified Indians may also apply to have lands they purchase taken into trust. The tribes do not have any control over allotted lands.

Appendix A

Minnesota Indian Reservations: Facts, Figures, and Maps

- ❏ Bois Forte
- ❏ Fond du Lac
- ❏ Grand Portage
- ❏ Leech Lake
- ❏ Lower Sioux
- ❏ Mille Lacs
- ❏ Prairie Island
- ❏ Red Lake Nation
- ❏ Shakopee Mdewakanton
- ❏ Upper Sioux Community
- ❏ White Earth

BOIS FORTE
Minnesota Chippewa Tribe Member
5344 Lakeshore Drive
PO Box 16
Nett Lake, MN 55772
(218) 757-3261
(800) 221-8129
www.boisforte.com

Tribal Enrollment (1999): 2,767
Tribal Land: 31,624 acres
Allotted Lands: 12,160 acres
Original Reservation Land: 127,000 acres

Unemployment Rate: 7.9%
Poverty Rate: 23.7%
Average Income: $28,214
Median Home Value: $41,400
(2000 U.S. Census Data)

Casinos:
Fortune Bay Resort Casino
1430 Bois Forte Road
Tower, MN 55790
(800) 922-7529 (Casino)
(800) 555-1714 (Resort)
www.fortunebay.com

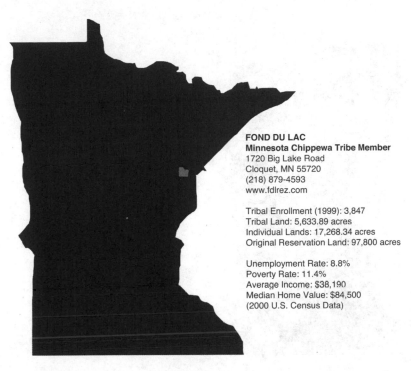

FOND DU LAC
Minnesota Chippewa Tribe Member
1720 Big Lake Road
Cloquet, MN 55720
(218) 879-4593
www.fdlrez.com

Tribal Enrollment (1999): 3,847
Tribal Land: 5,633.89 acres
Individual Lands: 17,268.34 acres
Original Reservation Land: 97,800 acres

Unemployment Rate: 8.8%
Poverty Rate: 11.4%
Average Income: $38,190
Median Home Value: $84,500
(2000 U.S. Census Data)

Schools:
Fond du Lac Tribal and Community College:
2101 14th St.
Cloquet, MN 55720
(800) 657-3712
www.fdl.cc.mn.us

Casinos:
Black Bear Casino and Hotel
1785 Highway 210
PO Box 777
Carlton, MN 55790
(888) 771-0777
www.blackbearcasinohotel.com

Fond-du-Luth Casino
129 East Superior Street
Duluth, MN 55802
(800) 873-0280
www.fondduluthcasino.com

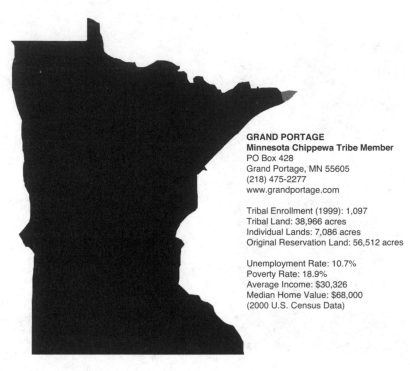

GRAND PORTAGE
Minnesota Chippewa Tribe Member
PO Box 428
Grand Portage, MN 55605
(218) 475-2277
www.grandportage.com

Tribal Enrollment (1999): 1,097
Tribal Land: 38,966 acres
Individual Lands: 7,086 acres
Original Reservation Land: 56,512 acres

Unemployment Rate: 10.7%
Poverty Rate: 18.9%
Average Income: $30,326
Median Home Value: $68,000
(2000 U.S. Census Data)

Casinos:
Grand Portage Lodge and Casino
PO Box 233
Grand Portage, MN 55605
(218) 475-2401
(800) 543-1385

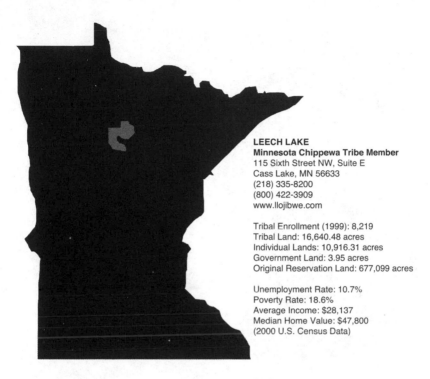

LEECH LAKE
Minnesota Chippewa Tribe Member
115 Sixth Street NW, Suite E
Cass Lake, MN 56633
(218) 335-8200
(800) 422-3909
www.llojibwe.com

Tribal Enrollment (1999): 8,219
Tribal Land: 16,640.48 acres
Individual Lands: 10,916.31 acres
Government Land: 3.95 acres
Original Reservation Land: 677,099 acres

Unemployment Rate: 10.7%
Poverty Rate: 18.6%
Average Income: $28,137
Median Home Value: $47,800
(2000 U.S. Census Data)

Schools:
Leech Lake Tribal College:
6945 Littlewolf Road NW
Cass Lake, MN 56633
(218) 335-4200
www.lltc.com

Bug-O-Nay-Ge-Shig Tribal School
15353 Silver Eagle Drive NW
Bena, MN 56626
(800) 265-5576
www.bugschool.bia.edu

Casinos:
Northern Lights Casino
6800 Y Frontage Road NW
Walker, MN 56484
(800) 252-7529
www.northernlightcasino.com

White Oak Casino
45830 US Highway 2
Deer River, MN 56636
(800) 653-2412
www.whiteoakcasino.com

Palace Hotel & Casino
6280 Upper Cass Frontage Road NW
Cass Lake, MN 56633
(800) 442-3910 (Hotel)
(877) 972-5223 (Casino)

LOWER SIOUX
PO Box 308
Morton, MN 56270
(507) 697-6185

Tribal Enrollment (1999): 930
Tribal Land: 1,785 acres

Unemployment Rate: 10.7%
Poverty Rate: 6.0%
Average Income: $69,792
Median Home Value: $66,400
(2000 U.S. Census Data)

Casino:
Jackpot Junction Casino and Hotel
39375 County Highway 24
PO Box 56270
Morton, MN 56270
(800) 946-2274
www.jackpotjunction.com

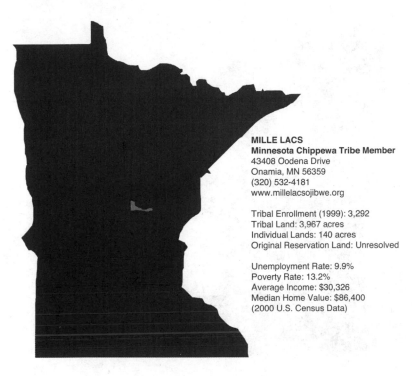

MILLE LACS
Minnesota Chippewa Tribe Member
43408 Oodena Drive
Onamia, MN 56359
(320) 532-4181
www.millelacsojibwe.org

Tribal Enrollment (1999): 3,292
Tribal Land: 3,967 acres
Individual Lands: 140 acres
Original Reservation Land: Unresolved

Unemployment Rate: 9.9%
Poverty Rate: 13.2%
Average Income: $30,326
Median Home Value: $86,400
(2000 U.S. Census Data)

Casinos:
Grand Casino Mille Lacs
777 Grand Avenue
Onamia, MN 56359
(800) 626-5825

Grand Casino Hinckley
777 Lady Luck Drive
Hinckley, MN 55037
(800) 472-6321
www.grandcasinomn.com

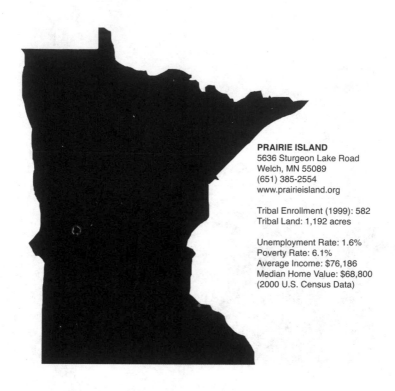

PRAIRIE ISLAND
5636 Sturgeon Lake Road
Welch, MN 55089
(651) 385-2554
www.prairieisland.org

Tribal Enrollment (1999): 582
Tribal Land: 1,192 acres

Unemployment Rate: 1.6%
Poverty Rate: 6.1%
Average Income: $76,186
Median Home Value: $68,800
(2000 U.S. Census Data)

Casino:
Treasure Island Resort & Casino
PO Box 75
Red Wing, MN 55066
(800) 222-7077
www.treasureislandcasino.com

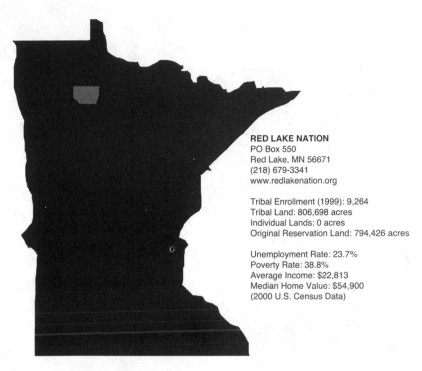

RED LAKE NATION
PO Box 550
Red Lake, MN 56671
(218) 679-3341
www.redlakenation.org

Tribal Enrollment (1999): 9,264
Tribal Land: 806,698 acres
Individual Lands: 0 acres
Original Reservation Land: 794,426 acres

Unemployment Rate: 23.7%
Poverty Rate: 38.8%
Average Income: $22,813
Median Home Value: $54,900
(2000 U.S. Census Data)

Schools:
Red Lake Nation Tribal College:
23750 Highway 1 East
PO Box 576
Red Lake, MN 56671
(218) 679-2860
www.redlakenationcollege.org

Casinos:
Seven Clans Casino (Red Lake)
(888) 679-2501

Seven Clans Casino (Warroad)
(800) 815-8293

Seven Clans Casino (Thief River Falls)
(800) 881-0712
www.sevenclanscasino.com

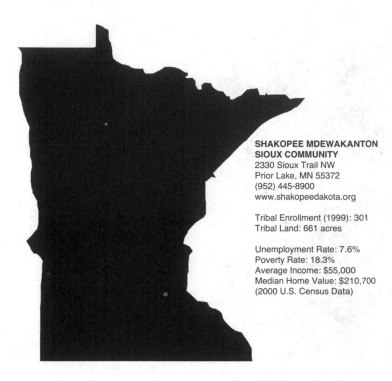

**SHAKOPEE MDEWAKANTON
SIOUX COMMUNITY**
2330 Sioux Trail NW
Prior Lake, MN 55372
(952) 445-8900
www.shakopeedakota.org

Tribal Enrollment (1999): 301
Tribal Land: 661 acres

Unemployment Rate: 7.6%
Poverty Rate: 18.3%
Average Income: $55,000
Median Home Value: $210,700
(2000 U.S. Census Data)

Casino:
Mystic Lake Casino Hotel
2400 Mystic Lake Boulevard
Prior Lake, MN 55372
(952) 445-9000
(800) 262-7799
www.mysticlake.com

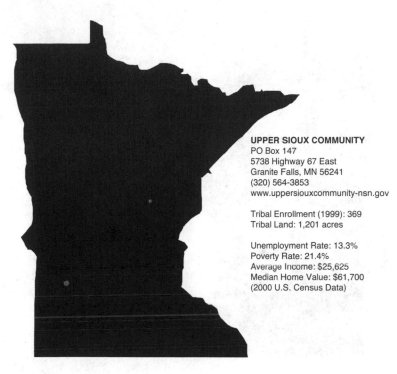

UPPER SIOUX COMMUNITY
PO Box 147
5738 Highway 67 East
Granite Falls, MN 56241
(320) 564-3853
www.uppersiouxcommunity-nsn.gov

Tribal Enrollment (1999): 369
Tribal Land: 1,201 acres

Unemployment Rate: 13.3%
Poverty Rate: 21.4%
Average Income: $25,625
Median Home Value: $61,700
(2000 U.S. Census Data)

Casino:
Prairie's Edge Casino Resort
5616 Prairie's Edge Lane
Granite Falls, MN 56241
(320) 564-2121
(866) 293-2121
www.prairiesedgecasino.com

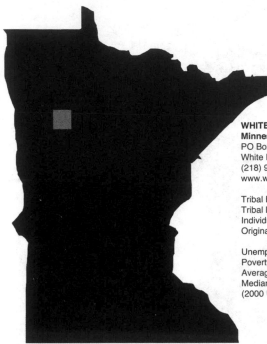

WHITE EARTH
Minnesota Chippewa Tribe Member
PO Box 418
White Earth, MN 56591
(218) 983-3285
www.whiteearth.com

Tribal Enrollment (1999): 21,083
Tribal Land: 56,116 acres
Individual Lands: 2,500 acres
Original Reservation Land: 709,467 acres

Unemployment Rate: 8.2%
Poverty Rate: 15.9%
Average Income: $28,487
Median Home Value: $51,500
(2000 U.S. Census Data)

Schools:
White Earth Tribal & Community College
202 South Main Street
Mahnomen, MN 56557
(218) 935-0417
www.wetcc.org

Circle of Life School
PO Box 418
White Earth, MN 56591
(218) 983-4180

Casino:
Shooting Star Casino & Hotel
777 Casino Road
Mahnomen, MN 56557-7902
(800) 453-7827
(218) 935-2711
www.starcasino.com

Appendix B

Treaties, Significant Federal Legislation, and Federal Court Decisions

Treaties, Significant Federal Legislation, and Federal Court Decisions

Treaties and Agreements

Establishing Minnesota's Reservations

1825   Treaty with the Chippewa, Sioux, and six other tribes signed at Prairie du Chien (7 Stat. 272; II Kappler 250). Established a boundary line between the Chippewa and Sioux (Article 5). A boundary also established between the Sioux, Sacs, and Foxes along Iowa border (Article 2). Tribes acknowledge the controlling power of the United States.

1826   Treaty with the Chippewa Nation signed at Fond du Lac (7 Stat. 291). Chippewa tribe gave the United States the right to search for and carry away minerals, but this would not affect the title of the land (Article 3).

1830   Treaty with the Sacs, Foxes, and other tribes (7 Stat. 328) ceded a small parcel in extreme southwestern and the extreme southeastern corner of Minnesota (along with land in Iowa and Missouri). Retained hunting and fishing rights were ceded in 1837 (7 Stat. 543).

Sioux (Dakota)

1808   Senate ratified 1805 Fort St. Anthony purchase (II Kappler 1031).

1830   Treaty with the Sioux, Sac, and Fox signed at Prairie du Chien (7 Stat. 328, II Kappler 305–309) ceded a twenty-mile-wide strip of land on the north side of the dividing line set in 1825 in attempt to keep peace. Small triangular parcel in southwestern Minnesota ceded; Sac and Fox ceded interest in the extreme southeastern corner of Minnesota.

1830   Sioux ceded land along the Mississippi River, near Red Wing, to be used for "half breeds." In 1851, this land was again ceded for non-Indian occupation.

1837   Treaty with the Sioux signed at Washington, D.C. (7 Stat. 538; Il Kappler 493). Ceded all Dakota lands east of the Mississippi River.

1851   Treaty with the Sisseton and Wahpeton bands signed at Traverse des Sioux (10 Stat. 949, II Kappler 588); treaty with Mdewakanton and Wahpekute bands signed at Mendota (10 Stat. 954; II Kappler 591). Ceded all Sioux lands in Minnesota and created two reservations 150 miles long and 10 miles wide, on either side of the Minnesota River. On ratification, the Senate struck the reservation from both treaties and inserted a payment of ten cents per acre.

1858   Treaty with the Mdewakanton and Wahpekute bands and treaty with Sisseton and Wahpeton Sioux signed at Washington, D.C. (12 Stat. 1031 and 1037; II Kappler 781, 785). Reservation land south of the Minnesota River allotted, and land north of the river to be sold. Indians received 30 cents per acre; settlers could buy at $1.25. Nearly all of the payment to the Lower Sioux and a large part to the Upper Sioux went to pay traders.

1858   Treaty with the Yankton Sioux signed at Washington, D.C. (11 Stat. 743; II Kappler 776). Ceded the pipestone quarry in Minnesota, with the provision that it be kept open to Indians "to visit and procure stone for pipes so long as they desire."

1863   Acts of Congress unilaterally abrogated all treaties with the four Minnesota Sioux bands and made payment to white victims (12 Stat. 652); ordered the Indian removal from Minnesota and the sale of their lands, while "meritorious" Indians who had befriended whites could have land on their old reservations (12 Stat. 819). Funding was authorized in 1865 (13 Stat. 427), but nothing happened. Legislation also ordered the Winnebagos removed "beyond the limits of any state" (12 Stat. 658).

1867   Treaty with Sisseton and Wahpeton Bands established reservations at Devil's Lake, North Dakota, and Sisseton (Lake Traverse), South Dakota, for the 1,200 to 1,500 Indians who remained friendly to the United States and put their lives in peril to help whites in 1862, and for the 1,000 to 1,200 Indians who did not participate in the conflict 1862 (II Kappler 956–959).

1884–   Purchase of land in Minnesota for Mdewakanton Sioux was
1890   authorized in annual Indian appropriation bills. In 1885, a qualifying member had to have been in Minnesota by October 1, 1883. In 1888, it was changed to those who were in the state before May 20, 1886 (25 Stat. 228-9). Additional land purchased under the Indian Reorganization Act (IRA; 1934) for Lower Sioux and Prairie Island communities. In 1981, Public Law 96-557 removed the restriction limiting settlement to those who qualified under the 1886 provision. Upper Sioux Indian Community land was purchased under the IRA; community was proclaimed on October 6, 1938.

Chippewa (Ojibwe)

1837   Treaty with the Chippewa signed at the mouth of the St. Peter River (Fort Snelling) (7 Stat. 536; 11 Kappler 491). This "Pine Tree Treaty" ceded a large area of Michigan and northern and western Wisconsin. In Minnesota it included land from north of the 1825 boundary to the Crow Wing River. Article 5 provided that "the privilege of hunting, fishing, and gathering the wild rice, upon the lands, the rivers and the lakes included in the territory ceded, is guaranteed to the Indians during the pleasure of the President."

1842   Treaty with the Chippewa of the Lake Superior and Mississippi Bands signed at La Pointe, Wisconsin, (7 Stat. 591, II Kappler 542) to get the mineral lands in northern Wisconsin, western Upper Peninsula of Michigan, and Isle Royale. Hunting and fishing rights were retained. Minnesota tribes who signed: Fond du Lac, Mille Lacs, Sandy Lake, Crow Wing River, and Gull Lake.

1847   Treaty with the Chippewa of the Mississippi and Lake Superior signed at Fond du Lac (9 Stat. 904, II Kappler 567). This and the 1847 treaty with the Pillager Band pertained to two adjacent parcels of land south and east of Fergus Falls. The land, to the east, was intended for a reservation for the Winnebago tribe, who instead first moved to Long Prairie, Minnesota, then, in 1855, to a reservation on the Blue Earth River south of Mankato (10 Stat. 1172).

1847   Treaty with Pillager Band signed at Leech Lake (9 Stat. 908; 1I Kappler 569). Ceded land intended for a Menominee reservation that was never established. Article 3 provided that "the country hereby ceded shall be held by the United States as Indian land, until otherwise ordered by the President." In 1848, the Menominee ceded their Wisconsin lands and were given this land as a reservation (9 Stat. 952). However, they never moved, and the Menominee ceded the land in 1854 (10 Stat. 1064). The land was then sold to whites.

1854   Treaty with Chippewa of the Lake Superior and Mississippi bands signed at La Pointe, Wisconsin (10 Stat. 1109; 1I Kappler 648). Ceded most of the Arrowhead country; created Grand Portage, Fond du Lac, and Lake Vermilion reservations. One section of land reserved for Chief Buffalo that ultimately became present-day downtown Duluth. Hunting and fishing rights were reserved on the ceded territory "until otherwise ordered by the President" (Article II). The treaty ended efforts to remove Wisconsin Indians to Minnesota.

1855   Treaty with the Chippewa of the Mississippi, Pillager, and Lake Winnibigoshish Bands signed at Washington, D.C. (10 Stat. 1165; 1I Kappler 685). Ceded north central Minnesota. Reservations created at Leech and Cass Lakes for the Pillagers; at Lake Winnibigoshish for that band; and at Mille Lacs, Sandy, Rice, Gull, Rabbit, and Pokegama Lakes for the Mississippi bands.

1863   Treaty with the Red Lake and Pembina Bands signed at Old Crossing of Red Lake River (13 Stat. 667;11 Kappler 835).

Amended in the supplementary treaty of 1864 (13 Stat. 689;11 Kappler 861). Ceded extensive land including eastern North Dakota. A large tract (approximately 8,000,000 acres) around Red Lake was retained.

1863   Treaty with the Mississippi, Pillager, and Lake Winnibigoshish Bands signed at Washington, D.C. (12 Stat. 1249, II Kappler 839), creating a single reservation at Cass, Leech, and Winnibigoshish Lakes, giving up Gull, Sandy, and Pokegama Lakes. Article 12 provides "that owing to the heretofore good conduct of the Mille Lac Indians, they shall not be compelled to remove so long as they shall not in any way interfere with . . . or molest whites." The treaty was ratified and proclaimed. However, there was Indian disapproval, and it was renegotiated in 1864 at Washington, D.C. (13 Stat. 693; 11 Kappler 862). Consolidated and expanded the Cass Lake, Lake Winnibigoshish, and Leech Lake reservations into Leech Lake. Indians from the other 1855 reservations were to move to Leech Lake; however, they could remain where they were until improvements were made at Leech Lake. The Mille Lacs and Sandy Lake Bands, because of support they gave to the whites during the 1862 uprising, could stay "as long as they shall not interfere with or in any manner molest the persons or property of the whites" (for Mille Lacs Indians) and "until the President so directs" (for Sandy Lake Indians) (Article XII).

1866   Treaty with the Bois Forte Band signed at Washington, D.C. (14 Stat. 765; 11 Kappler 916). Ceded Lake Vermilion Reservation and established the reservation at Nett Lake and a township on Deer Creek.

1867   Treaty with the Mississippi Band signed at Washington, D.C. (16 Stat. 719; II Kappler 974) to concentrate bands. White Earth Reservation was created. The 1864 expanded Leech Lake Reservation was reduced, retaining lands around Cass, Leech, and Winnibigoshish Lakes. Executive orders added land to Leech Lake Reservation in 1873 (numbers 549 and numbers 550, White Oak Point) and 1874 (numbers 567 and numbers 568).

1887   General Allotment Act (Dawes Act; 24 Stat. 388) authorized allotment of tribal lands to individual Indians. The land was to remain in trust for twenty-five years. (The IRA in 1934 extended trust status indefinitely.) Surplus lands remaining after allotment were to be sold, with proceeds used for Indian programs. Citizenship to be conferred upon allottees found competent and Indians who adopted "the habits of civilized life."

1889   Nelson Act (25 Stat. 642; I Kappler 301), the allotment act for Minnesota. The Rice Commission was to negotiate complete relinquishment of all reservations except Red Lake and White Earth, which were to be allotted. (Red Lake Band rejected allotment.) Residents on other reservations were to move to White Earth. However, if the Indians wished, they could take allotments on the existing reservations. The Red Lake Band sold the north part of its reservation, almost 3,000,000 acres. On July 29, 1889, White Earth Reservation ceded four northeastern townships.

Other laws followed: the Morris Act of 1902 and Clapp Acts of 1904 and 1906, which facilitated the rapid takeover of Indian land and timber resources by white business interests. The 1906 Clapp Act was especially destructive for White Earth Indians by allowing "mixed-bloods" to immediately take title to their allotments. Most were then sold.

1904   Red Lake Band sold eleven western townships, 256,000 acres, and was allowed to remain independent of other Chippewa reservations. The agreement had been reached in 1902 (31 Stat. 107). Additional Red Lake Reservation land adjustments were made by Executive Order on November 21, 1892, and legislation on February 8, 1905.

Winnebago

1837   Treaty with the Winnebago (7 Stat. 544) ceded their interest in the extreme southeastern corner of Minnesota, retaining hunting rights. These were ceded in 1846 (9 Stat. 878).

1847   Treaty with the Chippewa of the Mississippi and Lake Superior Bands signed at Fond du Lac (9 Stat. 904; II Kappler 567). Ceded land for a Winnebago reservation, south of Fergus Falls.

1855   Treaty with the Winnebago (10 Stat. 1172) ceded the 1847 lands, and they were given an area eighteen miles square on the Blue Earth River south of Mankato.

1859   Treaty with the Winnebago (12 Stat. 1101). The western portion of the Blue Earth land was taken to be sold to white settlers.

1863   Act of Congress for the "peaceful" removal from Minnesota of the Winnebago (12 Stat 658).

1865   Treaty with the Winnebago established Nebraska reservation (II Kappler 872).

Significant Federal Legislation

1787   Northwest Ordinance passed by Congress of the Confederation. Recognized Indian sovereignty over the Northwest Territory; attempted to protect rights of Indians in the land they occupied.

1789   Constitution of the United States, art. I, § 8 (the commerce clause) gave Congress power "to regulate commerce with . . . Indian tribes." This became basis of Congress' plenary power over tribes. Amendment XIV, § 2, provided the Representatives shall be apportioned among the several states according to their population, excluding Indians not taxed. Since Indians were all made citizens in 1924, this provision does not affect present-day Indian legal status.

1789   Department of War established with responsibility to handle matters relating to Indian affairs. In 1824, the Bureau of Indian Affairs (BIA) was established by order of the secretary of war. In 1849, the BIA was transferred to the Department of the Interior.

1871   Abolishment of treaty-making method of dealing with Indians (16 Stat. 566). Instead agreements were negotiated that required approval by both houses of Congress. No treaties previously made were invalidated.

1885   Major Crimes Act (23 Stat. 385;18 U.S.C. 1153). Federal courts given jurisdiction over major crimes committed by Indians on reservations.

1887   General Allotment Act (Dawes Act; 24 Stat. 388) authorized allotment of tribal lands to individual Indians. (See previous listing under Treaties and Agreements, Chippewa [Ojibwe].)

1921   Snyder Act (42 Stat. 208; 25 U.S.C. 13), the primary authorization for BIA programs for the benefit, care, and assistance of Indians throughout the United States. Authorization is open-ended and permanent, limited by congressional appropriations.

1924   Citizenship Act (43 Stat. 253). Indians made citizens of the United States.

1934   Indian Reorganization Act (IRA; Wheeler-Howard Act) (48 Stat. 984; 25 U.S.C. 470). Recognized inherent right of tribes to operate through governments of their own creation. Tribes given the right to engage in business; a revolving loan fund established. Indians given preference in BIA employment. Vocational education and student loan programs begun. Allotment process ended; land up for sale but not sold reverted to the tribes; trust land status extended indefinitely. Each tribe voted whether or not to accept the act.

1934   Johnson-O'Malley Act (JOM) (48 Stat. 596; 25 U.S.C. 52) authorized the secretary of the interior to enter into contracts with states to provide education, medical attention, agricultural assistance, and social welfare.

1942   Segregation Bill (56 Stat 1039). Separated the resources of the Minnesota Chippewa Tribe reservations and the Red Lake Tribe. Claims to each others' ceded lands were extinguished, and funds derived from land and timber sales would be the property of the respective tribe. This divided the Minnesota Chippewa Trust Fund. The law allowed Minnesota Indians for the first time to sell live timber from their lands.

1946   Indian Claims Commission (60 Stat. 1049; 25 U.S.C. 70) established to consolidate and speed up Indian claims. Ended on December 31, 1983 (Pub.L. 96-217), with unresolved claims transferred to the U.S. Court of Claims.

1953   House of Representatives Concurrent Resolution 108, Senate concurring. Established the policy of termination. Several tribes were terminated, with land removed from trust status and federal services stopped. Indians disagreed strongly with the policy, which proposed to end [Indians'] status as wards of the United States and to grant them all of the rights and prerogatives pertaining to American citizenship [by freeing them] from Federal supervision and control and from all disabilities and limitations specially applicable to Indians.

1953   Civil and Criminal Jurisdiction on Reservation, Pub. L. 83-280 (18 U.S.C. 1162; 28 U.S.C. 1360), known as Public Law 280. Transferred to five states, including Minnesota, civil and criminal jurisdiction on reservations, without tribal or state approval. Red Lake Reservation was excluded. States were not authorized to tax real or personal property. Indian rights to hunt, fish, trap, and harvest wild rice were exempted from state jurisdiction.

1954   Indian Health Service (IHS) transferred from BIA to the Department of Health, Education, and Welfare, now Health and Human Services (68 Stat. 674; 42 U.S.C. 2001). Snyder Act authorization procedures continued.

1968   Indian Civil Rights Act, Pub. L. 90-284 (82 Stat. 73; 25 U.S.C. 1301). Extended to individual Indians some protections of the U.S. Bill of Rights in their relations with their tribal governments (25 U.S.C. 1302). Tribes may, however, have an established religion, and free counsel is not required in court cases. Writs of habeas corpus may be sought in federal court. Public Law 280 amended so that states cannot assume legal jurisdiction over tribes without their consent (25 U.S.C. 1321), and responsibility can be retroceded from state to federal government if requested by the state (25 U.S.C. 1323).

1970   Presidential Message (President Nixon, H.R. Doc. No. 91-363). A major change in policy, urging Indians be allowed to become independent of federal control without being cut off from federal concern and support. Proposed were repeal of House of Representatives Concurrent Resolution 108, allowing Indians to control their own programs, helping urban Indians, expanding programs in economic development and health, and elevation of Indian affairs with the Department of the Interior.

1972   Indian Education Act, Title IV (86 Stat. 334). A greatly
        expanded program to meet special and culturally related
        education needs of reservation and nonreservation students
        with as little as one-eighth Indian ancestry. Indian parents
        given a major voice in program decisions (20 U.S.C. 241aa).

1975   Indian Self-Determination and Education Assistance Act, Pub.
        L. 93-638 (25 U.S.C. 450). Declared commitment to maintain
        the unique and continuing federal relationship, with
        responsibility to the Indian people and orderly transition
        from federal domination to Indian control of programs.
        Tribes can contract on a program-by-program basis to
        administer many BIA and IHS programs (Title I). Federal
        funding to continue, with additional money provided for
        administration. If requested by tribes, the agencies must
        resume administration. Indians to be given preference in
        contracts and hiring.

1978   Indian Child Welfare Act, Pub. L. 95-608 (25 U.S.C. 1901).
        Requires that tribes be notified and given a say when tribal
        children are brought to court for placement decisions.

1988   Indian Gaming Regulatory Act, Pub. L. 100-497 (25 U.S.C.
        §§ 2701). Provides a statutory basis for gaming. The purpose
        is to "promote tribal economic development, self-sufficiency
        and strong tribal governments." Three categories of gaming
        are defined. Type III, casino games, requires a tribal–state
        compact. Tribes pay 5 percent of gross earnings to fund the
        National Gaming Commission; per capita payments made
        from gaming profits are subject to federal income tax. Minn.
        Stat. 3.9221 authorized the state–tribal compact.

1988   Indian Self-Determination and Education Assistance Act of
        1988, authorizing demonstration tribal self-governance
        projects. Tribes negotiate directly with the BIA in
        Washington, D.C., for funding of the programs they want to
        run themselves. This removes dealing with the BIA area and
        agency levels and makes more money available.

1989–   Native American Languages Act (NALA) 1990. This federal
1990   policy statement recognizing the language rights of
        American Indians, Alaska Natives, Native Hawaiians, and

Pacific Islanders was passed to preserve, protect, and promote the rights and freedom of Native Americans to use, practice, and develop Native American languages and to encourage and support the use of Native American languages as a medium of instruction in order to encourage and support Native American language survival, equal educational opportunity, increased student success and performance, increased student awareness and knowledge of their culture and history, and increased student and community pride.

1990   Native American Grave Protection and Repatriation Act (NAGPR) 1990 was passed to clarify the ownership and control of Native American cultural items that are excavated or discovered on federal or tribal land after the passage of the Act.

1996   American Indian Religious Freedom Act (AIRFA) 1996 sets policy of the United States to protect and preserve for American Indians their inherent right to freedom to believe, express, and exercise the traditional religions of the American Indian, Eskimo, Aleut, and Native Hawaiians, including but not limited to access to sites, use and possession of sacred objects, and freedom to worship through ceremonial and traditional rites.

Significant Federal Court Decisions

Principles of legal construction important in Indian court decisions:

1. Laws are to be liberally construed, and doubtful expressions are to be resolved in favor of the Indians (cited in *Bryan v. Itasca*, 426 U.S. 392 (1973)).
2. Treaties and agreements are to be interpreted as the Indians understood them (cited in *State v. Clark*, 282 N.W.2d 909 (Minn. 1979)).
3. Implicit Indian treaty rights and jurisdiction are not lost by inference. They cannot be taken unless specifically stated by Congress (cited in *U.S. v. White*, 508 F.2d 453 (8th Cir. 1974)).
4. Treaty and statutory provisions that are not clear on their face may be clear from the surrounding circumstances and legislative history (cited in *Oliphant v. Suquamish*, 435 U.S. 191 (1978)).

5. Exhaustion doctrine: If tribal courts have jurisdiction, claims must first be heard there rather than in federal courts (*National Farmers Union Insurance Co. v. Crow Tribe of Indians*, 417 U.S. 845 (1985) and *Burlington Northern Railroad Co. v. Crow Tribal Council*, 940 F.2d 1239 (1991)).

Federal Cases

Fletcher v. Peck, 6 Cranch 87 (1810). This first Indian case before the U.S. Supreme Court stated that tribes had lost the right to govern every person within their limits except themselves. Cited in *Oliphant v. Suquamish* (1978).

Johnson v. McIntosh, 21 U.S. (8 Wheat) 543 (1823). "Discovery gave exclusive title to those who made it" (at 573). This gave the Europeans "an exclusive right to extinguish the Indian title of occupancy, either by purchase or by conquest" (at 587). This greatly limited Indian rights to control their land.

Cherokee Nation v. Georgia, 30 U.S. (5 Pet.) 1 (1831). The decision, written by Chief Justice Marshall, stated, "The Constitution by declaring treaties . . . to be the supreme law of the land, has adopted and sanctioned the previous treaties with the Indian nations, and consequently admits their rank among those powers who are capable of making treaties" (at 17). Tribes are called "domestic dependent nations." "Their relation to the United States resembles that of a ward to his guardian. They look to our government for protection; rely upon its kindness and its power; appeal to it for relief of their wants" (at 17). This special relationship is the basis of the trust relationship.

Worcester v. Georgia, 31 U.S. (6 Pet.) 515 (1832). Georgia had illegally and unconstitutionally extended control over Indians within the state. Tribes were declared to have inherent sovereign powers. They were distinct, independent, political communities with territorial boundaries within which their authority was exclusive. This is considered the single most important decision pertaining to Indians.

Ex parte Crow Dog, 109 U.S. 556 (1883). When an Indian was murdered on a reservation, it was realized that federal courts had no jurisdiction. The passage of the Major Crimes Act of 1885 gave jurisdiction over certain crimes to the federal government, marking the first overt congressional intrusion into Indian sovereignty.

U.S. v. Winans, 198 U.S. 371 (1905). Treaties are not a grant of rights to Indians but are rather a grant of rights from them and a reservation of those rights not granted.

Morton v. Ruiz, 415 U.S. 199 (1974). Indians living near reservations who maintain close economic and social ties and have not been assimilated into the general society are to receive federal Indian services.

Morton v. Mancari, 415 U.S. 535 (1974). Indians are not a racial group but members of quasi–sovereign tribal entities whose lives and activities are governed by the BIA in a unique fashion. Indian preference in employment by the agency as stated in the law is not invidious racial discrimination but is reasonable and rationally designed to further Indian self-government.

Bryan v. Itasca, 426 U.S. 373 (1976), reversing Minnesota Supreme Court (228 N.W.2d 249). Public Law 280 granted to the states only civil jurisdiction in court proceedings, not civil regulation such as taxing and zoning powers.

Santa Clara Pueblo v. Martinez, 436 U.S. 49 (1978). Even if a tribal government discriminates in a manner that would be in violation of federal law, the Indian Civil Rights Act does not give the federal courts jurisdiction to deal with the issues. (Federal jurisdiction is specifically granted only in criminal cases involving petitions for writs of habeas corpus.)

Oliphant v. Suquamish, 435 U.S. 191 (1978). By submitting to the overriding sovereignty of the United States, Indian tribes gave up the power to try non-Indians in criminal cases. The Court imposed its judgment without any Congressional language limiting tribal powers. The decision greatly limited tribal jurisdiction.

California v. Cabazon Band, 480 U.S. 202 (1987), on gaming. The issue was whether state/county law was "criminal law" or "regulatory" and thus exempted by the *Bryan v. Itasca* decision. The ruling was that Indian gaming in California was not subject to state jurisdiction since gambling was not a prohibited activity. "If the state generally prohibits a type of conduct, it falls within PL 280's grant of criminal jurisdiction, however if the state law generally permits the conduct at issue, subject to regulation, it is a civil/regulatory law and PL 280 does not authorize its enforcement on an Indian reservation" (at 209).

Cobell v. Babbitt, 1996 (renamed *Cobell v. Norton* in 2001), seeking historical accounting to determine the balances for all Individual Indian Money (IIM) accounts managed by the United States as trustee for the Indian beneficiaries. This suit is still within the court system.

Cass County, Minnesota, et al., Petitioners v. Leech Lake Band of Chippewa Indians on writ of certiorari to the United States Court of Appeals for the Eighth Circuit (No. 97–174 June 8, 1998). The Court granted certiorari in this case to resolve whether state and local governments may tax reservation land that was made alienable by Congress and sold to non-Indians by the federal government, but was later repurchased by a tribe. The U.S. Supreme Court held that ad valorem taxes may be imposed upon such land because, under the test established by precedents, Congress has made "unmistakably clear" its intent to allow such taxation.

Minnesota et al. v. Mille Lacs Band of Chippewa Indians et al. (No. 97–1337, decided March 24, 1999). The U.S. Supreme Court upheld the treaty rights of the Mille Lacs Band of Chippewa Indians and other Chippewa and Ojibwe tribes to hunt, fish, and gather on land currently outside of their reservations.

Notes

Introduction

1. House Concurrent Resolution 331, Oct. 4, 1988, passed by the U.S. Senate on Oct. 21, 1988.
2. Dr. Jack Weatherford, *Indian Givers: How the Indians of the Americas Transformed the World* (New York: Fawcett Columbine, 1988).
3. Talk by Alan R. Woolworth, research fellow, Minnesota Historical Society, St. Paul, Minn. at Grand Portage, Minn., Aug. 13, 1993; see also Alan R. Woolworth, *An Historical Study of the Grand Portage* (St. Paul: Minnesota Historical Society, 1993).
4. Warren Upham, *Minnesota Geographic Names* (St. Paul: Minnesota Historical Society, 1920; reissue 1969); William Burnson, "How Did Your County Get Its Name?" *Minnesota Volunteer* (Jan.–Feb. 1982), 56–63.
5. Janice Command, *Minnesota Daily*, Feb. 1, 1982.
6. Dr. Jack Weatherford, speech, National Indian Education Association meeting, St. Paul, Minn., Oct. 18, 1994.
7. John Poupart, with Dr. Cecilia Martinez, Dr. John Red Horse, and Dawn Scharnberg, *To Build a Bridge: Working with American Indian Communities* (St. Paul, Minn.: American Indian Policy Center, 2001), 29.

1. Indian People and Their Culture

1. Kimberly Blaeser, professor of English, University of Wisconsin–Milwaukee, quoted in Donna Halvorsen, "A New Perspective: Blaeser Brings Experience to Bench as Only Indian Judge in Minnesota," *Star Tribune*, Aug. 21, 1995.
2. Larry Aitken, professor, Itasca Community College, interview Mar. 24, 2005.
3. Rosemary Christensen, American Indian Associates, Duluth, Minn., interview June 15, 2004.
4. Earl Nyholm, professor, Bemidji State University, interview Apr. 29, 1994.
5. John Poupart, interview Apr. 23, 2004; also in *To Build a Bridge: Working with American Indian Communities*, American Indian Policy Center, 2001, 30.

6. Marge Anderson, former chief executive, Mille Lacs Band of Ojibwe, "Our Children, Our Future," keynote address for National I Family Preservation Conference, reprinted in *Ojibwe News,* Apr. 28, 1995, 4–5.

7. Gary Green, "Wig-I-Wam," Division of Indian Work, Minneapolis, Minn., Sept. 1980.

8. Ibid.

9. Stacy G. Smith (LL), Bemidji State University student, letter to the editor, "Another Aboriginal Thought," *Ojibwe News,* May 19, 1995, 4.

10. Tony LookingElk, quoted in Paul Levy, "Taught by Elders, They Listen and Lead," *Star Tribune,* Mar. 29, 2004.

11. Myron Rosebear, owner Bear-Hawk Store, Franklin Ave., Minneapolis, quoted in Suzanne P. Kelly, "Middle-class Indians Torn between Age-old Values and Modern Comforts," *Star Tribune,* Mar. 27, 1991.

12. Earl Nyholm, retired professor, Bemidji State University, interview Apr. 29, 1994.

13. Christopher Vessey, *Traditional Ojibway Religion and Its Historical Changes* (Philadelphia: American Philosophical Society, 1983). Henry Warren Bowden, *American Indians and Christian Missions, Studies in Cultural Conflict,* Chicago History of American Religion Series (Chicago: University of Chicago Press, 1981). Carol Devens, *Countering Colonization* (Chicago: Newbery Library, 1992). Timothy G. Roufs and Larry P Aitken, "Information Relating to Chippewa Peoples," in Frederick Webb Hodge, ed., *Handbook of American Indians, North of Mexico, 1907/1910* (Duluth, Minn.: Lake Superior Basin Studies Center, University of Minnesota, January 1984).

14. Roy W. Meyer, *History of the Santee Sioux* (Lincoln: University of Nebraska Press, 1993), 362–63.

2. Shifting Governmental Relationships

1. *Johnson v. M'Intosh* (21 U.S. 543–605, 1823; 8 Wheat 681–696).

2. Sylvia Van Kirk, *Many Tender Ties: Women in Fur-Trade Society in Western Canada, 1670–1870* (Winnipeg, Canada: Shillingford J. Gordon Pub. Ltd., Oct. 2000), 9.

3. Stephen Cornell, *The Return of the Native, American Indian Political Resurgence* (New York: Oxford University Press, 1990), 19.

4. President Andrew Jackson; quoted in Alexis de Tocqueville, *Democracy in America,* J. P. Mayer ed., translation by George Lawrence, New York: Anchor Books, 1969), 337.

5. *Democracy in America,* 1:355.

6. Northwest Ordinance of 1787, Article 3.

7. Lee Antell, "Indian Education: Involvement of Federal, State and Tribal Governments," Report 135 of the Education Commission of the States (Denver, Colo.: Education Commission,1980), 37.

8. William Folwell, *History of Minnesota* (St. Paul: Minnesota Historical Society, 1930), 4:201.

9. Harold Fey and D'Arcy McNickle, *Indians and Other Americans* (New York: Harper & Row, 1959).

10. Folwell, *History of Minnesota*, 4:323.

11. Lewis Meriam, *The Problem of Indian Administration*, report by the Institute for Government Research (Baltimore: Johns Hopkins Press, 1928) (hereafter cited as Meriam, *Report*).

12. George S. Grossman, *The Sovereignty of American Indian Tribes: A Matter of Legal History* (Minneapolis, Minn.: Minnesota Civil Liberties Union Foundation, 1979), 11.

13. "Urban Indians," Proceedings of the 3rd Annual Conference on Problems and Issues Concerning American Indians Today, Center for the History of the American Indian, The Newberry Library, Chicago, Illinois, Sept. 27, 1980.

14. The Declaration of Indian Purpose is discussed in David Beaulieu's "A Place among Nations: Experiences of Indian People," in Clifford E. Clark, Jr., *Minnesota in a Century of Change: The State and Its People since 1900* (St. Paul: Minnesota Historical Society Press, 1989), 421.

15. President Nixon, Presidential Statement, "Recommendations for Indian Policy," 91st Cong., 2d sess., July 8, 1970, H. Doc. 91–363.

16. President Reagan, 19 *Weekly Compilation of Presidential Documents* 98–99, 1983, 52.

17. President Bill Clinton, "Federal Indian Policy," 59 *Federal Register* 22951, May 4, 1994.

18. Senate Concurrent Resolution 76; House Concurrent Resolution 331, 1988.

19. Brent Simcosky, *Proud Nations: Celebrating Tribal Self-Governance*, (Self Governance Communication and Education, Bellingham, WA, 2005), 12.

20. Robert N. Clinton, professor of law, University of Iowa and an Associate Justice for the Cheyenne River Sioux Tribal Court of Appeals, "Once Again, Indian Tribes Are Losing Ground," *The National Law Journal*, Dec. 19, 1994, A21.

21. Interview with James Genia, May 27, 2004.

22. Daniel L. Boxberger, quoted in Russel Lawrence Barsh, "Progressive Era Bureaucrats and the Unity of Twentieth Century Indian Policy," Native American Studies Program, University of California at Berkeley. *American Indian Quarterly* 15, no. 1 (Winter 1991): 29–30.

23. Dr. John Red Horse, professor, University of Duluth, speech at the Seminar on Indian Children, American Indian Policy Institute, Hamline University, St. Paul, Minn., May 19, 1994.

24. Mary B. Magnuson, attorney, Jacobson, Buffalo, Schoessler & Magnuson, Ltd., representing Indian casinos, address at the Minnesota

Institute of Legal Education Conference on State-Tribal Relations, Bloomington, Minn., June 24, 1997.

25. Ashely Grant, Associated Press reporter, *Star Tribune*, Mar. 7, 2004.
26. Interview with James Genia, May 27, 2004.

3. The Tribes and the Land

1. Roy W. Meyer, *History of the Santee Sioux*, rev. ed. (Lincoln: University of Nebraska Press, 1993), 274.
2. Josephine Robinson, White Earth Reservation, quoted in the *Minneapolis Star*, Dec. 23, 1978, 10.
3. Alban Fruth, *A Century of Missionary Work among the Red Lake Chippewa Indians: 1858–1958* (Red Lake, Minn.: St. Mary's Mission, 1958), 35–36.
4. Minnesota Indian Affairs Council, Web site, Apr. 2004.
5. For the detailed history of how the Dakota people returned to their homelands and organized their governments, see Roy W. Meyer, *History of the Santee Sioux.*
6. Meyer, *History of the Santee Sioux*, 279, 282–83.
7. Meyer, ibid.
8. "Account of a Journey to the Coteau des Prairies," by George Catlin, reprinted in Alan R. Woolworth, comp./ed., "The Red Pipestone Quarry of Minnesota: Archaeological and Historical Reports," *The Minnesota Archaeologist* 42, no. 1 and 2 (St. Paul, Minn.: The Minnesota Archaeological Society, 1983), 4.
9. Reprinted in Woolworth, Alan R., comp./ed., "The Red Pipestone Quarry of Minnesota: Archaeological and Historical Reports." *The Minnesota Archaeologist* 42, no. 1 and 2 (St. Paul, Minn.: The Minnesota Archaeological Society, 1983), 39.
10. Steve Compton, "Pipestone Quarry Site Long Sacred to Indian Peoples," *Session Weekly*, Minnesota House of Representatives, May 2, 1997, 20 (16 U.S.C. 445 (a) & (d)).
11. Interview with Sam Gurnoe, director of Indian resources, counseling, The City Inc., Minneapolis, and pipemaker, June 14, 1994.
12. Ibid.
13. "Partial Settlement Reached in the Red Lake Band's Historic Indian Claims Commission Case," *The Red Lake Nation*, June 11, 1997, 1–2.
14. William Folwell, *History of Minnesota* (St. Paul: Minnesota Historical Society, 1930), 260–61, 307.
15. Anna Brooks, "A Brief History of Tamarac National Wildlife Refuge, Mino-Bimadiziwin," White Earth Land Recovery Project, Fall/Winter 1993.
16. Jack McNeel, *Indian Country*, Feb. 23, 2004.
17. Laura J. Smith, "Native American Trust Land Transfers in Minnesota," *CURA Reporter*, Center for Urban and Regional Affairs, Spring 2004.

18. See *Indians in Minnesota*, Elizabeth Ebbott, ed., 1985, 34–38, for the types of cases in 1983. Mariana Shulstad, former Field Solicitor, U.S. Department of the Interior, Minnesota, presented seminars on the complex legal history of Indian land status at Minnesota Institute of Continuing Legal Education.
19. Lorna Lague, White Earth Band of Ojibwe, interview, Apr. 18, 2005.
20. Mariana Shulstad, Field Solicitor, Office of Solicitor, U.S. Department of the Interior, "Performing Land Transactions in Indian Country," presentation of "Indian Legal Issues in Today's World," Minnesota Institute of Continuing Legal Education, Minneapolis, Feb. 1994.
21. Larry Morrin, Deputy Director, BIA, Minneapolis Area, interview, Aug. 24, 1995.
22. Priscilla Wilfarht, Solicitor General, U.S. Department of the Interior, Minneapolis Area, interview, Aug. 7, 1996.
23. Anishinabe Legal Services, quoted in "Pine Point Perspective," *Native American Press*, Feb. 24, 1995.

4. Tribal Governments, Sovereignty, and Relations with the U.S. Government

1. Gilman, Carolyn, *The Grand Portage Story* (St. Paul: Minnesota Historical Society Press, 1992), 99.
2. William W. Warren, *History of the Ojibway People*, written 1852, first published by the Minnesota Historical Society in 1885 (St. Paul: Minnesota Historical Society Press, 2000), 135.
3. Felix Cohen, *Handbook of Federal Indian Law*, quoted in "The Indian Civil Rights Act," A Report of the U.S. Commission on Civil Rights, June 1991, 36.
4. Cohen, *Handbook*, 123.
5. Ada Pecos Melton and Jerry Gardner, "Public Law 280: Issues and Concerns for Victims of Crime in Indian Country," American Indian Development Associates Web site, 2004; Don Weddl, interview, Mar. 21, 2005.
6. "Indians, Indian Tribes, and State Government," St. Paul: Minnesota House of Representatives, Jan. 2003.
7. Carole Goldberg-Ambrose, "Planting Tail Feathers: Tribal Survival and Public Law 280," University of California Los Angeles, American Indian Studies Center, 1997, 12.
8. Some major Minnesota cases: *Gayle v. Little Six* (Minn. Supreme Court, 1996); *Cohen v. Little Six* (Minn. Ct. App., 1996); *Setchell v. Little Six* (Minn. Ct. App., 1996).
9. Quoted in Laura Waterman Wittstock, "Minnesota Tribal Sovereignty," published on laurawatermanwittstock.com, May 21, 2004, and in *One Nation Lies* (Ardmore: OK) vol. 22, 2004.
10. Marge Anderson, Mille Lacs Band of Ojibwe Indians, "State of the Band Address: Rebuilding a Nation: A Partnership between Our

Government and Our People," *Speaking of Ourselves,* Minnesota Chippewa Tribe, Cass Lake, Jan./Feb. 1994, 14–16.

11. Henry Buffalo, attorney, speech, St. Thomas University, St. Paul, Minn., Aug. 23, 1996.

12. Joseph Kalt, Harvard Project on American Indian Economic Development, statement to the U.S. Senate Committee on Indian Affairs, Sept. 17, 1996, printed in *The Red Lake Nation,* Oct. 1996, 25–29.

13. Joseph Kalt and Stephen Cornell, "Sovereignty and Nation-Building: The Development Challenge in Indian Country Today," Harvard Project on American Indian Economic Development, 1998.

14. Dr. Robert Powless, speech, Jan. 26, 1994; interview, May 3, 2004.

15. Vine Deloria, professor, University of Colorado, speech at "Tribal Sovereignty" forum sponsored by the American Indian Research and Policy Institute, Hamline University, St. Paul, Minn., May 26, 1995.

16. Minnesota Indian Gaming Association, "So Where Does All the Money Go?" Mar. 2004.

17. Ron Libertus, interview, Nov. 22, 1994.

18. White Earth Band Chairman Wadena, quoted in 1989 by Pat Doyle, "Big Money Doesn't Impress Reservation Rife with Poverty," *Star Tribune,* Oct. 22, 1995.

19. Eugene McArthur, chairman, White Earth Band of Ojibwe, *Anishinaabeg Today,* News from the White Earth Reservation, Sept. 11, 1996.

20. Paul Levy, "Wadena Pursues Political Comeback," *Star Tribune,* May 3, 2004.

21. Eugene McArthur, elected Chairman of the White Earth Tribe, "A Letter to the People," *Anishinabe Dee-Bah-Gee-Mo-Win,* White Earth Reservation, July 1996, 3.

22. Paul Levy, "Wadena Pursues Political Comeback," *Star Tribune,* May 3, 2004.

23. Melanie Benjamin, quoted in *The Woodland Voice,* Mille Lacs Band of Ojibwe, Winter 2004, 1.

24. Robert N. Clinton, "Once Again, Indian Tribes Are Losing Ground," *The National Law Journal,* Dec. 19, 1994, A21.

25. 1988 House Concurrent Resolution 331, 100th Cong., 2d Sess., passed the House Oct. 4, 1988; 1986 Senate Concurrent Resolution 76 made the same commitment.

26. Laura Waterman Wittstock, "Bureau of Indian Affairs: King Kong of American Bureaucracies," *Star Tribune,* Nov. 9, 1995; interview, May 5, 2004.

27. "Major Management Challenges and Program Risks: Department of the Interior," U.S. General Accounting Office, Performance and Accountability Series, Jan. 2001.

28. "Four Reservations of MCT to Pursue Self-Governance; Mille Lacs and Leech Lake Already Self-governing," *Nahgahchiwanong Dibahjimowinnan,* April 1995; interview, June 27, 1994.

29. Jerry Reynolds, *Indian Country Today*, Apr. 9, 2004.
30. Donald R. Wharton, "Implementation of EPA's Indian Policy," Native American Rights Fund, Boulder, Colo., *NARF Legal Review* 17, no. 1 (winter 1992): 8–9.
31. Environmental Protection Agency, Clean Water Act, Section 404 Tribal Regulations, *Federal Register,* February 11, 1993, Part IV.
32. *Federal Register,* May 4, 1994.
33. Melissa Boney, Director, Twin Cities Healthy Nations Project, Minneapolis, Minn., interview, Apr. 2004.
34. Senator Daniel Inouye, Chairman Select Commission on Indian Affairs, U.S. Senate Hearing on FY 1992 Budget, 102nd Cong. 1st Sess., Feb. 21, 1991, 2.
35. Philip Norrgard, Director of Human Services, Fond du Lac Reservation, interview, Feb. 3, 2005.
36. "A Quiet Crisis: Federal Funding and Unmet Needs in Indian Country," U.S. Commission on Civil Rights, July 2003.
37. Sheila White Eagle, St. Paul Council of Churches, interview, Sept. 20, 1994.
38. Joyce Kramer, professor, Department of Sociology, University of Minnesota Duluth, interview, Sept. 26, 1995.
39. *To Build a Bridge: Working with American Indian Communities*, American Indian Policy Center, 2001, 44–45.

5. State and Local Relations

1. *United States v. Kagama*, U.S. S. Ct. 30 (1887), 325.
2. Meriam, *Report*, 93.
3. Sonny Myers, Executive Director, 1854 Authority, *Moccasin Telegraph*, Grand Portage Tribe, June 1997, 4.
4. Andrea Wilkins, National Conference of State Legislatures, "State and Tribes Building New Traditions," Jan. 2004.
5. The elections are administered by the Indian Affairs Council, with the Secretary of State's Office observing. Notices of elections are placed in Indian newspapers. The ballots are counted on Apr. 14.
6. *Minnesota Mining Tax Guide,* Minnesota Department of Revenue, Sept. 2004, 48.
7. U.S. Equal Employment Opportunity Commission, *Job Patterns for Minorities and Women in State and Local Government 1991* (Washington, D.C.: U.S. Equal Employment Opportunity Commission, 1992), 244.
8. Scott Strand, attorney, Robins Miller Kaplan and Ciresi, and former deputy counsel, Minnesota Attorney General's Office, interview, May 26, 2004.
9. Presentations, The Institute of Legal Education Conference on State-Tribal Relations, Bloomington, June 24, 1997.
10. Laura Waterman Wittstock, President, Migizi Communications, interview May 20, 2004.

11. Pat Doyle, "Against the Odds: Casinos Unlikely to Finance a New Stadium," *Star Tribune*, Sept. 27, 1995.
12. James Genia, attorney, Lockridge Grindal Nauen, interview May 27, 2004.
13. "Tribal and State Judges to Meet," *Anishinaabeg Today*, July 9, 1997.
14. Loa Porter, Director of Tribal Human Services, Grand Portage, interview Sept. 27, 1994.
15. Nadine Chase, Leech Lake Band, interview Sept. 15, 1982.
16. Mike McGuire, City Manager, Prior Lake, quoted in *Minneapolis Star and Tribune*, Aug. 10, 1983.
17. Shira Kantor, "Deal Would Mean Land for Tribe, Fields for Prior Lake," *Star Tribune*, July 14, 2004.
18. Joel Patenaude, quoted by Stephanie Hemphill, reporter, on Minnesota Public Radio, Mar. 8, 2004.
19. Michael Stetzler, Local Advisory Councils, Minnesota Department of Human Services, Adult and Children Mental Health Division, interview July 1, 1996.
20. Gary Revier, Mayor, Redwood Falls, quoted in Wayne Washington, "Casinos' Benefits Go Beyond Economics," *Star Tribune*, Apr. 5, 1994.
21. "The Economic Impact of the Mille Lacs Band's Grand Casino Mille Lacs and Grand Casino Hinckley as of September 2003," fact sheet, Mille Lacs Band of Ojibwe.
22. Renee Ruble, "Upper Sioux Casino Brings Change to Tribe," *Duluth News Tribune*, May 30, 2004.
23. Minnesota Indian Gaming Association, Web site, Jan. 2005.
24. Liz Johnson, Greater Twin Cities United Way, interview Jan. 13, 2005.
25. First Nations Development Institute, Web site data, Nov. 20, 2005.
26. Study done by Native Americans in Philanthropy, reported in "Minnesota Leads in Grants for Natives," *The Native American Press*, Apr. 25, 1997, 5.

6. Characteristics of the Indian Population of Minnesota

1. Larry Aitken, Professor, Itasca Community College, interview, Mar. 24, 2005.
2. Children's Defense Fund, Census Report, 2000.
3. U.S. Census, 2000.
4. Minnesota Department of Heath, Minnesota Health Statistics, 2001.
5. U.S. Census, 2000.
6. Minneapolis Planning Department, Oct. 2001.
7. Melissa Boney, Director, Twin Cities Healthy Nations Project, Minneapolis American Indian Center, interview, May 24, 2004.
8. Minneapolis Vital Statistics, Aug. 2001.
9. Minnesota Department of Children, Families and Learning, 2001.

10. Dr. Terrel H. Hart, Indian Health Board of Minneapolis, interview, Sept. 17, 2004.
11. U.S. Census, 2000.
12. William Means, Executive Director, Minnesota Opportunities Industrialization Center State Council, interview, Feb. 22, 2005.
13. Andriana Abariotes, focus group participant, American Indian Research & Policy Institute, "American Indians and Home Ownership," Hamline University, St. Paul, Minn., 1995, 4.
14. Student panel, Seminar on Indian Children, American Indian Policy Center, Hamline University, St. Paul, Minn., May 19, 1994.
15. Meriam, *Report,* 728.
16. Andriana Abariotes, focus group participant, American Indian Research & Policy Institute, "American Indians and Home Ownership," Hamline University, St. Paul, Minn., 1995, 5.
17. Shelley McIntire, interview, Feb. 17, 1994.
18. American Indian Policy Review Commission, *Report on Urban and Rural Non-Reservation Indians* (Washington, D.C., 1976).
19. Barbara Lickness, Minneapolis Neighborhood Revitalization Program, interview, Jan. 24, 2005.
20. National Congress of American Indians Web site, May 2004.
21. Verna Graves, National Indian Education Association meeting, Oct. 18, 1994.
22. Darelynn Lehto, Vice President of the Prairie Island Tribal Council, quoted by Todd LeGarde, "White History Month on KSTP AM," *The Circle,* Mar. 1995, 19.
23. "Indian Nicknames: They're Offensive and Needless," editorial, *Star Tribune,* June 9, 2003.

7. Natural Resources

1. Dennis Anderson, "Big Concerns at the Big Lake," *Star Tribune,* Jan. 31, 1997.
2. Sue Erickson, "Seasons of the Chippewa," Great Lakes Indian Fish and Wildlife Commission, 1996, 33.
3. Ronald Satz, "Chippewa Treaty Rights; The Reserved Rights of Wisconsin's Chippewa Indians," *Transactions, Wisconsin Academy of Sciences, Arts and Letters* 79, no. 1, (1991): 113, 115.
4. James Genia, Solicitor General, Mille Lacs Band, presentation at the Minnesota Institute of Legal Education Conference on State–Tribal Relations, Bloomington, Minn., June 24, 1997.
5. John Ringley, Director of Natural Resources, Leech Lake Tribe, interview, June 20, 1997.
6. John Echohawk, Executive Director, Native American Rights Fund, 1993.
7. Martin Topper, National Indian Program Coordinator, Environment Protection Agency, quoted in Tom Meersman, "An Indian

Priority: More Tribes Are Working to Clean Up Their Land," *Star Tribune*, Sept. 12, 1993.

8. For discussions of the complexity of jurisdiction over environmental laws on reservations see, "Environmental Protection Agency, 40 C.F.R. § 404 Tribal Regulations, 58 Fed. Reg. 8172–8184 (Feb. 11, 1993); Beverly M. Conerton, Minnesota Attorney General's Office, "Tribal 'Treatment as a State' Under Federal Environmental Laws and a Developing State–Tribal–Federal Collaborative Model," Minnesota Institute of Legal Education Conference on State–Tribal Relations, Bloomington, Minn., June 24, 1997, Section IV; and Linda Taylor, "Environmental Regulation in Indian Country," Minnesota House of Representatives; "Indians, Indian Tribes and State Government," Research Department, Minnesota House of Representatives, St. Paul, Minn., Feb. 1992.

9. 55 Fed. Reg. 43407–43408 (Oct. 29, 1990).

10. James Pearson, Executive Director, Petrofund Program, Minnesota Department of Commerce; Chai Insook, interviews, Feb. 18, 2005.

11. Great Lakes Indian Fish & Wildlife Commission, Odanah, Wis., "Bishigendan Akii Respect the Earth," 22.

12. Major sources include "Staff Report to the Minnesota Environmental Quality Board on the Siting of a Dry Cask Storage Facility in Goodhue County," Minnesota Planning, June 1996 and Randel Hanson, "Race Against the Nuclear Clock: NSP's Deal with Prairie Island Community Called Off," *The Circle*, Mar. 1996, 7.

13. Roger Moe, Minnesota Senate Majority Leader, comments at Minnesota Institute of Legal Education Conference on State–Tribal Relations, Bloomington, Minn., June 24, 1997.

14. *The Circle*, Apr. 1994, 17.

15. Minnesota Department of Natural Resources, Web site data, Nov. 2004.

16. U.S. Fish and Wildlife Service, 2001.

17. For a detailed history of Minnesota's Indian forests, see Historical Research Associates, Inc., Missoula, Mont., "The Forests of Anishinabe: A History of Minnesota Chippewa Tribal Forestry 1854–1991, 1992." Prepared for the U.S. Dept of the Interior, Bureau of Indian Affairs, Branch of Forestry, Minneapolis Area Office.

18. Ibid., 4–13.

19. Minnesota Forest Resource Council, Web site data, Nov. 2004.

20. Tom Meersman, "More Timber Harvesting Will Help Economy, But Also Affect Tourism, Wildlife," *Star Tribune*, May 19, 1993, 18A–19A.

21. Firewise Communities Report, Fall 2003.

22. Timothy G. Roufs, *The Anishinabe of the Minnesota Chippewa Tribe*, Phoenix, Ariz.: Indian Tribal Series, 1975.

23. Timothy G. Roufs, "Early Indian Life in the Lake Superior Region." Reprinted from, *Duluth: Sketches of the Past,* ed. Ryck Lydecker, Lawrence J. Sommer, and Arthur Larsen, Special bicentennial volume of Duluth's Legacy Series, Duluth, Minn., 1976, 53.

24. Ervin Oelke, agronomist, University of Minnesota, interview, July 2, 1982.

25. Frank Bibeau, partner in a small wild rice processing company, quoted in Jeremy Iggers, "Wild Rice: Much Isn't Native and Much Isn't Wild," *Star Tribune,* Sept. 25, 1988.

26. Joe Lagarde, "Sacred Wild Rice Must Be Protected," *Star Tribune,* Aug. 1, 2004.

27. Quoted by Cornel Pewewardy, "What Happens to One . . . Affects Another," *Colors,* July/Aug. 1992, 37.

8. Economic Development

1. Melanie Benjamin, interview, June 28, 2004.

2. Winona LaDuke Kapashesit, "White Earth Anishinabeg Economy: From Self-Reliance to Dependence and Back Again" (masters thesis, Antioch University, Osage, Minn., Feb. 1988), 98.

3. Karri Plowman, Director, Minnesota American Indian Chamber of Commerce, interview, Jan. 24, 2005.

4. Stephen Hoenack and Gary Renz, "Effects of the Indian-Owned Casinos on Self-Generating Economic Development in Non-Urban Areas of Minnesota," Plymouth, Minn: Stephen A. Hoenack and Associated Economic Research, May 9, 1995, 3.

5. Mirian Jorgensen and Jonathan B. Taylor, "What Determines Indian Economic Success? Evidence from Tribal and Individual Indian Enterprises," Harvard Project on American Indian Economic Development, John F. Kennedy School of Government, Harvard University, June 2000.

6. Joseph P. Kalt and Joseph William Singer, "Myths and Realities of Tribal Sovereignty: The Law and Economics of Indian Self-Rule," Harvard Law School Native Issues Research Symposium, John F. Kennedy School of Government, Harvard University, Dec. 2003.

7. Joseph Kalt, Harvard Project on American Indian Economic Development, Harvard University, statement before the U.S. Senate Committee on Indian Affairs, Sept. 17, 1996, printed in *The Red Lake Nation,* Oct. 1996, 26.

8. "Main Street Minnesota Is Finally Dealt a Winning Hand," Mille Lacs Band of Ojibwe, Onamia, ca. 1996, 13.

9. Mille Lacs Band of Ojibwe, report from Commissioner of Finance, July 13, 2004.

10. U.S. Census, 2000.

11. Metropolitan Business Development Association, 2002.

12. Kay Gudmafta, Director, Twin Cities Women Ventures, interview, Feb. 8, 1996.

13. Michael W. Myhre, State Director, Minnesota Small Business Development Center, interview, July 12, 2004.

14. Julie Murphy, Metropolitan Economic Development Association, interview, July 12, 2004.

15. Melvin Boser, U.S. Small Business Administration, Minnesota District Office, Minneapolis, interview, July 12, 2004.

16. Randy Czaia, Small Business Administration, Minnesota District Office, interview, July 12, 2004.

17. Carrie Ferlita, Assistant District for Minority Economic Development, Small Business Administration, Minneapolis, interview, Jan. 25, 1996.

18. Tran T. Nhon, Executive Director, Minnesota Minority Development Supply Council, interview, July 14, 2004.

19. John McCarthy, Minnesota Indian Gaming Association, interview, Nov. 11, 2003.

20. George Anderson, Director, Minnesota State Lottery, 2002.

21. Mark Brunswick, "Report: State's Indian Casinos Had Third-highest Take in U.S.," *Star Tribune,* July 8, 2004.

22. Ibid.

23. *International Gaming & Wagering Business,* cited in Tracey A. Reeves, "Playing the Odds on Casino Fever: High-stakes Games Pull in Big Money at Indian Reservations," Knight Ridder News Service, *The Oregonian,* Nov. 18, 1994, 3M.

24. Hubert H. Humphrey III, "Gambling on Indian Reservations," Memorandum to Governor Arne Carlson, Feb. 1, 1991, 7.

25. Mordecai Specktor, "State Wants Better Gaming Deal with Tribes," *The Circle,* June 1997, 6.

26. Patricia Lopez, "Fund for Poor Tribes Proposed," *Star Tribune,* Jan. 12, 2005.

27. Minnesota Indian Gaming Association, "So Where Does All the Money Go?" Mar. 2004.

28. Marquette Advisors, 2000, for the Minnesota Indian Gaming Association.

29. Ibid.

30. Lorna LaGue, Tribal Administrator, Shooting Star Casino, Mahnomen, Minn., interview, June 21, 1994.

31. Douglas Clements, "Milking the New Buffalo," *fedgazette,* Minneapolis Federal Reserve Bank, Mar. 2003.

32. Mille Lacs Band of Ojibwe, Fact Sheet: "The Economic Impact of the Mille Lacs Band's Grand Casino Mille Lacs and Grand Casino Hinckley," Sept. 2003.

33. Minnesota Planning, Minnesota Gambling 1993, 15–19.

34. Hoenack and Renz, "Effects of the Indian-Owned Casinos on Self-Generating Economic Development in Non-Urban Areas of Minnesota," Executive Summary, 2–3.
35. Minnesota Economic Trends, 2003.
36. Minnesota Indian Gaming Association, "So Where Does All the Money Go?" Mar. 2004.
37. Marquette Advisors, 2000, for the Minnesota Indian Gaming Association.
38. Ibid.
39. Ibid.
40. Mark Brunswick, "Tribes Betting on Goodwill Ads," *Star Tribune*, Mar. 7, 2004.
41. Phillip H. Norrgard, Director of Human Services, Fond du Lac Reservation, interview, Feb. 10, 2005.
42. William Means, Executive Director, Minnesota Opportunities and Industrialization Centers State Council, interview, Feb. 12, 2005.
43. Laura Waterman Wittstock, interview, May 20, 2004.
44. Ron Libertus, interview, Nov. 22, 1994.
45. Jim Northrup Jr., quoted in Irl Carter, "Gambling with Their Lives: American Indians and the Casinos," *CURA Reporter* 22, no. (Aug. 2, 1992): 3.
46. Chris Ison and Lou Kilzer, "Outside Managers Are Big Winners in Indian Gaming," *Star Tribune*, Dec. 18, 1994.
47. Keith Clark, Inspector General's Office, quoted in Chris Ison and Lou Kilzer, "Outside Managers Are Big Winners in Indian Gaming," *Star Tribune*, Dec. 18, 1994.
48. The Lower Sioux Community and its casino are in Redwood County. The address is usually given as Morton, which is across the Minnesota River in Renville County.
49. Pat Doyle, "Law Meant Casino Profits for Tribal Use," *Star Tribune*, May 1997.
50. Helen Blue-Redner, Chair, Upper Sioux Community, interview, Mar. 25, 2005.
51. William Eadington, Director, Institute for the Study of Gambling and Commercial Gaming, University of Nevada, Reno, at "Minnesota Gambling: The Research Connection" Symposium, Humphrey Institute of Public Affairs, University of Minnesota, 1994.
52. Quoted in Irl Carter, "Gambling with Their Lives: American Indians and the Casinos," *CURA Reporter*, University of Minnesota, Aug. 1992, 6.
53. Hoenack and Renz, "Effects of the Indian-Owned Casinos on Self-Generating Economic Development in Non-Urban Areas of Minnesota," 2.
54. Larry Kitto, quoted in *Star Tribune*, Jan. 19, 1996.

9. Employment Patterns and Opportunities

1. U.S. Census, 2000.
2. Department of Employment and Economic Development, 2002.
3. John McCarthy, Minnesota Indian Gaming Association, interview, Feb. 2004.
4. "Casino Gaming in Minnesota: A Winning Job Generator," Department of Employment and Economic Development, July/Aug. 2002.
5. Figures from the Minnesota Department of Employment and Economic Development, Web site data from 1990–2000.
6. Minnesota Indian Gaming Association, Marquette Advisors, 2002.
7. Roger Aitken, Executive Director, Leech Lake Reservation, interview, June 10, 2004.
8. Minnesota Indian Gaming Association, Web site, July 2004.
9. "Casino Gaming in Minnesota: A Winning Job Generator."
10. U.S. Glass Ceiling Commission Report, in Mike Meyers, "American Indians Mostly Have Been Left Off Corporate Ladder," *Star Tribune,* Mar. 24, 1995.
11. In the 2000 U.S. Census, Sample Count, the state unemployment rate was 4.7 percent; the five counties with the highest rate were in the north and included Clearwater (10.7 percent) and Red Lake (9.3 percent), both counties with reservations.
12. Minnesota Department of Employment and Economic Development, Web site, 2004.
13. Center for Law and Social Policy, 2002.
14. "Detailed Information on the Workforce Investment Act: Youth Activities Assessment," ExpectMore.gov, Aug. 3, 2006; Theresa Cox, Minneapolis American Indian Center, interview, Aug. 17, 2004.
15. "FY 2002: Minnesota Workforce Investment Act Annual Report," Minnesota Department of Employment and Economic Development, Feb. 2004, 11.
16. American Indian Families Project, "A Look at American Indians in Hennepin County," 2003.
17. Theresa Cox, ibid.

10. Education

1. Minnesota Department of Children, Families, and Learning (now Minnesota Department of Education), 2001–2002 school year data. These figures are based upon completing high school (grades 9–12) in four years.
2. Hearings of the House Committee on Indian Affairs, Jan. 22, 1818, 1.

3. Meriam, *Report*, 11–14.
4. Interviews with former students who had positive experiences at the White Earth School, Barb Nelson-Agnew, "The Final Chapter, St. Ben's a Part of Many People's Lives," *Anishinabe Dee-Bah-Gee-Mo-Win*, Mar. 1996, 12–17.
5. Folwell, *History of Minnesota*, 4:324
6. "2004 State of Students of Color: Building Alliances for Student Success," Minnesota Minority Education Partnership, 9, 12.
7. U.S. Department of Health and Human Services, Web site data, 2003.
8. Ibid.
9. Racial Disparities in Test Scores (from 2000 data provided by the Department of Children, Families and Learning), University of Minnesota, Hubert H. Humphrey Institute of Public Affairs, Oct. 16, 2000.
10. Minneapolis Public Schools, Minnesota Basic Standards Test Results, 2002.
11. "2004 State of Students of Color: Building Alliances for Student Success," Minnesota Minority Education Partnership, 25.
12. Minnesota Higher Education Office, 2000 data tracking high school freshman class of 1996.
13. Minnesota Department of Education, 2003 data.
14. "2004 State of Students of Color: Building Alliances for Student Success," Minnesota Minority Education Partnership, 23.
15. Minneapolis Public Schools, Department of Student Accounting, Dropout Rate Sheet, 2002.
16. Paul Tosto, "When Race, Discipline Meet," *St. Paul Pioneer Press*, May 6, 2002.
17. "2004 State of Students of Color: Building Alliances for Student Success," Minnesota Minority Education Partnership, 12.
18. Minnesota Department of Children, Families and Learning, 1999–2000 data.
19. Dr. Hal Gritzmacher, Bemidji State University, "Referral, Assessment, and Placement Practices Used in Northern Minnesota with Native American Students in Special Education," a report prepared for the Minnesota Department of Education, July 1993.
20. Wayne Erickson, Director of Special Education, Minnesota Depart-ment of Children, Families and Learning, interview, May 3, 1996.
21. Donald Allery, Chairman, Indian School Council, "Preliminary Report to the Minnesota State Legislature," Dec. 1, 1988, 1.
22. Indian School Council, "We Are Losing Our Children, Our Future," Final Report to the State of Minnesota Legislature, 1989, 19.
23. Robert Franklin, "Blandin Foundation Will Help Overhaul Indian Education System in Minnesota," *Star Tribune*, May 7, 1996.

24. Tony Looking Elk, Metropolitan Urban Indian Directors, interview, July 18, 2004.

25. The Saint Paul Foundation, "Lessons Learned Supporting Diversity in Schools," Sept. 1996.

26. Dr. Robert Fairbanks, Leech Lake member, educator, attorney, interview, Dec. 18, 1994.

27. Dr. David Baines, address; Edwin Haller and Larry Aitken, Conference Summation, *Mashkiki: Old Medicine Nourishing the New,* University of Minnesota–Duluth, 1988 (Lanham, Md: University Press of America, 1992), 171–73; 186–87.

28. Quoted by Will Antell, Manager of Indian Education, Minnesota Department of Education, in Doug Grow, "Have We Learned Our Lesson Regarding Indian History?" *Star Tribune,* June 25, 1993.

29. Dr. Robert Ferrera, Superintendent, Minneapolis Public Schools, testimony to the Minnesota Advisory Committee to the U.S. Commission on Civil Rights, "Educational Opportunities for American Indians in Minneapolis and St. Paul Public Schools," July 1992, 11.

30. U.S. Census, 2000.

31. Dr. Tom Peacock, Professor of Education, University of Minnesota– Duluth, interview, Sept. 13, 2004; also reported in "Our Children's Songs: American Indian Students and the Schools," *CURA Reporter,* Jan. 2000.

32. Dr. Robert Ferrera, ibid.

33. Minnesota Desegregation Rules, 3535–0180, Apr. 2, 1997.

34. Dr. Thomas Peacock, ibid.; Loretta Gagnon, Program Manager, Indian Education, St. Paul Public Schools, Seminar on Indian Children, American Indian Policy Institute, May 19, 1994; Flo Wiger, interview, May 23, 1994; Dr. Sally Hunter, Associate Professor, University of St. Thomas, interview, Mar. 25, 2005; "The American Indian Student Success Model: A New Direction Building on Past Efforts," Metropolitan Urban Indian Directors, Nov. 3, 2004; Laura Waterman Wittstock, former president, MIGIZI, interview, Mar. 23, 2005.

35. This program was originally Title IV, later changed to Title V. In the mid-1990s, it became Title IX.

36. Title I was the original designation; through the years the name was changed to Chapter I. In the mid-1990s, the name was changed back to Title I.

37. "Title I Funds: Who's Gaining, Who's Losing & Why," Center on Education Policy, June 2004.

38. Minnesota Indian Affairs Council, Annual Report, 2002, 21.

39. "Fiscal Analysis Report: Understanding the General Education Funding Program 2001–2002," Minnesota House of Representatives.

40. "Financing Education in Minnesota 2002–2003," Minnesota House of Representatives Fiscal Analysis Department, Aug. 2002.

41. Article C.
42. Minnesota Department of Education, 2002–2003 school year data.
43. Minnesota Department of Education, 2001 Student Survey and 2001 statewide enrollment data.
44. Quoting Phil Heffner, Indian Counselor, Redwood School District, *Star Tribune,* Feb. 1994; Tom Ellis, Lead Teacher, Dakota Open School, Morton, Minn., Apr. 18, 1996.
45. Norman Draper, "A $1 Million Boost for Indian Education in Minneapolis," *Star Tribune,* Aug. 13, 2004.
46. Karen Baldwin, Superintendent, Bug-O-Nay-Ge-Shig School, interview, Aug. 20, 2004.
47. Minnesota Association of Educational Opportunity Program Personnel, Trio Aggregate Data, 2001–2002.
48. "Collaborating for Change: New Directions for Meeting the Higher Education Needs of Urban American Indians," American Indian Urban Higher Education Initiative, Jan. 1999, 47.
49. Red Lake Nation, AmeriCorps Web site, 2004.
50. Minnesota Association of Educational Opportunity Program Personnel, Trio Aggregate Data, 2001–2002.
51. "2004 State of Students of Color: Building Alliances for Student Success," Minnesota Minority Education Partnership, 2004, 28; statistic provided by Minnesota Higher Education Service Office.
52. Minnesota Public Radio, Web site, Aug. 2004.
53. Ibid.
54. "2004 State of Students of Color: Building Alliances for Student Success," ibid.
55. Minnesota Higher Education Services, enrollment data for American Indians, 2002.
56. Minnesota Department of Higher Education, 2002 data.
57. "2004 State of Students of Color: Building Alliances for Student Success," ibid.
58. Minnesota Department of Higher Education, 2002 data.
59. "2004 State of Students of Color: Building Alliances for Student Success," ibid., 30; statistics provided by Minnesota Higher Education Service Office.
60. Holly Markwardt, research project, reported in *OMSSA,* magazine of the Office for Minority and Special Student Affairs, University of Minnesota–Twin Cities, June 1994, 26.
61. "Collaborating for Change: New Directions for Meeting the Higher Education Needs of Urban American Indians," American Indian Urban Higher Education Initiative, Jan. 1999.
62. LaDonna Mustin, Minnesota American Indian Scholarship Fund, interview, Aug. 24, 2004.
63. Mehgan Lee, "American Indian Scholarship Created," *Minnesota Daily,* Nov. 8, 2004.

64. "Collaborating for Change: New Directions for Meeting the Higher Education Needs of Urban American Indians," American Indian Urban Higher Education Initiative, Jan. 1999, 127.
65. Vicki Howard, American Indian Studies Department Coordinator, University of Minnesota–Twin Cities, interview, Aug. 11, 2004.
66. William Means, Director American Indian Opportunities and Industrialization Center, interview, May 24, 1994.
67. "Collaborating for Change: New Directions for Meeting the Higher Education Needs of Urban American Indians," American Indian Urban Higher Education Initiative, Jan. 1999, 108.
68. John Archibald, Director, Leadership Fellows Program, Bush Foundation, interview, Sept. 21, 1994.
69. Larry Aitken, Professor, Itasca Community College, interview, Feb. 23, 2005.
70. "Red Lake Nation College Officially in Business," *Red Lake Net News*, Jan. 12, 2004.
71. Steve Chapman, former director, American Indian Support Program, Minneapolis Community College, interview, May 13, 1994.
72. Information on the salt lands and the endowed chair of Indian education at the University of Minnesota–Duluth came from Mitzi Doane, Dean of the College of Education, UMD, interview, Nov. 21, 1994; Ruth Myers, interview, June 28, 1994; "The 'Seed' Was Sown in Salt Lands," *Ourselves,* Oct.–Nov. 1993, 5; Sheila Dillon, "Peacock Appointed to Endowed Chair," *Duluth News-Tribune,* Oct. 7, 1993; Samuel Trask Dana, John H. Allison, and Russell N. Cunningham, American Forestry Association, Minnesota Lands, 1960, 93, 141; William Lass, "Minnesota's Quest for Salt" and "Minnesota's Salt Lands Saga," *Minnesota History,* Minnesota Historical Society, Winter 1990, 130–43 and Spring 1992, 9–24.
73. University of Minnesota, Web site, 2004.

11. Social Services

1. Meriam, *Report,* 88–89.
2. Marge Anderson, Chief Executive of the Mille Lacs Band of Ojibwe, "Our Children, Our Future," keynote address for National Indian Family Preservation Conference, reprinted in *The Ojibwe News,* Apr. 28, 1995, 4–5.
3. U.S. Census, 2000.
4. Minnesota House Research Department, 2003.
5. Interview with Melanie Benjamin, June 28, 2004.
6. Nisha Patel and Mark Greenberg, Center for Law and Social Policy, Oct. 2002.
7. "Characteristics of Dec. 2002 Minnesota Family Investment Program Cases and Eligible Adults," Program Assessment and

Integrity Division, Minnesota Department of Human Services, Apr. 2003.

8. "Issues Behind the Outcomes for American Indian Welfare Participants," Wilder Research Center, Apr. 2003.

9. "State of Minnesota's Child and Family Services Plan," Minnesota Department of Human Services, June 2004, 52.

10. Julia Jaakola, Director of Social Services, Fond du Lac Tribe, interview, July 30, 1996.

11. U.S. Census, 2000; Minnesota Department of Human Services, interview with staff, Aug. 30, 2004.

12. Minnesota Department of Human Services, interview with staff, Aug. 30, 2004.

13. Noya Woodrich, Executive Director, Division of Indian Work, interview, Sept. 29, 2004.

14. Mark Kaszynski, Weatherization/Energy Assistance, Minnesota Department of Economic Security, interview, Jan. 16, 1996.

15. Minnesota Department of Commerce, Energy Office Division, interview with staff, Aug. 30, 2004.

16. "Minnesota Statewide Survey of People without Permanent Shelter," Wilder Research Center, Aug. 2001.

17. Sam Gurnoe, Director of Indian Resources, The City, Inc., Minneapolis, interview, Dec. 20, 1995.

18. Thomas D. Peacock, interview, Sept. 6, 2004; previously reported by Priscilla A. Day and Thomas D. Peacock, "Child Abuse and Neglect in Indian Country: A Look Back as We Move Ahead," *Colors*, May–June 1995, 12–13.

19. "Minnesota's Child Welfare Report for 2001," Report to the Minnesota Legislature, Apr. 2003; data from Social Services Information System.

20. U.S. Census, 2000.

21. Betty Greencrow, social worker and member of the St. Paul Indian community, interview, Sept. 22, 1994.

22. Noya Goodrich, Executive Director, Division of Indian Work, interview, Feb. 16, 2005.

23. Roger Toogood, Executive Director, Children's Home Society of Minnesota and former member of the Child Welfare League of America's Minority Adoption Committee, interview, Nov. 18, 1995.

24. *Holyfield*, 490 U.S. 30 (1989), U.S. Supreme Court, Indian Child Welfare Program, Hearings before the Subcommittee on Indian Affairs of the Senate Committee on Interior and Insular Affairs, 93rd Congress, 2nd Sess., 75–83.

25. Ann MacEachron, Nora Gustavsson, Suzanne Cross, and Allison Lewis, "The Effectiveness of the Indian Child Welfare Act of 1978," *Social Services Review* 70, no. 3 (1996): 460.

26. Ibid.

27. The data used to explain Indian involvement in the child protection system are from various sources: Minnesota Department of Human Services annual reports, Hennepin County Community Services, American Indian Families Project, and tribal social services departments.

28. Minnesota Department of Human Services, Legislature Statute Web site.

29. Minnesota Department of Human Services, Child Safety and Permanency Division, Feb. 2005.

30. National Indian Child Welfare Association, Oct. 2003.

31. Minnesota Supreme Court Task Force on Racial Bias in the Judicial System, "Final Report," May 1993, 84.

32. "Monitoring of Hennepin County Compliance with Laws Respecting Cultural Heritage," County Monitoring and Policy Coordination Division, Minnesota Department of Human Services, Jan. 1991; "Response to the January 1991 DHS Report, Feb. 1991.

33. "A Look at American Indian Families in Hennepin County: Part Two," American Indian Families Project," Feb. 2004, 8.

34. Loa Porter, Director of Tribal Human Services, Grand Portage Tribe, interview, Sept. 27, 1994.

35. Minnesota Supreme Court Task Force on Racial Bias in the Judicial System, "Final Report," May 1993, 90, 91, 84.

36. MacEachron, Gustavsson, Cross, and Lewis, "The Effectiveness of the Indian Child Welfare Act of 1978," 460.

37. Esther Wattenberg, Professor, University of Minnesota School of Social Work; coordinator for outreach, Center for Advanced Studies in Child Welfare, interview, Jan. 30, 2005.

38. Gabrielle Strong, Director, Ain Dah Yung, St. Paul, interview, Oct. 4, 1996.

39. Mark Fidler, Director, Indian Child Welfare Law Center, quoted by Kurt Chandler, "Budget Concerns Prompt Counties to Cut Foster Care," *Star Tribune,* Sept. 10, 1995.

40. Minnesota Department of Human Services, "Administration of Children & Families Data: 2000 Annual Report."

41. Minnesota Department of Human Services, "Report to the Legislature," Apr. 2002.

42. Dr. John Red Horse, Dean, College of Liberal Arts, University of Minnesota–Duluth, talk at American Indian Research and Policy Institute Seminar on Indian Youth, May 19, 1994.

43. Elizabeth Ebbott, *Indians in Minnesota* (Minneapolis: University of Minnesota Press, 1985) 183.

44. Marge Anderson, Chief Executive of the Mille Lacs Band of Ojibwe, "Our Children, Our Future," keynote address for National Family Preservation Conference, reprinted in *The Ojibwe News,* Apr. 28, 1995, 4–5.

12. Health

1. The 1782 epidemic and the charges that whites used gifts of blankets from small pox patients to infect Indians are discussed in William W. Warren, *History of the Ojibway People* (Minnesota Historical Society, 1885, reprinted in *Borealis,* St. Paul: Minnesota Historical Society Press, 1984), 260, 344; Arthur J. Ray, *Indians in the Fur Trade* (Toronto, Canada: University of Toronto Press, 1974); Carolyn Gilman, *The Grand Portage Story* (St. Paul: Minnesota Historical Society Press, 1992), 63–64.
2. Meriam, *Report,* 88.
3. Minnesota Department of Heath, Minnesota Health Statistics, 2001.
4. Ibid.
5. Ibid.
6. Minnesota Department of Planning, "Minnesota Milestones," Oct. 2002.
7. Minnesota Department of Health, Center for Health Statistics, 2002.
8. U.S. Census, 2000.
9. Minnesota Department of Heath, "Disparities in the Health Status of American Indians in Minnesota," May 2003.
10. U.S. Census, 2000.
11. Pauline Mendola, Germaine Buck, and Edward R. Starr, "Developmental Disabilities Prevention and the Distribution of Risk among American Indians," *American Indian and Alaska Native Mental Health Research* 5, no. 3. (1994): 30–44.
12. Minnesota Department of Health, "Eliminating Health Disparities: Injury and Violence," Mar. 2001, 8.
13. Pamela Adelman, Minnesota Department of Human Services, "Substance Use among Indians in Minnesota," Oct. 2000.
14. Ibid.
15. Minnesota Department of Health, "Healthy Minnesotans: A Progress Report on Minnesota's Public Health Improvement Goals," Oct. 2003.
16. Minnesota Department of Health, "Eliminating Health Disparities Initiative: 2003 Report to the Legislature," Jan. 2003, 20.
17. Minnesota Department of Heath, "Disparities in the Health Status of American Indians in Minnesota," May 2003.
18. H. Mitzi Doane, "Historical Approach to Diet and Community Support Systems for Chronic Disease," in Edwin W. Haller and Larry P. Aitken, *Mashkiki Old Medicine: Nourishing the New* (Lanhem, Md.: University Press of America, 1992), 107.
19. Thomas D. Peacock, interview, Sept. 8, 2004; also quoted by Priscilla A. Day and Thomas D. Peacock, "Child Abuse and Neglect in Indian Country: A Look Back as We Move Ahead," *Colors,* May–June 1995, 12–13.

20. Minnesota Department of Health, American Indian Symposium on Mental Health and Chemical Dependency, *Briefing Book,* Aug. 2000, 11.

21. "Population of Color in Minnesota, Health Status Report," Minnesota Department of Health, Spring 1997, 59, 64, 66.

22. Minnesota Department of Human Services, "Minnesota's Chemical Health System: A Report to the Minnesota Legislature," Feb. 21, 2003.

23. Ibid.

24. Ibid.

25. Dennis Hisgun, Coordinator, White Earth Chemical Dependency Program, testimony, Apr. 1, 1997, reported in *Anishinaabeg Today,* Apr. 9, 1997, 4.

26. "Estimate of the Need for Alcohol/Drug-Related Services for Adolescents in Minnesota: Implications for Managed Care Organizations and Health Care Providers," St. Paul: Minnesota Department of Human Services, Performance Measurement and Quality Improvement Division, 1997.

27. "Brief Interventions for Mild-Drug Abusing Adolescents," Ken Winters, University of Minnesota, 2000.

28. Hennepin County, Public Affairs, 2003.

29. National Alliance to End Homelessness, "Conference on Harm Reduction Strategies 2002."

30. James W. Thompson, MD, member of the Association of American Indian Physicians, testimony at the Oversight Hearing on a Community-based Mental Health Initiative for Indian People, U.S. Senate Select Committee on Indian Affairs, July 7, 1988.

31. "Tracking the Rate of Fetal Alcohol Syndrome," Minnesota Department of Health, Mar. 2003.

32. Jean Mellum, Maternal Child Health Program Coordinator for Fond du Lac Human Services, reported by Rocky Wilkinson, "Fetal Alcohol Exposed: The Invisible Impairment," *Nahgahchiwanong Dibahjimowinnan,* Oct. 1995, 8.

33. Douglas Benson, "Minority Health in Minnesota: Environmental Health—Lead," Minnesota Department of Health, 1992; Group Health Foundation, "Lead Exposure in Young Children from Seventeen Metropolitan Health Organizations: A Community Collaboration," Final and Summary Report, Mar. 24, 1995.

34. Minnesota Pollution Control Agency, "Estimated Mercury Emissions in Minnesota, 1990, 1995 & 2000," Mar. 2004, 1.

35. "Nuclear Power and Nuclear Waste," Prairie Island Indian Community, statement before the Minnesota Senate Committee on Local and Metropolitan Government, Feb. 14, 1997.

36. "Breast Cancer Rates and Trends Around Nuclear Power Plants in Minnesota," in *The Occurrence of Cancer in Minnesota 1988–1992,*

Minnesota Cancer Surveillance System, Minnesota Department of Health, 1995, 5–8.

37. Rita Messinger, toxicologist, Minnesota Department of Health, Nov. 11, 1994.

38. The fact that Congress intends the services to be freely available is underlined by the provision that the Indian Health Service is not to charge Indians who may have the economic means to pay unless and until such a time as Congress has agreed upon a specific policy to do so and has directed IHS to implement such a policy (25 U.S.C. 1681, added by legislation Sept. 30, 1994).

39. Ralph Forquera, "Urban Indian Health," Seattle Health Board for the Henry J. Kaiser Family Foundation, Nov. 2001.

40. "A Quiet Crisis: Federal Funding and Unmet Needs in Indian Country," U.S. Commission on Civil Rights, July 2003, 11, 50.

41. Minnesota Department of Health, "Eliminating Health Disparities Initiative: 2003 Report to the Legislature," Jan. 2003, 28.

42. Dr. Terrel H. Hart, Indian Health Board of Minneapolis, interview, Sept. 17, 2004.

43. Betsy Clarke, Commodities Program, interview, Jan. 10, 2005.

44. Community Development Section, Division of Community Health Services, Minnesota Department of Health, "Community Health Services in Minnesota," Mar. 1995.

45. Gerald L. Hill, MD, Director, University of Minnesota Center of American Indian and Minority Health, interview, Apr. 26, 1994, quoted in Richard Broderick, "Medicine Woman," University of Minnesota, *Update* 21, no. 1 (Jan. 1994): 6–7.

46. Gerald L. Hill, MD, Director, University of Minnesota's Center of American Indian and Minority Health, presentation "Challenge of Improving Indian Health Care," printed in "Returning to a Natural State of Good Health," National Summit on Indian Health Care Reform, Washington, D.C., Mar. 1993, 8.

13. Housing

1. U.S. Census, 2000.

2. Minnesota Indian Gaming Association, 2004.

3. Samuel L. Myers, Jr., "Race and Housing Policies in the Midwest," a report submitted to Fannie Mae on discrimination in mortgage lending, from the Fannie Mae University Colloquium, Hubert H. Humphrey Institute of Public Affairs, University of Minnesota, Dec. 3, 1993, 51.

4. "The Effect of Substandard and Overcrowded Housing Conditions on Native Americans and Their Children," survey by National American Indian Housing Council, Sept. 2004.

5. U.S. Census, 2000.

6. "The Cost of Living in Minnesota 2002," JOBS NOW Coalition, 2003.

7. Median home price from 2001–2002 data on arm's length sales of existing housing, Minnesota Department of Revenue, Property Tax Division; income needed to afford median home price based on 5 percent down payment, 21 percent of gross income for principle/interest and 6 percent, 360-month mortgage term.

8. Federal Financial Institutions Examination Council (FFIEC), 2003 Home Mortgage Disclosure Act data, July 2004.

9. Reported at a conference on "Race, Poverty and Housing Policy" at the Hubert Humphrey Institute, Dec. 3–4, 1993; "Census Analysis Update," The Urban Coalition, Minneapolis, Minn., 3.

10. Robert Ley and Patrick Welle, "The Economic Impact of Red Lake Reservation on the Regional Economy," Addendum B, Dec. 1995.

11. Eric Nalder, Deborah Nelson, and Alex Tizon, "HUD Missed Signs of Waste, Then Gave Tribe More Money," *Seattle Times/Seattle Post Intelligencer,* Dec. 4, 1996, and subsequent articles reprinted in *Anishinaabeg Today.*

12. Native Housing Council, "Rural Voices," Spring 2004.

13. National Commission on American Indian, Alaska Native, and Native Hawaiian Housing, "Building the Future: A Blueprint for Change," 1992, 62.

14. U.S. General Accounting Office, "Native American Housing: VA Could Address Some Barriers to Participation in Direct Loan Program," Aug. 2002.

15. Dr. Terrel H. Hart, Indian Health Board, interview, Oct. 4, 2004.

16. Pat Faherty, "City Urged to Address American Indian Housing Needs," *Duluth Budgeteer News,* Apr. 9, 2004.

17. Kevin Diaz, "City Grant to Aid Indian Ownership of Little Earth," *Star Tribune,* Oct. 1, 1994.

18. *Red Lake Net News,* www.rlnn.com, 2004.

19. National American Indian Housing Council report, based on 2000 U.S. Census, 2003.

20. Andriana Abariotes and John Poupart, "American Indians & Home Ownership," The American Indian Research and Policy Institute, 1996, 8–10; also reported in *CURA Reporter,* June 1996, 8–11.

21. Scott Beckman, University of Minnesota Extension Service, "Cass County/Leech Lake, Minnesota Comprehensive Housing Affordability Strategy," 1993, Appendix B: Survey Results, 4, 13.

22. Larry Leventhal, attorney, letter to the executive director of the Minnesota Housing Finance Agency, May 27, 1983.

23. Henry Cisneros, Secretary of Housing and Urban Development, letter, July 24, 1993; Clyde Bellecourt, AIM founder, interview, Nov. 14, 1994.

14. The Criminal Justice System

1. The 1883 "Rules Governing the Court of Indian Offenses" authorized action to stop and punish such activities as "old heathenish dances" or ceremonies, plural marriage, usual practices of medicine men, destruction of property at a burial, and the use of any intoxicants. Among the offenses defined by BIA regulations in 1904 were: Fourth. The "sun dance," and all other similar dances and so-called religious ceremonies, shall be considered "Indian offenses," and any Indian found guilty of being a participant in any one or more of these offenses shall . . . be punished by withholding from him his rations for a period of not exceeding ten days. . . . Sixth. The usual practices of so-called medicine men shall be considered Indian offenses [punishable by confinement] in the agency guardhouse . . . until such time as he shall produce evidence satisfactory to the court, and approved by the agent, that he will forever abandon all practices styled Indian offense under this rule." Regulations of the Indian Office, effective Apr. 1, 1904, Secretary of the Interior (Washington: Government Printing Office, 1904), 102–3.

2. "Minnesota Study Finds Indians Charged at High Rates," Adult Major Criminal Case Filings by Race and Ethnicity, Sept. 2, 2003.

3. U.S. Census, 2000; Minnesota Bureau of Criminal Apprehension Arrest Records, 2002.

4. Bureau of Criminal Apprehension, Minnesota Department of Public Safety, 2003 data.

5. Sam Gurnoe, Director of Indian Resources, The City, Inc., interview, Dec. 20, 1995.

6. Michael LeGarde, "Majority of Survey Participants Concerned about Crime and Violence and Yet Many Crimes Still Go Unreported," *Nahgahchiwanong Dibahjimowinnan*, Sept. 1995, 10–12.

7. Lawrence A. Greenfeld and Steven K. Smith, "American Indians and Crime," U.S. Department of Justice, Feb. 1999.

8. Joe Day, Indian Affairs Council, interview, July 8, 2004.

9. Paul Thiebeault, Director, Anishinabe Legal Services, quoted by Associated Press, "Indians Testify Racial Bias Rampant in State's Courts," *Star Tribune*, Oct. 1, 1991.

10. "Sentencing Practices: Annual Summary Statistics for Felony Offenders Sentenced in 2002," Minnesota Sentencing Guidelines Commission report, Jan. 2004, 12.

11. Tom Robertson, Minnesota Public Radio, Aug. 30, 2004.

12. Ibid.

13. "2003 Racial Profiling Study," Council on Crime and Justice and the Institute on Race and Poverty, University of Minnesota Law School, 2003.

14. "Minneapolis Police Traffic Stops and Driver's Race Analysis and Recommendations," Council on Crime and Justice, Apr. 2001.

15. Minnesota Supreme Court Task Force on Racial Bias in the Judicial System, Final Report, May 1993, S–3.

16. "Minnesota Judicial Branch Releases Data Collection Project," Minnesota State Courts, Aug. 29, 2002.

17. Ibid.

18. Ibid.

19. Minnesota State Courts, 2004 Web site data.

20. "Ministers' Plan Helps People Help Themselves in Violent Time," *Star Tribune,* June 5, 1996.

21. Minnesota Department of Corrections, Human Relations Office, Oct. 11, 1996.

22. "Diversity in Law Firms," Equal Employment Opportunity report, 2003, 14.

23. Minnesota Judicial Branch, 2004 Web site data.

24. Minnesota Department of Corrections, "The State of the Prison Population," 2001 Commissioner's Report.

25. Gertrude Buckanaga, Director, Upper Midwest Indian Center, interview, Sept. 23, 1993.

26. Sandra Gardebring, Minnesota Supreme Court Justice, presentation, American Indian Research and Policy Institute meeting, May 19, 1994.

27. "Residential Facilities for Juvenile Offenders," Program Evaluation Division, Office of the Legislative Auditor, State of Minnesota, Feb. 1995, xi, 71.

28. Ibid., 29, 48–49.

29. Tammy Laurer, "Institute Completes Juvenile Justice Study," American Indian Research and Policy Institute, Fall 1996, 2, 6–7.

30. Office of Justice Programs, Annual Report, Mar. 2004.

31. Clara Niiska, *Native American Press,* Mar. 7, 2003; Minnesota Supreme Court Ruling, Mar. 5, 2003.

32. Arthur A. Fletcher, Chairman, U.S. Commission on Civil Rights, testimony before the Select Committee on Indian Affairs of the U.S. Senate, 102d Congress, 1st Sess., Sept. 10, 1991, 4–5.

33. "The Indian Civil Rights Act," U.S. Commission on Civil Rights, June 1991, 51.

34. Judge David Harding, Coeur D'Alene Tribe, testimony, U.S. Commission on Civil Rights, The Indian Civil Rights Act, June 1991, 39.

35. Margaret Treuer, Chief Judge, Bois Forte Tribe, interview, July 23, 1996.

36. "The Indian Civil Rights Act," U.S. Commission on Civil Rights, June 1991, 72–73.

37. "A Quiet Crisis: Federal Funding and Unmet Needs in Indian Country," U.S. Commission on Civil Rights, June 2003.

38. Ibid.

39. Associated Press, CNN.com report, Jan. 2, 2004.

40. John Buckanaga, White Earth councilman, testimony in Washington, D.C., Aug. 1997, reported by the Associated Press; reprinted as "Officials Seek Ways to Control Crime on Reservations," *Star Tribune,* Aug. 20, 1997, A5.

41. Tom Robertson, "Tribal Justice—But Not For All," Minnesota Public Radio, Apr. 2001.

Conclusion

1. "A Quiet Crisis: Federal Funding and Unmet Needs in Indian Country," U.S. Commission on Civil Rights, July 2003.

2. Marge Anderson, Chief Executive of the Mille Lacs Band of Ojibwe, "Our Children, Our Future," keynote address for National Family Preservation Conference, reprinted in *The Ojibwe News,* Apr. 28, 1995, 4–5.

Selected Bibliography

Ahern, Wilbert H. *Indian Education and Bureaucracy: The School at Morris, 1887–1909.* St. Paul: Minnesota Historical Society, Fall 1984.

American Indian Law Center. *Felix S. Cohen's Handbook of Federal Indian Law.* Albuquerque: University of New Mexico Press, 1982 (reprint of original 1942 edition). An edition published by the federal government in 1958, during the termination era, was edited to eliminate many of the unresolved issues and stress federal plenary power over tribes. The 1958 edition is not Cohen's work.

Anderson, Gary C., and Alan R. Woolworth, eds. *Through Dakota Eyes: Narrative Accounts of the Minnesota Indian War of 1862.* St. Paul: Minnesota Historical Society Press, 1988.

Baraga, Frederic. *A Dictionary of the Ojibway Language.* Minneapolis: University of Minnesota Press, 1992. First published in 1878; reprinted by the University of Minnesota Press, 1992. It remains the most comprehensive lexicon available of the Ojibway language.

Beaulieu, David. "A Place among Nations: Experiences of Indian People." In Clifford E. Clark Jr., ed., *Minnesota in a Century of Change: The State and Its People since 1900.* St. Paul: Minnesota Historical Society Press, 1989.

Bemis, Samuel Flagg. *Jay's Treaty: A Study in Commerce and Diplomacy.* New York: The Macmillan Company, 1923.

Bowden, Henry Warren. *American Indians and Christian Missions: Studies in Cultural Conflict.* Chicago: University of Chicago Press, 1981.

Broker, Ignatia. *Night Flying Woman: An Ojibway Narrative.* St. Paul: Minnesota Historical Society Press, 1983.

Brown, Jennifer S. H. *Strangers in Blood: Fur Trade Company Families in Indian Country.* Vancouver: University of British Columbia Press, 1990; reprint, Norman: University of Oklahoma Press, 1997.

Buffalohead, Priscilla K. *A Fresh Look at Ojibway Women.* St. Paul: Minnesota Historical Society Press, Summer 1983.

Densmore, Frances. *Chippewa Customs.* Introduction by Nina Archabal. St. Paul: Minnesota Historical Society Press, 1979. Originally published in Smithsonian Institution Bureau of American Ethnology, Bulletin 86, 1929.

Folwell, William. *A History of Minnesota.* Vol. 4, St. Paul: Minnesota Historical Society, 1930.

Hickerson, Harold. *Ethnohistory of the Chippewa in Central Minnesota.* Vol. I–VII. Edited and compiled by Davis Agee Horr. New York and London: Garland

Publishing Inc., 1974. Seven volumes on the Chippewa Indians include documents and testimony presented at the Indian Claims Commission hearings as part of the first step of determining the location of Indian groups at the time the treaty was made. Volume 7 presents the commission's findings.

Great Lakes Indian Fish and Wildlife Commission. *A Guide to Understanding Chippewa Treaty Rights,* Minnesota ed. Odanah, Wisconsin: Great Lakes Indian Fish and Wildlife Commission, July 1995. Texts of the 1837, 1854, and 1855 treaties with Ojibwe tribes in Minnesota.

Heidenreich, Conrad, and Arthur J. Ray. *The Early Fur Trades: A Study in Cultural Interaction.* Toronto: McClelland and Stewart Limited, 1976.

Historical Research Associates, Inc. *The Forests of Anishinabe: A History of Minnesota Chippewa Tribal Forestry, 1854–1991.* Missoula, Mont.: Historical Research Associates, Inc., 1992. Prepared for the U.S. Department of the Interior, Bureau of Indian Affairs, Branch of Forestry, Minneapolis Area Office.

Johnston, Basil. *Ojibway Ceremonies.* Lincoln: University of Nebraska Press, 1990–1982.

Kegg, Maude. *Portage Lake: Memories of an Ojibwe Childhood.* Edited by John D. Nichols. Minneapolis: University of Minnesota Press, 1993.

Meyer, Roy W. *History of the Santee Sioux: United States Indian Policy on Trial,* rev. ed. Lincoln: University of Nebraska Press, 1993.

Moquin, Wayne. *Great Documents in American Indian History.* Edited by Charles Van Doren. New York: Da Capo Press, 1995. Originally published 1973; reprinted 1995.

Nichols, John D., and Earl Nyholm. *A Concise Dictionary of Minnesota Ojibwe.* Minneapolis: University of Minnesota Press, 1995.

Omer, Stewart. *Peyote Religion: A History.* Norman: University of Oklahoma Press, 1987.

Poupart, John, Cecilia Martinez, John Red Horse, and Dawn Scharnberg. *To Build a Bridge: Working with American Indian Communities.* St. Paul: American Indian Policy Center, 2001.

Ray, Arthur J. *Indians in the Fur Trade.* Toronto: University of Toronto Press, 1974.

Riggs, Stephen R. *A Dakota–English Dictionary.* St. Paul: Borealis Books, Minnesota Historical Society Press, 1992. First published in 1890.

Rogers, John. *Red World and White: Memories of a Chippewa Boyhood.* Norman: University of Oklahoma Press, 1974.

Roufs, Timothy G. "Early Indian Life in the Lake Superior Region." Reprinted from Ryck Lydecker, Lawrence J. Sommer, and Arthur Larsen, eds., *Duluth: Sketches of the Past,* Special Bicentennial Volume of Duluth's Legacy Series. Duluth, Minnesota: American Revolution Bicentennial Commission, 1976.

Rubinstein, Mitchell E., and Alan R. Woolworth. "The Dakota and Ojibway." In *They Chose Minnesota: A Survey of the State's Ethnic Groups,* Chapter 1. St. Paul: Minnesota Historical Society Press, 1981.

Satz, Ronald N. "Chippewa Treaty Rights: The Reserved Rights of Wisconsin's Chippewa Indians in Historical Perspective, Transactions." *Wisconsin Academy of Sciences, Arts, and Letters* 79, no. 1 (1991). Detailed analysis of the 1837 treaty from records of the proceedings.

Slabbaert-Norrgard, Lorraine, and Phillip H. Norrgard, producers. *A Gift to One, a Gift to Many.* Video of James Jackson, Sr., Ojibwe Medicine Man, 1913–1992.

Tanner, Helen. *Atlas of Great Lakes Indian History.* Norman: University of Oklahoma, 1986.

Traditional Ojibway Religion and Its Historical Changes. Philadelphia: American Philosophical Society, 1983.

Van Kirk, Sylvia. *Many Tender Ties: Women in Fur Trade Society in Western Canada, 1670–1870.* Winnipeg: Watson and Dwyer Publishing Ltd., 1980; reprint, Norman: University of Oklahoma Press, 1983.

Vessey, Christopher. *Handbook of American Indian Religious Freedom.* New York: Cross Road, 1993.

Warren, William W. *History of the Ojibway People.* Introduction by Roger Buffalohead. St. Paul: Minnesota Historical Society Press, 1984. Originally published in *Collections of the Minnesota Historical Society* 5 (1885).

Weatherford, Jack. *Indian Givers: How the Indians of the Americas Transformed the World.* New York: Fawcett Columbine, 1988.

White, Richard. *The Middle Ground: Indians, Empires, and Republics in the Great Lakes Region, 1650–1815.* New York: Cambridge University Press, 1991.

Williamson, John P. *An English–Dakota Dictionary.* St. Paul: Borealis Books, Minnesota Historical Society Press, 1992. First published in 1902.

Internet Resources

Minnesota American Indian Internet Resources

American Indian Community Development Corporation
www.aicdc.org
> The American Indian Community Development Corporation provides housing and supportive services to the American Indian community in the Twin Cities metropolitan area.

American Indian Policy Center
www.airpi.org
> The mission of the American Indian Policy Center (AIPC) is to provide government leaders, policy-makers, and the public with accurate information about the legal and political history of American Indian nations and the contemporary situation for American Indians. By providing knowledge and education, the AIPC seeks to foster better informed and culturally sensitive responses to the challenges of American Indian life.

Circle of Indigenous Nations
www.mcae.umn.edu/circle
> The mission of the Circle of Indigenous Nations at the University of Minnesota is to recruit, retain, and graduate American Indian students. The Circle achieves these goals by promoting cultural values that help American Indian students become self-directed, excel academically, and succeed in all areas of individual matriculation, academic pursuits, and career aspirations.

Minnesota American Indian Bar Association
www.maiba.org
> The Minnesota American Indian Bar Association (MAIBA) is a nonprofit organization of American Indian and law students and non-Indian attorneys and law students, who are interested in Indian law, and American Indians who serve as advocates, prosecutors, or judicial officers in tribal courts.

Minnesota American Indian Chamber of Commerce
www.maicc.org
> The mission of the Minnesota American Indian Chamber of Commerce is to promote entrepreneurial partnerships among American Indian businesses, professionals, and tribal governmental enterprises.

Minnesota Department of Health

www.health.state.mn.us

> This site provides health data and statistics on the Minnesota American Indian population.

Minnesota Indian Affairs Council

www.mniac.org

> The Minnesota Indian Affairs Council (MIAC) is the official liaison between state and tribal governments. The mission of the MIAC is to protect the sovereignty of the eleven Minnesota tribes and the well-being of American Indian people throughout the state of Minnesota.

Minnesota Indian Gaming Association

www.mnindiangaming.org

> The Minnesota Indian Gaming Association (MIGA) represents nine of the eleven gaming tribes in Minnesota. Its role is not to dictate policy to its sovereign members but to provide a forum where tribes can exchange information and address shared concerns. MIGA also educates the public, the media, and elected officials on tribal gaming, tribal governments, and the nature of sovereignty.

Minnesota Indian Women's Resource Center

miwrc.org

> The mission of the Minnesota Indian Women's Resource Center is to educate and empower American Indian women and their families.

Federal Government Web Sites

Bureau of Indian Affairs

www.doi.gov/bureau-indian-affairs

> The Bureau of Indian Affairs (BIA) is responsible for the administration and management of 55.7 million acres of land held in trust by the United States for American Indians, Indian tribes, and Alaska Natives. There are 561 federally recognized tribal governments in the United States. Developing forest lands, leasing assets on these lands, directing agricultural programs, protecting water and land rights, developing and maintaining infrastructure, and economic development are all part of the agency's responsibility. The Bureau of Indian Affairs also provides education services to approximately 48,000 Indian students.

U.S. Census Bureau

www.census.gov

> The U.S. Census Bureau provides social and economic tables, graphs, and numbers for all American Indian tribes, based on 2000 U.S. Census data.

U.S. Commission on Civil Rights

www.usccr.gov

> This Web site features two in-depth reports on American Indians. *A Quiet Crisis: Federal Funding and Unmet Needs in Indian Country,* published in

July 2003, looks at the breach of federal funding with the American Indian community and shows federal mandates versus their actual funding levels and the needs in Indian lands. *Broken Promises: Evaluating the Native American Health Care System* was published in July 2004 and reviews the American Indian health systems in this country.

U.S. Department of Health and Human Services: Indian Health Service
www.ihs.gov
> The mission of Indian Health Service (IHS) is to raise the physical, mental, social, and spiritual health of American Indians and Alaska Natives to the highest level and to assure that comprehensive, culturally acceptable personal and public health services are available and accessible to American Indians and Alaska Natives.

U.S. Small Business Administration: Office of Native American Affairs
www.sba.gov/naa
> The mission of the Office of Native American Affairs (ONAA) is to ensure that American Indians, Native Alaskans, and Native Hawaiians seeking to create, develop, and expand small businesses have full access to the necessary business development and expansion tools available through the agency's entrepreneurial development, lending, and procurement programs.

National American Indian Web Sites

American Indian Movement
www.aimovement.org
> The American Indian Movement (AIM) is dedicated to "fight White Man's injustice to Indians, his oppression, persecution, discrimination, and malfeasance in the handling of Indian Affairs. . . . AIM shall be there to help the Native People regain human rights and achieve restitutions and restorations."

American Indian Resource Directory
www.indians.org
> This directory is a Web site resource for American Indians.

Indian Health Council, Inc.
www.indianhealth.com
> The Indian Health Council's mission is to nurture a balance of physical, mental, emotional, and spiritual well-being.

National Congress of American Indians
www.ncai.org
> The National Congress of American Indians (NCAI), founded in 1944, is the oldest and largest tribal government organization in the United States. NCAI serves as a forum for consensus-based policy development among its membership of more than 250 tribal governments from every

region of the country. Its mission is to inform the public and the federal government on tribal self-government, treaty rights, and a broad range of federal policy issues affecting tribal governments.

National Indian Child Welfare Association
www.nicwa.org

The National Indian Child Welfare Association (NICWA) is the most comprehensive source of information on American Indian child welfare and works on behalf of Indian children and families. NICWA provides public policy, research, and advocacy; information and training on Indian child welfare; and community development services to a broad national audience, including tribal governments and programs, state child welfare agencies, and other organizations, agencies, and professionals interested in the field of Indian child welfare.

National Museum of the American Indian
www.nmai.si.edu

The National Museum of the American Indian is the sixteenth museum of the Smithsonian Institution and the first national museum dedicated to the preservation, study, and exhibition of the life, languages, literature, history, and arts of Native Americans. Established by an act of Congress in 1989, the museum works in collaboration with the Native peoples of the Western Hemisphere to protect and foster their cultures by reaffirming traditions and beliefs, encouraging contemporary artistic expression, and empowering the Indian voice.

Media Outlets

The Circle
www.thecirclenews.org

The Circle is an award-winning Native publication based in Minneapolis.

Indian Country
www.indiancountry.com

Indian Country is the nation's leading American Indian newspaper and news source.

Native Web
www.nativeweb.org

Native Web provides a directory of links to tribal home pages and Indian organizations.

Other Newspapers

Anishinaabeg Today, White Earth Reservation, White Earth, Minnesota
Bois Forte News, Nett Lake, Minnesota
De-Bah-Ji-Mon, Leech Lake Tribe, Cass Lake, Minnesota
The Mille Lacs Band News, St. Paul, Minnesota

The Moccasin Telegraph, Grand Portage Indian Reservation, Grand Portage, Minnesota

Nahgahchiwanong Dibahjimowinnan, Fond du Lac Reservation News, Cloquet, Minnesota

Native American Press/Ojibwe News, Bemidji, Minnesota

News from Indian Country, Wisconsin: The Nation's Native Newspaper, Hayward, Wisconsin

Red Lake News, Red Lake, Minnesota

Speaking of Ourselves Ni-Mi-Kwa-Zoo-Min, Minnesota Chippewa Tribe, Cass Lake, Minnesota

The Woodland Voice, Mille Lacs Band, St. Paul, Minnesota

Minnesota Indian Tribes

Minnesota Chippewa Tribe
www.mnchippewatribe.org
> The Minnesota Chippewa Tribe, comprised of the Bois Forte, Fond du Lac, Grand Portage, Leech Lake, Mille Lacs, and White Earth Reservations, is a federally recognized tribal government that, through unified leadership, promotes and protects the member bands while providing quality services and technical assistance to the reservation governments and tribal people.

Bois Forte Band of Chippewa
www.boisforte.com

Fond du Lac Band of Chippewa
www.fdlrez.com

Grand Portage Band of Chippewa
www.grandportage.com

Leech Lake Band of Ojibwe
www.llojibwe.com

Lower Sioux Indian Community
www.jackpotjunction.com

Mille Lacs Band of Ojibwe
www.millelacsojibwe.org

Prairie Island Indian Community
www.prairieisland.org

Red Lake Nation
www.redlakenation.org

Shakopee Mdewakanton Sioux Community
www.shakopeedakota.org

Upper Sioux Community
www.uppersiouxcommunity.org

White Earth Band of Chippewa
www.whiteearth.com

Index

traditional Indian medicine,
256–57; tribal programs, 261–62;
urban Indians, 262–63; veterans,
262; women, 264; youth, 246–47,
252–53. *See also* Indian Health
Service; specific diseases
HIP. *See* Housing Improvement
Program
HIV/AIDS, 255
Ho-Chunk tribe, 26–27, 331–32
Hogan, Vanya, 61
homelessness, 217, 279
housing, 269–82; characteristics,
269–71; and community, 280–81;
financing, 271–73, 275, 280;
issues, 280–81; programs,
273–78; reservation needs,
270–71, 281; rural, 277; special
needs, 279–80; on trust lands,
276–77; urban, 278–79, 281
Housing and Urban Development
(HUD), 72, 132, 170, 272,
273–75
Housing Improvement Program
(HIP), 275
HUD. *See* Housing and Urban
Development
Humanity Center casino, 40
humor, 1
hunting rights, 82, 107–14

IAC. *See* Indian Affairs Council
ICRA. *See* Indian Civil Rights Act
immunization rates, 245
income, 93
Indian Affairs Council (IAC), 7,
78–79
Indian Appropriation Act (*1871*), 14
Indian Arts and Crafts Act (*1990*), 6
Indian Child Welfare Act (*1978*),
56, 83–84, 99, 226–37
Indian Civil Rights Act (*1968*),
298–99, 300
Indian Claims Commission, 18, 44
Indian Education Act (*1972*),
179, 184

Indian Gaming Regulatory Act
(*1988*), 22, 145
Indian Health Care Improvement
Act (*1976*), 242
Indian Health Service, 20, 73, 99,
242, 258–60
Indian mascots and logos, 106
Indian Reorganization Act (*1934*),
16, 17–18, 29, 30, 57, 62, 165
Indian Self-Determination and
Education Assistance Act (*1975*),
20–21, 70, 165
Indian Trust Fund Reform Act
(*1994*), 71
infant mortality, 244
inheritance, 52–53
Inouyi, Daniel, 74
International Falls, Minn., 104
IRA. *See* Indian
Reorganization Act
iron ore, 28
Isanti tribe, 25

Jackpot Junction Casino, 42, 154–55
Jackson, Andrew (U.S. president),
12
Jackson, Jimmy, 89, 107
JOBS programs, 212
Johnson-O'Malley Act (*1934*), 78,
99, 172, 179, 184
Joseph (Nez Percé chief), 12

Kalt, Joseph, 131
Kitto, Larry, 157
Kramer, Joyce, 75

La Duke, Winona, 48
Lagarde, Joe, 127
Lakota. *See* Teton tribe
lands, 25; allotments, 15–16, 29–30,
50–52; appropriation, 11;
inheritance, 52–53; secretarial
transfers, 51–52; tribal lands, 30,
47; and tribes in Minnesota,
25–53; trust lands, 30, 48–50,
276–77. *See also* treaties

Kathy Davis Graves is a partner of Parenteau Graves Communications, a company that provides writing, marketing, and public relations services for nonprofit organizations. She is the author of several research reports for the League of Women Voters, including a groundbreaking study on violence prevention. She writes for the Jungle Theater, Mixed Blood Theatre, Minneapolis Public Schools, and the Minneapolis Department of Health and Family Support, and teaches writing at Metropolitan State University. She serves on the board of directors for the Friends of the Minneapolis Library and PACER Center.

Elizabeth Ebbott completed the draft of the manuscript for this book shortly before her death in 1998. She was the author of the fourth edition of *Indians in Minnesota* (1985) and assisted with the preparation of the earlier editions as well. She played a key role in establishing the State of Minnesota Ethical Practices Board in 1974 and also helped organize and served on the board of the national Council on Government Ethics Laws. Her civic service included involvement with the League of Women Voters of Minnesota, Minnesota Board of Education Sex Bias Advisory Committee, American Lung Association, Minnesota Museum of Art, and her local school board.